THE FABLIAU IN ENGLISH

LONGMAN MEDIEVAL AND RENAISSANCE LIBRARY

General Editors:
CHARLOTTE BREWER, Hertford College, Oxford
N. H. KEEBLE, University of Stirling

Published Titles:

Piers Plowman: An Introduction to the B-Text
James Simpson

Shakespeare's Mouldy Tales: Recurrent Plot Motifs in Shakespearian Drama
Leah Scragg

English Medieval Mystics: Games of Faith
Marion Glasscoe

The Fabliau in English
John Hines

Frontispiece: An early image of fabliau?

This book starts with literature of the twelfth century and ends with James Joyce in the twentieth. It is remarkable, however, how many echoes of the role and perception of fabliau that this book traces in and through this long period can also be discerned in the later eleventh-century, early Norman English Bayeux Tapestry. Brief scenes from perhaps indecent tales never to be told, of 'a certain cleric' and a lady Ælfgyva for instance, or of the couple here, counterpoint the Tapestry's predominantly noble images of knightly actions, heraldic and fabulous beasts and the like. While for a time these may seem to expose, comically though vigorously, what lies underneath the nobler trappings, a sadder theme may be revealed in the final lower borders of the Tapestry, where the earlier erotic nudes – all found in the borders – are recalled by ignominiously stripped and dismembered bodies of men who have fallen in the Battle of Hastings.

(Section 1314 from the Bayeux Tapestry, reproduced by kind permission of Fotomas Index.)

John Hines

THE FABLIAU IN ENGLISH

LONGMAN
LONDON AND NEW YORK

Longman Group UK Limited,
Longman House, Burnt Mill,
Harlow, Essex CM20 2JE, England
and Associated Companies throughout the world.

Published in the United States of America
by Longman Publishing, New York

First published 1993

ISBN 0 582 037328 CSD
ISBN 0 582 037336 PPR

British Library Cataloguing-in-Publication Data

A catalogue record for this book is
available from the British Library

Library of Congress Cataloging-in-Publication Data

Hines, John 1956–
    The Fabliau in English / John Hines.
        p. cm. – (Longman medieval and Renaissance library)
    Includes bibliographical references and index.
    ISBN 0-582-03732-8 (CSD). – ISBN 0-582-03733-6 (PPR)
    1. English poetry – Middle English, 1100–1500 –History and criticism. 2.
Narrative poetry, English – History and criticism. 3. Chaucer, Geoffrey, d.1400.
Canterbury tales. 4. Tales, Medieval – History and criticism. 5. English poetry –
French influences. 6. Fabliaux – History and criticism. I. Title. II. Series.
PR317.N28H56 1993   92-33700
    821'.03–dc20   CIP

Set by 7pp in 10/12 Benbo
Produced by Longman Singapore Publishers (Pte) Ltd.
Printed in Singapore

Contents

Preface

Fabliau is a precise literary term. It derives from a word found in the Picard dialect of medieval French. This word and its contemporary Central French counterparts *fablel*, *flabel* and sometimes even *flablel* clearly denoted a particular type of verse story that is quite numerously represented in twelfth- to fourteenth-century French literature; the term was eventually revived in later French literary scholarship and in due course adopted by English as well. Unlike a term such as *short story*, which uses basic vocabulary and is therefore self-explanatory at least at an introductory level, at the start of a book on the fabliau the reader can reasonably demand an early answer to the straightforward query 'What is a fabliau?'

This question is more complicated than it would seem if it were conceived of as a simple factual question seeking a concrete answer. This is because it implies a more theoretical, prior question: what class of thing is fabliau? The easy answer to this is that fabliau is a literary *genre* (in very simple terms a 'type', as already stated); but here the cycle of questions revolves again: what actually is a genre? Conceptualizing 'genre' has proved a considerably thornier problem for literary scholars than describing the primary characteristics of fabliau.

It would be false to pretend that investigating the problem of the nature of genre was the *raison d'être* for this book, or indeed that this preliminary problem is not really rather unwelcome: a distracting and abstract obstacle in the scheme of this study. In a sense, however, this whole book does offer an answer to the question of what a genre is, at least in the form of an assessment of the place of the history of fabliau within the history of literary genres in Europe from the Middle Ages to the modern era. More appropriate than trying to offer a summary of the answer to this very general question at the outset, then, is to indicate how such an answer can be found here.

In practice, the position adopted in relation to the problem coincides closely with that described by Hans Robert Jauss:[1] that literary genres are not static entities defined by fixed and timeless models or formulae but rather are historical phenomena that can grow, expand and mutate. Jauss indeed suggests these may live (and die) in accordance with some recurrent life cycle. Most pertinently, this implies that genres are properly to be described before being defined (or even instead of being defined). Attention should therefore be paid first to the recurrent characteristics of the 'type', the body of literature that seems *de facto* to form the genre, and secondarily to its taxonomic relationships with different literature, contrastive or similar, and how genres thus function in relation to one another in the whole body of literature.

In the same practical terms, the medieval French fabliaux have unquestionable priority in characterizing this genre. Medieval fabliau was most clearly conceptually recognized as a genre in France. Texts related to the medieval French fabliaux are also found in England, in Anglo-Norman and Middle English for instance, and in other medieval European literatures. This book in fact will argue very much for the critical and historical independence of the English (and some other) fabliaux from the French tradition. The evidence for French sources either for individual tales or for the whole tradition in England turns out to be limited. Individual fabliaux, it is argued, and the development of fabliau equivalents in individual literatures, can and should be appreciated individually. It is often more productive to refer to the spectrum of other types of literature in which the fabliaux in English take their place and to their immediate historical context to achieve a critical understanding and appreciation of this literature than to compare them with foreign-language counterparts.

Nevertheless, we shall look to build to begin with upon the substantial foundations of the medieval French fabliaux and modern scholarship concerned with these tales; we shall examine the range and general characteristics of these texts, and the more contentious

1. See Jauss H R 'Theory of Genres and Medieval Literature' in *idem* 1982 *Towards an Aesthetic of Reception*, translated by Timothy Bahti (University of Minnesota Press, Minneapolis) pp. 79–109, especially pp. 93–4, and Hertog *Chaucer's Fabliaux as Analogues, passim.*

questions of their origins and their tone. Attention then moves, via the French fabliaux in England, to the Middle English fabliaux. These are few, but all worth studying in careful detail. Inevitably the centre of this book is occupied by a study of Chaucer's fabliaux, considering both the interpretation of these tales and the use Chaucer made of them especially in the general context of the Canterbury Tales. The perspective then widens again in the final chapter, to set the picture drawn of the Middle English fabliaux in a literary–historical context that includes both a survey of fabliaux (and their equivalents) in other medieval literatures of western Europe and the post-medieval history of fabliau tales.

Ultimately this study seeks to do nothing more earnest than to contribute to the informed enjoyment of a body of literature which practical teaching experience shows can give a great deal of pleasure. If this book has at its heart any particular thesis to promote, I would claim that that thesis is that such pleasure is often sophisticated in a way that matches the sophistication inherent both in the production and the reception of at least a significant number of the fabliaux in the Middle Ages. (Reception, here, is treated in terms of the reception and reproduction of the tradition by new generations of authors: no substantial attempts are made to reveal hitherto hidden details concerning the readership of the fabliaux.) It is hoped, of course, that the analysis of the material carried out here will prove accurate and rational enough to be of use to critics working in other schools of analysis and interpretation. The conclusions of this book remain literary; they concern the function of fabliau in a literary world of readers, writers, genres and texts, upon which more general observations about the nature and function of *comedy*, which fabliau can truly represent, can be based.

I acknowledge with gratitude the encouragement and advice given to me in the preparation of this book by Longman. Thanks are due to library staff around the country for assisting me with access to manuscripts and many less easily found books and periodicals. Particular thanks are due to a number of close colleagues, in Cardiff and abroad, for their interest in the project and guidance on matters of detail: to Dafydd Johnston, who read the whole typescript as well as putting his expertise on the Welsh material at my disposal; to W. A. (Bill) Sullivan, in respect of the Old French material and to Rolf Bremmer and Erik Hertog in respect of the Middle Dutch *et al*. The backing and co-operation of my home department, the School of English Studies in the University of Wales, Cardiff, is much appreciated, as, finally, is the enthusiasm and enjoyment of the fabliaux expressed by many students in Cardiff, without which this book would never have been thought of.

Wherever possible, quotations from Old French fabliaux in this book are taken from Noomen and van den Boogard, *Nouveau Recueil Complet des Fabliaux,* and quotations from Chaucer from L. D. Benson *et al., The Riverside Chaucer.*

To KFP and MBP
for their teaching

Chapter 1

The French fabliaux

THE CATEGORY OF *FABLIAU*

Discounting variant examples of what is fundamentally the same tale, there are at least 127 fabliaux in the medieval French corpus. This is the number of fabliaux accepted in a *Nouveau Recueil Complet des Fabliaux* which has been published in parts since 1983 and which is, at the time of writing, about half complete in terms of the number of fabliaux published. The earliest French works now accepted as fabliaux date from the last decade of the twelfth century and the latest seem to have been composed about 150 years later, somewhere around 1340. As the modern term for this genre the word *fabliau* can be traced back to scholarly writing of the seventeenth century. *Fabliau(s)* is in fact the form this word took in the dialect of the north-eastern corner of France in the twelfth to fourteenth century (the final -*s* is a nominative singular case marker that is lost during this period). The greatest geographical concentration of provenanced medieval French fabliaux lies in this area of Picardy, and the use of the resurrected dialectal form is thus justified.

The word *fabliau* itself is found as a label in roughly half of this group of texts. While there are also a number of texts that claim to be fabliaux but which are not now considered to belong to the genre, the common characteristics of the type (described below) are sufficiently clear for the same number of texts again to be identified with and added to the self-proclaimed fabliaux. It is difficult to estimate how many more of these medieval works may have once existed but have since been lost. Joseph Bédier, the French scholar whose book published exactly a hundred years ago proved to be the inception of modern fabliau studies, inferred from the number of known authors and the number of anonymous fabliaux that only about one-eighth of the original corpus survives. As the Danish scholar Per Nykrog has observed, however, the corpus of fabliaux seems to be constituted of a certain stock of recognized tales rather than being the product of widespread and prolific extemporization as Bédier was inclined to believe. This observation is based on the high number of copies that there are of certain fabliaux and the number of variants that there are of others. It implies that we have a higher proportion of the original corpus surviving than Bédier calculated, and therefore a more representative sample.

The etymology of the medieval French word carries some suggestion of what the characteristic features of tales of this genre were originally considered to be, although nothing detailed enough to form a definition. The root of the word is French *fable*, a term as broad and adaptable as Modern English 'story'. Amongst the term's more specialized medieval uses, however, is a sense that it shares with its Latin ancestor *fabula*. This is the sense that is represented by the title *Aesop's Fables*: used of unrealistic stories (Aesop's fables are unrealistic in that they present anthropomorphized beasts and birds) which may nonetheless present a valuable and pertinent moral to their readers. As we shall soon see, both realism and moral message are aspects of the French fabliaux that are much discussed. It is hard to read lines such as:

> Icil fableau ce est la voire

> (This fabliau is the truth)

which is the first line of the fabliau *Le Prestre qui ot mere a force*, 'The priest who had a mother forced upon him', without believing that medieval French writers and readers of fabliaux could also be highly conscious, however flippantly, of the problematic nature of terms such as 'truth' in the context of this genre.

CHARACTERISTICS OF THE FRENCH FABLIAU

"Contes à rire en vers"

Although, as we shall see, many varied and lengthy accounts of what may have been the distinguishing characteristics of the fabliaux have been produced, the short definition given by Bédier in 1893 still attracts support: the fabliaux, he declared, are "contes à rire en vers".

The success of this definition is surprising, for it is a somewhat artificial expression for Modern French, and on the testimony of native French speakers on whom the phrase has been sprung its meaning is not immediately obvious. One would most readily suppose that "à rire" means 'to be laughed at', throwing emphasis on to the author's intention, but it seems possible, too, that it could be interpreted as 'playful'. However we interpret the phrase it is too general: there are many 'contes à rire en vers' that have never been taken for fabliaux. This is to say nothing of the varied forms and objects of laughter that there may be: spontaneous hilarity; dark chuckles over black humour; knowing, ironic laughter; the nervous giggles of imperfect comprehension. But by listing such possibilities we can already see how Bédier's definition may be serviceable in structuring discussion: identifying a set of three basic traits of the fabliau, each of which may be elaborated upon to produce an informative description of the subject, *fabliaux*.

Primarily, then, the fabliaux are *contes*, narrative stories. We shall see, in fact, that it is upon relatively clear and simple structural properties of the plot that an initial identification of a text as fabliau-like depends. The writer's intention to amuse, or the reader's amusement, are not easy issues to deal with in any summary way, but various forms of surprise and shock which may well cause a laugh or a smile will emerge as essential in distinguishing the fabliau. The greatest significance of the fact that the fabliaux are *contes en vers* is actually obscured by Bédier's focusing on the regular use of the verse mode. Prose narrative of the Middle Ages is overwhelmingly in Latin; vernacular narrative is usually in verse. The fact that the fabliaux are versified is a reflex of the more important fact that these are stories *in the vernacular* to be laughed at.

Fabliau narrative is characteristically brief, and the plot is complicated and problematic only for some of the characters within the tales, not for the well-informed readers or audience of the piece. There are frequently one or more characters within the fabliau who are as well informed of the situation as the reader may be, and in control of it. The difference between the situation of such characters and the readers and that of the remaining characters within the fabliaux makes *irony* a typical feature of the experience of reading a fabliau. Such irony is, inevitably, part of the effect of what the fullest analysis of the narrative structure of the French fabliaux published to date, that of Mary Jane Stearns Schenk (1987), finds to be an indispensable element in the fabliaux: a *deception* played by one or more characters on one or more other characters followed by a *misdeed* committed by the deceiver(s). Such events can indeed conclude a fabliau.

Reading through the Old French fabliaux one finds persistently recurring examples of certain types of dramatic situation created and resolved by the deception and misdeed. Rather than pursuing the discussion at an abstract level, it seems sensible to give here a brief synopsis of a selection of French fabliaux which can be regarded as highly typical of the genre, and which represent a range of subtypes within the genre: tales of sensual appetite or greed, adultery and fornication, sexual naivety and sexual fetishism; a tale of robbers, the macabre joke of the corpse that apparently either cannot or will not lie still, and a lavatorial tale of turds.

Le Bouchier d'Abeville, 'The butcher of Abbeville', is found in five French manuscripts. It tells of a butcher returning home empty-handed from a market, and looking for lodgings in a village that lies on his route homewards as it is too late at night for him to reach home. He is refused hospitality by the rich village priest, who lives with a concubine. He comes across a flock of sheep belonging to the priest, one of which he takes; he then returns to the priest, pretending not to be the traveller already refused entry, and this time is accepted in as he offers the sheep in payment. The animal is slaughtered and skinned; after a fine meal a young servant girl is ordered to ensure the guest wants for nothing. The priest and his concubine retire; the guest soon seduces the girl with the promise of the sheepskin in payment. Early in the morning the priest leaves to say the offices in the church. The butcher goes to take his leave of his hostess, but finding her naked in bed soon has his will of her, again promising her the sheepskin. Then the butcher goes to the church to take leave of the priest, and as a token of his gratitude sells him the sheepskin at a knock-down price of two sous. By the time the priest arrives the two women are at blows over the sheepskin. The priest soon learns why they both claim the sheepskin. He collapses into a miserable heap, but to round things off his shepherd comes to report that one of the sheep is missing, and identifies the disputed sheepskin as that of this beast. The priest finally concludes that the sheepskin is properly his, as he paid for it in goods not services. The author finally asks of his readers/ audience which of the claimants had best title to the sheepskin.

Les Perdris, 'The partridges', is a shorter and rather gentler tale. A peasant catches two partridges, takes them home to his wife to cook and sets off to invite the village priest to join them. The birds are ready before he returns, and the wife takes a morsel of them, but cannot stop herself before she has eaten both birds. When her husband returns, she first pretends that the cat has taken them, but when he does not believe this reassures him that the birds are being kept hot and that he should fetch his knife to cut them. While he sharpens his knife the priest arrives. The wife, in a panic, tells him that her husband is whetting his knife in order to castrate him, implying that the husband has some grounds for suspecting a sexual relationship between the wife and the priest. The priest, understandably, flees; the wife tells her husband that he is running off with the partridges, with the result that the husband pursues the priest brandishing his knife, apparently confirming what the wife told the priest. This "fabliaus" ends by claiming to be an example of the innate deceptiveness of woman:

> Fame est fete por decevoir
> Mençonge fet devenir voir
> Et voir fet devenir mençonge.

> (Woman is made to deceive:
> lying she turns into truth
> and truth she turns into lying.)

Les Trois Boçus, 'The three hunchbacks', is a harsher tale, found, along with *Les Perdris*, in a single copy in the largest known collection of French fabliaux, in a manuscript in the Bibliothèque National in Paris. A rich but ugly hunchback is able to obtain a beautiful young girl to be his wife and then guards her with consuming jealousy. One day, three hunchback minstrels are allowed in to entertain them; they are subsequently sent off and forbidden ever to return. But the young wife has been charmed by their singing, and when her husband is out she calls them back; unfortunately the husband returns inopportunely. The minstrels are hastily hidden in trunks, where they suffocate. The woman discovers their bodies after the husband has departed again, and calls in a "porter" to remove and dispose of one of the bodies for a rich sum. When he returns for his payment she shows him another body, claiming the porter has not done the job asked of him. The astonished porter disposes of this body as the previous one, but returns for his payment only to find, apparently, the corpse waiting for him again. This third body is disposed of, but as the porter returns he encounters the hunchback husband who he supposes to be the corpse returning yet one more time. He seizes him and disposes of him in the river like the previous three bodies, and finally gets his pay, the wife being all the more glad for having got rid of her repugnant husband. A moral conclusion drawn is that money is powerful but harmful, and that:

> . . . onques Dieus ne fist meschine
> C'on ne puist por deniers avoir.
>
> (. . . God never made a woman
> that one could not have for money.)

Les quatre Souhais Saint Martin, 'The four wishes of St Martin', a fabliau found in four manuscripts, one copy being an Anglo-Norman version in an English manuscript, represents a distinctive subset of fabliaux with a supernatural and religious setting. A peasant who is especially devoted to St Martin meets the saint one day and is told that his devotion is rewarded by four wishes. He goes home, to be abused by his wife for not being at work, until he tells her of his heavenly gift. Eventually he allows his wife to make the first wish; she wishes for him:

> Que tot soiez chargiez de viz
>
> ('That you should be completely covered with penises')

(*vit*, *viz* in fact has much more the tone of modern colloquial English *prick(s)*: see further below). He retaliates by wishing:

> Que tu raies autretant cons
> Comme je ai de viz sor moi
>
> ('That you should have as many cunts
> as I have pricks on me')

The peasant then seeks to reverse these wishes by wishing:

> Q'ele n'ait con ne il n'ait vit
>
> (That she had no cunt and he had no prick)

which of course removes every single one of these organs from their bodies. The last wish then has to be used to restore one each of these to its proper place. Thus all the wishes have been wasted leaving the couple as they were. The brief moral drawn at the end of the original French version of this tale is that he who trusts his wife more than himself will frequently regret it.

Barat et Haimet is one of the robber's tales, relatively long and preserved in four large manuscript collections of fabliaux. It is datable to the late twelfth century and attributable to the earliest named fabliau author, Jean Bodel. Interestingly, the manuscript regarded as providing the best text of the poem, Bibliothèque National fr.19152, labels the work a "fable" in the first line while the other copies read "fabliaus" or "fableaus", suggesting that the category of fabliau may not have been so clearly defined and recognized at this early date as it was later to become. Barat and Haimet are two brothers, who at the start of the tale are passing through a forest with a companion called Travers. Haimet shows off by climbing a tree, first to steal eggs from a nest without the bird sitting there noticing, and then by returning the eggs likewise. While he does the latter, his brother, whose name means 'deceit', trumps him by stealing his trousers from him, much to Travers's amusement and Haimet's embarrassment. Travers realizes that he is not as skilled as these two and returns home to his wife, Marie, and a more honest way of making a living. At Christmas they are able to have a pig slaughtered. This is noticed by Barat and Haimet who happen to call on Travers while he is out, and they plan to steal the meat. Meanwhile Travers and his wife, though unsuspecting, move and cover the meat. Thus Barat and Haimet are nonplussed when they return in the dark of night, but Barat takes advantage of an absence of Travers to imitate his voice in the darkness and to elicit from Marie the secret of where the meat is. When the real Travers returns his wife chides him for being so forgetful, from which Travers deduces what has happened. He sets off after the brothers, succeeds in imitating Haimet, and relieves Barat of his burden. Barat discovers the trick played upon him when he finds the real Haimet without the meat. Barat then returns, encounters Travers, and succeeds in imitating Marie and obtaining the meat in order to perform a bizarre ritual to preserve it from theft:

> Et cul et con trois foiz touchier

> (To touch both arse and cunt three times)

Travers soon discovers that he has been deceived again, and sets off once more to retrieve his property. This time he imitates a man hanging from a tree, which Barat and Haimet take for the ghost of their hanged father, drop their booty and flee. Returning with the meat, Travers and Marie decide to cook it there and then. Unfortunately both he and Marie fall asleep, and Haimet now spears and steals a piece of bacon from the boiling cauldron. Just then, Travers awakes, and to put an end to this to-ing and fro-ing invites his former companions to share the meat with him. It is divided into three; the brothers take two pieces leaving Travers and Marie with one. The conclusion of the tale is:

> Por ce fut dit, segnor baron,
> Male compaigne a en larron.

> (For this reason is this told, my lords:
> a robber makes bad company.)

The final example of the French fabliau to be summarized here is *Jouglet*, of interest to us both as an example of the scope for lavatory humour in the fabliau and for making a *jongleur*, a stereotyped character who is a sort of disreputable wandering entertainer, its central character. *Jouglet* is a personal name based upon *jongleur*, which is frequently written in the form *jougler* in medieval French. The tale begins with a retarded youth, Robin, whose mother succeeds in arranging for him a marriage with a beautiful young woman, Mahaut. The mother then hires a jongleur, Jouglet, to teach her son the facts of life; i.e. what he is expected to do on his wedding night and thereafter. Jouglet first gets Robin to eat masses of pears. As a result Robin's stomach is in turmoil throughout the ceremony and the evening of the wedding; in the marital bed he tells his new wife what has happened. To avenge herself on Jouglet, she directs Robin to relieve his bowels over the sleeping Jouglet, which he does, again and again, covering his sheets and clothes, filling his fireplace, water bucket and the bag for his *violle*, with excrement. In the morning, Mahaut wakes Jouglet for some music; he discovers, Midas-like, the shit everywhere he turns and in or on everything he touches: he leaves in a rage of humiliation. But as he goes, he passes a village where the villagers insist on some music from him. Eventually he orders them to unpack his instrument themselves: two of them then plunge their hands into the contents of his bag. He is then soundly beaten. The moral conclusion is:

Tel cuide conchier autrui
Qui assez miez conchie lui

(He thought to shit on another
but was shitted on much more himself.)

The six fabliaux selected for summarizing here are, if in any way at all, only slightly untypical in being generally longer than average, this being an efficient way of conveying something of the range of what is to be found amongst the French fabliaux. The most frequent type of tale found in these fabliaux is that dealing with the range of experiences of sexual gratification, marriage and adultery. In these situations, the characters are related to one another by a basic set of human relationships: desire, friendship, hatred and rivalry. The subset containing fabliaux with lavatory humour, tales concerning basic bodily functions of excretion or flatulence, are fewer in number. Most of these have tales which turn around such bodily necessities alone, but *Jouglet* shows how this type of tale can be made to co-act with a sexual one, the motif of the sexually incompetent young husband.

Characterization and the target figure

The brevity, or, rather, the efficiency, of French fabliau narrative is reflected by the typical forms of characterization in these tales. Most characters are simply sketched types rather than carefully constructed characters: the beautiful young wife, either licentious or honest but nearly always cunning; the prostitute; the husband, more often foolish than wise; the lover, more likely to be clever than a husband is. The sex of the character is usually the most prominent and significant variable in characterization. Most characters too are briefly designated in the tales by their social role: the townsman or townswoman, the peasant and the peasant's wife; the *jongleur*, the clerk, the priest, the knight, the squire. Beyond this, characterization rarely goes further than the creation of characters sufficient for the roles they play within the fabliau; there is very rarely the slightest pretence at verisimilitude in the form of feigning that the characters have experiences beyond or after those of the narrative given. There is nothing to encourage any speculation on what the butcher of Abbeville, the peasants, their wives or the priest in *Les Perdris* or *Les quatre Souhais Saint Martin*, Barat, Haimet and Travers, or Jouglet *et al.* did before or after the events we are told of in the tales, and this holds for the great majority of the fabliaux.

The deception, trick or ruse that forms the one essential element in the interaction of the fabliau characters is most frequently an impromptu action, very commonly occurring in the first instance as an example of a native cunning attributed to women, an ingenuity in lying and deceit that women have. This attribute has a place in an adverse stereotype of the woman that was promoted by a medieval tradition of *antifeminist* writing. The fabliaux, however, show very much less interest in exposing the wickedness of the tricksters than in ridiculing the tricked. Laughter is a means of expressing judgement that is directed at the characters who fail in some way in the text. The ridicule to which the dupes are condemned may be explicitly orchestrated by the author, by providing characters within the text to laugh at the victim. An especially clear example is in the fabliau *Boivin de Provins*, in which the hero, Boivin, having deluded a household of whores into providing him with a meal and a girl for free, and having set them at each other's throats, goes off to tell the provost of the town the tale, who in turn spreads the tale around, producing much mirth and laughter. An additional irony at the very end of this fabliau resides in the claim that Boivin himself 'made' this fabliau, and was paid ten sous by the provost for it. The provost, then, may be the last dupe of the character Boivin − or of the author? − although if the provost seeks only entertainment, not truth, out of the tale, he is hardly a ridiculous victim of this enhanced narratorial persona. This complication is a special extension to the range of the fabliau plot rather than an incongruous exception to the confinement of the 'life' of a character to the events of the fabliau story.

It has been a point frequently made that the characters exposed to ridicule are never given attributes that can have been designed to evoke sympathy from the reader; frequently quite the contrary. The target figure is usually a character whose comeuppance, in terms of simple poetic justice, is most likely to be reassuring: types such as the avaricious or preoccupied merchant, the boorish peasant, the selfish priest, in the roles of jealous husband or cohabitor, or selfish would-be seducer. We may note that in its targeting of a number of these figures, the fabliaux present a morality that does not offer a blanket indulgence to sexual desires; in some respects fabliau morality is very conventional.

With the illicit amorous adventures of wives in the situation of the eternal triangle (husband, wife, lover) being the most common single dramatic type in the fabliaux, the most frequent type as the object of ridicule is the deceived husband, often not merely cuckolded but on occasion beaten or otherwise degraded or abused as well; and what is more after all this sometimes so utterly deceived that he remains happy in the delusion that his wife has proved herself faithful to him. An elegant example of this is *La Bourgoise d'Orliens*, 'The townswoman of Orléans', in which the husband, a merchant, suspecting his wife of having a clerk as a lover (which she has) tests her by pretending to go away but returning in the guise of a clerk. She sees through the ruse and has the supposed clerk locked away, then beaten by her servants and dumped on a dungheap. Meanwhile she spends the night with her lover. The battered husband returns to be told and "reconforté", 'comforted', by the tale of the treatment meted out to the would-be seducer. The underlying value-system is clear, as the dream of a world in which the unconstrained sexuality of the favoured male and female characters converges, and is expressed without shame.

In technical terms, irony is, as noted, an important element in the amusement that can be felt at the plight of characters like this merchant of Orléans. Irony exists as a relationship between writer and reader (two further characters?), usually created by the writer, with regard to the characters and events within the fabliau. The two basic forms of irony found in these tales are verbal irony and dramatic irony. It is a case of dramatic irony when we as readers recognize and share with the fabliau author a knowledge of the 'realities' of the fictitious situation denied to the merchant of Orléans and may laugh at the merchant's misguided belief as a result. It is verbal irony when some character comes out with a statement or a choice of words which have a meaning to those in the know, either within the text or outside it, that is significantly different or even contradictory to that which the character may be supposed to have in mind. Especially rich in irony is *Le Prestre et Alison*, 'The Priest and Alison', in which a lecherous priest believes he has succeeded in bedding a beautiful young girl but has had, in the darkness, an elderly whore substituted for her. When he arrives for his pleasure he is asked by the girl's mother:

Avez vos l'avoir aporté
Que vos devez doner ma fille?

('Have you brought the goods
that you are to give to my girl?')

and he replies:

Dame, ne sui pas ci par gile!
J'ai les garnemenz aportez:
Veez les ci! Or esgardez
Quar il sont et bel et plaisant.
Vos me tenroiz a voir disant
Ainz que parte de vo maison.
Foi que ge doie a seint Simon,
Ge n'amai onques a trichier.

('Lady, I am not here by a trick!
I have brought the garments.
See them here! Now, look
for they are both fine and pleasing.
You shall see that I am truthful
before I leave your house.
By the faith that I owe St Simon,
I have never liked cheating.')

On top of the irony within the tales of these kinds, Schenk notes a more serious irony, involving the reader as a character or a 'subject' moulded by the text, in some of the laughter that the tales may provoke. Besides laughing with a comforting or gratifying sense of superiority when confronted with pictures of the incompetence of figures who the readers may recognize as representing their fellow men, the readers may also be regarded, she suggests, as laughing at common humankind and thus also (unconsciously) at themselves. This is linked in her book to schools of intellectual speculation, both medieval and modern, of a kind that will be further discussed later in this chapter. In advance of that, however, it can be noted here that as a generalization about the fabliaux, rather than a point to consider in relation to some fabliaux, her claim may go too far. The real problem for Schenk's case is the question of how far the target figures of the fabliaux can be identified with the real humanity that both authors and readers/listeners must be part of. The simple realism of any characters in the fabliaux is very limited: often no more than the characters being given recognizable and common social functions.

The sort of rebounding abuse, the trickster tricked, the reader (ironically) laughing at an image he does not realize is his own, that she describes, is indeed a pattern that is found in *some* fabliaux. Simple examples have been shown, for instance, in *Barat et Haimet* and *Jouglet*. In the discussion of Chaucer's Reeve's Tale in Chapter 4 of this book, however, we shall find an argument that this sort of 'measure for measure' reading has sometimes been imputed by modern critics to texts in a way that is neither strongly supported by the text itself nor an enhancement of the reading of the text.

Realism

The fabliaux do, however, maintain a number of prominent characteristics that can be called 'realistic'. Characters are most frequently involved in actions as they actively or passively deserve. It is important to note that chance plays virtually no part in the unfolding of events within these tales. As was noted in the context of *Les quatre Souhais Saint Martin*, supernatural settings and in particular the agency of supernatural forces are quite rare. In this way the fabliaux present a consistent world of characters and events, a world that in terms of the motivation and execution of actions, of the basic set of relationships noted above, is very much a human world. This anthropocentric view and attitude is one facet of what is frequently identified as the realism of the fabliaux.

Realism is also a feature of the characterization of time and place. The French fabliaux are generally consistent in the setting of the action. Most common are settings that are both urban and domestic, events taking place in or around private homes in the towns. These form a larger group than fabliaux set in the country, largely in villages, although the latter group is still a substantial one. It is rare for the scene to shift to a setting of higher status, in a castle, manor or abbey, etc., though some such examples can be found. Emblematic of the limited but crucial shift the fabliaux make use of from a thoroughly familiar world to one that is somewhat different is the extent to which the stories take place in the deep darkness of the medieval French night: as, for instance, all the tit-for-tat stealing and impersonation of *Barat et Haimet*. Darkness aids deception, of course, although the tricks played and misdeeds committed seem to lose little of their quality of daring for being performed under the cover of night.

Les quatre Souhais Saint Martin stands at the edge of a relatively small, distinctive subset of irreverent fabliaux, fabliaux which powerfully exploit the inherent realism of the genre by reducing the characters and setting of the Christian heaven to a comically mundane and very human level: Heaven and Hell become just two alternatives amongst the familiar *loci* of the fabliaux. A very clear example of this is *Le Vilain qui conquist Paradis par plait*, 'The peasant who conquered Paradise by arguing'. This tale starts with an unmistakably satirical point, on how the soul of a dead peasant is ignored:

> Tels aventure li avint
> Q'angles ne deables ne vint
> A cele eure que il fu mors.
> Qant l'ame s'en isci del cors
> Ne trueve qui rien li demant
> Ne nule cosse li commant.

> (It so befell him
> that neither angel nor devil came
> at the hour that he was dead.
> When the spirit parted from the body
> it found no one asking anything of it
> nor giving it any directions.)

St Peter first rebuffs the soul:

> Nos n'avons cure de vilain

> ('We are not concerned with a peasant')

but the unflappable soul gradually argues its way in past Peter, Thomas, Paul and finally God, nonplussing the saints by reminding them of their faults in life, but making a moral and liturgical claim on God's final grace. The conclusion of the tale:

> Miels valt engiens que ne fait fors

> (Trickery achieves more than force can do)

could stand as the epitome of the whole fabliau corpus.

Considerably more sacrilegious, albeit in a flippant way, is *Du Con qui fu fait a la besche*, 'Of the cunt, which was made with a spade', in which God is presented as having forgotten to give Eve genitals and then allowing the Devil to remedy this, on the condition that he neither adds to nor takes anything away from God's creature. The Devil chooses to model the appropriate part with a spade, and for good measure farts on the woman's tongue, rendering woman innately garrulous (another antifeminist commonplace). This fabliau makes explicit a linkage between vagina and mouth that we find implied elsewhere amongst the fabliaux: e.g. in *Le Chevalier qui fist parler les cons*, 'The knight who made the cunts talk', or *Berengier au lonc cul*, 'Berengier of the long arse', where a woman disguised as a knight makes her recreant husband kiss what seems to him to be her exceptionally long arse. Despite the damage the enticing vagina causes, it is essential not to slander women, for worse in the way of verbal retribution will come back in return.

More seriously sacrilegious is surely *Saint Pierre et le jongleur*, 'Saint Peter and the jongleur', in which a jongleur's soul goes off to Hell with a number of other satirically identified characters – jousting men, usurers, thieves, bishops, priests, monks, abbots, knights – but presents itself, incongruously, as that of a relatively good character, anxious, for instance, to please its new infernal master (in a witty parody of the Orpheus story) by singing. The jongleur is left to watch over some souls, but is approached by St Peter, with whom he plays two different games of dice, gambling for the souls. This aspect of the story has shocking implications as a representative of what might appear to be the random and unjust way by which salvation may be achieved – although St Peter always wins. A refrain-like line:

"Hé" dit Saint Pierre. . .

("Hey", said Saint Peter. . .)

renders Peter as a familiar *ribaud*, a colloquially-speaking gambler. "Hé" is also put into God's mouth in *Du Con qui fu fait a la besche*. The games end in a brawl between the jongleur, who feels he is being cheated, and the saint. To his further credit the jongleur has the sense to know when he is beaten. The poem represents the interests of the poet/jongleur's party: the denouement is that the Devil bars all jongleurs from Hell.

The image of God as a cosmic gambler can also be found in *Brunain*, where a simple peasant and his wife find God to be good *doublere*, 'doubler', giving them a second beast when they naively give their own cow to the priest who has told them that God repays gifts twofold. 'Doubling' in the context of gambling is clearly shown in *Saint Pierre et le jongleur*, where during the two games the stakes played for are steadily doubled.[1] The verb *dobler* can also, significantly, carry the sense of 'to deceive'. *Le Prestre et les deus ribaus*, 'The priest and the two wastrels', presents us with sacrilegious puns on 'dé/Dé' (die [plural *dice*]/God) and 'douze/Dieus' (twelve [=double-six]/God).

Language

The characteristic styles of discourse and the linguistic comic devices of the French fabliaux are also related fundamentally to the tales' narrative character. If the narrative is to be presented relatively rapidly, then brevity must be a feature of the style expected. As with gratuitous elaboration of character or place, it is not the case that the rhetorical ornamentation of text, or emphasis of passages of text, is generally absent; rather that these are used sparingly and therefore to particular effect. Although it is true, as Charles Muscatine has recently pointed out,[2] that it is inappropriate and impossible to seek to classify fabliaux *in toto* as representing one of the styles of Latin rhetoric recognized in the medieval schools – *humilis, medius* or *gravis*: low, middle or high – fabliau authors can call up such a range of styles for good local effect. The low style is surely recalled by the colloquial "Hé" given to God and St Peter as noted above, and the high by the description of the young wife in *Les Trois Boçus*:

> une belle fille
> Si bele que c'ert uns delis
> Et se le voir vous en devis
> Je ne cuit qu'ainz feist Nature
> Nule plus bele creature.

> (a beautiful girl
> So beautiful that she was a delight
> And if I should tell you the truth
> I do not think that Nature ever made
> Any more beautiful creature.)

1. See MacGillavry K 1978 Le jeu de dés dans le fabliau de *St Pierre et le Jongleur, Marche romane* XXVIII pp 175–9, for a discussion of the mathematics of gambling stakes in such literature.
2. Muscatine *Old French Fabliaux* p 58.

But the most significant point to make is that to attempt to force the fabliaux to fit some standard rhetorical classification is not just (perhaps) irrelevant, but, more seriously, distracting in respect of the frequently clever and significant exploitation of language in these texts. In a fabliau called *La Saineresse*, 'The female blood-letter', for instance, the deceptive actions performed by the deceiving character are actions entirely of speech, as a wife who has had sexual intercourse with a man her dull-witted husband believes to be a female blood-letter describes her act of illicit fornication to her duped and satisfied husband entirely in metaphors:

Sire, merci por amor Dé
Ja ai je esté trop traveillie.
Si ne pooie estre sainie
Et m'a plus de cent cops ferue
Tant que je sui toute molue.

(Sir, thank you by the love of God,
I have indeed been in hard labour.
I could not be bled
and have been dealt more than a hundred blows
so that I got a thorough grinding.)

A nice example of sophisticated linguistic play lies at the heart of *Cele qui fu foutue et desfoutue*: a tale in which a beautiful young woman, locked away in a tower by her jealous father, one day desires to buy a bird (a crane) from a young man passing by, and is told it will cost a *foutre*, a 'fuck'. She assures him she has no such thing; he enters the tower to look for a *foutre* and indeed finds one beneath the lady's clothes. Subsequently the young man passes the tower again, and the lady asks to exchange the bird for her *foutre* back. The fellow readily agrees; the lady subsequently tells her female guardian that he "desfoutue m'a", he 'has unfucked me'. The man has managed to *foutre* the girl twice, and keep his bird into the bargain. Although *desfoutre* is a perfectly proper grammatical construction, it is, of course, in real-world terms impossible to be 'unfucked', except perhaps in the mind of a naive woman who imagines that a second *foutre* can annul or return the first . . . or does she?

The notion of the fabliau being a form of linguistic game is one that has been extensively and productively explored in relatively recent scholarship. Roy J. Pearcy (1977) suggested that the fundamental comic structure of the French fabliau lay in epistemological problems: that is in failures and deceptions in understanding and communication, usually verbal as in the examples here, but by no means exclusively so. This he further suggested was a product of the same currents that saw intense conderation of such aspects of Logic in the schools and universities of the later Middle Ages. In her book *Les fabliaux*, Dominque Boutet (1985) emphasized the predominance of the 'low' discursive style and the comic exploitation of antagonisms in these texts, including antagonism between low and high culture. She describes a teasing, textual–linguistic game where, for instance, a conventionally solemn and important event such as death becomes contextually banal: just one accident amongst a hundred possible accidents that may befall Man. This may leave the reader of the fabliau puzzling over whether this is a matter of a subconscious anarchistic attitude or a conscious perception governing the composition of the fabliaux. For Boutet, the concluding morals of the fabliaux are a final inscription of the truth of traditional values; an ultimate retraction of such a challenge to the conventional order.

One of the most striking features of the diction of the fabliaux which the reader of this book should already have noted, and, perhaps, one of the most intriguing and intermittently popular features of the genre across the centuries, is the use of scurrilous language. To label and discuss – or suppress – this feature of the fabliaux as 'obscenity' has proved in the past to be unproductive, and it is perhaps better to talk instead of 'marked terms': colloquial and familiar terms for parts of the body or basic bodily acts which are labelled to varying degrees as vulgar and indecent, and not, normally, to be admitted into serious, careful or respectable discourse. Frequently these words are purportedly used by the characters within the fabliaux, such as the examples quoted above from *Les quatre Souhais Saint Martin*, but such terms are also quite often used by the narrators *propria voce*: in *Le Pescheor de Pont seur Saine*, 'The Fisherman of Pont-sur-Seine', for instance, a tale of sexual envy in a marriage, the narrator soon bluntly tells us of the couple that the man:

> A son poeir la maintenoit
> Et la fouti au mieus qu'il pot:
> Qui ce ne fait, l'amour se tot

De jane fame, quant i l'a,
Ja bone joie n'en ava,
Car jane fame bien peue
Vodroit sovent estre foutue.
Un soir gesoient en lor lit,
Au bacheler tendi le vit
Que il avoit et lonc et gros . . .

(He held her down
and gave the best fucking he could:
if a man does not do this, a young woman's love will
disappear when he has her,
and he will not find ecstasy with her:
for a young woman, properly brought up,
wants to be fucked often.
One evening they lay in their bed.
She held the young man's prick
– and he had a long and a thick one . . .)

It has been noted also that a particular salacious title for a fabliau, irrespective of the nature of the fabliau's contents, may have been the secret of the contemporary success of some, as measured by the number of extant manuscript copies. We may note *Le Chevalier qui fist parler les cons* (seven manuscript copies), *Cele qui se fist foutre sur la fosse de son mari*, 'The woman who got fucked on the tomb of her husband' (six copies), *Cele qui fu foutue et desfoutue* (six copies), *La Damoiselle qui ne pooit oïr parler de foutre*, 'The maid who could not bear hearing talk of fucking' (five copies), *La Coille noire*, 'The black balls' (six copies) or *La Dame escoillee*, 'The woman who had her balls cut off' (six copies). Only the innocently entitled *Auburee*, still a thoroughly sexual tale, exceeds all of these with eight manuscript copies. Of the remaining 120 fabliaux recognized in the *Nouveau Recueil Complet des Fabliaux*, more than half exist in a single copy, and fewer than twenty of the more innocently titled fabliaux exist in four or more manuscript copies.

The list of such marked words is not a particularly long one: for the relevant parts of the body we have *vit, coilles, con* and *cul* which correspond in meaning and, as far as one can tell, in tone, to current English *prick, balls, cunt* and *arse*; as actions *foutre* (*fuck*) or occasionally alternatives such as *corber* (*lay*); as bodily excretions *merde* and *pet* (*shit; fart*). Just as the current English equivalents suggested here, it would appear that the Old French terms bore

different degrees of markedness. A fine illustration of how these
terms are marked occurs in *L'Esquiriel*, 'The Squirrel', one of a set
of fabliaux, such as *Le Damoisselle qui ne pooit oïr parler de foutre* or
Cele qui fu foutue et desfoutue noted above, in which the markedness
or a related ignorance of such words is used as the basis of the
drama forming the narrative. A girl asks her mother 'What is the
name of the dangling thing that men have?'; the mother is
unwilling to tell her. Eventually, after some effort to put her off
with euphemisms she reveals the forbidden word: *vit*. The girl
bursts into incredulous laughter:

> Vit, dist ele, Dieu merci, vit!
> Vit, dirai je, cui qu'il anuit!
> Vit, chétive, vit dit mon pere,
> Vit dist ma suer, vit dist mon frere,
> Et vit dist nostre chamberiere
> Et vit avant et vit arriere
> Nomme chascuns a son voloir!

> ('"Vit'," she said, "Lord have mercy, 'vit'!
> 'Vit', I shall say, whoever likes it or not!
> 'Vit', dear me, 'vit' says my father,
> my sister says 'vit' and my brother says 'vit',
> and our chambermaid says 'vit';
> and 'vit' this way and 'vit' that:
> everyone says 'vit' whenever they want!")

Vit is a frequent homonym in Old French, appearing, as in Modern
French, as the *passé simple* of the verb *voir*, 'to see', and being nearly
homophonic with the nouns *vis*, 'face', and *vie*, 'life'.

The deployment of these marked terms appears virtually always
to be carefully controlled. There are few examples of their being
scattered extensively and repeatedly used within a single text; where
this does happen, as for instance in *Les quatre Souhais Saint Martin*,
the practice can readily be justified by its thematic significance (on
which see further below), as again can be seen to be the case with
the cornucopia of excrement that Robin drops on to the deservedly
victimized Jouglet.

Although the employment of such terms can be regarded as a
distinctive feature of fabliau language, there are several fabliaux
which treat of sexual adventures even in a bawdy way without
using this language. A range of euphemisms or metaphors may be
used, such as the device already noted employed by the wife to

hoodwink her husband in *La Saineresse* and to render him yet more ridiculous. The tale of *L'Esquiriel* goes on to tell of how the girl is approached by a young man playing with his erect penis; she asks him what he has there – a squirrel, is the answer; does she want it? – yes please, let me hold it; not yet, put your hand on it carefully; it's hot! – ah, it's just got out of its nest – and so on, until, after further euphemisms and foreplay, we return to the blunt world of crude speech as the squirrel enters the girl's *con* to seek from her stomach the nuts she ate the day before.

The combination of such marked terms with a widespread use of word play is what we can regard as the typical exploitation of language in the French fabliaux. The list of single words or phrases substituting for the sexual or scatological items listed above is considerably longer than the basic list; e.g. 'taking medicine' for having sexual intercourse, 'pipe' for penis, 'nest', 'eggs' and 'purse' for scrotum and testicles, 'fountain' for vagina. One of the most fascinating features of linguistic use in these works is the way in which words or syllables are used to enhance either the sensual atmosphere of the tales or the sense of scatological exposure within them. The latter situation may be illustrated by examples of the use of the word *cul*, which can, as in Modern French, have a simple sense of 'back'. In *La Male Honte*, 'Foul shame' (although the title itself is ambiguous, representing Anglo-French 'The purse of Honte', and the fabliau itself revolves around this ambiguity), the deceased Honte's friend carries the legacy due to the crown to the king "a son col": simply, 'on his back', although since we know that we are reading a "fablel" we are especially prepared for a word such as *col* = 'arse', and have to carry forward in our minds to the rest of the fabliau the notion that it might be significant that the friend carries what is due to the king on his backside. The same ambiguity is much more richly exploited in *Estula*, a robbers' tale, again turning on the verbal confusion between *Estula*, the extraordinary name of a dog, and *es tu la?*, 'are you there?' When a robber's voice responds to the calling of the dog's name, "Oui, voirement sui je ci", 'Yes, I am indeed here', the astonished dog's owner sends his son for the priest to witness this marvel. The priest, somewhat contrivedly, has to have a piggy-back to the house:

Et monte sanz plus de parole
Au col celui. . .

(And mounts without any more words
On the 'cul' of the boy. . .)

A similar effect of, on the one hand, challenging the reader to
take up an alert and interpretative role, and, on the other,
gratuitously creating an amorphous but strong atmosphere peculiar
to the fabliau through the text, is achieved by extensive use of the
homonyms *vit* and *con*, and *com-/con-* as a common suffix in the
Romance languages:

Ne sai que feisse lonc conte:
En cel chastel avoit un conte,
Et la contesse avuec, sa feme,
Qui mout ert bele et vaillant dame;
Si ot chevaliers plus de trente.
De maintenant el chastel entre
Cil qui faisoit les cons paller.
Tuit le corurent saluer,
Que mout le vuelent conjoir,
Dont il se puet mout esjoir.

(I cannot make a long tale:
in this castle there was a count
and with him the countess, his wife,
who was a very beautiful and worthy woman;
and there were [*or* she had] more than thirty knights.
He who made the cunts talk
went straightaway into the castle;
all ran to salute him
and wished to welcome him warmly,
in which he could take great pleasure.)

(*Le Chevalier qui fist parler les cons*, 337–46; cf.
Bloch *The Scandal of the Fabliaux* pp 107–10.)

This sort of process can be taken even further by exploiting the
suggestive potential of the bodily or sexual euphemisms. Co-acting
with the syllable *con-* in the passage above is the suggestive use of
joie (*joir*) (cf. the passage from *Le Pescheor de Pont seur Saine*, above,
where it has the clear sense of sexual ecstasy), the equally suggestive
emphasis on the 'entering' of the castle by the knight, and the
ambiguity of the past tense of *avoir, ot*, meaning either 'there were'
or 'she had'. In *Barat et Haimet* the sexual innuendo of Barat
approaching Marie's bed in the dark, and successfully imitating her
husband, Travers, is difficult to miss, and since we may know that

bacon, the term generally used for the meat that is stolen and stolen back over and over again, can also be used of a girl's thighs, there is a strong suggestion that the actions are really a sexual allegory: is it Marie that the three men are trying to appropriate? The final answer is no, for the text does not support a coherent allegorical interpretation, as the reader is generally aware. This does not detract from the pleasure there may be both in recognizing the possibilities and in being able to judge them unambiguously. Comparable psuedo–allegorizing may be found in, for example, *Constant du Hamel*, where Constant's wife extorts from her would be seducers a *sachet* (cf. *bourse* 'purse' - 'scrotum'), a *corroie* ('belt', 'money-pouch', therefore parallel to *bourse*) and an *anel* ('ring' - 'anus', 'labia' and ?'foreskin'), or in *Les trois Dames qui troverent l'anel*, 'The three women who found the 'ring'', which has an obvious basic parallel in *Les trois Dames qui troverent un vit*.

Language thus contributes to an atmosphere in the fabliaux that lies above and outside the describable details of character and setting: an all-enveloping 'feeling' of sensuality, shared by the real people involved – the authors and their anticipated readers/audiences – via the medium of the tale. That people delight in and desire the excitement and sensual pleasure found in sexual contact, food, bathing and money is an essential and straightforward assumption made in the fabliaux. The shifting sign-value of the terms tends to emphasize the overlap, or the common power, of three of these basic sources or types of sensual pleasure: sex, food and money; of these it is sexuality that is central, overlapping with both of the others. Philosophically, this implied recognition of the existence and power of such common pleasures could be Epicurean, or some other form of hedonism: that is, the holding of pleasure (which can be obtained in various ways, including abstinence) to be the greatest good. We can now focus more directly on the philosophical potential of the fabliaux.

SOURCES AND TONE

Theories of social origins

Amongst many other ways in which Joseph Bédier set the pattern for subsequent scholarly study of the French fabliaux in his book of

1893, he elevated the question of the social origins of this literary form. He saw the question of how such contrarious genres as fabliau and romance could co-exist in medieval French literature as a critical problem, and consequently tried to identify a source for a *taste* which could explain the proliferation and regularization of fabliau, the narrative and comical substance of which he accepted as being ubiquitous. Amongst the most pertinent critical observations he makes of the fabliaux is that they are neither truly crude and naive, nor pretentious. His cohesive solution was to see the spirit of the fabliaux, "le description ironique de la vie quotidienne et moyenne", as having been born with the *bourgeoisie*, the town dwellers, and to propose that fabliaux were the literary expression of this social class, romance that of the aristocracy.

More than sixty years later, in 1957, Per Nykrog was the first to publish a thorough critique of Bédier's theory. He, like Bédier, identified the fundamental problem posed by fabliaux to the scholar as that of identifying the social condition of the audience they were addressed to. Rather than a bourgeois audience, however, he saw the fabliau as belonging primarily to a seigneurial, aristocratic milieu, and to be closely related to romance precisely as the antithesis of romance; as being very largely parodic. Having done away with an earlier one-to-one social class to genre relationship, it is not so very surprising that Nykrog's substitute for it proved considerably less persuasive and durable than Bédier's had. By 1960 Jean Rychner produced a valuable study of how certain types of variation in the textual transmission of what were essentially the same fabliaux could be explained in terms of their being aimed at specific, and differing, audiences rather than through random mutilation and degeneration. Nonetheless Nykrog's work does demonstrate substantially the extent to which these fabliaux support and respect relative status in the existing late-feudal social scale.

More recent studies have revived the question, and tended, after a fashion, to move closer to Bédier's view. Charles Muscatine (1986) notes that the self-indulgence and materialism of the fabliaux were symptomatic of ideas that contributed to (perhaps he should have said attitudes that flourished along with) the growth of urbanism and a concurrent commercialization of the French countryside. Mary Jane Stearns Schenk (1987) completed the set of social classes to which the rise of the fabliaux had been attributed by proposing that an economically emancipated peasantry in north-eastern France provided the right conditions for the genre to prosper; a group whose primary values were competence and ambition, and success in the form of profit.

The clerkly tone

The analysis of the French fabliaux up to this point has included recurrent references to the roles of readers and writers involved with these texts. As the scholars just reviewed generally note, the social identity of the fabliau writers need not be the same as that of their typical audience. Nonetheless the characterization of the fabliau writer in the text is a worthwhile subject of study, for an assessment of the *tone* of the fabliau beyond anything it might tell us of the usual origins of such texts. The notion of 'tone' here reflects a sense of the word expressed by I. A. Richards: that *tone* resides in the relationship between the author and his readers.[3] Tone here comprises implicit communications and attitudes conveyed from the author to an informed and enquiring readership through the refractive medium of the text.

The writers of fabliaux commonly draw attention to themselves by naming themselves, signing their work at beginning or end, and they don a limited number of disguises as their narratorial *personae* – as in the case of *Boivin de Provins* described above. The most common disguise is that of the *jongleur* or *menestrel* (within the fabliau tales there is barely any discernible difference in status or respectability between these two although conventionally it is supposed that the former is lower than the latter): a disreputable itinerant entertainer living, creditably, off his wits and his talents, but only too vulnerable, and given to wasting what he gains on the temporary pleasures of drinking and gambling in the taverns; a social outcast but at the same time one called upon by the members of normal society, as Jouglet is, both to instruct the ignorant young man and to play for the villagers. This image of the jongleur is unquestionably a stereotype, a caricature, but at the same time it is historically neither entirely true nor entirely false.

Perhaps the most important aspect of this persona is the extent to which, in terms of intratextual characterization, it overlaps with the

3. Richards I A 1929 *Practical Criticism* (Cambridge University Press) p 182; cf. Ricks C 1988 *T. S. Eliot and Prejudice* (Faber and Faber) especially pp 132–3.

figure of the *clerc/clers*, a term that can best be translated as 'student' in this context. Clerks too tend to be travellers, temporary incomers to the towns where they study or just stay; they are indigent, and they are shown in the fabliaux to supply their wants, in terms of food, sex and entertainment, by dint of their wits. A useful review of the *clers* of the Old French fabliaux by Phillipe Ménard (1983) indicates that to be a clerk is a matter of attitude and behaviour rather than simply an occupation. A pertinent statistical table produced by Nykrog shows how clerks are always successful in the eternal triangle of sexual competition, pitted against husbands ranging from knights to peasants.

Through the clerkly sympathies of the fabliau corpus we can justifiably reach back to other forms of literature and literary theory associated with students and the universities and assess the fabliaux in that light. Several studies have been produced that point to correspondences between French fabliaux and intellectual (scholarly) currents of the twelfth to fourteenth centuries. Pearcy (1974) investigated the functional contrasts between explicit marked language or its detailed figurative substitutes and euphemistic language, and interpreted the results in terms of the nominalist–realist opposition in medieval philosophy.[4] Schenk (1987) supported her arguments on the importance of problems of language, reality and illusion by invoking "a rising interest in the thirteenth century in the power of language and the complexities of its interpretation".

Particularly productive, however, is comparison with Latin literature of the twelfth century and later, all of which must belong to a learned milieu. This includes much which has gone under the name of 'students' songs': acerbic goliardic and satiric verse, as well as a set of narrative–dramatic *comoediae* modelled in the twelfth century on the ancient Latin comedy plays. For the detailed discussion of theories that have been advanced concerning the relationship of the fabliaux to these slightly earlier Latin works, the reader is best directed to studies by Edmund Faral, Jürgen Beyer and Peter Dronke, and responses in the books of Ménard and

---

4. This, in brief, is an opposition between a view that the mental experience of grouping discrete phenomena or events into sets proceeds via a process of abstraction from the real phenomena themselves (whereby the general category is just a 'name') and a view of the category as having a 'real' pre-existence, present to the mind, thus enabling recognition of its individual manifestations.

Muscatine.[5] Whatever the role, if any, of this medieval Latin work in the genesis of the fabliaux, such similarities as can be found between these works and the fabliaux validate the reading of the fabliaux in the light of the medieval scholarly milieu. As an interim measure of the significance of so doing we may recall, briefly, the irreverent verses such as *Saint Pierre et le jongleur*, discussed above. In this light, these appear less as vulgar reductions of the divine from a profane angle, but sharp satires, not so much of God's ordinance of the cosmos, but rather of human understanding of the scope for salvation and damnation.

Exempla

Of quite fundamental importance to our understanding of the special nature of the fabliau is an appreciation of its relationship with the *exempla* (singular *exemplum*). These were anecdotes, like the parables of the gospels, which were intended and used to illustrate, explain or emphasize some moral argument. The transmission of such exempla could take any form from the imitation of an exemplum heard or read to the compilation and dissemination of greater or lesser collections of exempla intended, for a variety of possible reasons, to provide a wide-ranging, or even comprehensive, corpus of moral precept. An important collection of exempla which we shall have reason to refer to on several occasions is the *Disciplina Clericalis*, an early twelfth-century collection of instructive tales put together by Petrus Alphonsus, a converted Jew, for his son. Besides being labelled as "fabliaus", "fablel", etc., the tales recognized as fabliaux in Old French are often also called "essemple". We shall see, by the end of this book, that a simple and practical distinction between fabliau and exemplum can be drawn, but that the same stories often do service in both categories. Most fabliaux, as can be seen in the summaries already given in this chapter, end on an explicit moral. Like Boutet (above), most French fabliau scholars are inclined to take the explicit moralizing of the fabliaux very much at face value. This includes Schenk, despite her stated belief in the essentially ironic character of wisdom

5. Faral E 1924, Le fabliau latin au Moyen Age, *Romania* 50, pp 321–85; Beyer, *Schwank und Moral*; Dronke P 1973 The Rise of the Medieval Fabliau, *Romanische Forschungen* 85 pp 275–97; Ménard *Les Fabliaux* pp 212 and 225; Muscatine *Old French Fabliaux* pp 14–15.

literature; a belief which seems to imply that the best lesson one can ever be taught is to be cynical (which might, sadly, be true). The morals one finds at the end of the fabliaux are generally relevant at least in part to the tales that have been told, and on the whole appear ironic only in the sense of the contrast between the worldly-wise, pragmatic and cynical counselling they most frequently offer and the idealistic norms of Christian moralizing that the reader is otherwise prepared for. Commonly, the tales of adulterous wives end with counsel to men not to trust what their wives tell them, not to let them out, and so on. Warning rather than exhortation to virtue is the style of the fabliau morals.

Schenk's study accepted the fabliaux' morals as a proper element of fabliau structure, which should imply that they make a more positive contribution to the overall significance of the fabliaux than several writers on the subject would have us believe. Nykrog, for instance, suggested the morals were a redundant, fossilized feature inherited by the fabliaux from twelfth-century precursors that were *fables*; Ménard sees the moral largely as a façade and Charles Muscatine is most inclined to see the moral simply as a convenient, traditional way of closing a text. Taking the moral seriously, however, does not mean taking it at face value and ignoring the potentially ironic and certainly easily seen limitations of morals of the kind just noted. An unquizzical synthesis of the fabliaux' explicit morals produces at best an alternative moral scheme to that which was conventional in the Christian Middle Ages – and is still, largely, conventional today; a scheme that various critics have described either as the morality of efficacy, the liberation of the instinct, a morality of pleasure, hedonistic materialism, or pragmatic warnings of the need to avoid deception and the promise or threat of retributive justice. Yet we have already noted how, in terms of poetic justice for instance, fabliau morality is often conventional in precisely these terms.

There are several fabliaux in which the explicit moral seems to be so incongruous in relation to the narrative it accompanies as to be facetious, if not sarcastic. This moral incongruency can draw attention to, and throw light upon, the very process of moralizing and the role of literature therein; which indeed are themselves well evidenced and clearly focused aspects of twelfth- to fourteenth-century intellectual speculation. Approaching the fabliaux with a mind prepared to find moral instruction in the texts, however unpromising they might superficially seem to be for such interpretation, is something that we can reconstruct as an authentic medieval mode of reading – "All that is written is written for our doctrine" as St Paul has it – although there is little direct evidence for the application of such literary theory to vernacular literature as well as the classics before the fourteenth century, and even then the extent of such application is difficult to assess.[6] The common claim made for classical secular literature in response to the analytical question *cui parte philosophiae supponitur?*, 'to what branch of philosophy does it pertain?', is *ethice supponitur*, 'it pertains to ethics', and the reason: 'because it treats of human behaviour'. As we have seen, the fabliaux treat very much of human behaviour, and regarded in the light of ethical ideals present an image of the very baseness of which humankind is capable. As examples we may take the grotesque sexual extravagance, and the intense foolishness, of the peasant and his wife in *Les quatre Souhais Saint Martin*, or the state of the peasant in *Le Vilain asnier*, 'The peasant ass-driver', who is overpowered and anaesthetized by the beautiful scent of flowers and brought back to himself only by having dung thrust under his nose. If we take these as emblematic of the human condition, the morals drawn at the end of these tales look conspicuously, even deliberately, inadequate. In *Les quatre Souhais Saint Martin*:

> Par cest fablel poez savoir
> Que cil ne fet mie savoir
> Qui mieus croit sa fame que lui
> Souvent l'en vient honte et anui.

> (Through this fabliau you may know
> that he does not act at all wisely
> who trusts his wife rather than himself:
> often he suffers shame and grief.)

(MS BN Paris fr. 837)

and in *Le Vilain asnier*:

> Et por ce vos veuil ge monstrer
> Qui cil fait [n]e sens [n]e mesure

6. See further Chapter 3, also Minnis A J 1988 *Medieval Theory of Authorship* 2nd edn. (Wildwood House) p 110 and Minnis A J, Scott A B and Wallace D 1988 *Medieval Literary Theory and Criticism* c.1100–c.1375 (Oxford University Press), especially pp 324–34.

Qui d'orgueil se desennature:
ne se doit nus desnaturer.

(And through this I wish to show you
that he acts without sense or measure
who, through pride, acts beyond his nature:
nobody should disnature himself.)

The very incongruency between moral and tale in these (and other) cases can draw the reader to reconsider the moral 'sentence' of both those parts of the fabliaux: initially, possibly, to see if or how far they match one another, but ultimately in respect of their own nature – to see how the narrative tale of humanity implies human baseness, while explicit human moralizing fails to match the height, or depth, of that depravity. In so far as such tales are written for our doctrine they must be actively morally interpreted by the reader; they act through revelation, not mere instruction.

In a recent article, Pearcy (1990) has suggested that a general function of the explicit moral in a fabliau, where there is one, is to express a dialectical opposition between social convention – in particular the supposedly sanctifying constraints of Christian marriage – and individual libertarianism, in particular extra-marital sexual indulgence. These are conflicting principles for the government of human life, the "legitimacy" of both of which, Pearcy claims, is recognized by the fabliaux. Unfortunately, this is an observation made briefly at the end of his paper, and not expanded upon. We may, however, dispute any implication that serious unresolved moral uncertainty is shared with the audience by the fabliau writer, without necessarily following Boutet in her ultimate respect for the authority of the conventional moral closure. The fabliau through which Pearcy approaches this point, *Connebert*, is crystal clear in its poetic justice, with a lecherous priest being forced to castrate himself. A recognition of the power of sexual instinct is undoubtedly implied virtually every time the fabliau form is selected by an author. But while the breaking of convention may be agreeable, and therefore laughable (cf. certain views of Freud, below), there is never any questioning of what is 'right' and what is 'wrong': for that sort of conundrum one should look rather to a romance like Marie de France's lay *Eliduc*.

Antifeminism

Material characteristic of medieval Latin writing that is widely
exploited in the fabliaux in ways that are often both entertaining
and probing is the dogma of antifeminist traditions: traditions which
present woman, the daughters of Eve, as generally morally
reprehensible and dangerous to man; insatiable and extravagant
sexual sirens with their bodies, and perjurers, temptresses or endless
naggers with their tongues. The association of this material with the
clerk is clearly exemplified by Chaucer's Wife of Bath's fifth
husband, the clerk Jankyn, who, in the Wife of Bath's Prologue,
reads antifeminist material to her from his book "Valerie and
Theofraste". The commonplace accusations of medieval antifeminism came to the Middle Ages as an ecclesiastical tradition. At
the root of most medieval writing on the subject was the late
fourth-century figure of St Jerome, who wrote a tract *adversus
Jovinianum*, attacking the arguments of a relatively liberal-minded
monk, Jovinianus, who had denied the superiority of virginity to
marriage. Jerome included here material designed as a rhetorical
dissuasion to men from marriage by warning of the weaknesses and
vices of wives. By the thirteenth century such material makes a
substantial penetration of vernacular literature, with important
examples in texts which we shall later meet in connection with
Chaucer's fabliaux in *The Romance of the Rose* (8455ff.) and Eustache
Deschamps' *Miroir de Mariage*, 'Mirror of Marriage'.[7] It is probably a
minority of medieval antifeminist writing that was meant to be
taken literally rather than metaphorically; even Jerome's model
diatribe was a rhetorical exercise designed for the refutation of
Jovinianus and the assertion of the value of celibacy. The
antifeminist teaching of Repertoire de Science ('the Body of
Knowledge') in the *Miroir de Mariage* is similarly designed to turn
the male character Franc Vouloir from contemplation of an earthly
marriage to contemplation of a spiritual and divine one.

No doubt there were medieval men, and women too, who took
and applied the clumsy generalizations of this tradition literally.

7. A helpful account of the diffusion of antifeminist material in the Latin and
vernacular literature of the Middle Ages is given by Mann *Geoffrey Chaucer* pp
1–3 and 49–55. See also Bloch, R H 1987 Medieval Misogyny, *Representations* 20 pp
1–24. A wide ranging anthology of relevant texts is available in Blamires A 1992
(ed) *Woman Defamed and Woman Defended* (Clarendon Press).

Anything really resembling such unalloyed antifeminism is, however, rare in the French fabliaux. One good example of it is a fabliau called *Sire Hain et Dame Anieuse*, 'Sir Hatred and Lady Obnoxious', where an antagonistic husband and wife fight a crudely physical and violent battle, literally over who should have the trousers. The trousers are destroyed; the wife is eventually overcome and forced to promise submissiveness. A moral is drawn advising husbands:

> Mes fetes ausi fetement
> Commes Hains fist de sa moillier,
> Qui ainc ne le vout adaignier
> Fors tout le mains que ele pot,
> Dusques atant que il li ot
> Batu et les os et l'eschine!

> (Do just as Hain did with his wife,
> who would only ever show him the slightest respect,
> until he had beaten her to the core.)

The garrulity of women – one of St Jerome's first objections – clearly underlies the crude joke of *Du Con qui fu fait a la besche*, noted above, and woman's moral weakness is apparent in *Cele qui se fist foutre sur la fosse de son mari*, a version of a tale known as the Matron of Ephesus that can be traced as far back as to the classical author Petronius. But more often than not the women of the fabliau are presented with admiration and respect. They are morally no worse on the whole than the lecherous men who inhabit these tales, and intellectually much superior to them on most occasions. There are several examples like *Les Perdris*, quoted earlier on in this chapter, where the conventional, antifeminist moral counterpoints the wit and ingenuity of the woman of the tale which is, after all, what makes the tale interesting and amusing – what makes it a tale at all. A good number of fabliaux advise the husband simply to accept his inferiority to his wife and to allow her to continue to keep the passage of the world smooth; at the end of *Le Chevalier a la robe vermeille*, 'The Knight with the scarlet robe', a husband who has surprised his wife and made the compromising discovery of her lover's horse and robe is hoodwinked by her, and the tale concludes:

Mes cil qui tient la droite voie
Doit bien croirre sanz contredit
Toit ce que sa fame li dit.

(But he who keeps to the right path
should believe fully, without dispute,
everything that his wife tells him.)

Some women, like Constant du Hamel's wife, are splendidly loyal
to their husbands; more are loyal to their lovers – and are, indeed,
their saviours.

In his study of 'Medieval Misogyny', R. Howard Bloch makes
the point that male distrust may depend less on a sense of the utter
difference of women than on a sense of how similar women are:
gender boundaries can be crossed, and men can become feminized
– as Eve was created from Adam. The fabliaux generally retain a
strong sense of the sexual difference, so that either sex can find
fulfilment only with the other. But they minimize the difference in
so far as they propound a thoroughgoing assimilation of male and
female desires. The fabliaux' fantasies may clearly be male ones, but
fabliau attitudes are far removed from those implied by the
conscious and formulaic antifeminism of medieval tradition.

Laughter: conventional morality, indecent comedy and pornography

Although defining fabliaux as "contes à rire", Bédier did not define
the comedy of the fabliaux by any positive attributes. He presented
it rather as what was left in tales that were not any of the supposed
binary opposites of simple comedy, i.e. religious miracles, moralities
or satire. By the time we conclude our comparison of fabliau and
exemplum at the end of this book we shall face a very similar
formulation of the difference between the two as lying in the
fabliau's divergence from the normal modes of exemplum, which
may in itself be funny, rather than in an all-preceding intention to
be funny. Even though, as readers of the fabliaux, we may spend a
good deal of time smiling at the preposterous ingenuity of gross
deceptions and misdeeds – in other words things that are generically
wrongs in terms of conventional Christian morality – we have
already seen that substantial elements of positive Christian
spirituality and conventional morality are widely represented
amongst the French fabliaux.

It is undeniable that most readers find amusement to be part of their experience of these texts. The superficial nature of such humour varies considerably. There are for instance extreme examples of the inhibition or punishment of the sexual act in which laughter cannot be other than inhumane if it can be found at all: for example in *Connebert*, where a lecherous priest has to castrate himself in order to save his life, or *Le Prestre et le leu*, 'The priest and the wolf', a laconically brief tale of just twenty-eight lines relating how a peasant digs a trap for a lecherous priest, into which first a wolf, then the priest, and then the wife's maid sent to see if the priest is coming fall in turn, after which the peasant kills the wolf, castrates the priest, and chases off the maid. The fabliaux as a whole clearly imply a system of values that in many respects is quite conventional, and it is one of these values that directs that the lecherous priest should be the type that suffers most from the poetic justice of these texts.

Writing about comedy, a term used here in its commonest current English sense of some pleasantly amusing drama, has never been easy. Jokes that have to be explained lose nearly all their force, and no one ever laughs spontaneously at the explication of a joke; even the terms we have at our disposal in English to discuss literature of this kind – *comedy, humour, amusement, ridicule* – are full of ambiguities demanding pedantic caution on the part of anyone who uses them in an analytical way. It is easy enough to identify features that are likely to provoke laughter and were presumably intended to do so amongst the common attributes of the fabliaux. The use of marked language is a familiar enough device of modern television comedy or stage farce to raise a laugh, be that in the mild form of so-called 'family entertainment' – words like *knickers, pratt, plonker*, etc. – or in the form of more marked terms used in later night viewing on the supposedly more serious channels. The milder range in fact serves not to challenge but to define the limits of propriety; they set a horizon beyond which 'improper' linguistic use will not go, and the audience can laugh with relief at the reassurance that they will not be shocked, as well as at the impudence of these terms. The more marked terms, conversely, represent pretensions of freedom and anarchy in writer, performer and audience alike. It is interesting to note how even euphemisms, symbolizing but not presenting marked terms, can be the more amusing for the conspiracy between scriptwriter, actors and audience in recognizing the term signified at the same time as superficially recognizing that its use is a taboo not to be broken. One thinks of examples such as "shorthouse" (for *shortarse*) or "naff off" (for *fuck off*) from post-war British comedy. An intellectual amusement resides in the interplay between what for simplicity's sake we can represent as just two contrasting ranges of marked and unmarked language – although *arse* is undoubtedly less marked than *fuck*.[8] Ironically, the linguistic difference (in markedness) between the terms is emphasized at the same time as their functional equivalence – with the milder signifying the stronger – is blatantly evident. The comic process here is conscious and intellectual rather than unconscious and psychological. Something very similar is found in *L'Esquiriel*, in which the boy's figurative euphemisms – squirrel, nest, eggs – are not simply comic as signifiers of 'real' objects – penis, scrotum or pubic hair, testicles – but as signifiers of the sort of language that the girl has already talked about – *vit, coilles*, etc. – but is discouraged from using. Usually, however, the dividing lines in this sort of linguistic stratification are simply annihilated in the fabliaux.

With their characteristic and pervasive atmosphere of sexuality and sensuality and their erotic tales presented or disguised within verbal play, it is hardly surprising that many have considered 'pornography' to be an appropriate term to describe at least a good part of what is found in these fabliaux. Whether one agrees with this or not depends, of course, on how one defines 'pornography'. A substantial essay by Thomas D. Cooke on the subject in relation to fabliau defines pornography in conventionally evaluative and political terms as a modern form of misogyny: it is a branch of art that represents or reflects aggressive male sexuality, concerned wholly with the physical aspects of sexual experience and reducing women to the status of objects of sexual actions.[9] It is claimed that the fabliaux can reduce human characters to merely their genitals – perhaps best represented by the excitement of the three women who find an isolated *vit* – linking brutal violence with crude language and excluding emotion or affection. One answer to this

8. In Pearcy 1974, a distinction between the figurative and the euphemistic in unmarked language is crucial to the argument. The distinction does not, however, appear to be a very clear-cut one.
9. Cooke T D 'Pornography, the Comic Spirit, and the Fabliaux'. In Cooke and Honeycutt *The Humor of the Fabliaux* pp 137–62.

point is that of Ménard, who notes that anything that could be interpreted as such writing belongs very much on the extreme fringes of fabliaux writing; detailed brutality is quite rare, and such as there is is not primarily sexual.

An alternative conventional definition of pornography is that it is art designed to excite and to some degree to satisfy sexual arousal. The vision of the fabliaux offered by R. Howard Bloch (1986) seems to fit this definition squarely: he sees fabliau narrative as the origin and catalyst of sexual desire; in reading, or writing, the fabliaux, sexual experience is purely linguistic: "if any pleasure is attached to sex in the fabliaux it comes from the deferral in speech, of speech, substituting for the act". But one may reasonably dispute that the French fabliaux are pornographic by this definition either. The euphemistic linguistic representation of sexual foreplay as in *L'Esquiriel* may be titillating to different readers to various possible degrees, but in general such presentations in the fabliaux are either too absurd or too blatant, or both of these, for the fabliaux to stand any serious comparison with the verbal eroticism of modern pornographic narrative.

On the surface, neither of these definitions of pornography could apply to the fabliaux if the fabliaux really are, as Bédier's definition would suggest, simply meant to be laughed at. One general psychological theory of the intrinsic nature of indecent jokes is, however, of considerable relevance and practical value here. This is Sigmund Freud's, as presented in a study *Der Witz und seine Beziehung zum Unbewussten*.[10] Freud included a study of sexual jokes as a subcategory of a major class of jokes he characterized as 'tendentious'. He traced a chain of development in the verbalization of sexual material from 'smut', "Zote", which is characteristically used, he claims, by a man to excite a woman, to the joke itself as a covert expression of thwarted male sexual aggression and desire. In 'ideal' circumstances, the male joker releases his frustration by joking about the woman with a second male — an inhibitor of the desired intimacy — who thereby becomes a conspirator with the teller in the indulgence in smut as a substitute for the sexual act. In culturally more refined society, a joke supersedes overt indecency,

---

10. In English translation, *Jokes and their Relation to the Unconscious*, translated by James Strachey, Penguin Books (The Pelican Freud Library volume 6). See especially section III, 'The Purposes of Jokes'.

and is able to satisfy baser instincts in a relatively sophisticated way. Jokes thus both acknowledge and circumvent conventional restrictions; the breaking of conventional restraint increases the pleasure of the sexual joke. Thus comedy may merge, 'pornographically', with eroticism.

This is a useful model for an analysis and description of the use of indecent comedy in the fabliaux. It is in the first place striking that in the Old French fabliaux, a male rival or spoiler is more commonly the butt of the humour than a female, though examples of the latter situation are reasonably numerous. Thus a considerable proportion of the fabliaux may appear less inhibited in expressing their underlying desires than the more sophisticated sexual joke envisaged by Freud. Freud's graded system of classification of jokes, from the crude and explicit to the refined and more abstract, implies that many of the fabliaux achieve an intriguing conflation of basic smut – in their overt expression of the dreams of masculine sexuality, with women, often other men's wives, freely available, especially to the lover who spices his indulgence with daring and danger, and their insistence on the use of diction which is the opposite of refined – and the circumstances of the more sophisticated joke: where there is an inhibitor, he becomes the butt of the joke. In respect of the supposed vicarious eroticism of the genre, however, we may argue that the unembarrassed and disembarrassed honesty of the fabliaux' sexual fantasies largely precludes any lingering upon the process of arousal in the form of a gradual uncovering of the tale's sexual core.

Muscatine's book (1986) treats these topics in a persuasive way. He commences upon the dismantling of assumptions of where the texts are funny or obscene based on modern suppositions of what constitutes obscenity *et al.*, and puts forward a theory that picks up a suggestion of Nykrog's concerning the relationship of fabliau and romance: that the fabliaux flourished as a conservative reaction to new notions of gentility and decency in behaviour and especially in language; new notions that are found most clearly in the literary cult of *fin amour*.

THE FRENCH FABLIAU IN ENGLAND

The Norman Conquest introduced a French-speaking community and aspects of Norman French culture into England. The full assimilation of this population to the native English and the submergence of Anglo-Norman culture within English culture took several centuries to complete, while the political separation of English and French territory was not complete until the loss of Calais to the English crown in the mid-sixteenth century. Anglo-Norman literature composed in what became an increasingly distinctive Anglo-Norman dialect of French was flourishing by the second half of the twelfth century.

The French fabliau in England may take one of two basic forms: fabliaux composed in Old French in France of which copies made their way to England, and fabliaux composed (in most cases re-composed) in the Anglo-Norman dialect, presumably in England. It is difficult to ascertain whether any known examples fall into the former category. Three manuscripts containing genuinely French fabliaux are known in English collections: in the British Library, London (Additional MS 10289), the Bodleian Library, Oxford (Douce 111) and the Middleton Library, University of Nottingham (Middleton LM6). Douce 111 is a fifteenth-century manuscript that seems to have remained in France until being obtained by the nineteenth-century collector, Douce, and it has been deduced that the Middleton manuscript was taken as plunder from the French town of Laval during the later stages of the Hundred Years' War, between March 1428 and September 1429.[11] BL Additional MS 10289, which contains a copy of *Jouglet*, is more interesting in that it shows distinct traces of particularly Norman interest, beginning for instance with a long *Roman du Mont St Michel*, St Michael's Mount being situated on the coast of Normandy. There is no record of the history of this manuscript before it was bought for the British Museum in 1836, but it appears possible that the *Jouglet* it contains could be one text forming a bridge between the French fabliaux and the Anglo-Norman.

A bridge of a different kind is represented by French fabliaux taking Englishmen – and their poor French – as their characters. Examples are *La Male Honte*, noted already, and *Les deux Anglois et l'anel*, 'The two Englishmen and the *anel*', which turns around a joke based on an Englishman's inability to make *a[g]nel* (lamb) distinct from *a[s]niel* (young ass) in his attempt to speak French. A

---

11. Cowper F A G 1959 Origins and Peregrinations of the Laval-Middleton Manuscript, *Nottingham Medieval Studies* III pp 3–18.

more scurrilous comic innuendo comes with the fact that these two
words can be (and are in the one manuscript copy of this text)
turned into phonetic or graphic homonyms with *anel*, 'ring', with
its sexual connotations as noted above. Similarly the text is written
so as to bring out comic connotations of the word *fut*, the *passé
simple* of the verb 'to be' by writing it with a characteristically
Anglo-Norman spelling as "fout", recalling *foutre*. Not only does
the Englishman confuse terms; he appears ridiculously ignorant of the
comic implications of his bewilderment to the initiates in French
fabliau slang. *Asnele* is also recorded as an adjective meaning 'stupid'.

The Anglo-Norman fabliaux had been thoroughly neglected
before Nico van den Boogard had a conference paper devoted to
the subject published in 1981. This paper listed seven
Anglo-Norman fabliaux, collected in four manuscripts.[12] All bar a
fragment of the Anglo-Norman version of *Cele qui fu foutue et
desfoutue*, found on an isolated leaf in a library in Clermont-Ferrand,
are in manuscripts still in British libraries. The largest collection is
of four works in a manuscript of the British Library famous,
amongst other things, for a collection of English medieval lyrics it
contains, British Library MS Harley 2253 (a facsimile of this
manuscript has been published by the Early English Text Society,
Original Series no.255). This manuscript is dated *circa* 1330–1350, and
was written by a scribe based in or near Ludlow, Shropshire. The
fabliaux in this manuscript are *Le Chevalier qui fist parler les cons*,
'The knight who made the cunts talk', *Les trois Dames qui troverent
un vit*, 'The three ladies who found a prick', *Le Chevalier a la
corbeille*, 'The knight of the basket', and *La Gageure*, 'The wager'.
The first two of these are also found in genuinely French versions,
but not the latter two. Manuscripts containing single
Anglo-Norman fabliaux are Bodleian Library, Oxford, MS Digby
86, with a version of *Les quatre Souhais Saint Martin*, a manuscript
which also contains our one Middle English fabliau found outside
of Chaucer's works, *Dame Sirith*, and Corpus Christi College
Cambridge MS 50, with a fabliau, *Un Chevalier, sa dame et un clerc*,

---

12. One might add an Anglo-Norman version of *La Housse partie*, 'The divided
blanket', in a further manuscript. This moralistic work, in which a child's 'ruse'
teaches a father to treat his own father better, and which is only labelled an
"ensaumple" within the text, does not have a strong claim to be included
amongst the fabliaux, although it is included in NRCF.

'A knight, his lady and a clerk', a variant of the story found in *La Bourgeoise d'Orliens*.[13]

Van den Boogard concentrated his study on revealing characteristics shared by the Anglo-Norman fabliaux which could be explained by reference to the peculiar situation of the Anglo-Norman community. This echoes the general case made by Rychner for variation between closely related fabliau texts to be explicable on the basis of different intended audiences, although van den Boogard actually contradicted Rychner's specific findings on the Anglo-Norman fabliaux, which Rychner found to represent only the common degeneration typical of "transmission memorielle". The Anglo-Norman community was a socially isolated but powerful group: the higher aristocracy of England with their households and retinues. Not every member of the Anglo-Norman-speaking community would have been an aristocrat, but virtually all would be linked to and dependent upon the aristocracy. This appears to be reflected in the character of the Anglo-Norman fabliaux, which – small though their number is and therefore a rather unreliable basis for generalizations – tend to concentrate upon the adventures of knightly characters, and to develop the characters they contain in terms which, however facile, represent the aristocratic or courtly ethos: characters are frequently identified as "bel", 'fine', for instance, and given 'noble' motives for their actions, such as the lady of *Un Chevalier, sa dame et un clerc*, who, superficially at least, gives herself to the clerk as an act of pity, in order to avoid his dying of his "maladie" of love. Van den Boogard suggested that in the Anglo-Norman fabliaux the author assumes what he calls the *persona* of the clerk, i.e. a character looking for respect and admiration for his ability to tell a fascinating tale of intrigue (*inter alia*), whereas a French author is more likely to adopt the *persona* of the *jongleur*, shocking by his anarchism but amusing at the same time through his self-mockery.

Both Rychner (1960) and van den Boogaard note that the five Anglo-Norman fabliaux with identifiable French counterparts tend to appear to be further removed from hypothetical original forms. This stands in striking contrast with the *Jouglet* of British Library MS Additional 10289, which is described in the *Nouveau Recueil Complet des Fabliaux* as "sans doute la plus proche de l'original".

---

13. For studies of this text, see Nykrog *Les Fabliaux* pp 66–9, and Wailes 1972.

Van den Boogaard argued that in entering Anglo-Norman, fabliaux underwent a radical transformation because they were aimed at such an isolated audience; an audience isolated from the full French literary frame of reference that a truly French audience would have had. As his principal example (to which the effacement of the *jongleur persona* could be added) he noted the removal of deliberate and witty echoes of the characteristic diction of the Breton lay from the French version of *Le Chevalier qui fist parler les cons*: the fairy *lande* disappears in the Anglo-Norman version, the magic *don*, 'gift', becomes a mundane *guerdon*, 'reward', and the *fées*, 'fairies', become *desmoisselles*. The impact of French literary tradition on the Anglo-Norman fabliaux seems to have been rather crude: van den Boogard indicates that Anglo-Norman poets saw the fabliau primarily as a mode of 'obscene' entertainment. The influence of French literary tradition was thus limited, but not, as he rather loosely stated in his article, entirely absent.

Emphasizing the isolation of the Anglo-Norman literary community can also be misleading in another respect. The Anglo-Norman fabliaux are preserved in manuscripts that are miscellaneous literary anthologies. Irrespective of the circumstances of their composition, the Anglo-Norman fabliaux were transmitted, eventually, and preserved for posterity because the fabliau was recognized as a genre which had its place in the full range of new and recent vernacular literary production in England. The great majority of French fabliaux too are to be found in manuscripts that contain extensive collections of fabliaux, and other genres, reflecting a development in manuscript production of the thirteenth century that it is difficult to believe is not connected in some general way to the growth of scholarly 'compilations' (*compilationes*) at the same time.[14] But the assembling of separate tales to form some larger whole is a distinctive feature of medieval literature with a history of its own, apart from the history of what can properly be called *compilationes*. A range of such collections seems to develop from earlier collections with either no framework at all, or an apparently

14. Parkes M B 1976 The Influence of the Concepts of Ordinatio and Compilatio on the Development of the Book, in Alexander J J G and Gibson M T (eds) *Medieval Literature and Learning. Essays presented to Richard William Hunt* (Clarendon Press) pp 115–41. See also Minnis, *Medieval Theory of Authorship* pp 190–210, and on MS BM Harley 2253 specifically Revard C 1982 *Gilote et Johane*: an Interlude in B.L. MS Harley 2253, SP79(2) pp 122–46.

genuine, utilitarian one, as in the *Disciplina Clericalis* (see above), to more imaginative and narratologically significant frameworks created by Boccaccio for his *Decameron* and, *par excellence*, Chaucer for his Canterbury Tales.

The subject of this book is the fabliau in English. That is, it is about works of a genre that can be identified as equivalent to the fabliau in French or in Anglo-Norman. We shall see that there is evidence that this was perceived as a genre in its own right in England, and in English. The medieval fabliaux in English belong in the first instance to the context of medieval England, and are not to be seen as foreign intruders disguised in the clothing of the Middle English language. One of the issues for discussion is whether or not, or how far, the Anglo-Norman fabliaux formed a bridge between the French fabliaux and the English. We shall see, in fact, that the case for French sources and thus a possible Anglo-Norman bridge is most persuasive and pertinent in respect of the fabliaux in English with what we shall be able to identify as the 'earliest' features: *Dame Sirith* and Chaucer's Shipman's Tale. (Norman) French influence may also have introduced the fabliau to medieval Welsh literature.[15] Anglo-Norman literature was not constituted of the random dregs and splashes of French literature that landed in England; it formed an organic literary corpus of its own, and, most significantly in this context, formed part of a trilingual medieval English literary corpus, as exemplified by certain great English, Latin and Anglo-Norman manuscript miscellanies of the late thirteenth and fourteenth centuries. It is in Anglo-Norman that we find the earliest evidence of the concept of fabliau in England, and it is appropriate, therefore, that our earliest English fabliau is labelled a "fablel" in an Anglo-Norman rubric. This is *Dame Sirith*, the subject of the next chapter.

15. See below, Chapter 6 pp 247–50.

Chapter 2

Dame Sirith

DAME SIRITH

A study of the poem

Dame Sirith is the only extant Middle English fabliau by an author
other than Chaucer. It is found in a manuscript in the Bodleian
Library, Oxford (MS Digby 86), that appears to have been written
within the diocese of Worcester both for, and, arguably, by, a
layman and is datable between the accession of Edward I in 1272 and
the end of the eleventh year of his reign in November 1283.[1] This
manuscript contains many English, Anglo-Norman and Latin works
besides *Dame Sirith*, a clear majority of which are thoroughly
serious and religious. However, this collection also gives a good
impression of the effective presence of the fabliau in the
Anglo-Norman literary corpus and its context. It contains the sole
copy of the Anglo-Norman version of *Les quatre Souhais Saint
Martin*. The fact that *Dame Sirith* was introduced to this collection
as a representative of a genre otherwise known as a French genre is
indicated by the rubric in the manuscript which marks the
beginning of the poem. In French, this reads "Cil comence le fablel
e la cointise de dame Siriz", 'Here begins the fabliau and the
trickery of Dame Sirith'.[2] Besides these true fabliaux, the fabliau
voice and tone are to be heard in a text rubricated *Le fablel del
gelous*, 'The fabliau of the jealous man', which includes observations
such as:

1. Miller B D H 1963 The Early History of Bodleian MS Digby 86, *Annuale
   Mediaevale* IV pp 23–56.
2. The name *Sirith* is frequently represented as "Siriz" in the text. The sporadic
   use of the graph <z> for sounds we should write <th> is a medieval English
   practice deriving from the unfamiliarity of Francophones with the <th> sounds.
   Sirith is an identifiable personal name while a *Siriz* pronounced with a *z* at the
   end is not; the pronunciation *Sirith* is confirmed by rhymes in the text.

Gelous doit gisir en la merde

(The jealous should lie in the shit)

and in the salacious *La vie de un vallet amerous*, 'The life of a lusty lad', which includes the lines:

'Amie chere
Oiez ore ma priere
Wous hos jeo foutre
E mun vit en toun coun boutre.'

('Dearly beloved one
now hear my prayer;
I'm brave enough to fuck you
and to shove my prick up your cunt.')

The tale of *Dame Sirith* is as follows. A clerk lusts after a woman who is married to a merchant. One day, when the merchant is away on business, the clerk approaches the woman, and being courteously welcomed by her, and encouraged to state what he wants, he declares his 'love' for her. The wife, Margery, refuses him; the clerk departs and on a friend's advice takes his problem to an older woman, Dame Sirith. She at first refuses to help him, suspecting a trap to catch her out in witchery, but as the clerk, Wilekin, persists she finally agrees to solve the problem, accepting twenty shillings in payment. She then feeds her dog mustard, to make its eyes run, and goes to Margery's house, where she starts to lament her poverty and need. Margery charitably takes notice of her, whereupon she continues to lament, claiming her daughter was turned into the dog Margery sees weeping by a clerk whose advances she refused. At this Margery panics, expecting the same fate for herself, and soon begs the old woman to try to find Wilekin and bring him to her. This is quickly done, and Wilekin prepares to bed Margery, dismissing Dame Sirith, who is no longer needed and who leaves urging Wilekin to take his pleasure of Margery aggressively:

'. . . loke þat þu her tille
And strek out hire þes. . . '

('. . . see that you plough her
and stretch out her thighs. . . ')

(440–1)

and offering her services more generally to any man who is failing to 'get' the object of his desires.

There is not a substantial critical tradition relating to *Dame Sirith*. It tends to be noticed in simple literary-historical terms as representative of the fabliau genre in thirteenth-century English, and presented simply as a work of little art. The most substantial and recent discussion of the poem is that of Michael Swanton (1987), where the terminology used is amply clear and quite typical. The story is "frivolous" and "short", the plot, "such as it is", simply concerns the trick; the style is one of "informed immediacy", with stock phrasing and stock characters; there is a "characteristically narrow" field of vision; speech is "plain" and "colloquial"; the tale, in this form, is a "straightforward enough tale of unedifying bawdry", an "unadorned anecdote". Swanton's presentation of the poem is an exercise in detailed précis and commentary; the only complexity of any credit that is found added to "pure narrative at its simplest and barest" is a little irony in the incredible moral comment passed by the narrator on the clerk's desires:

þerof he hevede wrong!

(In this he was wrong!: this might, however, be translated
'This caused him grief!')

(9)

The artistry of the poem, however, deserves far more credit than this. The prosody of *Dame Sirith* may be unobtrusive, but as such it represents a smooth and polished performance that itself contributes to the tone of the work. Most of the work is composed in six-line tail-rhyme stanzas, rhyming A A B C C B. There are usually two main stresses within the line of at least six syllables which may also be made coherent by the use of alliteration, internal rhyme and assonance, as, for instance, in the first stanza:

As *I* com b*i* an waie
*H*of on Ich *h*erde saie
    Ful *mo*di *mon* and *proud*
Wis he *wes* of lore
And *g*ouþliche under *g*ore
    And clothed in fair sroud.

(As I travelled along a path
I heard the tale of one,
    a spirited man, and proud;

he was wise in learning
and splendid under his clothes,
and clothed in fine array.)

(1–6)

There are also passages of the work in octosyllabic couplets, the typical French fabliau measure. The author of *Dame Sirith* was fully able to exploit such prosodic devices to good effect. A sequence of six lines with the same rhyme are given to Dame Sirith as, initially, she professes her conventional goodness and innocence to Wilekin:

'Ich am on holi wimmon
On wicchecraft nout I ne con
Both wiþ gode men almesdede
Ilke dai me lif I fede
And bidde mi paternoster and mi crede
Þat Goed hem helpe at hore nede
Þat helpen me mi lif to lede
And leve þat hem mote wel spede. . . '

('I am a holy woman;
I know nothing of witchcraft
but with almsgiving to good men
I sustain my life each day,
and offer my paternoster and my creed
that God should help those in their need
who help me my life to lead
and should grant that all should go well with them. . .)

(205–12)

This conveys the glib emptiness of the persona with which Dame Sirith attempts to clothe herself. When she finishes speaking, the blunt colloquialism of Wilekin's response emphasizes the facile and artificial nature of her self-portrait:

'Leve nelde, bilef al þis!'

('Dear woman, give over!')

(217)

The author is thus not just skilled in the use of form; he also enjoys a very productive skill in characterization: that is in the exploitation of the literary phenomenon of the production and manipulation of characters within a series of dramatic events for his own effects, rather than in the production of 'memorable' or 'realistic' characters.

The principal way in which characterization is thus exploited in

Dame Sirith lies in the use of formulaic language, in particular in the use of terms appropriate to the romance of *fin amour*. Indeed before we even come to the characterization of characters within the drama we find the poem itself being apparently characterized one way but then characterized another in the opening three stanzas:

As I com bi an waie
Hof on Ich herde saie
     Ful modi mon and proud
Wis he wes of lore
And goupliche under gore
     And clothed in fair sroud.

To lovien he bigon
One wedded wimmon;
     þerof he hevede wrong!
His herte hire wes al on,
Þat reste nevede he non –
     Þe love was so strong.

Wel 3erne he him biþoute
Hou he hire gete moute
     In ani cunnes wise.
Þat befel on an day
Þe loverd wend away
     Hon his marchaundise.

(As I travelled along a path
I heard the tale of one,
     a spirited man, and proud;
he was wise in learning
and splendid under his clothes,
     and clothed in fine array.

He began to love
a married woman;
     there he was wrong!
His heart was set on her
so that he could never relax –
     this love was so strong.

Anxiously he bethought himself
how he might get her
     in any way at all.
It happened one day
that the master went away
     upon his business.)

(1–18)

If we set the poem's rubric, which informs us that we shall be
reading a fabliau, on one side for the moment, we could in the first
stanza be looking at a tail-rhyme romance – a type familiar in
English literature from the fourteenth century. No respectable
knight could object to being described as "modi" and "proud",
"wis of lore", "goupliche under gore" and well dressed. This
possibility gradually breaks down in the next two stanzas. Firstly we
learn that this 'one' fell for a wedded woman. This does not
disqualify the character from honourable knightly status – think of
Tristram and Yseult, or Lancelot and Guinevere – but it does create
a degree of tension: the *service* of a knight to another man's lady
wife is, as the Lancelot–Guinevere tale shows, the classically
subversive element within the knightly ethos. Indeed lines 10–12
describe the restless wretched lover in terms fully appropriate to any
sincere romance. It is with stanza 3 that we really discover that we
are in the fabliau mode, not the romance. The crudity of:

> Hou he hire gete moute

could just be an unfortunate clumsiness on the part of a romance
versifier, but the uncourtly range of the lover's plotting:

> In any cunnes wise

can only be fabliau. And then we learn that the wife is a
townswoman, a merchant's wife, not a fine lady, and the stage is set
for the fabliau drama by the absence of the husband on business.

The assumption of the persona of a courtly suitor is particularly
striking in the clerk's language. One should note that within the
text it is not until a good three-quarters of the tale has passed that
Wilekin is identified as a clerk, in the exchange between Margery
and Dame Sirith over the weeping bitch. Before that, he is simply
a libidinous man. He opens his wooing with a courteous regard for
the lady's feelings (at the same time as with a pragmatic eye on the
best route to success):

> 'Min hernde will I to þe bede
> Bote wraþþen þe for ani dede
>   Were me loþ.'

> ('I will tell you what I have to say,
> but to make you angry by any deed
>   I should be loath.')

(40–2)

Similarly both courtly and ironically pragmatic is the clerk's offer to love Margery:

Boþ derneliche and stille

(Both secretly and quietly)

(86)

and with "derne love" ('secret love': 130). Wilekin appeals to the lady to show pity on him by an appeal to her "curteisi" and her Christian pity:

'Dame, dame, torn þi mod
Þi curteisi wes ever god
    And ʒet shal be.
For þe Loverd þat ous haveþ wrout
Amend þi mod and torn þi þout
    And rew on me.'

('Lady, lady, change your heart:
your courtesy was ever good
    and shall remain so.
For the Lord who has made us
amend your heart and change your mind
    and take pity on me.')

(109–14)

It is particularly ironic, then, that the next lady to whom Wilekin must plead, Dame Sirith, does heed his perseverance in pleading, which includes some good courtly motifs:

'But if hoe wende hire mod
For serewe mon Ich wakese wod
    Oþer miselve quelle.'

('Unless she changes her mind
I shall go mad with sorrow
    or kill myself.')

(181–3)

and responds in the terms he asks of Margery:

'Wat God, Wilekin, me reweþ þi scape'

('God knows, Wilekin, your distress finds my pity')

(235)

Wilekin, appropriately, responds by 'plighting his troth' (252) to seal the contract with Dame Sirith.

Margery is the most carefully, cleverly and unexpectedly constructed character in *Dame Sirith*: not much more than a dumb blonde, admittedly, but a character through which the author revels in presenting to his readers or audience a detailed comic portrayal of how a dumb blonde can act. She has little in her mind or in her mouth other than platitudes. Such clichés fill her first speech of welcome to Wilekin with a set of offers that for the reader and writer are ironically naive in the context of which we are aware:

'His hit þi wille, com and sit,
And wat is þi wille lat me wite,
    Mi leve lif.

Bi houre Loverd, hevene king,
If I mai don aniþing
    Þat þe is lef
þou miȝtt finden me ful fre
Fol bleþeli wil I don for þe
    Wiþhouten gref.'

('If you like, come and sit,
and what your will is, let me know,
    my dear life.

By our Lord, the king of heaven,
if I can do anything
you want
you may find me most generous;
most happily will I perform for you
    without grudging.')

(28–36)

Within these lines, language and style combine to highlight both the fabliau context and the construction of the character. Margery's description of herself as "fre" is highly ambiguous. The term can mean 'noble', and 'generous', and no doubt in realistic terms this should be what Margery wishes to say of herself. It can also mean 'unrestrained' in the sense either of freedom to act or prodigality in giving: what Wilekin wants is that she give herself. "Fol bleþeli", in the manuscript's spelling with an <o>, provides the reader of the text with the hint of a bilingual compound adverb, following the model of Middle English *fol-hardi*, *fol-hardili*, etc., allowing a reading of line 35 as:

Fool-gladly shall I perform for you

which is indeed what Wilekin would like to hear. Potentially more poignant and serious is the rhyme *lef/gref*, 'desired, loved'/'grief'; a linkage of glee, licence and distress that we find again shortly afterwards, with a different but phonetically similar word, "leve", 'leave', 'licence', and the verb "greve", 'grieve', where Wilekin takes the risk of declaring himself:

'Nou Ich have wonne leve
3if þat I me shulde greve
    Hit were hounlawe.'

('Now that I have won leave
for me to cause myself grief
    would be wrong.')

(58–60)

But the whole thrust of the poem militates against serious meditation here on the transient and subverted joys of human sexual liberty; rather it identifies those as facts for us to note and to submerge within the same sardonic amusement at human folly that Margery, in particular, seems to invite.

The ill-endowed Margery fails to maintain any very good face before the world. Even when she puts an important and sensible condition upon her offers to do Wilekin's will:

'if þat þou me tellest skil
I shal don after þi wil'

('if your request is reasonable
I shall do your will')

(52–3)

she immediately undercuts herself:

'And þau þou saie me ani same
Ne shal I þe noui3t blame'

('And even if you say something shameful to me
I shall blame you in no way at all')

(55–6)

Ironic, then, is Wilekin's immediate comment:

'Certes, dame, þou seist as hende'

('Indeed, lady, you speak as a gracious person')

(61)

as, indeed, in the sense of 'like' rather than 'being'. We might note that the adjective *hende*, which we shall find extensively exploited in Chaucer's Miller's Tale, is also used of Dame Sirith, when she is first mentioned in the text, in line 154. It is in fact when Margery is put on the spot, to produce her shocked rejection of Wilekin's advance, that the clever pitching of her character is revealed. The immediate rebuff is in conventional and predictable terms:

'Þat wold I don for non þing
Bi houre Loverd, hevene king
      Þat ous is bove.'

('That I would do in no circumstances
by our Lord, king of heaven,
who is above us.')

(88–90)

Line 89 is a repetition of one of Margery's first lines, line 31. She goes on in formulaic terms:

'He loveþ me and Ich him wel
Oure love is also trewe as stel. . . '

('He [my husband] loves me and I love him well;
our love is as true as steel')

(94–5)

Equally dull rhetoric appears in:

'Nevermore his lif-wile
Þau he were an hondred mile
      Biȝende Rome
For noþing ne shuld I take
Mon on erþe to ben mi make. . . '

('Never during his life time
though he were a hundred miles
      the other side of Rome
in any circumstances would I take
a mortal man to be my mate. . . ')

(103–7)

culminating in a banal image of the perfect married couple:

'Mi loverd is curteis mon and hende
      And mon of pris
And Ich am wif boþe god and trewe. . . '

> ('My master is a courteous and gracious man
> and a man of worth
> and I am a wife both good and faithful. . . ')

> (119–21)

In the meantime Margery has exposed her ability to think and
indeed picture herself in the vulgar, crude terms of the fabliau
world:

> 'Þat ne shal nevere be
> Þat I shal don selk falsete
>   On bedde ne on flore.'

> ('That shall never be
> that I shall do such falsity
>   in bed or on the floor.')

> (100–2)

And in her final words to Wilekin in this exchange she manages to
give an ambiguous hint that she may be prepared to entertain
Wilekin – along with her husband:

> 'Þou miȝt gon home, leve broþer.
> For wille Ich þe love ne non oþer
> Bote mi wedde houssebonde
> To tellen hit þe ne wille Ich wonde.'

> ('You could go home, dear brother.
> For if I should wish to love you and no other
> except for my wedded husband
> I shall not fail to tell you.')

> (135–8)

In all of this giving away of herself (which can be taken in two
modern senses), this revelation of a coarser character beneath the
courtly exterior she tries to sustain, Margery follows the movement
of the opening stanzas of the text down from the character of the
courtly dame to the level of the townswoman, a stereotyped
bourgeois *Vxor*, 'Wife': the label that seems to be given her by the
letter "V" alongside some of her speeches in the manuscript copy of
Dame Sirith.

After Dame Sirith is introduced as a character (line 154), the
terms of courtship in the conventions of *fin amour* become blended
with persistently repeated terms of an altogether different register
and semantic field: that of the marketplace and brothel. Wilekin

wastes no time in offering Dame Sirith "ful riche mede", 'a most rich reward/payment' (166) if she will help him. The term "riche mede" is repeated at line 191, thus enveloping Wilekin's opening speech in this dialogue and emphasizing the meretricious nature of the contract he proposes with Dame Sirith. At the beginning of his next speech, after Sirith's defensive demurral, he has to be more specific, and perhaps more generous:

> 'Ich wille geve þe gift ful stark
> Moni a pound and moni a mark
> Warme pilche and warme shon.'

> ('I will give you a mighty gift,
> many a pound and many a mark,
> warm clothing and warm shoes.')

(223–5)

although in fact he ends up paying just twenty shillings (one pound) when Dame Sirith agrees to help (270).

Wilekin's offers to Dame Sirith are inverted in the next dialogue, where Dame Sirith goes to Margery and speaks with her. Firstly, as noted, Dame Sirith laments the "poverte" of all old women and wins Margery's ready – and formulaic – Christian sympathy:

> 'For love of Goed
> Ich have reuþe of þi wo
> For evele iclothed I se þe go
>   And evele ishoed.'

> ('For the love of God
> I pity your misery
> for I see you go ill-clothed
>   and ill-shod.')

(317–20)

Dame Sirith's response is immediate and tellingly worded:

> 'Goed almiȝtten do þe *mede*'

> ('God Almighty *reward* you')

(322)

> '. . . þilke Loverd þe *forȝelde*'

> ('. . . that same Lord *repay* you')

(326)

and yet more ironically Margery replies in precisely the same terms:

'Goed do þe *mede* for þi swinke'

('God *reward* you for your labour')

(330)

And so it goes on. After Margery has swallowed Dame Sirith's trick she has recourse to the same commercial means of gaining what she thinks she needs and what she therefore now wants – indeed yearns for with an eagerness that the clerk himself could hardly have hoped for!

'Loverd Crist, þat me is wo
Þat þe clerc me hede fro
   Ar he me hevede biwonne.
Me were levere þen ani fe
That he hevede enes leien bi me
   And efftsoones bigunne.

Evermore, nelde, Ich wille be þin
Wiþ þat þou feche me Willekin,
   Þe clarc of wam I telle.
Giftes will I geve þe
Þat þou miȝt ever þe betere be. . . '

('Lord Christ, it grieves me
that the clerk went from me
   before he had won me.
I would rather than any payment
that he had once lain with me
   and got at it straightaway.

Evermore, old woman, I will be yours
if you bring me Wilekin,
   the clerk of whom I speak.
I will give you gifts
so that you are better off for ever. . . ')

(379–89)

What is perhaps most curious about the characterization of Margery after the trick has been played is that she very soon drops all reference to – and therefore seems to be portrayed as forgetting – the threat she believes the clerk to pose. By her next words to Dame Sirith all she says of her feelings towards Wilekin is:

'Bote þat þou me Wilekin bringe
Ne mai I never lawe ne singe
  Ne be glad.'

('Unless you bring me Wilekin
I can never laugh nor sing
  nor be glad.')

(400–2)

and her next speech welcomes Wilekin:

'Welcome Wilekin swete þing!
Þou art welcomore þen þe king.

Wilekin þe swete
Mi love I þe bihete
  To don al þine wille.'

('Welcome, Wilekin, sweet thing.
You are more welcome than the king.

Sweet Wilekin,
I promise you my love,
  to do all your will.')

(425–9)

Line 428 in particular − 'I promise you all my love' − may be interpreted in various ways, and it is worth reviewing, briefly, the possibilities. Is Margery's love truly so fickle? And does this reflect generally on womankind? But it has also been apparent from the very beginning of the tale, where Wilekin 'began to love a married woman' that 'love' in this text may mean nothing more than carnal desire. Around such points it is possible to construct a reading of *Dame Sirith* as an antifeminist text. The two female characters could be read as established types of women, untrustworthy to, or just unworthy of, men, paralleled in fact in the French fabliaux. Margery, in her swift change of attitude abandoning her loyalty to her absent husband in favour of a sexual liaison with Wilekin, is a parallel to the woman in *Cele qui se fist foutre sur la fosse de son mari*; and as an elderly procuress, operating through feigning grief and gaining sympathy, Dame Sirith finds a parallel in Auberee, "la vieille maquerel", 'the old bawd', in the fabliau of the same name.[3]

But it is a heavily biased reading of *Dame Sirith* to see only the

---

3. See below, Chapter 3 pp 82.

antifeminist direction and to ignore the unfavourable reflections upon Wilekin's base attitude and desires. It is in the midst of the cloud of images and references to money, after Wilekin has opened negotiations with Dame Sirith, that we get the most carefully constructed implicit observation on the whole business of the procurement that Wilekin is about. After Dame Sirith has agreed to help, Wilekin pays her:

> 'Have her twenti shiling
> Þis Ich ʒeve þe to meding
>   To buggen þe sep and swin.'

> ('Take, here, twenty shillings:
> this I give you in reward
>   to buy sheep and swine for yourself.')

(270–2)

Apart from the metrical need to round off the stanza, there is no contextual requirement for Wilekin to suggest Dame Sirith buy animals with the money. The detail, then, is in this sense gratuitous, but it has its effect: Wilekin buys Margery with the same money that Dame Sirith can use to buy animals; the bargains, and the items bought, are reduced to the same level. With this in mind it is hard to overlook Margery's first, charitable gift to the needy old lady that she sees:

> 'Have her *fles* and eke bred. . . '

> ('Take, here, *flesh* [meat] and bread as well. . . ')

(327)

We should not blindly make the easy moralistic assumption that whores are disgraceful and so are their customers, of course. The French fabliau *Boivin de Provins*, for instance, treats the prostitutes just as one source of sexually desirable and available women, and laughs with the man who is able to con them into providing him with a whore for free. Similar in effect is *Le Bouchier d'Abeville*, with his sexual purchases with the stolen sheepskin. It is, however, the case that the man who approaches the whore as a client, on her terms that is, is usually mocked in the fabliau: see, for example, *Le Prestre et Alison*, described in Chapter 1, or *La vieille Truande*, 'The old beggarwoman', in which an old woman manipulates an attractive young squire into either 'embracing' her or carrying her across a river — an act which in fact becomes a physical embrace — to "la grans risee", 'the great laughter', of the witnesses. In the next chapter too we shall see female prostitution presented in a morally adverse manner, in Chaucer's Shipman's Tale and its Italian analogues.[4]

The least obtrusive character in *Dame Sirith* — the dog and the merchant excepted — but still one that is distinctly constructed, is the narrator. He is a character easily overlooked by the reader of the text, for the bulk of the drama is conveyed in a series of dialogues between the other three characters, and attention is naturally attracted — or rather distracted — by the probability that this text is a script for a simple sort of play and thus very different from a straightforwardly narrative text. Nonetheless the narrator retains about 50 lines out of 450, and if, as is likely, the form of drama here is that which requires only one actor, shifting his voice to declaim all the lines, perhaps miming the actions and reactions of the characters, then the narrator's voice has to be a distinct presence in the performance of the text. The narrator makes his presence most felt by a series of moralistic or sacrilegious apostrophes: comments on events within the text. We have already seen how in line 6 he wrily notes of Wilekin's passion:

Þerof he hevede wrong

A further moral comment appears on Dame Sirith's deceit of Margery:

Crist awarie hire lif!

(Christ damn her life!)

(332)

and a mild, though still blasphemous oath appears in the brief narrative transition from Dame Sirith's dialogue with Margery to her reporting of her success to Wilekin. Margery has begged her to try to find the clerk:

Hoe wente hire to hire inne;
Þer hoe founde Wilekinne,
    Bi houre Driȝtte!

4. A useful survey of attitudes to the prostitute in French fabliaux is found in Lorcin *Façons de sentir et de penser: les fabliaux* pp 51–67.

(She took herself to her home;
and there she found Wilekin,
   by our Lord!)

(406–8)

What a surprise! All of the narrator's rhetoric is to be taken ironically, not at face value. There is a self-characterization here that is comic, and sophisticated, all the more so for being so unobtrusive that it is usually missed.

The last three verses of *Dame Sirith* form a fitting climax to this skilfully constructed fabliau. The first is spoken by Wilekin, the remaining two by Dame Sirith:

'Dame, so Ich evere bide noen,
and Ich am redi and iboen
   To don al þat þou saie.
Nelde, *par ma fai*,
Þou moste gange awai,
   Wile Ich and hoe shulen plaie.'

'Goddot, so I wille;
And loke þat þou hire tille
   And strek out hire þes.
God ȝeve þe muchel kare
ȝeif þat þou hire spare
   Þe wile þou mid hire bes.

And wose is onwis
And for non pris
   Ne con geten his levemon,
I shal, for mi mede,
Garen him to spede,
   For ful wel I con.'

('Lady, as I hope to live until nones,
I also am ready and well prepared
   to do all that you say.
Old woman, by my faith,
you must go away
   while I and she are to play.'

'God knows, so I shall;
and look that you plough her
   and stretch out her thighs.
God give you great care
if you should her spare
   for the time that you are with her.

And whoever is not clever enough
and not at any price
    can get the object of his desires,
I shall, for my fee,
make sure he succeeds,
    for I am very skillful.')

(433–50)

Wilekin reverts here to speaking in his courtly manner. He is
Margery's servant, eager and prepared to do her behest. He
addresses Dame Sirith imperiously, and with a French expression:

'Nelde, *par ma fai*,
    Þou most gange awai. . . '

But Dame Sirith's final words remind us that this courtliness of
expression is located in a fabliau in which the actions and attitudes
are as commercial (*pris, mede*) and as crude, sexually, as in any
French counterpart:

'And loke þat þou hire tille
And strek out hire þes'

These lines do not quite move into the register of marked language
that we have seen in the French fabliaux and shall see in Chaucer's
English fabliaux except in so far as references to women's thighs do
not find a place in the conventional rhetorical portrayal of a courtly
lady. The sentiment, however, is unmistakably marked in the same
way as is marked vulgar language. The last verse is a masterpiece.
Not only does Dame Sirith advertise her professional ability to
repeat the trick, or to obtain for a man the woman he wants in the
way he wants, and thus anticipate her ability to star in an extended
series of fabliaux that the poet may tell, but the language and
prosody convey certain points that lie at the heart of the fabliau
perspective. We have seen already how rhymes in this text can
create telling juxtapositions: here we have the linkage of *wis* and
pris, 'wise' and 'price', i.e. wisdom means knowing the price of
something or being able to buy it, or alternatively *onwis* and *pris*,
i.e. the unwise can be bought.   There is a comparable linkage of
mede and *spede*, 'payment' and 'success'. Moreover the word *con*,
whose French meaning we are unlikely to forget, appears twice in
this verse, once as the final, rhyming word of the tale. This clearly
allows the bilingual audience – and one's knowledge of a language

does not have to be particularly broad for one to know the rude words – to appreciate a pun that tells us much of the character of the fabliau: the essential place of the *con* in the *conte*.

Dame Sirith in literary history

How far does this Middle English "fablel" correspond to the French or Anglo-Norman fabliaux? In terms of basic structure there is no doubt that Dame Sirith belongs to the same genre. The situation for the fabliau, the clerk's desire for the wife, and her vulnerability with her husband away, is rapidly set up with no superfluous details or distractions. The plot is concluded by a deception which we see leading to a misdeed, although that misdeed is only anticipated in the speech of all three *dramatis personae* at the end rather than enacted in the text. *Dame Sirith* also has a clear target figure, the butt of the humour. This is not, as it might have been with such a tale, the cuckolded merchant, but rather Margery, the stupid wife, who is particularly funny because she is so unthinkingly conventionally good and who effaces any real self she may be imagined to have within a cluster of clichés. She has no sense of her own sexuality – which stimulates the clerk – or of the value of her sexuality: though promised to her husband it becomes an easy counter to pay on the threat of being changed into an animal. In Freud's terms, this becomes a joke when both teller and listener, writer and reader, share an appreciation of at least the potential value of that sexuality. We also find something close to the marked language characteristic of fabliaux in Dame Sirith's parting words to Wilekin.

The performable format of Dame Sirith, however, is not what one would expect in light of the French tradition. Although dialogue can be deftly used in scenes within the French and Anglo-Norman fabliaux, none of those fabliaux as a whole seems as well suited to performance as this. Here we have what is clearly a well set-up series of dialogues: Wilekin with Margery; Wilekin with Dame Sirith; Dame Sirith with Margery; only in the last five stanzas do we get anything more complicated, with three characters present in the same scene. The sort of one-man performance of such a text is neatly encapsulated in a description of the 'mime' artist's skills by Vitalis of Blois, a writer in Medieval Latin:

Fingebam vultus, habitus, ac verba loquentum,
   Ut plures uno crederes ore loqui.

(I feigned the countenance, clothing and words of speaking characters,
So that you should suppose several to speak through one mouth.)

It is, in fact, in twelfth-century Latin *comoediae* and some
thirteenth-century Old French works that one finds the most
convincing examples of works composed for performance of this kind;
in the present context it is particularly interesting to note that Edmond
Faral identified as Anglo-Latin comedies the two extant twelfth-
century *comoediae* written entirely in dialogue. On the other hand,
thirteenth-century French 'dramatic monologues' which provide
parallels to the mixture of metres – octosyllabic couplets and
tail-rhyme stanzas – of *Dame Sirith* have been discovered, and it is
difficult to resist the case that these had some contributory influence
on the form of Dame Sirith. Of considerable potential importance too
is fragmentary evidence of Anglo-Norman 'plays' of the late thirteenth
and fourteenth century. These regularly include at least one actor
standing in a position intermediary between the dramatic characters
proper and the audience by acting as a narrator or declaiming a
prologue.[5] The issue of theatrical performance is an important one,
and one that will appear again in the next chapter.

   One is obliged to note, however, that *Dame Sirith* does very
little else to support the case that the Anglo-Norman fabliaux stand
between the French tradition and English fabliaux. The existence of
possible bilingual wordplay within the poem – *fol* and *con* – suggests
that *Dame Sirith* may have been composed with a bilingual audience
in mind, but it does not match the features of the Anglo-Norman
fabliaux identified by van den Boogard. There is nothing to suggest
any direct seigneurial interest in the plot or characters of the tale;
although the comedy of *Dame Sirith* does at least assume knowledge
and recognition of the conventions of chivalric behaviour, it would
be absurd to suggest that knowledge of such conventions was
socially limited in any significant way in the later thirteenth
century. What is more, the narrator can be seen to strike a
ridiculous pose within this text in a way supposedly omitted from
the Anglo-Norman fabliaux: drawing attention to himself with his
unnecessary, insincere or ignored apostrophes. The use of rhetoric

---

5. See Legge D M 1963 *Anglo-Norman Literature and its Background* (Oxford
   University Press) pp 328–31 and Revard 1982, as Ch.1 n.14.

and the extensive deployment of irony are very much characteristic features of the original French tradition. One does not, however, need to know that in order to be able to appreciate their use in *Dame Sirith*.

Dame Sirith does not end with a brief moral in the way that so many of the French fabliaux do. And it is not easy to discover any more covert or sophisticated moral view of the characters and the events of the poem: it does not dwell in any suggestive way on the irremediable carnality of human desires, and only with a degree of distortion and uncalled for determination could we assert that the poem is significantly antifeminist or anticlerical. If anything, the poem seems to create a deliberate breach of moral conventions – hence the irrelevance of the narrator's moral apostrophes – and to proclaim, in the clerk's success, the *carpe diem*, 'take your chance', theme. One might surmise that *Dame Sirith* was written to create and fill a brief space of moral relaxation for an audience who knew well both the moral and the social conventions the tale plays with. But one cannot overlook the point that all other known medieval European versions of this tale, written in or translated from Latin prose, present it as a moral example; it can be allegorized, with the housewife as the Christian soul, the absent husband Christ, the lover worldly vanity, the procuress the Devil.[6] It is in fact possible to find passages in *Dame Sirith* which may again recognize, and irreverently exploit, a knowledge that such was a possible presentation of this tale. This appears, for instance, where Margery first rejects Wilekin's advances, referring to "houre Loverd, hevene king" and going straight on to:

> 'Ich habe mi loverd þat is mi spouse
> Þat maiden brouȝte me to house. . . '
>
> ('I have my lord who is my spouse
> who brought me a virgin to his house. . . ')
>
> (91–2)

This multiplies the humour for those in the know, at the same time as it enhances the potentially shocking behaviour of the poet–narrator.

The text itself tells us more about the origins of *Dame Sirith*.

6. For example Petrus Alfonsus *Disciplina Clericalis*, exemplum XIII, 'De canicula lacrimante', 'Of the weeping bitch'; Jacques de Vitry, Exempla, no.CCL. See also Chapter 6 p 214.

Localization of the tale in the eastern Midlands is suggested by the reference to the husband being absent at the fair of Boston, in southern Lincolnshire, and it is also the case that the poem was composed in the East Midland dialect. The manuscript, however, can be attributed to the West Midlands, to the diocese of Worcester, and a small number of spellings in the text appropriate to the dialect of this region can be found, as indeed can an equally small number of spellings appropriate to the south-east of England. The language of the text is Middle English with a typical medieval admixture of words derived from the Scandinavian language of Viking-period settlers in England and from Old French, the language of the post-Conquest aristocracy. The level of Norse and French influence is equal in terms of a simple count of loanwords – about thirty words adopted from each language are found in *Dame Sirith* – but the presence of Scandinavian loanwords is dialectally more diagnostic, in this case again confirming an East Midland origin. More noteworthy are a small number of words and phrases apparently adopted from Middle Dutch, including the name Wilekin, which has the Dutch diminutive suffix *-kin*. Dame Sirith's name is of Scandinavian origin, *Sigríðr*.

Should it surprise us that this tale from the East Midlands should be taken into a largely religious anthology produced in the West Midlands? The dialectally divergent spellings suggest that at the very least three written English versions of the tale existed: an East Midland original, a south-eastern copy and the West Midland copy that we now have. It is also relevant here that the story of the weeping bitch was a widely known one, albeit in moralized versions, as an exemplum, rather than simply as a fabliau. There is, however, only a fugitive, implicit (and comic) reference to the tale being an *exemplum* within the text, and no reference to it as it is presented in the manuscript; the tale is identified in the manuscript by the name of the character peculiar to this basically East Midland version, Dame Sirith. The case must be, then, that the tale stands in the manuscript to represent the fabliau, in this case as an English rather than an Anglo-Norman fabliau. The fact that the tale is such a familiar one suggests that *Dame Sirith* may not represent, by random survival, a substantial stock of late thirteenth-century English fabliaux. Had a more diverse stock existed it would have been more likely for a less familiar tale to have been selected. Thus there is no evidence as yet for any imaginative creation, development and writing up of a range of stories within the English fabliau corpus.

THE *INTERLUDIUM DE CLERICO ET PUELLA*

The *Interludium de Clerico et Puella*, 'The interlude of the clerk and the girl', appears to be a fragment of the tale of *Dame Sirith*, presented quite explicitly as the text of a play and preserved in an early fourteenth-century copy in a manuscript in the collection of the British Library (Additional MS 23986). The manuscript is a strip of a vellum roll with the extant text of the *Interludium* on one side and an earlier eighty-line fragment of Anglo-Norman poetry on the other.[7] The *Interludium* therefore occurs in a later copy than the extant copy of *Dame Sirith*, and since *Dame Sirith* contains details that are also found in the other European versions of the tale, such as the object of the clerk's desires being a married woman, not a 'girl', it is regarded as impossible for *Dame Sirith* to be derived from the *Interludium*. That the *Interludium* could derive directly from *Dame Sirith* is possible. The dialect of the *Interludium* is distinctly Northumbrian, but derivation of a Northumbrian text from a source located in Lincolnshire presents no difficulties. There are some remarkable verbal correspondences between the *Interludium* and *Dame Sirith*, such as the clerk's plea to the girl to "mend þi mode" (I. 25), appearing in *Dame Sirith* as "Amend þi mod" (DS. 113), and in the denial by Mome Elwis (the *Interludium*'s counterpart to Dame Sirith) of her ability to perform the tricks the clerk requires:

(*Interludium*)
    'A son! Vat saystu? Benedicite!
    Lift hup þin hand and blis þe!
    For it es boyt syn and scam
    Þat þu on me hafs leyt thys blam
    For Hic am an old quyne and a lam
    Y led my lyf wit Godis love

7. Published in Wright T 1839 *The Political Songs of England, from the Reign of John to that of Edward II*, Camden Society O.S.6, pp 59–63. A curious parallel to the preservation of the *Interludium de Clerico et Puella* in this form is found with one of the Anglo-Norman plays described by Dominica Legge (*op.cit.* footnote 5) which was written on the back of a manorial roll, which "seems to have been a piece of scrap parchment". See further, below, on the completeness or fragmentariness of the extant text of the *Interludium*.

Wit my roc Y me fede
Can I do non othir dede
Bot my pater noster and my crede
To say Crist for missedede. . . '

('A son! What are you saying? Benedicite!
Lift up your hand and cross yourself!
For it is both sinful and shameful
that you have laid this accusation against me,
for I am an old woman, and lame.
I lead my life in God's love;
I support myself by my spinning.
I cannot do anything else
except for saying my paternoster and my creed
to Christ, for my sins . . . ')

(I. 63–72)

which can be compared with *Dame Sirith*:

'Benedicite be herinne. . . '

(DS. 193)

'Þou servest affter Godes grame
Wen þou seist on me silk blame,
For Ich am old, and sek, and lame . . . '

(DS. 197–9)

'Blesse þe, blesse þe, leve knave . . . '

(DS. 201)

'On wicchecrafft nout I ne con
Bot wiþ gode almesdede
Ilke dai mi lif I fede
And bidde mi paternoster and mi crede . . . '

(DS. 206–9)

Yet there are details of the *Interludium* that would appear very strange if solely attributable to a northern English redaction of an East Midland text identifiable as the source of the *Dame Sirith* that we know. There is, in particular, the introduction of two French saints within the text: St Leonard (I. 7), a sixth-century hermit from near Limoges, and St Denis (I. 38), the first bishop of Paris in the sixth century. Since other versions of the weeping bitch tale are known from the continent, and France is unquestionably home to the fabliaux, the divergent descent of the known *Dame Sirith* and

the *Interludium* from an English descendant of a French source –
perhaps an Anglo-Norman play text – rather than the one from the
other looks most likely.

It is generally assumed that both texts on British Library
Additional MS 23986 are preserved there as fragments of longer
originals, and this is certainly true of the Anglo-Norman ballad first
written on the roll. Regrettably this manuscript has been lost within
the British Library for the last twenty years, and studies of it at
present have to be based on photographic records. The text of the
Interludium ends, at the end of a sentence, about half an inch from
the bottom of the roll, leaving space for at least three more lines of
text. It is impossible, from the photograph, to tell whether the
surface of the vellum has been erased here. It is quite clear that
nothing is missing from the other end of the *Interludium* as it was
copied on to this vellum: the vellum had already been cut to its
surviving top edge by the time the *Interludium* came to be written
on to it. The start of the text is clearly signalled by a rubric about
five and a half inches from the top edge of the roll: "Hic incipit
interludium de clerico et puella", 'Here begins the interlude of the
clerk and the girl'. While the opening exchanges between the clerk
and the girl are very cursory, they are sufficient to introduce all that
is necessary for an audience to know: the girl is a "damishel" (I. 1),
the interlocutor a man ("sir", I. 2), and the girl is vulnerable as she
is alone:

> 'Wer es ty sire, wer es ty dame?'
> 'By Gode, es noþer her at hame.'
>
> ('Where is your master, where is your mistress?'
> 'By God, neither is here at home')

(I. 3–4)

(Line 3 could be read 'Where is your father, where is your
mother?'). The man's desires are immediately revealed:

> 'Wel war suilc a man to life
> þat suilc a may mithe have to wyfe'
>
> ('That man would be well off indeed
> who might have such a maiden as his wife')

(I. 5–6)

and the girl's reaction is just as immediate and direct, revealing to
the reader or audience too the identity of the man as a "clerc":

'Do way! By Crist and Leonard
No wyl Y lufe na clerc fayllard
Ne kep I herbherg clerc in huse no y flore
Bot his hers ly wituten dore.
Go forth þi way . . .'

('Get off! By Christ and Leonard
I shall love no failing clerk
nor do I care to receive a clerk within the house nor on the floor;
let him keep his arse outside the door!
Be on your way . . .')

(I. 7–11)

The girl remains witty and determined throughout the extant text, and thus quite the opposite of Margery in *Dame Sirith*. Individualizing traits are the girl's witty use of "fayllard", meaning both 'unsuccessful' (with her) and 'good-for-nothing' (generally) and her vulgar but effective way of telling the clerk his place lies on the other side of the door to her.

From line 13 of the text onwards, after his sudden advance upon the girl has been rejected, the clerk becomes verbose and directionless. His self-pitying speech reveals his worthlessness:

'Y may say "Hay, wayleway":
Y luf þe mor þan mi lif,
Þu hates me mor þan gayt dos chnief.'

('I may say "Alas, woe is me":
I love you more than my life,
you hate me more than a goat hates the knife.')

(I. 18–20)

His opening compliment to the girl may backfire:

'In al þis land ne . . . Hi none
Mayden þat Hi luf mor þan þe . . .'

('In all this land I [know] not one
maiden that I love more than thee . . .')

(I. 14–15)

depending on whether we take the "mayden" as a vocative (i.e. 'girl, I love no one more than thee') or as the object of the lost verb of line 14, whereby the þat-clause becomes a restrictive relative clause ('I love no maiden more than you . . .' [but I might love some just as much or only a bit less]). The clerk pleads:

A! suythe mayden, reu of me . . . '

('Ah, wonderful maiden, take pity on me . . . ')

(I. 23)

but cannot sustain a courtly approach with the articulacy of Wilekin: line 23, quoted here, could easily come from a prayer to the Virgin Mary, and the clerk soon concludes by a sacrilegious plea in Marian terms:

'For þe luf of þe moder of efne
þu mend þi mode and her my stevene!'

('For the love of the mother of heaven,
change your mind and hear my plea!')

(I. 25–6)

Like Margery in *Dame Sirith*, he cannot maintain the courtly role he attempts to appropriate, and cuts a most unimpressive figure.

The girl, fittingly, is quite unmoved, giving him two clear rejections, ending with a fine rhetorical flourish:

'Go nu, truan! Go nu, go!'

('Go now, beggar! Go now, go!')

(I. 35)

In so far as the *Interludium* is amusing, up to this point and beyond it, the humour is very much at the expense of the clerk. He has been soundly scourged, verbally, by the girl, and can only respond by going off to Mome Elwis, and giving her another verbose and self-pitying plea (lines 39–62), repetitiously anticipating his own death if his sexual desires are not gratified. Within this text, which ends after Mome Elwis's speech in reply, a speech that matches that of Dame Sirith when she initially protects herself, the wretched clerk finds that the only answer he gets is a speech that matches his own for its wordiness and clichéd character – a speech in which Mome Elwis well may mouth the same formulae as Dame Sirith in the equivalent situation, as quoted above. And what is more, the clichés used by Mome Elwis are at least better suited to the cleric than anything the clerk can come out with:

'Can I do non oþir dede
Bot my pater noster and my crede
To say Crist for missedede
And myn Avy Mary;

For my scynnes Hic am sory
And my *De profundis*
For al þat in sin lys,
For can I me non oþir þink –
þat wot Crist of hevene kync.'

('I can do no other deed
but say my paternoster and my creed
to Christ for my misdeeds,
and my Ave Maria –
I am sorry for my sins –
and my *de profundis*
for all who remain in sin,
for I am good for nothing else –
Christ knows that, the king of heaven.')

(I. 70–78)

The result is that the surviving text of the *Interludium de Clerico et Puella* looks quite different from *Dame Sirith*: it looks like an anticlerical play. It does appear as if there is an incomplete text of the play surviving: we could sketch in the rest from the analogue in *Dame Sirith* and the continental analogues reached through that text, but what we have here is sufficiently individual to counsel caution in assuming we know what is missing. Interrupted or not, the extant text of the *Interludium* ends exactly at the end of a line and sentence, which by reference to *Dame Sirith* we can argue is the end of this particular speech from Mome Elwis. If the play did end at this point, the real anticlerical joke would be that the *Interludium* does not go on to the successful trick as the audience might have expected and the clerk might have hoped. As well as being fully adequate at the beginning, the text ends at a suitable and sufficient point; the possible significance of this can evidently easily be missed.

Chapter 3

Chaucer's Shipman's Tale

THE SHIPMAN'S TALE AS A FABLIAU

All of the remaining medieval English examples of the fabliau are found in Chaucer's Canterbury Tales. We shall start our study of these with the Shipman's Tale, as that tale forms a good bridge between the non-Chaucerian fabliaux and Chaucer's other examples of this genre in certain ways, and it is as good a starting point as any for a discussion of Chaucer's complex response to the norms of fabliau tradition within the Canterbury Tales.

The Shipman's Tale and its analogues

The Shipman's Tale tells of a lovers' triangle, involving a merchant who lives at St Denis (France), his wife, and a Parisian monk who was regarded as their friend: indeed the monk and the merchant call each other cousin, as both are from the same village. It comes about that the merchant has to go to the fair at Bruges on his business, and while he spends part of a day before departure in his counting-house reviewing his affairs the monk meets and converses with the wife. She responds to a comment by the monk on how she appears to have passed the night in sexual 'labour' by bemoaning what she suffers as a wife, implying that her husband gives her no pleasure in bed and is mean with his money. Finally she states that she needs a hundred francs to pay a bill for her clothing. Should the monk provide her with this money she will repay him in whatever way he pleases. The monk subsequently borrows a hundred francs from the merchant, pays it to the wife and enjoys a night in bed with her while the husband is away. The merchant goes from Bruges to Paris, via his home at St Denis, to raise the cash to pay a pledge made in Bruges, and in Paris asks the

monk for his hundred francs. The monk tells him that the money
has already been returned to the wife. Later, after returning home,
in bed with his wife, the merchant taxes her about not having told
him the monk had given her the money; she claims that she
thought the money the monk gave her was gift, and that she has
already used it to buy clothing; she will pay, she says, her debts to
her husband in bed. The husband demurs only to tell his wife, in
the form of a brief moral conclusion, to:

> . . . ne be namoore so large,
> Keep bet thy good. . .

(431-2)

> *large*: extravagant; *keep bet*: look after better

after which the narrative ends with a concluding flourish:

> Thus endeth my tale, and God us sende
> Taillynge ynough unto oure lives ende.

(433-4)

> *taillynge*: this word is a significant pun, explained below

The only real parallels to this tale in continental literature come
from Italy; in the first and second tales on Day Eight in Boccaccio's
Decameron and in one of the *novelle* of Giovanni Sercambi. It has
been suggested that Chaucer had come across and drew upon all of
these sources for his Shipman's Tale.[1] The circumstantial case for a
related but lost version in French being the ancestor of Chaucer's
tale is, however, more persuasive. Chaucer's tale is set in the
north-east of France, the true home of the French fabliaux, its
geographical range stretching from Paris to Bruges. A French
ambient is added to the tale by the invocation of French saints – St
Martin, St Denis and possibly St Ivo of Chartres – and by providing
the merchant with a snatch of French in his conversation: "Quy
la?", "Who's there?" (214). Technically, however, the tale is
distinctly similar to *Dame Sirith* in the use that is made of dialogue
and the patterning of scenes. More than half of the Shipman's Tale
consists of dialogue (237 lines out of 434), a figure that increases if
we count odd lines introducing a change of speaker or place in
dialogue as part of the dialogue. *Dame Sirith* has 397 lines of
dialogue out of a total of 450. Like *Dame Sirith*, the dialogue of the

---

1. For Sercambi, De avaratia et lussurie, see Benson and Andersen, *Literary Context*
   pp 312-19; on Chaucer's possible debt to these Italian works, see Guerin 1971.

Shipman's Tale sets in front of the reader or audience a set of vignettes in which only two characters are present at any one time: the monk and the wife (89–208), the wife and the husband (212–48), the monk and the husband (255–92 and 342–64) and the husband and the wife (380–432). The line numbers given here give a better sense of the preponderance of dialogue over narrative in the Shipman's Tale, a ratio of about 2:1. There is very little use of dialogue in Boccaccio's tales. Dialogue is deftly used in Sercambi's novella, as sometimes in the French fabliaux, but, as has been noted, none of the French fabliaux are suited to performance in the way that *Dame Sirith* is, and as an inferrable source for the Shipman's Tale may have been. One may tentatively suggest that at least one English fabliau version of the tale given by Chaucer to the Shipman stood between a French source and Chaucer. The majority of the truly narrative lines are found at the start of the Shipman's Tale, where we have a careful introduction of the characters and setting of the tale. If the Shipman's Tale is a redaction of a dramatized fabliau of the same kind as the English *Dame Sirith* we can expect these opening lines to convey at least some particular characteristics of the fabliau as conceived and used by Chaucer.

The merchant as target figure

All of the Italian versions of this tale make the lady the dupe, the victim of the male lover's ruse, prostituting herself for money that simply circulates from the husband to the wife via the lover. The husband is also, of course, the victim of this ruse, but in none of the Italian versions is he built up in any way to provide a substantial target figure. Traditional readings of the Shipman's Tale, however, suppose the husband to be a, or even the, target figure, and not without reason. The husband's preoccupation with his commercial affairs, which might imply a neglect of his wife's conjugal and material desires, is repeatedly hinted at. The opening couplet of the tale introduces and immediately impugns the merchant by making an obviously facile equation of wealth and imputed wisdom:

> A merchant whilom dwelled at Seint-Denys
> That riche was, for which men heeld him wys.
>
> (1–2)

whilom: once

His wisdom is not revealed by manifestly wise behaviour. We are soon informed of how his wealth is made public knowledge in lines that suggest his generosity with his riches could be extravagance; an imprudent use and showing of wealth — and his wife — rather than a wise one:

> This noble marchaunt heeld a worthy hous
> For which he hadde alday so great repair
> For his largesse (and for his wyf was fair)
> That wonder is. . .

> (20–3)

> > *alday*: all the time; *largesse*: generosity

The preoccupied merchant, whose attention is totally bound up with his commercial affairs and who consequently neglects his wife, is a stock figure of fabliau-type narrative (compare, for instance, *La Bourgoise d'Orliens*, *Le Cuvier*, 'The bathtub', or *L'Enfant qui fu remis au soleil*, 'The child who was given back to the sun'). Here, the wife is left exposed to the monk's attentions when the husband shuts himself up in his counting-house (75–88); he delivers his wife a lecture on his "curious bisynesse" when she asks him to come down to eat (224–48); he must settle his affairs in Paris before he can settle back at home after his trip to Bruges (365–9). The latter lines are introduced with an echo of the opening couplet:

> This merchant, which that was ful war and wys

> (365)

> > *war*: prudent, wary

with the complimentary epithets "war and wys" now ironic: "war and wys" he is, evidently, in business life, but not in keeping his wife.

The Shipman's merchant is far from uncomplicated and satisfactory as a target figure. A perfectly rational case can be made for the merchant to be carefully and conspicuously established as the innocent and undeserving victim of a conspiracy between his wife and the monk. Generous merchants are rare beasts in the literature of any age, and to see this merchant's generosity as entirely foolish, or purely representative of commercial self-interest, is to make a severe assumption. This merchant refuses to be a caricature in the form of the character without individual 'character' that his wife attempts to portray him as. At one point, the wife enumerates to the monk six qualities that women supposedly 'desire' in their husbands:

> 'They wolde that hir housbondes sholde be
> Hardy and wise, and riche, and therto free,
> And buxom unto his wyf and fressh abedde'
>
> (175–7)
>
> *hardy*: firm, tough, vigorous; *free*: generous; *buxom*: submissive, obedient

This is itself a formulaic list (cf. the Nun's Priest's Tale: VII: 2912–17). The wife implies that her husband fails in every way:

> 'As helpe me God, he is noght worth at al
> In no degree the value of a flye.'
>
> (170–1)

But with the exception of a little doubt as to what the relatively vague adjective *hardy* might mean, the husband eventually proves a worthy man against all of these criteria: clever enough to be a successful merchant and therefore rich; hospitable and generous; and apparently able to fulfil his wife's demands of him in bed. An engagement of sympathy on the side of the character who seems superficially to be the target figure constructs for the reader an unusual angle of vision on the events and characters of this fabliau.

The merchant is, however, a typical fabliau target figure in so far as he is ridiculous in his ignorance of how his wife and friend have deceived and cuckolded him. This final ignorance is anticipated by an innocence in the merchant that takes the form of his persistent lack of awareness of the loaded nature of particular forms of language use, of double meanings and innuendo. Before leaving for Bruges, he invites the monk, John:

> That he sholde come to Seint-Denys to pleye
> With him and with his wyf. . .
>
> (59–60)

where "pleye" is clearly intended by the merchant in what the modern reader can identify as a particularly childish sense — 'to play, have fun' — but which in Middle English, not unlike Modern English, also carries an additional sense of sexual play, and can also, appropriately, be used in the sense of playing tricks (a semantic range similar to that of Old French *dobler*: cf. Chapter 1). Naively, too, the merchant tells his wife to be "buxom", 'obedient, biddable', to "every wight" while he is away in Flanders.

Linguistically, thereby, the merchant weaves a number of strands into the net in which he is eventually caught, innocent and unknowing to the last. He seems crucially unconscious of potential sexual double meaning in imagery he uses to describe the commercial world: the world he faces is called a "queynte world" (236) (*queynte* as a noun is used to represent *cunt* in Chaucer) and he uses an obviously phallic image of merchants:

> '. . . hir moneie is hir plogh.'

> (288)

(cf. *Dame Sirith* lines 440–1: 'And loke þat þou hire tille/And strek out hire þes'). The merchant's contribution to linguistic play becomes especially distinct in the final dialogue, in bed with his wife. He kindly but firmly remonstrates with his wife:

> 'Telle me alwey, er that I fro thee go,
> If any dettour hath in myn absence
> Ypayed thee . . .'

> (396–8)

> *er*: before; *ypayed*: paid

'Paying the debt' has a clear double meaning in the sexual/conjugal context which the wife, who is made to respond to her husband's ignorance not by laughing at him but rather by underlining his innocence/ignorance in a play of irony for the tale's readers/listeners to respond to as they think fit, picks up upon and develops into a crude pun:

> 'Ye han mo slakkere dettours than am I . . .

> (412)

> I am youre wyf; score it upon my taille,
> And I shall paye as soone as ever I may . . .

> (416–17)

> By God, I wol nat paye yow but abedde!'

> (424)

> *mo*: more

"taille" here is polysemous, reflecting two homonyms, *taille*, 'tally, bill', whereby line 416 reads:

> 'I am your wife; notch it up on my account'

and *taille*, 'tail', thus 'rear parts, genitals', thus giving something like:

'I am your wife; notch it up on my crotch'

Here, we might note, the *wife* enunciates the aggressive sexual joke that Freud supposed to originate with the man.

The subtler of the recent readings of the Shipman's Tale keeps the merchant in the position of target figure by treating him not as a realistic character, but as a functional one: a figure representing the interplay of more abstract themes and factors affecting human life. His apparent personality as an ungeneralized individual is a literary illusion; he is regarded instead as an object of a form of general moral evaluation and judgement that probes the *mores* of medieval commercial and commercialized life from a conventional standpoint that is, paradoxically, radical and fundamentalist. Common to these readings is the observation of fundamental connections and parallels between the merchant and the monk, not just as individuals but as representatives of late medieval culture in a very broad form: of economic and religious life. Pioneering in this respect was the interpretation of the Shipman's Tale by Janette Richardson (1970), who claimed that the merchant was tied by the imagery of the tale into an inseparable pairing with the monk, and thus although "overtly" morally superior to the monk in several ways still essentially one with him. At the heart of her case lies the claim that the merchant, like the monk, is not generous as a virtue but rather as a matter of "calculated business policy", for the sake of appearing creditworthy:

> We may creaunce whil we have a name,
> But goldlees for to be, it is no game.
>
> (289–90)

> *creaunce*: be granted financial credit

At the end of the tale, the wife underlines this aspect of the merchant's lifestyle by suggesting that her spending on clothing serves the same purpose:

> . . . I have on myn aray,
> And not on wast bistowed every deel;
> And for I have bistowed it so weel,
> For youre honour, for Goddes sake, I seye,
> As be nat wrooth.
>
> (418–22)

> *wast*: waste; *as be nat*: do not be

This understanding provides a fundamentally important gloss to the *moot*, 'must', of the lines spoken, apparently by a female speaker, very early on in the Shipman's Tale:

> The sely housbonde, algate he moot paye,
> He moot us clothe, and he moot us arraye,
> Al for his owene worshipe richely,
> In which array we daunce jolily.
>
> (11–14)

> *sely*: innocent; *algate*: always, indeed; *jolily*: prettily

Both the merchant and the monk in the tale operate by borrowing money on credit in order to make profitable purchases. The monk takes his profit in the form of sexual gratification, the merchant, to begin with, in the form of "a thousand frankes". Thus when carnal and financial imagery in the tale finally merge in the puns *taille* and *taillynge* at the very end, it is an emblem of how much deeper the "bretherhede" and "cosynage" runs that the monk and the merchant imagine exists between them in the form of play, or as a polite figure of speech, and how concrete it is. The merchant, moreover, seems to be liberated by his financial success to take his own carnal reward:

> And al that nyght in myrthe they bisette
> For he was riche and cleerly out of dette
>
> (375–6)

These parallels between the monk and merchant should not, however, be allowed to obscure the differences between the two, especially the moral contrast. This contrast is most evident in the early presentation of the generosity of the monk and merchant respectively. The monk in this tale is soon presented as a witty and skilful fellow. Like the merchant – and, indeed, implicitly, his wife – an early-emphasized detail of his character is that he is "free" in the sense of 'generous', but in his case this is very much a means to an end rather than an end or a pleasure in itself:

> Free was daun John, and manly of dispence,
> As in that hous, and ful of diligence
> To doon plesaunce, and also greet costage.
> He noght forgat to yeve the leeste page
> In al that hous. . .

For which they were as glad of his comyng
As fowel is fayn whan that the sonne up riseth.

(43–7, 50–1)

doon plesaunce: give pleasure; *costage*: expenditure; *yeve*: give; *fowel*: foul, bird;
fayn: glad

The merchant's generosity, by contrast, is more genuinely *giving*:

. . . he seith nat ones nay
But was as glad therof as fowel of day,
For to his herte it was a great plesaunce.

(37–9)

The merchant is a professed and, as far as we are told, an honest
merchant: there is no case for any suggestion that the display of
wealth in his "largesse" (22) is a serious form of duplicity rather
than a worthy – if also pragmatic – use of his riches. The most
obvious moral interpretation of the assimilation of monk and
merchant does not lie in the drawing down of the merchant to the
level of the monk so much as in showing the monk to be
transgressing the bounds of his special profession by entering into
the commercial market place to procure a whore for himself. The
most telling point against Janette Richardson's methodical
interpretation may well be that no commercial benefits to the
merchant can be imputed to his generosity and hospitality towards
the monk; the monk is invited to his house simply "to pleye. . . in
alle wise", 'to have fun in every way' (59–61), and is able to borrow
a hundred francs from the merchant even at a time when cash in
hand would be particularly useful to him in his business (255–92):
this, significantly, is the immediate context of the merchant's
reflection:

'We may creaunce whil we have a name,
But goldlees for to be, it is no game.'

Derek Pearsall nicely describes the poignant ambivalence of a single
action that is motivated simultaneously by instinctive self-interest
and by the "inner springs" of human virtue in the Shipman's
merchant's desire both to be and to be recognized as generous.[2]

As David Aers has skilfully shown, the merchant, the monk and
the very language of the Shipman's Tale do co-act at a general level

2. Pearsall *The Canterbury Tales* pp 209-17.

to show a society where spiritual growth has been stunted, or rather deformed and directed away from an ideal moral and spiritual state.[3] The merchant unwittingly parodies Christ's resurrection in his withdrawal to his counting-house to review his affairs:

> The thridde day, this merchant up ariseth
> And on his nedes sadly hym avyseth
> And up into his countour-hous gooth he
>
> (75–7)
>
> *sadly hym avyseth*: solemnly/carefully contemplates

He descends only to join the rest of the household in a superficial scanting of Christian ritual between the call of the business world and the lure of socializing:

> And with that word his counter dore he shette
> And down he gooth, no longer wolde he lette.
> But hastily a messe was ther sayd
> And spedily the tables were ylayd
> And to the dyner faste they hem spedde . . .
>
> (249–53)
>
> *messe*: mass

Note the distraction and reluctance implied by the "But. . ." at the beginning of line 251 in comparison with the consecutive "And. . . ."'s that introduce more pleasing activities. While the secular merchant retires for contemplation, the 'religious' monk has been actively talking love and making a bargain with the wife. The monk, indeed, has commercial dealings as part of his duties as a monk, as

> . . . an officer, out for to ryde,
> To seen hir graunges and hire bernes wyde,
>
> (65–6)

and on this account he is able to request a loan of the merchant, without occasioning the slightest suspicion. He words his request in a particularly ironic way:

> '. . .lene me
> An hundred frankes, for a wyke or tweye,
> For certein beestes that I moste beye'
>
> (270–2)

3. Aers *Chaucer* pp 20–4.

We may note here in passing the same coarse innuendo as in *Dame Sirith*, where the money is paid to the dame "To buggen þe sep and swin".

As wisdom is measured by wealth (see above), epithets from a human value-system, 'good', 'worthy' and 'noble' take on explicitly commercial significance. The worst instance of this sort of linguistic fall from grace would seem to be that of the terms 'debt' and 'paying the debt', from the figurative sense of penance due to God, through the literal sense of a financial repayment, to a figurative countersense to the religious one, of sexual indulgence.[4] Yet this scandalous polysemy is already potential in the words of one of Paul's New Testament Epistles, where in I Corinthians 7: 3 he creates the concept of the conjugal debt, writing *opheilēn apodidotō*, 'let [the husband] pay the debt' (*New English Bible*: "The husband must give the wife what is due to her, and the wife equally must give the husband his due").

The disruption of categories in the Shipman's Tale

If the merchant in the Shipman's Tale does not easily fall into the role of the target figure, could another character do so, for instance the wife, who is unquestionably put in this position in the Italian analogues to the tale? The most significant result of re-posing the question is to reveal how difficult it is to separate the different characters of the Shipman's Tale and to assess, and judge, them individually in these terms. One is faced in the text by a body of material that invites interpretation as a critical examination of human action, but as a general, not a selective, critical view, that can be antimercantile and antifeminist (with the merchant and wife as target figures) and anticlerical in the satirical exposure of the monk's behaviour. Beyond even this, however, it can be argued that the intrinsic nature of the fabliau that resides in the Shipman's Tale counteracts all of these 'anti-isms', and that the Shipman's Tale thus offers a critical disruption of these conventional categories. Such a disruption corresponds to the critical assessment by Chaucer of the features of another category, the genre of fabliau itself, through this tale. This in turn contributes to a thematized

4. Adams 1984.

exploration of literary types in fragment VII of the Canterbury Tales.

In the simple moralistic and realistic view, there can be little question that the interaction of the monk and the wife forms a dramatic exemplification of unworthiness in human behaviour. In the more symbolic terms, a damning inditement of medieval culture might be found in the situation and behaviour of the wife. Here is a character economically dependent on the opposite sex, and who has instant and sole recourse to her vagina as her bargaining counter in negotiations with these two men. But we cannot trust this wife's claim that she is starved of cash by her husband. We must also attribute some significance to the fact that the wife takes the lead in talking smut and negotiating with the monk.

The conspiracy of the wife and the monk is the matter of the first dialogue in the tale. It is a passage that clearly portrays an intimate similarity between the two characters, although the wife is in some telling respects the more subtle of the two, reflecting the feminine cunning that is so typical of fabliau wives. Her opening words, which echo a pair of lines in Chaucer's first fabliau in the sequence of the Canterbury Tales, the Miller's Tale (I: 3768–9), invite a dialogue charged with sexual connotations, not only in the obvious case of "ryse", but also in the detectable reference to a conventional love-sickness:

'O deere cosyn myn, daun John,' she sayde,
'What eyleth yow so rathe for to ryse?'

(98–9)

    eyleth: ails; *rathe*: soon, early

The monk's answer immediately confirms the sexual topic of the dialogue, and dispenses with any euphemistic disguises:

'But deere nece, why be ye so pale?
I trowe certes that oure goode man
Hath yow laboured sith the night bigan. . .'

(106–8)

This rapid movement to a contextually surprising level of familiarity on the topic of sexual intimacy is paralleled in the French fabliau *Auburee*, where the old bawd, Auburee, in procuring a young wife for a besotted admirer, visits the wife and moves smartly into the bedroom, declaring:

'Bien vodroie voer ton lit:
Lors savroie certainement
Se tu gis ausi richement
Com fesoit la premiere fame.'

('I should certainly like to see your bed:
then I should know for certain
if you lie in the same splendour
as the first wife did.')

Having surreptitiously placed the man's coat in the room, she says:

'Ne vi ge mes si riche lit!
Plus as asey de ton delit
C'onques n'ot l'autre, ca me semble!'

('I never saw so luxurious a bed!
You indeed have more of your delight
than ever the other did, it seems to me!')

Auburee, however, plays to the full here the apt role of a garrulous
and clumsy, but essentially thoughtless and harmless, old woman to
entrap the wife; the sexual connotations of her interest in and
comments on the bed are rather different from the explicit
insolence of the monk of the Shipman's Tale. Having spoken, the
monk undergoes a physical reaction to the utterance of his salacious
thoughts of the wife being exercised, sexually, in bed:

And with that word he lough ful murily
And of his owene thought he wax al reed.

                                                    (110–11)

      murily: merrily

This response to his own thought and speech on the monk's part
creates another novelty within this fabliau: a character who assumes
a role parallel to that of a real reader outside the text; a listener to
and responder to a text and its implications, and what is more a
reader who indulges in an interpretation of the text of his thoughts
as pornographic, i.e. capable of exciting vicarious, erotic sensation.
By locating the pornographic reading of these events within a
character within the tale, Chaucer encourages the reader to view
the pornographic relationship of text and reader with detachment
and therefore thematizes it.

The pornographic monologue of the monk's expressed thoughts
soon turns into a pornographic play, in the dialogue between monk

and wife whereby each tests and reassures the other that their desires, and their readiness to hide those desires under the dissimulation of a financial bargain, match. The slow deliberacy with which the wife commences her reply, with not a hint of offence in her reaction but rather a hint of care in selecting the right mode of reply, emphasizes her willingness to converse on the topic:

> This faire wyf gan for to shake hir heed
> And seyde thus, 'Ye, God woot al,' quod she,
> 'Nay, cosyn myn, it stant nat so with me. . .'
>
> (112–14)
>
>   *woot*: knows; *stant*: stands

So does her subsequent appropriation of a rhetorical device, the *occupatio*, a statement emphasized by the speaker feigning unwillingness or lack of freedom to express it:

> 'Dar I nat telle how that it stant with me'
>
> (120)
>
>   *dar*: dare

The monk too takes a moment's pause before replying:

> The monk bigan upon this wyf to stare
> And seyde. . .
>
> (124–5)

again seeming to digest the implications of the wife's words, or (and?) to express, silently but with an eloquent action, astonishment at the wife's ready invitation to him to continue to converse on this topic. The next necessary act in this play is for the two to reassure each other of their discretion; from the monk:

> '. . .telleth me
> Al youre anoy, for it shal been secree.
> For on my portehors I make an ooth
> That nevere in my lyf, for lief ne looth,
> Ne shal I of no conseil yow biwreye.'
>
> (129–33)
>
>   *anoy*: trouble; *portehors*: breviary (a book of liturgical texts); *for lief ne looth*:
>   whether I want to or not; *of no conseil yow biwreye*: reveal any secret concern-
>   ing you

And from the wife:

'The same agayn to yow,' quod she, 'I seye
By God and by this portehors I swere,
Though men me wolde al into pieces tere
Ne shal I nevere, for to goon to helle,
Biwreye a word of thyng that ye me telle. . .'

(134–8)

Agreement on the sexual exchange is thus sealed:

Thus been they sworn, and heereupon they kiste.

(141)

They can then indulge themselves in filling out the details of their play – and anticipating the events of the act to come – at a certain amount of leisure.

Although the monk does not tell the wife where the hundred francs have come from, and creates potential trouble for her by telling the husband that he has paid her this sum, the wife in the Shipman's Tale is quite the opposite of the foolish, deceived creature that Margery is in *Dame Sirith*. Unlike Margery, this wife knows exactly the power and value of her own sexuality – its power to allure and gratify men (and herself), and its current exchange value in direct cash terms. She makes the scenes in which she moves pornographic in the etymological sense of the word: prostitutes' tales (Greek *pornē/pornos* = prostitute). In substance and spirit there is much in her portrayal that coincides with the stereotype of woman found in medieval antifeminist literature: lascivious and insatiable, alluring to men, drawing them to a fall – e.g. tempting the monk to sin, and befooling her husband (or, more seriously, tempting him to indulge in sexual intercourse for its own pleasure and indeed for its cash value).

A further seam of antifeminism may be introduced by certain early lines of the Shipman's Tale which unmistakably imply a female speaker:

The sely housbond, algate he moot paye,
He moot us clothe, and he moot us arraye,
Al for his owene worshipe richely,
In which array we daunce jolily.
And if that he noght may, par aventure,
Or ellis list no swich dispence endure,
But thynketh it is wasted and ylost,

Thanne moot another payen for oure cost,
Or lene us gold, and that is perilous.

(11–19)

noght may: cannot; *ellis*: else; *list*: desires

Most critics have accepted the assumption that the Wife of Bath is
the only female pilgrim of the Canterbury Tales who would be a
suitable narrator of this scurrilous narrative, usually by weighing her
character up against the profession of the nuns, the only other
women amongst the Canterbury pilgrims.[5] If we ignore,
momentarily, the "murie wordes of the Hoost to the Shipman" at
the end of the tale, and assume that the narrator of the tale is a
woman – it really does not matter who she is – the narrator then
becomes a close parallel to the wife within the tale: a wordsmith; a
user of language who combines the sordid *matere* of carnal
indulgence with a gilded linguistic cover. The narration of the
Shipman's Tale has its fair measure of rhetoric. The apostrophe:

Who was so welcome as my lord daun John,
Oure deere cosyn, ful of curteisye?

(68–9)

is in the narrator's voice, but the greatest concentration of rhetorical
ornament comes in the dialogue between the wife and the monk,
particularly in the words of the woman. There is hyperbole:

'In al the reawme of France is ther no wyf
That lasse lust hath to that sory pley.'

(116–17)

reawme: realm; *lust*: desire

or:

'Thogh men me wolde al into pieces tere
Ne shal I nevere, for to goon to helle,
Biwreye a word of thyng that ye me telle.'

(136–8)

and *occupatio*:

'Cosyn,' quod she, 'if that I hadde a space,
As I have noon, and namely in this place,
Thanne wolde I telle a legende of my lyf. . .'

(143–5)

5. See below, Chapter 5 pp 196–9.

and exclamation:

> 'My deere love,' quod she, 'O my daun John. . .'

(158)

The wife's greatest linguistic *tour de force* is the climactic pun on *taille/taillynge* at the end of the tale. If, then, the narrator is characterized as a woman, and, moreover, a woman who boldly presents this tale of female prostitution and financial gain as a jape in which the wife as well as the monk triumphs at the husband's expense, the implication that women innately conform to the medieval antifeminist stereotype is doubled in strength.

A reading of the tale as a satire on merchants is usually supported by reference to the pilgrim-narrator to whom the tale is ultimately ascribed, the Shipman. For the Shipman, as a pirate, the merchant is a natural enemy:

> Ful many a draughte of wyn had he ydrawe
> Fro Burdeux-ward, whil that the chapman sleep. . .

(General Prologue. I: 396–7)

It is not particularly difficult, however, to reconcile the appearance of a female narrative voice in lines 11–19 of the tale with the male narrator that it has within the dramatic framework of the Canterbury Tales, and thus to preserve the presence of both of these voices and their critical implications. The simplest case was that put forward by Murray Copland in the 1960s, suggesting, simply, that in modern editorial terms inverted commas should be put around these lines so that we see that in these lines the Shipman is imitating (a) woman.[6] Contextual and generic considerations strengthen this case. The context of the Canterbury Tales is one in which Geoffrey Chaucer, a historical poet, feigns to speak through a fictitious mouthpiece, 'Chaucer' the pilgrim-narrator, who both, in turn, feign to speak through a further series of mouthpieces, the individual pilgrim-tellers. (Conversely they have those fictitious individuals speak through them, 'rehearsing every word as closely as he/they can' (I: 732–3).) It is not so difficult, in these circumstances, to accept that at least one of the pilgrim-tellers should be represented as speaking through an incongruously feigned mouthpiece, in this case strengthening the

6. Copland 1966.

antifeminist line of the tale by purporting to speak as a woman. And this need not be seen as a particularly innovative piece of verbal transvestism on the part of the Shipman. We have already seen how the adoption of voices for the performance of the text is appropriate to *Dame Sirith*, and how similar the structure of the Shipman's Tale is to *Dame Sirith* in just this respect. If the adoption of a female voice by a male character is a ruse intended, *inter alia*, to throw an oblique light upon the characteristics of womankind, the fabliau, with its characteristic representation of women in terms of their sexuality and such a capacity to allow overt changes of voice, would provide just the right mode.

But we cannot forget that in fabliau terms the wife of the Shipman's Tale can be credited as a successful trickster; in so far as the Shipman's Tale does develop an antifeminist perspective in the ways suggested above, it enhances the antifeminist possibilities of a genre that is characteristically only playfully antifeminist. The Shipman's Tale differs from its Italian analogues with their blatant antifeminism. It would be possible, temporarily, to laugh at the wife being landed in trouble by the monk after her meretricious bargain with him, but she extricates herself from this problem in true fabliau manner. In the Italian analogues the wife's punishment is her realization that she has been tricked, and the implication that her 'lover' did not consider her worth spending his own money on; there, this is reflected by the wife's helplessness when the trick is sprung – quite the opposite of what we have in the Shipman's Tale.

In the case of the monk, too, we have a conflict between satirical anticlericalism and creditworthiness in terms of the fabliau's comic and pragmatic standards. This appears strikingly in the words of the pilgrims' Host, commenting on the tale when the Shipman has finished. He condemns the monk:

> 'God yeve the monk a thousand last quade yeer'
>
> (438)

> *a thousand last quade yeer* : bad years a thousandfold

at the same time as he acknowledges the monk's ingenuity that has provided him with his sexual reward:

> 'Aha! Felawes beth ware of swich a jape. . .'
>
> (439–41)

This monk does not suffer the retributive poetic justice that is so frequently met with by lecherous clerics in the French fabliaux.

The teller of the tale – who in real historical terms is Chaucer the poet – presents the monk to his audience with a heavy use of irony. This is a familiar, even rather worn-out and wearisome form of irony. As with Wilekin in *Dame Sirith*, the teller is careful to describe the monk and his actions in terms of a courtly gentility, an affectation of the monk to be "free . . . and manly of dispense" (43), "a man of heigh prudence" (64), "ful of curteisye" (69), a "gentil monk" (195) who will be "trewe" to his lady (207). The hypocritical contrast between this elegant exterior and the sordid inner man is presented in a pedestrian and predictable manner. Between his speech which starts:

'Now, trewely, myn owene lady deere. . .'

(196)

and which ends:

' .. beth as trewe as I shal be'

(207)

there comes a direct restatement and physical demonstration of the meretricious contract:

'. . . For I wol bringe yow an hundred frankes'
And with that word he caughte hire by the flankes,
And hire embraceth harde, and kiste hire ofte.

(201–3)

Any aspect of his religious profession can be pressed into the service of his lechery. He cuts an elegant figure as he:

. . . in the garden walketh to and fro,
And hath his thynges seyd ful curteisly.

(90–1)

The ambiguous tone and register of *thynges* here, either 'prayers/intercessions' or just 'things', is an effective piece of wry irony – and he swears fidelity and discretion to the wife, whom he claims to love, on his breviary (131), and on his profession as a monk (155). It is only by overlooking details of the presentation of the monk within the verse and taking a very generalized and abstract view of the plot, as the Host does, that the monk can be mistaken for any sort of comic rogue.

While predictability in behaviour of this kind may enhance the anticlerical view of the monk, it also renders his portrait mundane. Mundanity is a variety of realism in so far as familiar and recurrent experiences are those which the mind most readily conceives of as 'real'. Equally familiar is the device which closes this fabliau drama. The concluding ruse of the tale, the wife's excuse for not returning the hundred francs to her husband, is not particularly novel or surprising. There is a reversion to a concept of Biblical antiquity, that of the conjugal debt; and, most significantly, in continuing the metamorphosing of sexual and monetary transactions, the wife presents the reader at the end with more of the same in the Shipman's Tale, nothing new or refreshing. Human turpitude of a personal kind is clearly visible in the activities of the wife and the monk – a sad human ignorance, lack of mastery and even spiritual failure in the case of the merchant – a turpitude that is not rendered comic in any distinguished way by some unexpectedly creative sleight of hand in the Shipman's Tale, nor artfully embodied in the sort of grotesque and rapid excesses that we have in *Les quatre Souhais Saint Martin*. In comparison with fabliaux like that, the misbehaviour of the monk and the wife is all too deliberate and plausible.

At the same time, the characteristic attitudes of the fabliau world countermand moral antifeminist and anticlerical perspectives on the wife and the monk. Finally, one must conclude, the tale is left in a state of moral indeterminacy and neutrality, and may thus emerge as a truly 'pointless' tale. The Shipman's Tale is quite close in its features to external models of the fabliau – to the French fabliaux and to *Dame Sirith*. We have seen, in the comparison of *Dame Sirith* with the *Interludium de Clerico et Puella*, that slight modifications can crucially change the meaning of a tale. From one interpretative angle, Chaucer makes the axioms and ethics of the fabliau models – the availability of beautiful women and their longing for fornication; the exaltation of practical cunning in the French fabliaux or the *carpe diem* theme of *Dame Sirith* – turn into a tale of prostitution with the deception of an undeserving husband who gains sympathy rather than scorn. There is, however, one further disruptive interpretation that can be made, rendering Chaucer's Shipman's Tale as fabliau taken to an ultimate, self-destructive point of fulfilment where the dichotomy between the witty trickster and the deluded target figure collapses. The merchant, so unsatisfactory as a target figure, can be seen as a fabliau champion: a man consummately successful in business and in bed, enjoying the good life, and able to 'cozen' a profit out of his usurious dealings. He could be the ultimate fabliau trickster, able to convert the target figure into the victor with his triumphant indifference to the facts of his wife's dealings with the monk. Here is a man, to anticipate terms we shall find in the next two chapters to be of lasting significance in respect of Chaucer's use of the fabliau, who can indeed find "Goddes foyson" in his wife's "queynte" without enquiring further.

THE SHIPMAN'S TALE AND FRAGMENT VII

Tales, genres and morals

The texts that we have of the whole Canterbury Tales are made up of a number of *fragments* or *groups*, which vary in contents from single isolated tales to sequences of several tales connected by link passages. Within the fragments only a limited amount of variance in the ordering of the tales is possible; rather more diverse is the order in which the fragments can be and are found to be arranged. From a very early date we witness the introduction of tales and links that Chaucer had not written himself, and reorganizations of the order of the tales.

The Shipman's Tale stands at the beginning of the second largest fragment of the Tales, fragment VII by the conventional numbering, a fragment which is consistently found in reliable manuscripts immediately after a fragment VI that includes the Physician's and the Pardoner's Tales. A single manuscript, Bodleian Library Arch. Selden B14, a later fifteenth-century and unquestionably unreliable example, makes the Shipman's Tale follow the Man of Law's Tale, and consequently names the Shipman in the Epilogue of the Man of Law's Tale where other manuscripts name either the Squire or the Summoner as the pilgrim offering to speak next. Nevertheless, a radical editorial reorganization called the Bradshaw shift, involving the moving of fragment VII as one large block back to the end of fragment II, with these fragments then relabelled groups B2 and B1 respectively, has been eagerly accepted by some editors and critics since the nineteenth century, wishing to solve thereby certain anomalies in the ordering of named places that the pilgrims would pass on their road to Canterbury.

Arguments over the female narrative voice in the Shipman's Tale have too often directed attention away from its usual and final context in the Canterbury Tales and its only certified narrator towards its hypothetical earlier association with the Wife of Bath. There is little justification for assuming the uncertain earlier attribution of the Shipman's Tale to be meaningful and its final attribution to be merely a convenient slot in which Chaucer parked his tale without even bothering to make a few simple revisions to make the tale fit its new narrator. The tale is in fact carefully tied in as the Shipman's Tale at the beginning of fragment VII, with an endlink that binds it to the Prioress's Tale that follows it. There are also various thematic connections between this tale and the following members of the group.[7] A reading of fragment VII that is most congruent with the interpretation of the Shipman's Tale offered here is a combination of elements of the so-called "surprise group" and "literary group" interpretations. Fragment VII, comprising the Shipman's, the Prioress's, 'Chaucer's', the Monk's and the Nun's Priest's Tales, can be seen as a group of consistently recalcitrant texts: texts which somehow contradict the expectations that may be brought to them, either in the light of the genre to which the tales belong or in the light of the character of the teller as we might suppose we know it before the tale is told. The Shipman's Tale not only is part of a larger text, it is most informatively read in the light of the details of that larger text. These show the Shipman's Tale to function as the opening section of a thoughtful exploration of the interdependent topics of narratorial character, genre and moralization.

There is a complex tension in the Prioress's Tale between the intense maternal sentimentality of the narrator's treatment of the child martyr of whom she tells, the deeply symbolic nature of the tale, and the sublimated violence meted out to the "cursed Jewes". Although no explanation is given of the stunned response of her fellow pilgrims at the end of her tale:

7. See P.F. Baum Chaucer: A Critical Appreciation pp 74–84; Gaylord 1967; Howard The Idea of the Canterbury Tales pp 271–84; Pearcy 'The Genre of Chaucer's Fabliau-Tales' p 375. See also Benson et al., The Riverside Chaucer, Explanatory Notes, p 910.

When seyd was al this miracle, every man
As sobre was that wondre was to se,
Til that oure Hooste japen tho bigan..

                                                                    (VII: 691–3)

   tho: then

their response is not difficult to understand. The way in which the
Prioress's Tale hangs like a shadow over the pilgrims is reflected by
the continuation of the rhyme-royal verse form from the tale into
the following link: a feature matched only once elsewhere in the
Tales, by an apparently repressed stanza at the end of the Clerk's
Tale (IV: 1212a–g).

   The form that the Host's japing takes here is to turn to
'Chaucer', the pilgrim-narrator, and to demand his tale. Chaucer
uses this opportunity to present two quite contrasting tales, *Sir
Thopas* and *Melibee*, the one a tail-rhyme romance, the other a
moral example in prose; two tales which in turn represent quite
contrasting aspects of the one narratorial character, being two quite
contrasting versions of what type of tale an audience or readership
might think Chaucer 'ought' to tell. *Sir Thopas* is the tale told by
the self-mocking comedian and parodist, producing as the Host so
richly puts it, "drasty rymyng" that "is nat worth a toord" (VII:
930). 'Chaucer' is the only interrupted character who is made to
take the opportunity to tell a second tale, although the Monk, too,
in this same fragment, is given a second chance. The second tale
'Chaucer' tells is the persistently solemn prose of the serious
moralist; a close, careful and caring translation of a French original.
It has occurred to some that *Melibee* too may be a self-mocking
parody[8] but to read the work like this is to read with little
sensitivity. Significantly, the tale is not interrupted either because it
is stylistically intolerable – like *Sir Thopas* is – or unbearably dull,
like the Monk's Tale, which follows it. There is a little wry irony
both in the prologue to the tale, where 'Chaucer' describes it as "a
litel thyng in prose" (VII: 937), and a touch of bathos in its
epilogue, the link passage leading to the Monk's Tale, where the
Host unfavourably compares his wife, with her lack of patience,
with Prudence, wife of Melibee. The point must not, however, be
missed that the Host is able to grasp a moral point made in the tale.

---

8. Cf. Benson *et al.*, *The Riverside Chaucer*, Explanatory Notes, p 924 for references.

Chaucer's self-image is that of a writer, and he reflects upon it by exploring extremes in literature. He asserts himself as a poet (note that we still today think of him primarily as a 'poet' rather than as a 'writer') superior to the ridiculous doggerel of *Sir Thopas*. But poetry can appear 'light', for instance if it lacks the explicitly solemn moralizations of a Langland. Chaucer makes this point on more than one occasion, nowhere more emphatically than at the end of the Canterbury Tales, after the Parson's Tale, where he 'revokes' in his 'retractions' "my translacions and endytinges of worldly vanitees" (*endytinges*: compositions) including "the tales of Caunterbury, thilke that sownen into synne" (*sownen into synne*: 'resonate with sin') (X: 1084–5). He wrote a number of serious prose works besides the Melibee.[9] It is quite possible Chaucer's attitude to such explicitly serious literature was uncertain, appreciating its moral worth but also sensing it to be more than the "litel hevynesse" that "is right ynogh for muche folk" (the Knight, in the epilogue of the Monk's Tale, VII: 2769–70), or to be preaching the "inportable" (the Clerk's Tale, IV: 1144). Nowhere do Chaucer or any of his characters mock solemn moral prose, but within the Canterbury Tales such prose always stands in a thought-provoking contrast with verse of a lighter tone.

Melibee is followed by the Monk's Tale, a collection of brief vignettes showing the tragic fall of men (and of one woman) from some high degree through the change of fortune. A form of structure can be found in the Monk's Tale in the grouping of examples of, for instance, those whose fall is attributable to women, those whose fall is attributable to sin, those who fall through treachery, etc., but repetition rather than variation is the wearisome experience of reading this tale. So the Knight says when he cuts the tale short.[10] Taking account of the full literary context of the Monk's Tale in the Canterbury Tales, it seems that the real disappointment of the Monk's performance comes from the contrast between his character as a narrator as revealed by his tale and the

---

9. See *The Legend of Good Women*, Prologue G 412–18.
10. It has, however, been suggested that the Knight's interruption is motivated by the Monk's survey having come to Peter of Cyprus, amongst the so-called Modern Instances. Peter, who had won Alexandria in 1365 with the help of English knights – including, in Chaucer's fiction, the Knight on the pilgrimage – was assassinated by three of his own knights a few years later, an incident which the Knight might be happy to suppress.

presuppositions that his appearance has created in the Host and apparently in 'Chaucer'. There can be little doubt as to what in the way of topics and register the Host expects in the Monk's Tale; he concludes his observations on *Melibee* with:

> But lat us passe awey fro this mateere
>
> (VII: 1923)

and continues with a description of the Monk that matches with the impression 'Chaucer' claims to have of the Monk in the General Prologue, of a "manly man", straining at the bounds of what is allowed to a monk (and not dissimilar to the monk of the Shipman's Tale):

> I vowe to God, thou hast a ful fair skin;
> It is a gentil pasture ther thow goost.
> Thou art nat lyk a penant or a goost:
> Upon my feith, thou art som officer,
> Som worthy sexteyn, or som celerer,
> For by my fader soule, as to my doom,
> Thou art a maister whan thou art at hoom;
> No povre cloystere, ne no novys,
> But a governour, wily and wys,
> And therwithal of brawnes and of bones
> A wel farynge persone for the nones.
> I pray to God, yeve hym confusioun
> That first thee broghte unto religioun!
> Thou woldest han been a tredefowel aright.
> Haddestow as greet a leeve as thou hast myght
> To parfourne al thy lust in engendrure,
> Thou haddest begeten ful many a creature.
> Allas, why werestow so wyd a cope?
> God yeve me sorwe, but, and I were a pope,
> Nat oonly thou, but every myghty man,
> Though he were shorn ful hye upon his pan,
> Sholde have a wyf; for al the world is lorn!
> Religioun hath take up al the corn
> Of tredyng, and we borel men been shrympes.
> Of fieble trees ther comen wrecched ympes.
> This maketh that oure heires been so sklendre
> And feble that they may nat wel engendre.
> This maketh that oure wyves wole assaye
> Religious folk, for ye mowe bettre paye
> Of Venus paiementz than mowe we;

God woot, no lussheburghes payen ye!
But be nat wrooth, my lord, though that I pleye.
Ful ofte in game a sooth I have herd seye!

(VII: 1932–64)

wel farynge: fine-looking; *for the nones*: indeed; *tredefowel*: stud cock; *leeve*: leave, permission; *engendrure*: fathering children; *werestow*: do you wear; *and I were*: if I were; *pan*: skull; *lorn*: lost; *borel*: common; *ympes*: shoots, especially cuttings; *mowe*: may; *lussheburghes*: Luxemburgers – coins of little value

After nearly a hundred stanzas of the Monk's tragedies, the Host is prepared to give him a second chance, as 'Chaucer' had, but feels this time he has to be more specific as to what is wanted:

Sire, sey somwhat of huntynge, I yow preye.

(VII: 2805)

But as soon as the Monk speaks we have the opportunity to see, firstly, that his reaction does not suggest he is flattered or pleased by the Host's appraisal of him, and secondly that he sounds quite different from the bold and thrusting 'man's man' that 'Chaucer' and the Host would make of him:

This worthy Monk took al in pacience
And seyde, 'I wol doon al my diligence
As fer as sowneth into honestee
To telle yow a tale, or two, or three. . .'

(VII: 1965–8)

Note how the Monk's desire to offer literature that "sowneth into honestee" anticipates Chaucer the prosist's retraction of the tales "that sownen into synne". And even if the Host is still able to hope that the Monk will show another side to his character as a tale-teller, the Monk will not, and retreats into a sort of sulky silence after being interrupted and asked for something less serious:

'Nay,' quod this Monk, 'I have no lust to pleye.
Now lat another telle, as I have told.'

(VII: 2806–7)

The Monk as a character is explicitly and repeatedly compared and contrasted with the teller who succeeds him, the Nun's Priest. The description of the Monk in the General Prologue is a full and detailed one, even if we are subsequently invited to conclude that it is a mistaken and misleading one; by contrast, the presence of three priests with the Prioress and her nun/chapeleyne is noted in just

three words at the end of line 164 of the General Prologue. Both
the Monk and the Nun's Priest are clerics. The first details we have
of the latter, in the Host's invitation to him to follow the Monk,
initially suggest, if we still believe appearances and associations can
be a sign of character, that he is as likely to turn out as the
threadbare and serious Clerk on his horse "as leene as is a rake" does
(I: 284) as to prove to be what the Monk has proved not to be:

> 'Com neer, thou preest, com hider, thou sir John.
> Telle us swich thing as may oure hertes glade.
> Be blithe, though thou ryde upon a jade.
> What thogh thyn hors be bothe foul and lene?'

> > (VII: 2810–13)

> *glade*: gladden

While the Monk, usually politely addressed as *ye*, declines the
invitation of the Host to "be myrie of cheere" as he tells his tale
(VII: 1924–5), the Nun's Priest, familiarly addressed as *thou*, is ready
and able to provide what is wanted:

> (Host) 'Looke that thyn herte be murie everemo.'
> 'Yis, sir,' quod he, 'yis, Hoost, so moot I go,
> But I be myrie, ywis I wol be blamed.'

> > (VII: 2815–17)

> *but I be*: unless I am; *ywis*: indeed

The tale the Nun's Priest tells is a beast-fable: a form of literature
that should observe and comment on human traits and manners in a
moral light, presenting those traits and manners in a fictional drama
in which the characters are of the animal world. The Nun's Priest's
Tale is a complex and supremely witty composition that has been
described as a microcosm of the Canterbury Tales as a whole;[11] I
shall seek only to illustrate those points of particular relevance to
our study of the Shipman's Tale's immediate literary context.

A fundamentally important way in which the Nun's Priest's Tale
reflects the overarching structure of the Canterbury Tales is by
inviting profound reflection on the two criteria by which the
tale-telling game on the pilgrimage is to be judged:

> And which of yow that bereth hym best of alle –
> That is to seyn, that telleth in this caas

---

11. Cooper *The Structure of the Canterbury Tales* pp 5–7 and 180–8.

Tales of best sentence and moost solaas —
Shal have a soper at oure aller cost. . .

(I: 796–9)

Shal have a soper. . .: will have a supper at the expense of us all. . .

'Sentence' and 'solaas' — a familiar pairing of *lust* and *loore*,
instruction and entertainment — are the two aspects of literature
supposed by the terms of the competition to produce the best tales.
The Nun's Priest ends his tale with a direction to the
reader/listener, purportedly indicating what they must do:

Taketh the moralite, goode men

(VII: 3440)

and supporting it with St Paul's dictum:

For Seint Paul seith that al that writen is,
To oure doctrine it is ywrite, ywis.

(VII: 3941–2)

In the Nun's Priest's Tale this is no simple directive, finally defining
the purpose of a tale which the narrator has introduced as a
"myrie" ('merry') exercise, and which is truly comic and lively.
The *folye* (line 3458) and the *doctrine* (3442) of the tale combine to
make it complex rather than contradicting one another. The use of
the animal characters is an unmistakable signal that the tale can be
read as a moral allegory and example. At the same time the use of
animal characters is clearly one of the persistently funny elements in
the Nun's Priest's Tale. It is through the use of animal characters
that epic or heroic imagery becomes mock-heroic; for instance of
Chauntecleer, the cock:

He looketh as it were a grim leoun
And on his toos he rometh up and doun
Hym deigned nat to sette his foot to grounde

(VII: 3179–81)

So too the solemnity of the debate over the significance of dreams,
introduced by Chauntecleer with a pompous "Madame" and
rhetorically conducted by the citation of a battery of learned
authorities, becomes a burlesque in the mouth of this proud bird.
The dignified pose struck by Chauntecleer in response to Pertelote's
unsympathetic reaction to his dream, in particular the
understandable offence he takes at the embarrassing suggestion that

what he really needs is a good laxative, would be comic in a human character; that the character is a bird provides an opportunity for a greater bathetic and comic deflation when the character ends his monologue by flying down from the perch to peck, chuck and 'tread' his favourite hens twenty times before dawn (3172–8).

The Nun's Priest's Tale might then offer a perfect rapprochement of *sentence* and *solaas* – qualities that are both, arguably, lacking in the Shipman's Tale. It certainly indicates that these two are not mutually exclusive in the way that the immediately preceding tales in fragment VII, and the Nun's Priest's concluding directive, seem to imply. But the difficulty with taking the Nun's Priest's Tale as a successful harmonization of instruction and entertainment is the fact that within the tale any explicit approaches to didactic seriousness are continually subverted. The capacity of any writing to act as an instructive *auctoritee* is scrutinized within the Nun's Priest's Tale in the *auctoritees* cited, all but one by Chauntecleer, in the 'debate' over dreams which in reality consists of two opposed monologues rather than a dialogue. It is one of the commonplaces of interpretation of the Nun's Priest's Tale that the reader/listener is spoilt for choice of morals to be drawn from the tale at the end, when the Nun's Priest refers to the moral with a throwaway carelessness that seems to suggest the moral is so obvious that he need not state it. These petty morals, partly overlapping, form a cascade of precepts none of which amounts to anything more than a trite platitude. Immediately before the Nun's Priest's parting instruction to his reader comes:

> Lo, swich it is for to be recchelees
> And necligent, and to truste on flaterye
>
> (VII: 3436–7)
>
> *recchelees*: heedless

Immediately before this, the fox, one of the victims of flattery in the tale, has drawn his own, slightly different moral from his deception:

> . . .God yeve him mischaunce
> That is so undiscreet of governaunce
> That jangleth whan he sholde holde his pees.
>
> (VII: 3433–5)
>
> *mischaunce*: misfortune; *jangleth*: chatters

Idle words may take the form either of praise or of abuse. Other issues on which morals can be drawn are whether dreams are forewarnings of events to come, and the image of woman as man's confusion: the latter point, though, the Nun's Priest himself refuses to present seriously:

> But for I noot to whom it myght displese
> If I conseil of wommen wolde blame,
> Passe over, for I seyde it in my game

(VII: 3259–61)

> *noot*: do not know

The burlesque treatment of matters of moral seriousness in the Nun's Priest's Tale reaches its climax in the middle of the tale, with a reference to one of the crucial dilemmas or mysteries for Christian philosophers: that of reconciling human free will with the necessary truth of God's Providence. If God foreknows all the events in the history of His creation, what real freedom is there on the part of His creatures, for us to act according to our wills not His? This is the subject of the largest stretch of commentary on the events of the tale by the narrator, some twenty lines in the verse paragraph in lines 3215–55. The burlesquing of the debate over this issue does not simply lie in the Nun's Priest's professions of inability to cope with such learned speculations:

> . . .in scole is greet altercatioun
> In this mateere, and greet disputisoun,
> And hath been of an hundred thousand men.
> But I ne kan nat bulte it to the bren. . .

(VII: 3237–40)

> *bulte it to the bren*: sift out the husks

or in his finally declaring the problem irrelevant:

> I wol nat han to do with swich mateere;
> My tale is of a cok as ye may here

(VII: 3251–2)

Learned in-joking on one of the authorities on the subject of freewill and providence, Boethius, is also found in the fox's ability to refer to Boethius' book on music (3293–4) and the fact that the fox breaks into Chauntecleer's yard "By heigh ymaginacioun forncast", 'Foreseen by High Imagination' (3217). 'Imagination' is the upper level of animal intellectual activity according to Boethius, as distinct from the *Reason* of humans and the *Intelligence* of God and angels (cf. Chaucer's *Boece*, Book V, prose 5). Briefly flashed into the minds of those in the know is the preposterous image of a doggy God foreseeing the world and events of the beast-fable.

This does not mean, however, that the Nun's Priest's Tale is an anti-academic parody. It is rather a display of witty dexterity, depending for its effect upon a sharing of specialized learning between author/narrator and readers/listeners. At the same time as the Nun's Priest is made to try to claim for himself in his tale the equivalent of:

My wit is short; ye may well understonde

(I: 746)

he, or Chaucer, reassures those who are able to share in the joke that the opposite is the case. The Nun's Priest therefore emerges from his tale as a character — a character who adopts an amusing *persona* as the teller of a tale just as Chaucer does in his narrator-pilgrim 'Chaucer'. The character of the Nun's Priest is a complex of knowledge, attitude and sympathy: knowledge of learning, literature and the *ars praedicandi* ('art of preaching'), attitudes of detachment from but understanding of the rarefied world of speculative learning, and of sympathy towards the commoner run of humanity for whom this learning is mystifying and in practical terms irrelevant. Helen Cooper notes that the inferrable character of the Nun's Priest is the same as the inferrable character of Chaucer. We might say that the Nun's Priest represents a human character standing at the intersection of various areas of human activity and experience mirrored within the text, and that the important attributes of the construct that this character is are not least life and humanity themselves; the real individual and communal life that has to compromise between animalistic anarchy (i.e. the fabliau world? — cf. Janette Richardson's commentary on animal imagery in the Shipman's Tale, and that to be found in the Miller's and Reeve's Tales (next chapter)) and sterile intellectualism; between the worlds of sensory *experience* and high *auctoritee*. The final and comprehensive pose struck by the Nun's Priest is one that exemplifies the high ethic of the Canterbury Tales — a pragmatic and tolerant attitude of human good fellowship — by virtue of the truly merry tale that the Nun's Priest tells, laughing at and with his characters and readers but scorning and destroying none. Every potential target in this tale, like Chauntecleer, survives to ponder the events that have happened and to consider their moral. The true moral of the Nun's Priest's Tale is a moral of character and attitude not of precept; and appropriately the Host responds by commenting on the Nun's Priest as a *character* who has proved to be what the Monk has turned out not to be. In praising the Nun's Priest, however, he is limited to a motif of sexual worth that inescapably recalls the fabliau:

> . . .if thou were seculer
> Thou woldest ben a tredefoul aright.

(VII: 3450–1)

which is what he had imagined of the Monk (VII: 1945). What we shall see in the next two chapters is that this limitation in the Host's response cannot be seen simply as a caricaturing of the Host as an intellectually limited churl, or as an endorsement of the undoubtedly vital fabliau ethos.

Consequently, we find that the relationship between teller (pilgrim-narrator) and tale, between tale and genre and between story and moral, are consistently to the fore in the tales of fragment VII. The importance of such aspects inferred from a reading of the Shipman's Tale is confirmed by the consistent treatment of these themes in the following group. The feminine voice at the start of the Shipman's Tale is a conundrum that draws attention to the teller. The conundrum may be solved, but what use is made of the character of the Shipman, thus emphasized? The answer may again lie in the tolerant perspective on the surrounding world taken by Chaucer and 'Chaucer' through and in the Canterbury Tales. This does not mean a suspension of judgement and uncritical acceptance of the thief and murderer the Shipman is suggested to be in the General Prologue (I: 388–410); a fitting teller for a graceless tale. It is rather a perspective that recognizes and takes full account of the reality of such crime within the world and which stands at a distance from it. The Shipman's portrait in the General Prologue is a case, like that of the Yeoman, where a distance and unfamiliarity between 'Chaucer' and the pilgrim is conveyed by a naive curiosity with which 'Chaucer's' description focuses and lingers on the sharp and pointed or menacing aspects of the pilgrim's accoutrements. With the Yeoman, attention falls rapidly on the

. . .sheef of pecock arwes, bright and kene

(I: 104)

and returns to:

Upon his arm he baar a gay bracer,
And by his side a swerd and a bokeler,
And on that oother syde a gay daggere
Harneised wel and sharp as point of spere

(I: 111–14)

baar: bore; *bracer*: arm guard; *bokeler*: buckler, shield; *harneised*: harnessed, strapped

After two lines on the horse and garb of the Shipman, the gaze focuses on:

A daggere hangynge on a laas hadde he
Aboute his nekke, under his arm adoun

(I: 392–3)

laas: lace, thong; *adoun*: down

The constant but controlled menace of these characters and their weapons is recognized and observed by Chaucer/'Chaucer' with a perception as keen as their daggers. But the approach is patient, curious and explorative, not a condemnation that could, all too easily, have been staged.

As we shall see more clearly after studying Chaucer's other fabliaux and uses of fabliau, the Shipman's Tale stands out as the particular instance when Chaucer uses a fabliau to place fabliau in a critical light, examining fabliau as an extant genre rather than exploiting it for some other purpose. This does not prevent it from functioning, at the same time, as a vehicle for social or cultural criticism. What we find is that the virtually unadapted fabliau of this kind, a version of the world of production, religion and sexual relationships (which do not in this case imply reproduction) is a literary genre that, allowed to follow its own logic to the very end, shames the active characters within the tale, which in this case includes the feigned narrator. One consequence of the exclusive pursuit of the selfish and self-indulgent ethos of the naked fabliau is that the Shipman's Tale, unlike the majority of the French fabliaux, contains no concluding moral, ending instead on the selfish prayer:

. . .God us sende
Taillynge ynogh unto oure lives ende. Amen

(433–4)

The failure of a moral to appear here is emphasized by the fact that the Host immediately tries to draw a moral from the tale – an appropriately pragmatic one:

A ha! Felawes beth war of swich a jape!

(VII: 439)

It could and has been held that the Shipman's Tale is thereby *amoral*. However, we have in fragment VII another example of amorality – the moral insignificance of the meaningless nonsense-rhyme of *Sir Thopas* – against which, and against the positive morality of *Melibee*, from which the Host is able to draw a more pertinent moral, the amorality of the Shipman's Tale becomes in itself a form of immorality, the failure of a tale to offer more than a licentious celebration of the terms of trade of the brothel and of pornography.

Fragment VII and the Man of Law's Tale

In the ways argued above, fragment VII on its own forms a rather more consistent group than that which is produced by the 'Bradshaw shift', which labels fragment VII as group B2 and places the Shipman's Tale immediately after the Man of Law's. Nonetheless the Introduction to the Man of Law's Tale (II: 1–98) is particularly relevant to the themes we have just identified in fragment VII. There is there a critical discussion of a sort of Chaucer's literary works, introduced by the Man of Law ironically declaring his own inability to tell a "thrifty tale" as Chaucer can with his "lewed" metre and "crafty" rhyming. He gives a survey of Chaucer's literary products, concentrating on works dealing with lovers and noble women. All this is supposed to contrast with his own offering, which appears to be introduced with the words "I speke in prose" (II: 96) although in fact his tale of a noble woman and wife, Custance (Constance), is told in rhyme-royal stanzas.

The direction in which the discussion of literature in the Introduction to the Man of Law's Tale points, however, is towards a comparison of Chaucer's writing with that of his contemporary John Gower rather than towards the survey of literary genres detached from the accidental circumstances of the identity of authors of specific examples of those genres that we find in fragment VII. This emerges particularly in the verse paragraph in lines 77–89 of the Introduction, in which the Man of Law is made to note certain tales which Chaucer has not versified – Canace and Machaire, and Appollonius of Tyre – which Gower did include amongst the tales of his *Confessio Amantis*. Both these tales involve incestuous sexual relationships, which is presumably what is meant by referring to them as "unkynde ('unnatural') abhomynaciouns" (II: 88). A great deal could be written on the contrast between Chaucer and Gower reflected here: one might note, for instance, that incest plays a relatively small part in the tale of Appollonius, and that it is hardly condoned in the Canace and Machaire story of Gower although it is romantically treated in a tragic and sympathetic manner. The significant point here is that this would itself be a distraction from the study of Chaucer's fabliaux, the Shipman's Tale, and fragment VII. It is, however, a worthwhile exercise to compare the Shipman's Tale with these tales of Gower to see where Chaucer may have drawn the line between permissible and even useful scurrility in literature and unconscionable sin.

The Man of Law's "I speke in prose" need not be a description of the tale he is about to tell – it may be read as equivalent to 'my speech is (normally) prosaic' – but several critics have looked for a prose work of Chaucer's which could be identified as the once-intended tale of the Man of Law. *Melibee*, one of our fragment VII tales, is a popular solution. If the Man of Law had a prose tale it should certainly have been a serious and learned tale like *Melibee*, the Parson's Tale, or Chaucer's translations of Boethius' *De consolatione philosophiae* or Pope Innocent III's *De miseria condicionis humane*, and thus a tale of the kind that found a place in fragment VII. Likewise the comic reference to Chaucer's poetic skill:

> . . .thogh he can but lewedly
> On metres and on ryming craftily
>
> (II: 47–8)

is echoed by the Host's comments on the "veray lewednesse" and "drasty speche" and "drasty ryming" of *Sir Thopas* (VII: 919–30). The Introduction to the Man of Law's Tale does thus anticipate some of the issues that will be raised in fragment VII. Evaluation of the editorial 'Bradshaw shift' is not simply a matter of deciding whether it is right or wrong. The Bradshaw grouping can be seen as a variant rather than an alternative ordering of the fragments. It makes a valid connection in a collection the order of which almost certainly varied during the process of composition and which was never completed. The reader may "Turn over the leef and chese another tale" (I: 3177) constructively as well as evasively.

Chapter 4

The Miller's and Reeve's Tales and their fictional context

THE MILLER'S AND REEVE'S TALES: A FABLIAU DIPTYCH

Cherles tales

While variation in the ordering of tales is not merely possible but can be a critically rewarding way of reading the fragments in and around the middle of the sequence of the Canterbury Tales, the fragments at the beginning and end (fragments I and X, and, generally, II and IX) are solidly fixed in place, challenging the reader to interpret them as and where they stand. Fragment I contains Chaucer's most highly prized and praised fabliaux, the Miller's and Reeve's Tales. These tales call out for assessment as a pair, and critics have responded appropriately. Extant interpretations of this diptych, however, vary radically, and the case that will be argued here appears to be the least orthodox view, at least to judge by the published criticism of the last thirty years or so.

The primary division amongst critical views lies between readings of these tales as fundamentally serious moral reflections on the state of humankind despite their undeniably comic appearance, and readings of them as essentially lighthearted tales, designed to amuse rather than to disturb, elevating *solaas* well above *sentence*. Many would concur with the case most recently and most substantially argued by V. A. Kolve, that the Miller's and Reeve's Tales contrast with one another in these terms: the former full of liberty and light; the latter replete with dark moral shades and tones. Several read both tales as moral dramas in which human sin is revealed, judged and punished. Distinctly the minority view is that which allows laughter at both tales to be free of moral implications and which thus allows the tales genuinely to be fun –

which would not, of course, imply that the two tales are vacuous exercises aimed at giving pleasure alone.[1]

The immediate dramatic context of the Miller's and Reeve's Tales is an argument between the Miller and the Reeve. It is not explicitly stated that the Miller demands to tell his tale out of spite to the Reeve. He in fact puts himself forward "to quite the Knyghtes tale" after the Host has asked the Monk to do that very thing (lines 3119 and 3127). But the synopsis that he offers of his tale:

> '. . .a legende and a lyf
> Bothe of a carpenter and of his wyf,
> How that a clerk hath set the wrightes cappe.'

(3141–3)

> *set the wrightes cappe*: made a fool of the artisan

is unmistakably that of a fabliau, and with the target figure appearing as a regular element within the fabliau it is understandable that the Reeve, a carpenter, should anticipate an attack upon himself:

> 'Stynt thy clappe!
> Lat be thy lewed dronken harlotrye.
> It is a synne and eek a greet folye
> To apeyren any man, or hym defame. . .'

(3144–7)

> *stynt thy clappe*: hold your noise; *apeyren*: libel

Fabliaux are thoroughly suitable textual weapons for the two churls, the Miller and the Reeve, to beat each other over the head with. There are, moreover, reasons for expecting an attack upon the Reeve, which in turn would mean that it is not solely his unsuccessful pre-emptive strike that establishes a state of enmity between these two characters. In the General Prologue portrait of the Reeve – a portrayal which leans heavily on conventional attitudes of hostility towards the lords' men, the peasant officials amongst the peasants, in medieval English satire – the Reeve is presented as a man who provokes suspicion and fear:

---

1. On the first view see, besides Kolve, Marsha Siegel 1985; for the second see Curry 1920, Robertson *A Preface to Chaucer* pp 382–6; P.A. Olson 1962 and 1963; Hill 1973; Copland 1962. The third view is represented by Glending Olson 1974; *idem* 1974 The Medieval Theory of Literature for Refreshment and its Use in the Fabliau Tradition, *SP* LXXI pp 291–313; and *idem Literature as Recreation in the Later Middle Ages*.

They were adrad of hym as of the deeth

(605)

and as a man who, by being identifiable as one of a type rather than an individual, attracts the prejudices associated with that type. Much of the critical antipathy towards the Reeve derives from the ingestion of such prejudice as opposed to detached examination of it.[2]

The proposition that the fabliau is an appropriate mode for an argument between two churls is explicitly Chaucer's. The only term he uses to characterize the content of these tales in advance is "harlotrye", and this appears after he has not once but twice emphasized the purported social origin of these tales. The Miller, he states:

tolde his cherles tale in his manere

(3169)

and immediately before the tale commences he repeats the point:

The Miller is a cherl; ye knowe wel this.
So was the Reve eek and othere mo,
And harlotrie they tolden bothe two

(3182–4)

However doubtful we should be about attempts to associate the emergence of the medieval fabliau with any particular social class, it is significant that Chaucer wishes to represent the fabliau in precisely such terms. The point is well made by Kolve, that what the Miller says does not, realistically, sound very much like an inebriated medieval churl. This is even true, *contra* Kolve, of what he says for most of his prologue. But what he has to say in his tale may represent what we might like to believe such a character's ribald attitudes towards women, towards his fellow men, and towards conventional morality would predictably be. A good part of the wit of these two fabliaux lies in the incongruous mixture of the urbane and sophisticated amusement they have to offer with the notionally rude and crude character of the churls' minds. The serious side of this entertaining situation lies in Chaucer's crediting these two churls with intellects far higher than those of brute beasts.

2. See Mann *Chaucer and Medieval Estates Satire* pp 163–5.

Of particular relevance to such a potentially egalitarian levelling of differences between social classes is the great emphasis that is laid upon role-playing in fragment I. Chaucer is especially concerned to draw attention to his *persona*, 'Chaucer', towards the end of the General Prologue and in the Miller's Prologue (725–6; 3170–86). His ironic protestations – "My wit is short; ye may well understonde"; "Blameth nat me. . ." – serve only to remind us of the fact that here we have a court poet playing first the pilgrim-narrator 'Chaucer' and then playing a churl. It seems, curiously, to have remained generally unnoted that there is no explicit change of speaker between the end of the Miller's Prologue, where 'Chaucer' is speaking:

> Avyseth yow, and put me out of blame;
> And eek men shal nat maken ernest of game.

(3185–6)

    avyseth yow: think about it

and the opening of the Miller's Tale:

> Whilom ther was dwellynge at Oxenford
> A riche gnof. . .

(3187–8)

perhaps because the transition is marked in written or printed editions by rubrics and headings such as the Ellesmere manuscript's "Heere bigynneth the Millere his tale". This unmarked transition from 'Chaucer' to another pilgram-narrator where a tale begins is unparalleled in the rest of the Canterbury Tales, and, be it by accident or design, it encourages us to reflect upon how far the Miller's Tale is also Chaucer's.

THE MILLER'S TALE

Narrative tone

Full comprehension of the Miller's Tale, by its teller or its audience, requires a mind well stored with esoteric, learned knowledge. Sophisticated technical vocabulary from medieval astrological procedures and psychology is deftly deployed, and even woven into the rhymes of the verse: thus "conclusiouns/interrogaciouns" (3193/4) and "affecioun/ymaginacioun. . . impressioun" (3611/12–13). An informed mind is needed to appreciate the circumstantial detail of this Oxford fabliau: the relationship between the town and Oseney, for example, and the carpenter's calling upon a local saint, St Frideswide. The narrator of the tale is made a rhetorician, apostrophizing both his audience:

> Now, sire, and eft, sire, so bifel the cas . . .
>
> (3271)

and one of his characters:

> Now ber thee wel, thou hende Nicholas . . .
>
> (3397)

It has been pointed out that a skilled mastery of the 'idiom of popular poetry', embodied in the witty appropriation of familiar poetic epithets such as *hende*, *jolif* and *gent*, which are used of Nicholas, Absolon and Alison respectively, is not simply a characteristic of Chaucerian style, but is especially exploited by Chaucer for this one tale.[3]

A role is created for the reader to play beyond that of the simple suspension of disbelief required by all fiction in the face, for instance, of such instances of an extraordinary control over his tale-telling by a supposedly drunken Miller as those just noted. By the very act of reading on into the tale from the Miller's Prologue we as readers allow ourselves to be manipulated into supposing ourselves somehow different from the readership of "every gentil wight" that is offered a warning and an invitation to:

> Turne over the leef and chese another tale
>
> (3177)
>
> *chese*: choose

We know ourselves to be more complex beings. In our case, of course, it is a mature, open and enquiring critical mind that leads us to read on into the churls' tales of 'harlotrie', not a degrading taste for such material and a lack of interest in:

> storial thyng that toucheth gentillesse,
> And eek moralitee and holynesse
>
> (3179–80)
>
> *storial*: historical, true; *gentillesse*: nobility

3. Donaldson 'Idiom of Popular Poetry in the Miller's Tale'.

We might see the combination of the intrinsically low status of the Miller and the consequently low expectations of what he will produce with the sophistication of his narrative performance as simply an entertaining absurdity, or perhaps a burlesque, like Chauntecleer's discursive pomp and display in the Nun's Priest's Tale. But Chauntecleer slips and gives himself away:

> For al so siker as *In principio*,
> *Mulier est hominis confusio* —
> Madame, the sentence of this Latyn is,
> 'Womman is mannes joye and al his blis'.

(VII: 3163–6)

The Latin '*Mulier est.* . .' in fact means 'Woman is man's confusion'.

and the Miller does not. A very much richer reading is obtained, by way of alternative, by stressing how a perception of the arbitrary nature of social divisions and of socio-cultural class stereotypes underlies Chaucer's composition here, and that he invites his readers – those who do not wish to conform to the naive stereotype of the "gentil wight" – to share this insight.

The construction of the fabliau

Exactly how far the Miller's Tale is Chaucer's composition we do not know. A number of close analogues to the tale are known, a particularly close one being a Middle Dutch fabliau *Heile van Beersele*, apparently virtually contemporary with Chaucer's composition. This tale is set in Antwerp, and the major difference between it and the Miller's Tale is that the woman concerned is not a wife but a prostitute, who lives in *Coperstraten* (apparently Merchant Street, although it has been suggested it should really be *Coeperstraten*, Cow Gate Street). Three further versions known in sixteenth-century copies from Germany combine the three major elements of the tale: the Second Flood, the kissing of the arse (in all cases the male lover's arse, not the woman's) and the retaliatory branding. The kiss and branding also appear in a fifteenth-century Italian novella.[4] It would not detract anything from Chaucer's achievement if the whole plot were derived from some external source: it is generally the case that Chaucer's skill lies in the

---

4. Bryan and Dempster *Sources and Analogues* pp 106–23; Benson and Andersson *Literary Context* pp 3–77. See also Boccaccio *Decameron*, Day 3 tale 4.

handling and shaping of extant material rather than in original composition. The plot of the Miller's Tale is, however, a complex one, more complex that either of the English fabliaux we have looked at so far in this book, and unsurpassed in complexity amongst the French fabliaux. There are multiple tricksters and dupes. The carpenter, John, Alison's "old" husband, is the most obvious target figure of the piece, but Absolon is tricked into kissing Alison's arse "savourly" and being farted upon, and Nicholas is led to put his bare behind out of the window little knowing he does so for it to be branded with a plough-coulter hot from the forge. The only character in the tale who cannot be regarded as the target figure in any way is Alison, the woman, who sails through "upright", laughing and unscathed.

An emphasis upon the characters within the tale is established from the start of the Miller's Tale, where there are three character portraits replete with significant detail. The carpenter, the "riche gnof", is mentioned in the first three lines but the narration moves swiftly on to the portrait of Nicholas. This portrayal confirms the expectations of a fabliau that have been raised in the Reeve, and with him the reader, by the Miller's Prologue. This principal character is a "poure scoler" (3190), a "clerk" (3199), liable, therefore, to be living by his wits, including, it is hinted (3191-6), by forecasting the weather on the strength of his astrology. This clerk is amorously alive and even experienced:

> Of deerne love he koude and of solas;
> And therto was he sleigh and ful privee

(3200-1)

> koude: knew

− "deerne love" is as double in meaning here as it is at the beginning of *Dame Sirith*, and the same must hold for the semantically similar "privee"; slyness is very much more the quality of a fabliau lover (cf. *Dame Sirith* 159) than of a courtly suitor. Evidently emblematic of Nicholas's priorities in life is the description of his psaltery, a stringed musical instrument, lying above all else in his chamber − his books, astrolabe and counters. After the introduction of Nicholas (3190–220) we turn back to the carpenter, of whom, too, we are instantly given details making him a perfect fabliau character: he is married, newly and ill-matchedly so, and thus perhaps green and inexperienced as well as old and jealous:

This carpenter hadde wedded newe a wyf,
Which that he lovede moore than his lyf;
Of eightetene yeer she was of age.
Jalous he was, and heeld hir narwe in cage,
For she was wylde and yong, and he was old
And demed hymself been lyk a cokewold.

(3221–6)

narwe: narrowly, close

The fabliau formulae themselves produce an unjust stereotyping in this case, as the carpenter's jealousy, although referred to again by Alison (3294), is nowhere evident in his words or actions in the tale. The carpenter's sincere love for his wife is, however, reflected in his subsequent actions (i.e. 3522–3; 3614–17).

From the description of the carpenter (3221–32) the narrative moves on to a glorious and often-analysed *effictio*, an external portrait such as was conventional in introducing ladies in romance literature, of the beautiful and sensuous young wife, Alison. She is a child of nature, likened to several animals, particularly, in some cases, to their young: a weasel (3234), a wether (3249), a kid and a calf (3260) and a colt (3263); and also to flowers (3268). Her whole self appeals to all the senses. She has an apron "whit as morne milk" (3236), a mouth as:

sweete as bragot or the meeth
Or hoord of apples leyd in hey or heeth

(3261–2)

She is "blisful on to see" (3247), soft to the touch (3249) and even present to the sense of hearing with her song (3257–8). Her clothing moulds itself to her body so as to reveal or to promise as much of the delights within as it conceals; it too includes silk, soft to the touch (3235) and the fresh warm taste of morning milk (3236). Both body and clothing are made up of the black and the white – uncomplicated but striking – and her complexion shines like gold (3236–41; 3246; 3255–6). Her clothing shows the shape of her body – her apron is seen "upon hir lendes" (3237), where it is "ful of many a goore": full, we may interpret this, of pleats, leading the attention further in to the apron, and towards what lies beyond/behind it. So too the embroidery on her smock leads the reader to turn her round in his gaze, "al bifoore/And eek bihynde" (3238–9). The mind's eye is drawn to move down, just a little, below her waist, where there "heeng a purs of lether" (3250) (compare, here, the sexual connotations of Old French *bourse*, 'purse'), and likewise up her legs from her shoes (3267). She is indeed a transcendent figment of the creative literary imagination:

> In al this world, to seken up and doun,
> Ther nys no man so wys that koude thenche
> So gay a popelote or swich a wenche.

(3252–4)

    thenche: think, imagine

According to Janette Richardson (1970), Alison escapes any punishment in the tale because she acts purely in accordance with 'nature'. Another difference between the characterization of Alison and that of the three men is that she is seen totally from the outside – one sees her appearance in her face and her clothes; we see what actions she does. All the men, by contrast, have some psychological character, however simple, associable with their actions – love, lust, malice, and so on; Alison's mind, her attitudes, what she "thoughte in hir herte" (cf. the Merchant's Tale, IV: 1851), remain absolute mysteries.

Many women in the French fabliaux are described as beautiful, and thus alluring in such a way as to motivate the fabliau plot, but none is made poetically truly so within the text to the extent that Chaucer's Alison is. Immediately after her portrait is completed Nicholas woos her in a typically crude, fabliau manner, presented by the narrator in appropriately marked, fabliau language:

> And prively he caughte hire by the queynte,
> And seyde, 'Ywis, but if ich have my wille,
> For deerne love of thee, lemman, I spille.'

(3276–8)

    spille: die

Alison puts up some resistance to this rude assault (3282–7) but as Nicholas persists, crying mercy and speaking fair, she seems in the end to be a relatively easy conquest for him (3288–93). From here, the notion that the husband's jealousy requires the lovers to perform a fabliau trick is made explicit (3294–302), after which Nicholas takes up his psaltery, excitedly making music as he mentally rejoices in his conquest and the promise of sexual delight it holds (3305–6).

That next we see Alison going to church:

> Cristes owene werkes for to wirche
>
> (3308)

yet prepared for adultery, and, who knows, anticipating it in her mind, and with one of her attractions, her shining complexion, emphasized with her newly-washed forehead, might well be taken as creating an adverse moral perspective on Alison. Equally we might take 'nature' as being so predominant in Alison's whole being and actions that we thus recognize church-going to be a part of medieval culture that has become so instinctive an act as to be part of the essential rhythm of medieval life. Whatever the case – and the religious context is a problem that will be considered with wider reference in due course – it is at church that the parish clerk, Absolon, is introduced. He, too, is presented with a description of his appearance, dress, behaviour and character that is clearly an exercise similar to the drawing of Alison, and which encourages the comparison of the figures thus drawn. In Absolon's case, this emphasizes, not quite his effeminacy, but rather his daintiness, with his Pre-Raphaelite fan of golden curly hair, his rosy cheeks and grey eyes, "yclad . . . ful smal and proprely", 'dressed tightly and fashionably', and his dancing, like Alison (3312–38). He has, however, the same sexual appetite as Nicholas – and, correspondingly, has his musical instruments: a "smal rubible" (there is, no doubt, a bawdy joke in the *smal*, 'thin', here) and a "giterne". Particularly striking is how far Absolon's image is the product of nurture, not nature: his hair "crul", 'curled', "strouted", 'made to stick out', and with a "shode", 'parting', which we read of him combing later on (3691); his shoes and clothing "corven", 'carved' and "set"; not, like Alison, skipping like a kid or a calf, but tripping and dancing "in twenty manere .. after the scole of Oxenforde tho" (a wonderful image of the 'school'!).

Absolon's portrait thus ends with particular bathos when it transpires that he still cannot escape the vulgar facts of the body's nature, try as he might:

> But sooth to seyn, he was somdeel squaymous
> Of fartyng. . .
>
> (3337–8)

> *somdeel sqaymous*: somewhat squeamish

This second instance of a marked word in the Miller's Tale encourages a recall of the context of the first, Nicholas's grabbing of Alison, and thus even before it has been dramatically explicated completes the second fabliau triangle, Nicholas–Alison–Absolon, which forms a symmetrical reflection of the first, Nicholas–Alison–John. If we are alert to textual detail – and all studies of the reverberations of imagery in the Miller's Tale tell us that it is a tale that encourages us to be so (see below) – then we can also find a suggestive parallel between Absolon's inability to detach himself entirely from the vulgarities of the human world and the Host's failure to impose an elegantly hierarchical structure on the tale-telling competition. "This gooth aright: unbokeled is the male", he says, praising the tale of the Knight, the highest-ranking pilgrim, and proceeding, with deferential patronization, to call on the Monk to "quite", to 'answer', the Knight's Tale (3115–19). The vulgar Miller intrudes, and, with his fabliau and the nature of the genre and of fabliau language in mind, we can find some amusement in contemplating the possible sexual reading of "unbokeled is the male", 'the purse is unbuckled', a vulgarity that the Host, playing the role given him at this point, would no doubt have considered excluded from his words. We see Absolon submit to nature once more, when despite his reported courtly wakefulness in his desire for Alison (3373), he decides upon a couple of hours' nap before his waking and playing on the fateful night (3685-6).

Absolon's artificiality can be seen as the root of his failure within the tale. He fails with all his devices to attract Alison:

Fro day to day this joly Absolon
So woweth hire than hym is wo bigon.
He waketh al the nyght and al the day;
He kembeth his lokkes brode, and made hym gay;
He woweth hire by meenes and brocage,
And swoor he wolde been hir owene page;
He syngeth, brokkynge as a nyghtyngale;
He sente hire pyment, meeth, and spiced ale,
And wafres, pipyng hoot out of the gleede;
And, for she was of town, he profred meede;
For som folk wol ben wonnen for richesse,
And somme for strokes, and somme for gentillesse.
    Somtyme, to shewe his lightnesse and maistrye,
He pleyeth Herodes upon a scaffold hye.
But what availleth hym as in this cas?

She loveth so this hende Nicholas
That Absolon may blowe the bukkes horn;
He ne hadde for his labour but a scorn.
And thus she maketh Absolon hire ape,
And al his ernest turneth til a jape.

(3371–90)

woweth: woos; meenes: intermediaries; brocage: agency; brokkynge: trilling; meeth:
mead; gleede: glowing ember; strokes: blows, possibly 'great deeds'

where Nicholas succeeds with his direct and unambiguous seizure
of Alison (3276–8). Absolon's unfortunate request for a kiss – which
he hopes will be a sign of things to come – itself comes as the
conclusion of a pastiche of literary models and sources including the
lover's complaint and the Old Testament's Song of Solomon
(3698–726). Nicholas succeeds because he is different, with naked and
unambiguous phallocentric maleness. Thus, too, Nicholas absolutely
displaces the deluded John:

Withoute wordes mo they goon to bedde,
Ther as the carpenter is wont to lye.

(3650–1)

There is a wealth of detail in the imagery of the Miller's Tale, a
wealth to be measured in terms of the narrative or thematic
relevance of the individual images. Charles Muscatine wrote
memorably of the fulfilment of a "fabliau entelechy" in this tale: an
actualization in the course of the fabliau of a potential residing in
the elements of its composition from the start.[5] Nicholas's weather-
forecasting (3193–6) anticipates the Flood trick. The "lycorys" that
Nicholas is as sweet as (3207) is echoed by the "likerous ye" of
Alison (3244) and the liquourice that Absolon, less favoured by
nature, chews:

To smellen sweet, er he hadde kembd his heer

(3691)

kembd: combed

before approaching Alison's window on the night of the
denouement of the tale. The inverse of the use of this sweet spice
comes with the kissing of Alison's arse, "ful savourly" (3734–5) and
Absolon's attempts to take the taste of that away:

5. Muscatine Chaucer and the French Tradition pp 224ff.

Who rubbeth now, who froteth now his lippes,
With dust, with sand, with straw, with clooth, with chippes

(3747–8)

    froteth: polishes

– note here the details appropriate to this action taking place in a carpenter's yard. "Woodnesse", 'madness', itself becomes a theme of the tale, as Nicholas screams "as he were wood" (3814) on being branded, and Alison and Nicholas assert that John was "wood" after crashing to the ground in his tub (3833). The pun on "wood" in its sole surviving modern sense makes the imputed insanity of the carpenter – a would-be second Noah, the shipwright – adhere to John the more firmly. When Alison requires Nicholas to be "ful deerne" (3297) we already know that he can be (3200).

The association of sex and musical imagery reaches a splendid climax in this tale as Alison and Nicholas enjoy "revel" and "melodye" in bed to a devout musical accompaniment as:

    the belle of laudes gan to rynge,
And freres in the chauncel gonne synge.

(3655–6)

The use of animal imagery to describe Alison prepares us for her response to Nicholas's first assault:

And she sprong as a colt dooth in the trave

(3282)

while the images of the *trave*, a frame for holding a horse to be shod, and of the final night of the tale "derk . . . as the cole", prepare us for the brief scene at Gerveys the blacksmith's forge (3760–85). Around the blacksmith's forge, too, there is assembled another cluster of imagery with sexual connotations. We have already seen the phallic symbolism of the plough in *Dame Sirith* and the Shipman's Tale; it is thematically appropriate that the Miller should swear by "the oxen in my plogh" when considering in his prologue whether he may be a cuckold or not (3151–62). When Absolon brands Nicholas with the hot coulter there is an unmistakable innuendo that he disgraces the rampant Nicholas, who has replaced Alison at the window, with a homosexual assault.[6]

  6. A paper by Folke Ström, 'Níð, ergi and Old Norse moral attitudes', The Dorothea Coke Memorial Lecture in Northern Studies, 1973 (Viking Society for Northern Research) provides relevant documentation of how a culture may stigmatize the 'female' (passive) position in homosexual intercourse as more disgraceful than taking the 'male'/active role.

Perhaps the most poignant echo in the tale comes towards the end where the townspeople, laughing at John, "kiken and . . . cape", 'peer and gape', into his roof (3841), repeating the verb used of Nicholas pretending to be transfixed by his astrological vision (3444): the "folk" here align themselves with Nicholas – and with Nicholas the trickster, not Nicholas of the branded bum. As at the end of *Dame Sirith*, the cycle of fabliau narrative is ready to roll around again.

Many more details of this kind of exploitation of imagery could be picked out of the Miller's Tale; the above, however, is sufficient to make the point that the composition of the tale is extremely well organized, wasting no details, and indeed harmonizing the disparate plots in the magnificent denouement of the tale. The dramatic climax of the tale is reached when Nicholas foolhardily puts his backside out of the window: he farts like thunder upon the "squaymous" Absolon, the roll of the "thunderdent" being an audible sign of the imminent storm. He is then "scalded in the towte" and screams for water; John wakes up and interprets Nicholas's cry in his own deluded way. It is several critics' testimony that John's awakening re-awakens the reader to John's sleeping presence (or, rather, immanence). As in the French *Jouglet*, it seems that Nicholas's tricks are rebounding on him. The comparison with *Jouglet,* however, helps us in our analysis to see the Miller's Tale as a pre-eminent example of a fabliau in which trickery really is the essence of the narrative. Despite, realistically, plenty of opportunity, there is no illicit sex between Nicholas and Alison until the pleasure of their union can be enhanced by Nicholas truly having replaced John by tricking him into a contrived 'absence'. Even the reported jealousy of John, which is the intratextual spur to Nicholas's applying his wits to "bigyle" him (3294–00), is left looking like a contrivance, validated by its function which is to excuse what is 'really' a gratuitous trick. The joke of the Miller's Tale is not the cuckolding of John; the bedding of Alison by Nicholas. Rather it is *how* those results are achieved, and the series of discomfitures that are a consequence of Absolon's intrusion and creation of an antitype to the cosy lovers' triangle in the carpenter's house. Sex, thus, is not a theme of the Miller's Tale in the way that it is of *Dame Sirith* and the Shipman's Tale.

In its complexity and coherency, however, the process of composition of the Miller's Tale mirrors the plotting and contrivances within the tale. This is a further twist to the problem of the identities of the tellers of the tale, which Chaucer conspicuously, and apparently ingenuously, labels with a subjective genitive as a "cherles tale". We do not need to wait for the Reeve's Tale for a fabliau in which the Miller can be identified with a target figure: the Miller's Tale itself links its dramatic teller, the Miller, with John the carpenter as John repeats the Miller's axiom found in the Miller's Prologue:

> An housbonde shal nat been inquisityf
> Of Goddes pryvetee
>
> (3163–4)

in his own homespun wisdom:

> Men sholde nat knowe of Goddes pryvetee
>
> (3454)

– a valuing of ignorance which Nicholas is able to play upon (3558). We can read this assimilation of characters either as an irony beyond the Miller's ken, confirming the limits of his churl's intellect, or as a droll piece of self-examination and reflection on the character's part: the Miller might, as he says in his prologue, be a cuckold as John is. Again the reader is offered *choice*; here a choice of what sort of Miller the reader wishes to have.

Very much part of the truly amusing comedy of the Miller's Tale is the swift chain of cause and effect that links the three familiar plots – what is euphemistically called 'the misdirected kiss', the branding, and the Second Flood trick – together in the dramatic climax in lines 3798 to 3823 of the tale. Here, we may claim, the clusters of imagery in the tale reach their fulfilment in a hilarious fabliau denouement, not in a climax in which they convert to solemn symbolic meanings in an implicit moral scheme. Ranges of imagery such as that of the plough may be symbolic, but are only so in a particular type of fabliau symbolism: disgraceful or phallic in their symbolic reference in a manner that is the very antitype of Christian moralization. The hilarious final rush of actions dominates the tale, and may provide a form of comic catharsis by which not only are potentially grave moral images and considerations emptied of their solemnity, but also the sympathy that it is difficult at times not to feel for the poor dupe, John, faithfully and helplessly in love with his wife, is overwhelmed by

the sheer absurdity of this all-embracing climax. What is more, the
funny side of John's situation is made explicit in the tale by lines
which indicate the fundamentally urbane and clerkly bias of the
humour of the fabliau:

> For every clerk anonright heeld with other.
> They seyde, 'The man is wood my leve brother';
> And every wight gan laughen at this stryf.

(3847–9)

> *wight*: creature, person; *gan laughen*: began to laugh, or did laugh

The laugh is on the uneducated man who thought his common
sense better than the clerks' sophistry (3448–91). We can, moreover,
hear the urbane inflection of the voice where Nicholas and Alison
briefly take up the fabliau narrative within the narrative, spinning
the yarn of John's foolishness:

> They tolden every man that he was wood;
> He was agast so of Nowelis flood
> Thurgh fantasie that of his vanytee
> He hadde yboght hym knedyng tubbes thre,
> And hadde hem hanged in the roof above,
> And that he preyede hem, for Goddes love,
> To sitten in the roof, *par compaignye*.

(3833–9)

The joke is enhanced by their attribution of the elegant French
phrase, *par compaignye*, to this "lewed" character. The Miller's tale
concludes as a fabliau, not only with appropriate, marked fabliau
language:

> Thus swyved was this carpenteris wyf,
> For al his kepyng and his jalousye,
> And Absolon hath kist hir nether ye,
> And Nicholas is scalded in the towte.

(3850–3)

> *swyved*: screwed; *nether ye:* lower eye; *towte*: bum

but also with a general and amiable benediction:

> . . . and God save al the rowte!

(3854)

Moral interpretation

The more recent moral–allegorical readings of the Miller's Tale have seen John, Nicholas and Absolon as type figures, representing the sins of Avarice, Lechery and Pride respectively, all of whom come to judgement and punishment in their discomfiture. It would clearly take considerable mental agility to square this reading with that emphasizing the comedy of the fabliau put forward here, even in terms of the black humour of the exposure of human baseness as suggested for the French *Les quatre Souhais Saint Martin*. More arresting are readings which note the inescapable presence of the Christian religion in the ambient of the tale, embodied in the church – to which Alison goes on the "haliday" and where Absolon "gooth with a sencer", or where the "freres in the chauncel gonne synge" – and in the Bible: echoes of the Song of Solomon in the descriptions of Alison and Absolon, and in Absolon's love song (3698–707). There is also the identification of John and Alison, an old carpenter and a young carpenter's wife, with Joseph and Mary, especially as Nicholas's early sweet singing includes the Anunciation, *Angelus ad virginem*, 'The angel [coming] to the Virgin. . .' (3216).[7] R. E. Kaske puts it extremely neatly by claiming only for the Miller's Tale an "implicit orientation" towards "a controlling set of [moral and religious] values" creating a framework within which, ultimately, the actions within the tale *and* the actions of writing, telling and reading the tale, are to be evaluated. Kolve, however, would argue even this moral content away, suggesting that possible religious images are systematically emptied of their moral potential in the telling of the tale, to celebrate "the possible sovereignty of comic order within the world of daily life, a world temporarily – by an act of imaginative exclusion – unshadowed by Last Things": Noah's Flood really is transformed into "Nowelis flood". This reading of the effect of the 'fabliau entelechy' on religious imagery can also be applied to what appears as a singularly stark, socially satirical statement in this tale, the concluding lines to the portrait of Alison:

> She was a prymerole, a piggesnye,
> For any lord to leggen in his bedde,

7. See Kaske 1962 and Rowland 1974.

Or yet for any good yeman to wedde.

(3268–70)

prymerole: primrose; *piggesnye*: pig's-eye [another flower]; *leggen*: lay

These could focus critically on the selfish pleasure-taking of lords with town 'wenches', whom yeomen of lower status have to wed. The lines could, of course, be read as reflecting on Alison: 'she was there for any man'. But they can also be interpreted in accordance with the overriding thematic interpretation of the Miller's Tale suggested here. Alison's favours break down the boundaries of class; any man who can lay her in his bed is like a lord, as Absolon says as he anticipates her kiss:

'I am a lord at alle degrees;
For after this I hope ther cometh moore.'

(3724–5)

at alle degrees: in every way

Kolve's interpretation of potentially religious images within the tale is fine as far as it goes, and can justly be quoted against the allegorizers, but there is at least one aspect of the tale that refers irreducibly to a moral frame within which the tale is set: recurrent swearing of oaths by "Seint Thomas of Kent", which reminds us of the framing narrative with its realistic and morally symbolic journey towards Becket's shrine in Canterbury and the judgement of the tale-telling game just as much as John's calling upon St Frideswide locates the tale effectively within Oxford. From here, a futher interpretation of the Miller's Tale may be proposed which is similar in form to that of *Les quatre Souhais Saint Martin* recalled just above, although far less severe, morally, than either that proposed for the French fabliau or that of the allegorizers. This takes as its theme "Goddes pryvetee": a phrase appearing three times in the Miller's Prologue and Tale (3164, 3454, 3558) and recalled again when John tells his wife his so-called "pryvetee" in line 3603. We can find in this tale a sharp focusing of the contrast between the far-off histories of the Old Testament and the mysteries of God's will and intelligence, and the vulgarities of the human condition and the spectrum of personal relationships with the church from Nicholas and Absolon through Alison to John. The tale thus appropriately represents an early station in the Canterbury pilgrim-community's road towards a religious goal that they can approach in fourteenth-century England, Becket's shrine. And prayer may span the divide between the mundane and the transcendental:

> God save al the rowte!
>
> (3854)

THE REEVE AND HIS TALE

When the Miller has finished telling his tale, Chaucer characterizes its contents once more, this time describing it as a "nyce cas", 'a foolish state of affairs' (3855): an apparently neutral moral description which nonetheless contrasts significantly with the more clearly marked "harlotrye" that has formerly been used to label the contents of the pair of fabliaux we are now halfway through. The responses of the pilgrims to the Miller's Tale, we are told, were various:

> Diverse folk diversely they seyde
>
> (3857)

but the majority of the pilgrims simply laugh (3858). If we imagine the situation at the end of the Miller's Tale in realistic terms, we can suppose that the divisions amongst the pilgrims in terms of their appreciation of the tale are as likely to reflect different sensibilities to the marked, fabliau language the Miller's Tale makes use of as shock at the possible moral implications of the tale (compare the response to the Prioress's Tale, noted in Chapter 3). The one dissenting voice that is made explicit to us is the Reeve's:

> Ne at this tale I saugh no man him greve,
> But hit were oonly Osewold the Reve,
> By cause he was of carpenteris craft
>
> (3859–61)

saugh: saw

As has been noted, the Reeve's Tale is often read as a much darker piece than the Miller's Tale, and such readings are usually rooted in the reading of the Reeve's character: a character who *may* be presented as corrupt, as well as frightening, in his General Prologue portrait. The elusiveness of the Reeve in this respect, while he knows fully the sleights of those around him (603–4), makes him the more troubling. He is then described as irous as he comes to tell his tale:

A litel ire is in his herte ylaft;
He gan to grucche, and blamed it [the Miller's Tale] a lite

(3862-3)

  grucche: grouch; *lite*: little

Kolve contrasts the obsessiveness of sin and punishment in the
Reeve's Tale with the freedom and lightheartedness of his Miller's
Tale. At the end of both the Reeve's Prologue and of his Tale, a
measure-for-measure attitude to the governing of human affairs,
and, most significantly, human relationships, is enunciated:

. . .leveful is with force force ofshowve

(3912)

(. . .force is permissibly resisted with force)

and:

A gylour shal himself bigyled be

(4321)

  gylour : beguiler

with no sense anywhere of grace, mercy or forgiveness, the
essentials for human salvation in the Christian view. Particular
attention has correspondingly been drawn to the manner in which
moral blemishes in Symkyn the miller and his relatives by blood
and marriage pervade the Reeve's Tale and govern – or are implicit
in – the unfolding of the narrative. Symkyn's father-in-law is the
village parson, which means, of course, that Symkyn's wife is of
illegitimate birth. This is the "noble kyn" of Symkyn's wife and
their daughter that Symkyn and his wife are so proud of. Symkyn's
daughter, Malyne, physically inherits from her father a characteristic
"kamus (pug) nose" (3934 and 3974), while the main feature of her
role in this fabliau, to be "swyved" by one of the clerks, mirrors
the extra-marital 'swyving' by which her mother was conceived.
An important question in our interpretation of the moral structure
of the tale must, however, be whether we regard the 'swyving' of
the two women as the visitation of some form of punishment upon
them. To insist that that is so would seem to be a hard claim to
substantiate. The women may be 'disparaged' (4271) but are not
shown to be outraged at what has happened to them. There is a
touch of pathos in the scene when the clerk leaves Malyne:

'. . . goode lemman, God thee save and kepe!'
And with that word almoost she gan to wepe.

(4247–8)

lemman: sweetheart

but it is Alayn's going, not his coming, that upsets her. In the case
of the miller's wife:

So myrie a fit ne hadde she ful yoore

(4230)

(She had not had so pleasant a time for many a long year)

The women appear rather to get a share of the compensation for
the "il fit", the 'unpleasant trick' (4184) that the clerks had suffered
during the preceding day.

P. A. Olson's article of 1962, identifying the Reeve's Tale as
Chaucer's *Measure for Measure*, was especially severe on the Reeve as
a character, and has proved to be the foundation stone for much
subsequent interpretation of the Reeve's Tale. In particular, Olson
suggested that the truly comic element in the tale is an ironic one:
that the moral criticism implicit within the tale applies more to the
Reeve that to his dramatic adversary, the Miller. He claimed too
that the Reeve is presented as indicting the Miller for a judgement
he does not make, i.e. that he had criticized the Reeve for being
over-ready to see himself as a priest, the agent of God's
punishment, through John's naive readiness to see himself as a
second Noah. Chaucer's Reeve, for Olson, is revealed as a judge
who will not temper strict retributive justice with mercy, and thus
becomes a character who is liable to strict justice himself. But in
casting himself as judge rather than criminal the Reeve himself is
the beguiler beguiled by the partiality of his moral vision: that is,
his own self-righteousness, and his ire towards his fellows.

It is undeniable that the individualized character of the Reeve is
very prominent as a result of his self-reflexions in his prologue, and
that the common theme of the scales of justice in Prologue and
Tale invites us to make our own assessments of characters and
actions there portrayed. Apart from the general fitness between
what most would see as a hostile and acerbic tale and a bitter and
unlovely character, one is constantly reminded of the Reeve's
provincial origins by his own dialect speech – in particular the
occasional use of the Scandinavian-derived first person pronoun *ik*,
'I', against Chaucer's standard *ich* – and by the northern speech of
his two clerks, Alayn and John of Strother (perhaps modelled on

two northern characters known to the English court),[8] which was yet further removed from the London standard of Chaucer's day. But if this reading of the Reeve's character, and of the relationship between teller and tale, were true, it would leave the Reeve almost uniquely condemned amongst the Canterbury pilgrims. He would not, of course, be alone in being exposed in the General Prologue and enhancing the adverse view of himself by his own Prologue – consider, for instance, the Pardoner – but he would be alone in then telling a tale which clinches the destruction of any claim to a good character he might have; a tale without any redeeming features, which the tales of even the worst of the corrupt clerics, the Friar and the Pardoner, have.

Reflexivity in the Reeve

After reminding ourselves, once more, that the General Prologue portrait of the Reeve contains its ambiguities – possibly sinister ones – we can start our examination of the portrayal of the Reeve with his Prologue. Most of what he says here is a reflection upon old age, which is also a reflection upon himself: "ik am oold" (3867). He considers the loss of physical potency and attractiveness with age, without any compensatory waning of physical lust, and lists four vices in which the old can still show some vitality:

> Avauntyng, liying, anger, coveitise

(3884)

    avauntyng: bragging

without, however, developing the discussion of these in any systematic and thematic way. Some of his self-portrayal is admittedly utterly unattractive:

> Myn herte is also mowled as myne heris,
> But if I fare as dooth an open-ers –
> That ilke fruyt is ever lenger the wers,
> Til it be roten in mullock or in stree.
> We olde men, I drede, so fare we:
> Til we be roten, kan we nat be rype.

(3870–5)

    also: just as; *mowled*: mouldy; *but if*: unless; *open-ers*: literally 'open-arse', the
    medlar fruit; *mullock*: rubbish; *stree*: straw

8. Robinson *The Works of Geoffrey Chaucer*, Explanatory Notes, The Reeve's Tale
    4014.

But are we required or invited to follow or even to surpass the Reeve in hostile judgement of his character? In the Miller's Prologue, the Miller's supposed drunkenness should not blind us to the measured good sense and balance of the mind implied within the character who speaks as the Miller. The Miller knows himself:

> '. . .I am dronke; I knowe it by my soun'
>
> (3138)

He recognizes too how it is that that his tale may offend the Reeve, and responds to the Reeve in conciliatory terms:

> 'Leve brother Osewold,
> Who hath no wyf, he is no cokewold.
> But I sey nat therfore that thou art oon. . .'
>
> (3151–3)

Most pertinently, he eschews the generalization of the fabliau image of the world:

> 'Ther been ful goode wyves many oon,
> And evere a thousand goode ayeyns oon badde.
> That knowestow wel thyself, but if thou madde.
> Why artow angry with my tale now?'
>
> (3154–7)

> *knowestow*: thou knowest; *madde*: art mad

The Reeve, too, in his Prologue, speaks more in relative than in absolute terms. Although he momentarily speaks of "eelde", 'old age', in general terms (3885) he is quite clearly presented as speaking of old age *as he knows it,* on the basis of his personal experience: he starts his speech with a reference to himself, "I", which by line 3874 is expanded to "we olde men". Immediately after his generalization about "eelde" he returns to the first person plural – "owre olde lemes" (3886) – and within two lines is back to "ik". The Reeve's speech is measured, not a splenetic outburst: only "a *litel* ire is in his herte ylaft" and he finds fault with the Miller's Tale just "a lite". The Reeve's speech is indeed serious, but it is serious because it is a reflective examination of his self; the Reeve's Prologue is precisely where the Reeve *does* judge himself. Or, one might say, the Reeve's Prologue is where the Reeve makes his confession, publicly, and thus frees himself from the charge of seeing motes in the eyes of others and ignoring a beam in his own: which is just the figure he ends his Prologue with in commenting upon the Miller.

Olson, however, sees this confession as ingratiating and artificial; a hypocritical show of feigned humility. He places particular stress upon contextual details which can be interpreted as the Reeve's appropriation of the role of priest. In the General Prologue the Reeve is thus described:

His top was dokked lyk a preest biforn

(590)

> dokked: cropped

and:

Tukked he was as is a frere aboute

(621)

> tukked: tucked up [of clothing]; frere: friar

and the Host responds to the serious reflections of the Reeve's Prologue accordingly:

The devel made a reve for to preche

(3903)

But the Host too has appropriated a character, as judge and ruler of the tale-telling game, that takes him beyond the predictable attributes of his normal station in life:

What that oure Hoost hadde herd this sermonyng,
He gan to speke as lordly as a kyng.

(3899–900)

while in the fiction of the Tales, the Miller has just been attributed with the strengths of the court poet Chaucer as a narrator. When the Reeve likens himself to an "open-ers" he associates himself with Nicholas in the tale just passed, and can thus be attributed with the same wry self-reflection as the Miller shows in attaching himself to John the carpenter. The Miller, in his tale, re-emerges in the target figure that superficially seems meant to represent the Reeve; the Reeve then retrospectively identifies himself with a trickster and target figure: the trickster who makes a fool of the character supposed to represent him but who is subsequently made a fool of himself from another quarter. Altogether, the ironies of the passage read far more plausibly as a challenge to the categories in which the Reeve, the Host and the Miller superficially belong than as a re-assertion of the impropriety of such characters acting out of their places.

The Reeve's Tale

The style of the Reeve's Tale is in keeping with the openness – the honesty, of a kind – that is introduced in his Prologue. The moral fault of his miller is stated directly and without delay:

> As any pecock he was proud and gay
>
> (3926)

a point which is equally straightforwardly repeated with reference to the miller's wife:

> And she was proud . . .
>
> (3950)

Conspicuous rhetorical devices are used to underline the moral viewpoint; sarcasm in treating of the magnificence of the miller's wife and daughter; the wife:

> was as digne as water in a dich
>
> (3964)

> *digne*: dignified

and the daughter:

> With kamus nose and eyen greye as glas
> With buttokes brode and brestes rounde and hye.
> But right fair was hire heer; I wol nat lye.
>
> (3974–6)

and amplification in treating of the parson's simoniac behaviour:

> For hooly chirches good moot been despended
> On hooly chirches blood, that is descended.
> Therfore he wolde his hooly blood honoure,
> Though that he hooly chirche sholde devoure.
>
> (3983–6)

Quite unlike anything in the Miller's Tale, the moral faults of the characters are explicit in the Reeve's Tale: simony, indeed, names itself in the name of the miller, Symkyn or Symond. Pride, which is the major of these two moral themes, emerges in some bizarre and therefore entertaining forms in the course of the fabliau narrative. When the absurdly naive theatricals by which the clerks seek to cloak their scheme for preventing the miller's stealing – which has increased from the 'curteis' to the 'outrageous' with the illness of their college's manciple – reveal their design to him, he determines to steal yet more, out of pride, and out of his own version of measure for measure, but not out of covetousness:

> '. . . by my thrift, yet shal I blere hir ye
> For al the sleighte in hir philosophye.
> The moore queynte crekes that they make
> The moore wol I stele whan I take.'

(4049–52)

> *blere*: deceive, blind; *queynte crekes*: elaborate tricks

As soon as the two clerks can stop and consider the trick that has been played on them, we see that the miller's action, motivated by his pride, hits directly at the pride of the clerks:

> 'Allas,' quod John, 'the day that I was born!
> Now are we dryve til hethyng and til scorn.
> Oure corn is stoln; men wil us fooles calle. . .'

(4109–11)

> *hethyng*: ridicule

Another offence to John's pride leads him later to attempt to bed the miller's wife, hearing the success of Alayn with the daughter (4199–209). And when the clerks have taken their "esement" by 'swyving' the miller's wife and daughter it is clear that this hurts the miller first and foremost in his family pride. Alayn, unwittingly, boasts to the miller himself of having three times "swyved" the miller's daughter. The miller roars in reply:

> 'Ye, false harlot,' quod the millere, 'hast?
> A, false traitour! False clerk!' quod he,
> 'Thow shalt be deed, by Goddes dignitee!
> Who dorste be so boold to disparage
> My doghter, that is come of swich lynage?'

(4268–72)

Thus pride answers pride. But can we turn the Reeve's Tale into a closed and exemplary moral piece showing how pride causes its own fall, and thus how one man's pride is corrected by conflict with another man's? Perhaps not; the tale hardly encourages us to suspend all other responses to indulge in such abstract mathematical balancing of measures of vice and their products. The inconclusive moral closure of the Reeve's Tale is nicely exemplified by the ambiguity of the word "ybete" in the tale's summing up of the miller's fate:

Thus is the proude millere wel ybete

(4313)

Ybete can mean either 'beaten' or 'corrected'.

In other respects, however, the style of the Reeve's Tale is very similar to that of the Miller's Tale, supporting the view that the tone of the two tales is more a matter of continuity than of contrast. Like the Miller's Tale, the Reeve's Tale is characterized by the coherent use and significant exploitation of certain fields of imagery. As in the Miller's Tale, most prominent amongst these is animal imagery. Not only are characters within the tale likened to animals – for instance the miller, proud as a peacock, with his skull "piled as an ape", or his wife, "peert as is a pye" (3926, 3935, 3950) – but an animal has a substantial role to play in the story: the clerk's horse, a stallion, who even has a name, Bayard. Interestingly, the two clerks are first introduced to us as "testif", 'testy', 'headstrong', a French-derived adjective with horsy connotations of its own and which can indeed be used of horses in French. It has often been noted that Chaucer differs from the various continental analogues of the Reeve's Tale[9] in having this horse a stallion, thematically an astute adaptation, if adaptation it be. Through the horse, we have emphasized for us the animalistic and instinctive nature of the male (or human?) sexual appetite. When the miller unleashes this stallion to plunge straight off after the wild mares in the fen (4057–66) he unwittingly unleashes the whole course of events that will lead to the 'swyvinges' in his family's bedchamber that night. As Janette Richardson has noted, the transition from the horse's frolics to the clerks' night-time escapades is marked by the collocation of the miller's retying the horse, and making the clerks a bed:

> [the miller] boond hire hors, it sholde namoore go loos,
> And in his owene chambre hem [the clerks] made a bed. . .

(4138–9)

To make the point absolutely explicit, when the clerk John has leapt on top of the miller's wife in bed:

9. Most attention is usually paid to two French fabliau analogues: see Bryan and Dempster *Sources and Analogues* pp 124–47; Benson and Andersson *Literary Context* pp 88–201. See Chapter 6, *passim,* for discussion of a sixteenth-century English version of a tale that may descend from a Middle English version different from Chaucer's, conceivably representing Chaucer's source, and for medieval German, Italian and Dutch analogues.

He priketh hard and depe as he were mad

(4231)

— the verb *priken*, in Middle English, is a standard term for riding or spurring a horse. Alayn, too, immediately afterwards, manages to remind us of the sexual sense of 'to ride' in his farewell to Malyne:

'But everemo, wher so I go or ryde,
I is thyn awen clerk. . .'

(4238–9)

      awen: own

The miller, too, is like a horse in his sleep; in his case, however, in his unselfconscious drunken snoring and farting (4162). In the same way as Bayard has, finally, been bound, the miller, for all his pride and show, is proved to be impotent and emasculated by event after event, image after image, in the tale.

Various effects can be attributed to other instances of recurrent imagery besides that of merely providing a satisfactory feeling of unity in the narrative performance. When Alayn, for instance, rouses the miller, who he thinks is John, to brag of his success with a familiar and confiding jest: ". . .thou swines heed, awake!" (4262), the epithet is ironically appropriate to the miller, especially as sixteen lines later the clerk and the miller are fighting ". . .as doon two pigges in a poke". Most important in terms of the overall interpretation of the Reeve's Tale in relation to the Miller's Tale, however, are examples of imagery that achieve some form of fulfilment in terms of the reading of the tale as a fabliau, complete with the characteristic fabliau attitudes, rather than as a moral example. Most prominent amongst these are terms that mock the miller as an impotent and inadequate cuckold. It is difficult to miss the phallic connotations of the weapons the miller seems to make such a show of having about his person:

Ay by his belt he baar a long panade,
And of a swerd ful trenchant was the blade.
A joly poppere baar he in his pouche

(3929–31)

    ay: ever; *panade*: cutlass; *joly poppere*: nice little dagger

— the diminution in scale to the "joly poppere" may already hint at the bawdy belittling the miller is to suffer. That the miller's knives substitute for his sexual potency rather than reflect it is indicated by the superiority of the clerk's performance in bed with his wife to anything he has managed for a long time:

> So myrie a fit ne hadde she nat ful yoore
>
> (4230)

He has fathered two children, but, like Bayard, his sexual energy is now exhausted. As a result, when it comes to his turn to be on top of his wife again, he falls down backwards on to her (4281), the wrong way around for sexual intercourse, as she sleeps with John after their night-time labours.

There are many elements which establish a broad and strong line of continuity from the Miller's Tale into and through the Reeve's Tale. Contrastive, in a sense, is the Varsity match they play, pitting an Oxford fabliau against a Cambridge one, but common to both is the urbane and clerkly perspective in which the comedy of the tales is made explicit. Just as 'every clerk's' unanimity of opinion directs the laughter of "every wight" at the end of the Miller's Tale (3847–9), the text of the Reeve's Tale brings its readers to view and laugh at the miller and his family through the clerks' perceptions, their attitudes and their frame of reference:

> The millere hath so wisely bibbed ale
> That as an hors he fnorteth in his sleep,
> Ne of his tayl behynde he took no keep.
> His wyf bar hym a burdon, a ful strong;
> Men myghte hir rowtyng heere two furlong;
> The wenche rowteth eek, *par compaignye*.
> Aleyn the clerk, that herde this melodye,
> He poked John, and seyde, 'Slepestow?
> Herdestow evere slyk a sang er now?
> Lo, swilk a complyn is ymel hem alle . . .'
>
> (4162–71)

> *wisely*: thoroughly; *bibbed*: drunk; *fnorteth*: snorts; *took no keep*: took no heed; *burdon*: refrain; *rowtyng*: snoring; *complyn*: compline; *ymel*: between

We may particularly note, for instance, how the incongruous "*par compaignye*" that Nicholas and Alison put in the mouth of the unfortunate John recurs in this urbane rendering of the family's vulgar cacophany, and how the somewhat different "melodye" recalls the "revel" and the "melodye" that Alison and Nicholas enjoy. Thus, too, the "complyn" in this passage, the last service of the monastic day, matches the "laudes" sung out by the bells and sung by the friars in Oxford as Nicholas and Alison consummate their passion. In this light, anyone who would still assert that the attribution of a northern dialect to the clerks by a London court poet was simply meant to render them intrinsically absurd must surely think again.

Continuity between the two fabliaux in the case of animal imagery is a matter of more than just a general resemblance. The ape that Alison makes of Absolon, the excluded potential lover (3389), re-emerges as John the clerk after Alayn has jumped into bed with Malyne (4202), while throughout the night the miller, with his skull "piled as an ape" (3935) is left in the same position. The drunken miller's incoherency, "as he were on the quakke" (4152) recalls how Nicholas puts the equivalent of an ass's head on John the carpenter by portraying him, absurdly, as a duck swimming above the Second Flood (3575–6). The linguistic echoes of the Miller's Tale in the Reeve's are intense, and, usually, located near the very heart of the tales' character as fabliaux. The marked language of the Miller's Tale, *swyve* and *pisse*, is found again in the Reeve's Tale; *fartynge* is not named as such in the Reeve's Tale, but is included with a circumlocution that uses a marked term we have seen in the Shipman's Tale:

> Ne of his tayl bihynde he took no keep
>
> (4164)

The miller's boast:

> Yet kan a millere make a clerkes berd
>
> (4096)

is no doubt intended to be simply proverbial, but has a richly ironic meaning in light of the 'beard' that Absolon finds upon obtaining his kiss from Alison (3730–43). Perhaps the most telling of such echoes is that between the stallion's ecstatic animal cry of "wehee" as it races off towards the mares (4066) and Alisons's gleeful cry of "tehee" after making such a fool, in her way, of Absolon (3740). One may truly get the sense of the Reeve's Tale being played by the same company with the same costumes on the same stage as the Miller's Tale: Absolon's red hose for the "halyday" (3319–40) re-appear early on (3952–5), and the daughter has the same grey eyes as the delicate Absolon (3317, 3974). The Absolon who mourns

'. . . as dooth a lamb after the tete'

(3704)

may be recalled when we see the suckling child in the cradle at the
foot of the miller and his wife's bed (4156-7).

For such reasons, one may argue that there is a continuity of
comic tone between the Miller's and Reeve's Tales which
counteracts such contrasts as may be produced by cold moral
calculation. It may be objected that the identification of such
continuities bases a far-fetched proposition on simple coincidences,
against which one can argue that it simply extends to the Reeve's
tale an alert manner of reading which has become absolutely
orthodox in respect of the Miller's Tale. One may indeed go
further, and find the tales to be firmly linked by some remarkable
but amusing instances of interference and confusion with one
another. Twice, in the Miller's Tale, we hear a cock crow, as
Absolon presents himself at the "shot-wyndowe" of Alison's
bedroom (3357, 3687). A crow is heard once more in the Reeve's
Tale, identified as the "thridde cock" (4233). It has been noted that
the grounds on which the miller's wife strikes her husband over the
head with a staff as he fights with John are somewhat absurdly
contrived:

> . . . at an hole in shoon the moone brighte,
> And by that light she saugh them bothe two,
> But sikerly she niste who was who,
> But as she saugh a whit thyng in hir ye.
> And whan she gan this white thyng espye
> She wende the clerk hadde wered a volupeer..

(4298–303)

sikerly: indeed; niste: knew not; volupeer: cap

This can be interpreted as the contrived excuse for the wife to help
her welcome lover to escape, as appears in some continental
analogues of the tale. Irrespective of this, we have seen a character
wearing a white volupeer earlier in the text: not in the Reeve's
Tale, but Alison, in the Miller's Tale (3241). It is as if the wife
remembers a detail out of the Miller's Tale but misattributes it
(deliberately or by accident) to the wrong context. Realistically, this
would be possible if the wife were on a different narrative 'level' to
the Miller's Tale, i.e. a character within the framing narrative rather
than within one of the tales. That she is in fact on the same

narrative level as Alison, but in a different tale, is a joke. Rather more serious, although not, therefore, more grave, is the way in which this draws attention to the conventional rather than the real distinction between characters — especially tale-tellers — at different levels of a framed narrative. The fiction may be spoken at different times by characters such as 'Chaucer', the Miller and the Reeve. But all the time it is Chaucer's composition.

These are not the only potentially significant examples of intertextual interference affecting the Reeve's Tale and its pairing with the Miller's Tale. Two further instances bring into the picture the various analogues to the Reeve's Tale. In many of the analogous medieval fabliaux of a miller and two clerks, the one clerk's designs upon the daughter are motivated by simple lust, because she is beautiful, and involve her deception too, as she is given, in the dark, what she is told is a gold ring but which is simply an iron ring off an andiron in the fireplace. There is no such ring in the Reeve's Tale, but it is hard not to notice that the motif seems to have been displaced and taken over by Absolon as he approaches Alison's window for the second time that night, in order to deceive her:

> 'I am thyn Absolon, my deerelyng.
> Of gold,' quod he, 'I have thee broght a ryng.
> My mooder yaf it me. . .'

$$(3793-5)$$

A sure example of intertextual inference is found in John's use of the cradle trick; he envies Alayn's success with Malyne, and decides he will "arise and auntre [chance] it" himself. So:

> . . .up he roos, and softely he wente
> Unto the cradel, and in his hand it hente,
> And baar it softe unto his beddes feet. . .

$$(4211-13)$$

> . . .Soone after this the wyf hir rowtyng leet,
> And gan awake, and wente hir out to pisse. . .

$$(4214-15)$$

>   leet: stopped

In most analogues, the cradle-switch is performed, quite logically, *after* one of the characters has gone out to relieve him or herself: an action which allows the cunning clerk to perceive an opportunity and to take advantage of it. What John 'auntres', by contrast, is a trick he must know from elsewhere – he decides to try out what he can have learnt only from a fabliau such as the related English, French, Dutch, Italian and German examples, banking on the sure expectation that either the miller or his wife will eventually get out of bed to allow the plot to be fulfilled. If we need any further confirmation of Chaucer's ability to play with and confuse levels of narrative in this sort of way, we can cite line 1685 of the Merchant's Tale, where Justinus reminds January of the teaching of the Wife of Bath's Prologue.

It would be silly to try to represent the duel between the Miller and the Reeve as merely good-natured fraternal leg-pulling. But just as the 'Miller's' energies are concentrated in his sustained and masterful display as a raconteur, the spleen of the Reeve is released in his self-reflection and in his pointed but ultimately harmless fabliau. The pair of fabliaux assimilates the two tellers; it leaves them standing virtually hand-in-hand rather than at blows; they are reconciled by the tit-for-tat of fabliau tale-telling. Such an interpretation is not merely a case of reading some preferred assumption into the silence on the subject of the Miller's relationship with the Reeve that descends after the Reeve has finished his tale. The Reeve is able to round his tale off by repeating the socially integrative prayer with which the Miller ends his tale, and stating that all is now square:

> And God that sitteth heighe in majestee,
> Save al this compaignye, grete and smale!
> Thus have I quyt the Millere in my tale.

(4322–4)

THE KNIGHT, THE MILLER AND THE REEVE

If we are to look for *sentence* in the Miller's and Reeve's contributions to the Canterbury Tales we have, then, to find it in other forms than in the reduction of characters to figures of unalloyed vice and their consequent condemnation. A great deal of significance can be seen in the relationship between these two tales and the tale that precedes them in fragment I, the Knight's Tale. We may remind ourselves that the Miller first sets out to "quite" the Knight rather than to abuse the Reeve.

The Knight's Tale

There are clear parallels between the Knight's Tale and the Miller's Tale. Both tell the stories of the rivalry of two men after the one girl, and many critics have reached the simple conclusion that the Miller's fabliau is an irreverent parody of the Knight's romance. The suggestion is quite valid, but it is unsubtle, and goes only so far in explaining details of the first three tales of fragment I. There are moments when the wording of the Miller's Tale explicitly and pertinently echoes what has been heard in the Knight's Tale, for instance the description of Nicholas's sole occupancy of his room in John the carpenter's house being the same as Arcite's description of the occupancy of the grave:

> Allone, withouten any compaignye
>
> (2779, 3204)

or when Absolon:

> . . .pleyeth Herodes upon a scaffold hye
>
> (3384)

which may recall the preliminaries of the tournament between Palamon and Arcite:

> An heraud on a scaffold made an 'Oo!'
>
> (2533)
>
> *heraud*: herald

but such parallels, of which more will be noted *passim*, are rarely located in such a way as to emphasize the similarities in the plots of the two tales. There are substantial differences between the two as well. Alison's situation is significantly different from Emily's in that she is promised to one of her suitors as well as married; there is no real contest between Nicholas and Absolon — Absolon is striving with Alison, not with his rival — until Nicholas arises to "amenden al the jape" (3799); the only parallel to Theseus's role in the Miller's Tale is Nicholas's construction of a 'theatre' for his fabliau, nor is there any very obvious counterpart to John the carpenter in the Knight's Tale, unless Theseus's "olde fader" Egeus, who comes out with one wise saw in the tale (2837–52), takes this role.

The cultured refinement of the *fin amour* felt by Palamon and Arcite — the engulfing passion for the unattainable object, the stern tests by which the suitors' worthiness is proved, and the coy

exclusion of consideration or anticipation of the carnal side of love
– certainly contrasts with the solidly physical lust of both Nicholas
and Absolon for Alison:

> 'Ywis, but if ich have my wille,
> For deerne love of thee, lemman, I spille.'

(3277–8)

and the indifference of the students in the Reeve's Tale to the
women they 'swyve': Malyne cannot be desired by Alayn for her
beauty, but only for her sex, pleasure in which is assessed in terms
of compensation for the miller's theft; John beds the miller's wife
simply so not to have been outdone by his colleague. Lest one
should be tempted into hostile feminist evaluations of the male
attitudes towards women thus displayed, however, one might note
that the attitudes of their bedfellows are all the same as far as the
women are concerned: in the fabliaux, they show a quite healthy
indifference to their lovers, who they appreciate simply in terms of
their ability to satisfy them physically; and Emily, of course, is quite
unaware of Palamon and Arcite's jealous passion for her for years.

Lessening the sharpness of such contrasts, however, are instances of
the sort of continuity between the Knight's and Miller's Tales that we
have just noted between the Miller's and Reeve's Tales. That the
courtliness of Palamon and Arcite's pursuit of Emily is appropriated by
Absolon in his efforts at 'complaining' to his lady in the Miller's Tale,
as is an *aube,* the morning parting song of lovers, in the Reeve's Tale,
could be regarded just as a matter of parody. But the Knight's Tale
conversely seems to anticipate the exploitation of various senses of the
homonym "queynt" in the following fabliaux: the word first appears as
'elaborate, rare' with reference to the "queynte geres" (which the
Riverside Chaucer renders "strange manners") of lovers, after which it
re-appears in the same sense, and in the sense of 'extinguished', four
more times, conspicuously concentrated in a passage of just fifteen lines
when Emily is in the temple of Diana, once in a pair of rhymes (2321,
2333/4, 2336). The Miller's Tale's first use of the terms is in another
rhyme-pair:

> . . .As clerkes been ful subtil and ful queynte
> And prively he caughte hir by the queynte

(3275–6)

besides using it in the sense of 'extinguished' (3754). Nicholas's "queynte cast" to beguile John (3605) definitely recalls the "queynte geres" of the Knight's Tale's lovers, as does the last occurrence of the term in the "queynte crekes" of the students endeavouring to prevent the miller's thieving in the Reeve's Tale (4051).[10]

The element of parody within the Miller's Tale seems serious if we take the attitudes and behaviour of the characters within the fabliau as being realistic while those in the Knight's Tale are idealistic to a fault. Nothing seems to be at stake other than one's dignity in the Miller's Tale, not even Alison's virtue. The Knight's Tale leads to a tragic and unnatural death, that of Arcite (see especially 2743-61); Absolon is "heeled of his maladye" (3757) but not Arcite (2706). Theseus's attempt to contain the violence of the tournament by limiting the weaponry to be used there (2537-57) seems to be of little effect when the fighting starts:

> Out goon the swerdes as the silver brighte;
> The helmes they tohewen and toshrede;
> Out brest the blood with stierne stremes rede;
> With myghty maces the bones they tobreste.

(2608–11)

tohewen, toshrede, tobreste: cut, shred and break to pieces

This description of the tournament is ironically recalled as the drunken Miller thrusts himself forward; one could imagine that this was the image in the Knight's Tale that most impressed itself upon him, and is guiding his otherwise wandering consciousness as he swears:

> 'By armes, and by blood and bones,
> I kan a noble tale for the nones,
> With which I wol now quite the Knyghtes tale.'

(3125–7)

The tournament, the climax of the violence in the Knight's Tale, is again recalled at the comic climax of the Miller's Tale:

> Ther stomblen steedes stronge, and doun gooth al. . .

(2613)

as John:

10. On Chaucer's use of "queynte" see Benson L D 1984 The "Queynte" Punnings of Chaucer's Critics. In Strohm P and Heffernan T (eds) *Reconstructing Chaucer, Studies in the Age of Chaucer: Proceedings No.* 1 pp 23–47.

. . .with his ax he smoot the corde atwo,
And doun gooth al . . .

(3820-1)

and in a fainter echo at the end of the Reeve's Tale, when
Symkyn's wife:

. . .smoot the millere on his piled skull,
That doun he gooth. . .

(4306-7)

The fabliaux have their violence, undoubtedly, but the broken arm
and cracked head of the carpenter and miller are made to seem minor
injuries, and the burnt bum of Nicholas absurdly unrealistic (although
the narrative comically maintains its meticulous attention to detail):

Of gooth the skyn an hande-brede aboute

(3811)

Altogether the violence of the fabliaux is submerged in their
preposterous humour. The characters concerned lose face not life.
But such absurdity of itself makes the point that in contrasting
romance with fabliau here, we are comparing two forms of
unreality, perhaps two forms of idealism, rather than idealism with
realism.

The Knight's Tale is altogether too complex and ambivalent a
work of literature to sit happily and satisfactorily in any simple
contrast with the tales that follow it. Ambivalent in particular is the
character who is arguably the most prominent in the Knight's Tale
– the one who gives his name to Chaucer's source for the tale,
Boccaccio's *Teseida*, Theseus, Duke of Athens, conqueror of
Femenia and of Thebes. An older view of Theseus as an
outstanding example of wisdom and virtue, chivalry and even
humanity, so pre-eminently so that he can even be quoted as a type
figure of Christ, has undergone a number of challenges recently,
from critics who have found fault in his violence and tyranny, or at
least seen him as distinctly limited in his ability to control the
violent forces of his world.[11] The true critical problem with

---

11. On the 'older' view see Muscatine *Chaucer and the French Tradition* pp 173-90;
Robertson *A Preface to Chaucer* pp 260-6; Pearsall *The Canterbury Tales* pp 115-38;
as the challengers, Scheps 1977; Jones *Chaucer's Knight* pp 192-211; Aers *Chaucer,
Langland and the Creative Imagination* pp 174-95; Cooper *The Structure of the
Canterbury Tales* pp 91-107.

Theseus's ambivalence may be not so much that of deciding which side of the argument we should come down on, pro- or anti-Theseus, but rather that of coming to terms with ambivalence as a regular attribute of truly exceptional political characters in literature – for instance Shakespeare's Henry v, Marvell's Cromwell or Virgil's Aeneas. In such cases the tension of the ambivalence itself becomes an emphatic factor in the construction of the special individuality of the supreme man of state and of destiny who is raised above the arithmetical pros and cons of mundane morality. But Chaucer's Theseus will not stay in place even in those apologetic terms: in one of the few scenes where he is distinctly to the fore and is closely examined, in a critical scene for the direction of the plot, he shows a virtue in his character in his ability to change – to temper what might alternately be called either brutal tyranny or unwavering justice, "juwise" in Palamon's words (1739), with "pitee" and "discrecioun" by substituting the tournament for Palamon and Arcite's immediate execution (1742–825).[12]

Thematically, the Knight's Tale explores the tensions between the set of rules governing man-to-man relationships in the world of chivalrous romance – both face-to-face in battle and side-by-side in fraternity – and the set of rules governing man-to-woman relationships: the rules of love. The tale poses as a form of *demande*, a literary puzzle, the question of which of these has the superior force, arms or love; a question that is allegorized in the conflict between Mars, to whom Arcite prays for victory, and Venus, to whom Palamon addresses his prayer. As the tale turns out, the answer is clear: Venus has the last word, and with Saturn's intervention trumps Mars, as Arcite is mortally injured at the moment of his triumph in the tournament.

An essential point to bear in mind in reading this allegorized conflict between arms and love is that it takes place in an utterly pagan setting; fittingly, the amphitheatre in which Arcite and Palamon's battle is to be staged is surrounded by altars or oratories to the pagan deities (1902–13). The characters within the tale know only this pantheon of deities that is a mythicization of the forces and experiences of humankind. They have no accurate sense of the one true God and thus no hope of the life to come, no higher

---

12. Mann, *Geoffrey Chaucer* pp 171–80, sees Theseus as an outstanding example of what she calls a 'feminised hero' for this capacity to change.

hope than that of attaining human perfection and bliss; of winning their Emily.

> O Cupide, out of alle charitee!
>
> (1623)

– the Christian virtue of *caritas* does not crown the scheme of different types of love in this world. The triumphant deities, Saturn and Venus, are no better than the unstable figure of Lady Fortune, the lowest power governing people's lives, below Providence and Fate in the Boethian scheme of things (1086–9, 1328, 1534–9).[13] It is, no doubt, to emphasize the Christian perspective on this world that Palamon, Arcite and Emily are shown to make their pagan obeisances on a Sunday (2209), with the tournament to take place on the following Tuesday, the day of Mars, the god of war, although Theseus seems to have stipulated a Saturday (the day after Friday, the day of Venus, the day upon which Palamon and Arcite first meet out of prison) as the day for their battle: "this day fifty wekes" (1850). Thus we see Arcite, whose only religious act within the tale is to sacrifice to Mars "in his payen (pagan) wise" (2368–70) to be horribly denatured as his death approaches (2743–60), after which his soul is left only under Mars's care (2815). His funeral, of which the narrative makes such play (2857–966), is conspicuously pagan – on ground hallowed only by being:

> ther as first Arcite and Palamoun
> Hadden for love the bataille hem bitwene
>
> (2858–9)

in a grove, that familiar locus of pagan rites, and his body is cremated along with expensive grave goods. Palamon is at least rewarded for his constant worship of Venus, praying, for instance, to Venus when first he sees Emily (1103–11). Arcite notes the difference between his worldliness and Palamon's religious devotion in this respect:

> Thyn is affeccioun of hoolynesse,
> And myn is love as to a creature. . .
>
> (1158–9)

affeccioun of hoolynesse: religious enthusiasm

---

13. Boethius *de Consolatione Philosophiae*, especially Book II and Book IV: 6–7.

The part of the Knight's Tale that would usually be cited to counter such a picture of the empty paganism of the lives of its characters is Theseus's famed "Firste Moevere" speech (2987–3089), a speech that draws substantially on the concepts of Boethius's *Consolation of Philosophy* to describe the fixed

> days and duracioun
> To al that is engendred in this place

> (2996–7)

the inevitably of death in other words (3027–34), and which concludes that they should

> maken vertu of necessitee

> (3042)

and

> make of sorwes two
> O parfit joye

> (3071–2)

> *o parfit*: one perfect

by marrying Emily to the surviving suitor, Palamon. Curiously, although several pertinent analyses have been made showing that one need not claim that Theseus here enunciates laudable wisdom from a state of Boethian enlightenment, it seems generally unnoted how different Theseus's conception of "the faire cheyne of love" that sets the bounds of elements such as fire, air, water and land is from anything in Boethius. What is in Boethius an image in which it is the *links* within the *rerum series*, the 'series of things', that are in focus, the harmonization of the conflicting elements of the universe, becomes instead an image of a fetter made by a prince who

> Hath stablissed in this wrecched world adoun
> Certeyne dayes and duracioun
> To al that is engendred in this place
> Over the whiche day they may not pace

> (2995–8)

Nicholas's abuse of astrology in the Miller's Tale clearly mocks the concern with providence and the universal natural order reflected by the planets of the Knight's Tale. But perhaps the most brilliantly witty echo of the Knight's Tale in the Miller's Tale is the way in which this Boethian stress on the linkage of the elements is preserved by the teller of the latter: the fire burning Nicholas's backside calls forth a cry for water which brings the carpenter crashing through the air to land. This is a witty pastiche both of Boethius's *Consolation* and of Theseus's speech; its satirical butt is Theseus alone, who is shown by his speech to have no conception of the perfection of the relationship of all with the One and the Good, only of power and of the limits of power. Enlightenment can come only into the Knight's Tale in the very last lines, when the Christian Knight prays for intercession:

> And God, that al this wyde world hath wroght,
> Sende him his love that hath it deere aboght
>
> (3099–100)

and where the verbs shift into the present tense and a picture of true happiness and harmony is presented:

> For now is Palamon in alle wele,
> Lyvynge in blisse, in richesse, and in heele,
> And Emelye hym loveth so tendrely,
> And he hire serveth so gentilly,
> That nevere was ther no word hem bitwene
> Of jalousie or any oother teene.
>
> (3101–6)

>   *wele*: prosperity and joy

So ends the tale, and in such a state end Palamon and Emily (3107). Then the Knight offers the same sociable prayer that the Miller and Reeve will utter:

> And God save al this faire compaignye! Amen.
>
> (3108)

Social and cultural implications

The relationship between the Knight's Tale and the following fabliaux, the Miller's and Reeve's Tales, is usually taken in terms of a clear order of precedence between the former and the latter, between type and antitype: that the Miller's and Reeve's Tales somehow pass comment upon the Knight's Tale. In the present context the pertinent question is rather what the romance implies about the fabliaux. It would be ideal, if it were possible, to find a new perspective, not one reversing the usual one, but one expelling the notion of hierarchy: setting the two types of tale absolutely side by side. In such a comparison one of the key topics to be tackled is that of social class; a topic which Chaucer clearly foregrounds by making the Knight, the highest in secular social rank amongst the pilgrims, be manoeuvred into telling the first tale by Harry Bailly, and by insisting that the tales that follow are "cherles tales". Very significantly, Chaucer does not make this last point only through his mouthpiece, 'Chaucer': he makes the Reeve repeat the point:

> '. . . by youre leve, I shal hym [the Miller] quite anoon;
> Right in his cherles termes wol I speke.'

> (3916–7)

This comes at the end of the Reeve's reflections upon himself in his Prologue. It emphatically makes the point that the Reeve speaks in these so-called "cherles termes" not because he is a churl and can do no other, but because he *chooses* to do so. The crucial notion that a romance is fitting for the Knight and the fabliaux for the churls not by the spontaneous workings of nature but rather by the dictates of social convention is thus recognized and expressed. These connections between character and genre are variable aspects of culture, and when revealed they can be challenged.

In terms of a social commentary, fragment I of the Canterbury Tales gives a sense of a difference between the high and the low in social class, but a sense of real antagonism only within the lower class. It should also be borne in mind here that peasants in positions of power such as a miller and a reeve are less representative of the real churl class in social identity than, say, the silent Ploughman would be. The assumption that the romance is fitting to the Knight is an expression of the ideology of the conservatives of an aristocratically ordered society; romance represents a set of ideal ethics which sets the aristocracy, the knightly class in its imaginary rather than its real state, apart from the other classes. This is a code of ethics that governs relations within that class – men-to-men and men-to-women – and may thus sustain the solidarity of that class. In feudal, and early post-feudal or sub-feudal medieval Europe it is a code that is *de facto* closely allied with Christianity, but it can cross the boundaries of faith, as much, perhaps, as the result of the efforts of the promoters of romance to make this ordering of society seem universal and thus 'natural' as the result of a naive inability to

construe geographically or temporally distant societies in terms
other than those of the formulae near to hand.

In the field of military virtues, correspondingly, the peculiarities
of medieval romance can be seen particularly in an emphasis on the
need for the warrior to be virtuous, and on the ties of fraternity
under arms; qualities that differ markedly from the isolation of the
hero of an earlier age of literature, and his dependence upon his
cunning as well as his strength, courage and determination to
succeed. In the field of love, medieval romances contain a host of
tales from which can be generalized a normative set of forms of
behaviour that is usually labelled 'fin amour' or 'courtly love'; a
normative set that expresses ideals of the delicacy and vulnerability
of love as an experience, the delight which it should be to those
who experience it, and how, consequently, those who desire to
experience it to the full must strive for perfection: a perfection for
men that is expressed in terms of beauty and chivalric virtue; for
women in terms of beauty and maidenly virtue. The testing of
Palamon and Arcite to see which will prove most worthy of Emily
is very evident in the Knight's Tale, yet a sense (at the very least) of
unease may be felt not only at the easy way in which heterosexual
love replaces the fraternity of Palamon and Arcite with enmity but
also in the way in which questions of love must constantly be
resolved by recourse to arms. In the Knight's Tale even the
declaration of the love of Palamon and Arcite to Emily is made in
this form, as she, Ypolita and Theseus discover Palamon and Arcite
fighting as they ride to hunt. The Knight is given an apostrophe to
suggest that he sees love as attaining perfection through the infusion
of arms:

> To fighte for a lady, benedicitee!
> It were a lusty sighte for to see.

> (2115–16)

The thoughtful reader, however, may justifiably observe the Knight
here rather than follow him sheepishly, and may see instead an
uneasy confusion of two areas of idealism that are kept in better
order by being kept separate – as the Knight is separated from his
son, the Squire, in the General Prologue, the former representing
martial chivalry, the latter, by contrast, amorous chivalry.

A teasing question is that of whether we should see the political
considerations of a noble marriage in the same disconcerting light.

We are certainly never allowed to forget that such is the way that most aristocratic marriages were decided upon in medieval Europe, and that Emily cannot be considered free from such terms. When Arcite is released, Palamon fears that he may win Emily "by some aventure or some tretee" (1288) and as soon as he has escaped from prison sees her as an object to be won by war (1475–86). Arcite, somewhat ambiguously, also sees that Emily needs to be constrained in some way by a display of force into marriage:

> And wel I woot, er she me mercy heete,
> I moot with strengthe wynne hire in the place.
>
> (2398–9)

> heete: promise; moot: must

Most conspicuously of all, all of Theseus's "Firste Moevere" speech that paves the way for the marriage of Palamon and Emily is based upon the politics of a parliament at Athens which determines:

> To have of certein countrees alliaunce,
> And have fully of Thebes obeisaunce.
>
> (2973–4)

> obeisaunce: obedience, submission

– the result of which is that Palamon and Emily are summoned (2975–80). Thus Theseus's consequent argument about love can be seen either as a cynical manipulation or a blindly egocentric misuse of a romantic term whose ideal connotations are thus textually stripped away. It is not, however, absolutely necessary to construe Theseus's argument in such hostile terms. An alternative is at least to acknowledge the subtlety of such a mind as can find in such an event the concurrent fulfilment of both private romantic and public political aspirations.

The point of all this is that the strains inherent within the chivalric ethos are evident enough within the Knight's Tale without recourse to the fabliaux as juxtaposed but subordinate commentaries. It would certainly be wrong to deny, or to dismiss as too crude, the fabliaux' sardonic reflection upon the absurd aspects of Palamon and Arcite's passion for the unknowing and largely indifferent Emily and its destructive consequences, but again this absurdity is made amply explicit within the Knight's Tale. It is soon recognized by the more worldly-wise Arcite:

We stryve as dide the houndes for the boon;
They foughte al day, and yet hir part was noon.

(1177–8)

it is underlined by Theseus:

But this is yet the beste game of alle,
That she for whom they han this jolitee
Kan hem therfore as muche thank as me.
She woot namoore of al this hoote fare,
By God, than woot a cokkow or an hare!

(1806–10)

jolitee: sport; hoote: hot

and it can still be repeated by Arcite in the temple of Mars on the
even of the tournament, when he describes himself as:

. . .with love offended moost
That evere was any lyves creature,
For she that dooth me al this wo endure
Ne reccheth nevere wher I synke or fleete.

(2394–7)

dooth: makes; wher: whether; fleete: float)

But while this portrayal of a love relationship and the fabliaux'
versions of amorous couplings are deeply antithetical, it is in the
end more a comparison of one unrealistic model with another than
a qualititative argument.

Nykrog's view of the French fabliaux was that they presented
their own ideal world – an ideal world of everything that was
contrary to the seigneurial elegance that found its expression in the
rarefied ethics of romance. For Muscatine the French fabliaux are
the expression of a system of hedonistic materialism that arose in a
appropriate phase of French cultural history, offering an imaginary
world of individualism and egalitarianism in opportunity, levelling
distinctions of social class and gender.[14] The very different social
settings of the Knight's Tale and the Miller's and Reeve's Tales are
an irreducible contrast between them. The juxtaposition of romance
and fabliaux in fragment I does not enact any form of social

14. Nykrog Les Fabliaux p 253; Muscatine The Old French Fabliaux pp 153–5.

levelling by the abusive parody of romance, however, even if the earthly simplicity of Nicholas and Absolon's desires may serve to demystify the precious passions of Palamon and Arcite. The real thrust of the Miller's and Reeve's fabliaux in terms of levelling social differences comes in the form of deflating the pride of the richer artisan churls – but this not from the viewpoint of those below them, rather from above; in terms that would appeal to the urbane and relatively well informed, and terms which would be perfectly tolerable to the existing order of society, in the circles of the highest in which Chaucer moved and worked.

The structure of fragment I of the Canterbury Tales does not thereby simply reinforce that existing social order. In the first three tales of this fragment Chaucer's writing produces a careful and explicit analysis of the nature of social order that is able to be quite comprehensive without crossing the boundary between analysis and criticism. These tales contain no imitation of the transformation of the social order considered therein, and anticipation of such transformation is left totally implicit – it remains an option available as a critical reader's response to the text. In this we might find a characteristically Chaucerian interest in and tolerance of the diversity of his world: what traditional criticism has referred to in the Miller's words – amusingly, ignoring their context – as 'God's plenty'. These three tales seem to represent the subjectivity of social norms: how the characteristics of knightliness and churlishness are not the unchangeable attributes of characters ranked in class by their intrinsic nature but are fictions perpetuated by continued compliance to cultural norms. In very simple terms this means that the Knight and the churls have freedom of choice whether to conform to their stereotypes or not. Whether they know this or not, and whether or not they would feel or be free to diverge from such stereotypes, are the more pertinent ethical questions.

Such issues lie at the heart of the multilevelled drama that contains the most profound *sentence* of fragment I; the ironic context created by Chaucer's emphasized authorship of all of these supposed reflections of different social orders; by the Miller, possibly, in his ironic re-creation of some of himself in John the carpenter, and the Reeve, certainly, at the end of the triad, being given a 'reflexive' consciousness emphatically lacking in the Knight. The Knight's frequent use of the device of *occupatio*, purportedly to try to summarize relevant information without dwelling upon detail, on some eight occasions from the seventeenth line of the tale onwards (875–85, 1187–9, 1198–201, 1380, 1459–61, 2197–207, 2284–6, 2931–66) in a manner that seems to become increasingly lengthy and therefore ironic, besides one use of the opposite of *occupatio* (1881ff), emphasizes how the romance formulae are taking over and drawing the Knight along in their train: the tale begins to tell the Knight, rather than the Knight the tale. The Reeve, we may claim, and perhaps the Miller too, have the insight to understand this relationship between the subject and its appearance and behaviour; in this way we find a critically maligned character to be attributed by his maker, Chaucer, with one of the author's own potentially very powerful perceptions. The Reeve and the Miller declare their independence in the form of individualism: they transcend the Saturnine "cherles rebellyng" that is all the scheme of the Knight's Tale can envisage for them (2459). Marsha Siegel has claimed that the Knight's and the Miller's Tales represent two opposing views of the human capacity to understand and order the world: the Miller's Tale offering a world of physical objects with discoverable properties and of persons with psychological traits distinct enough for their behaviour to be predicted and understood; the Knight's Tale a world dominated by *fortune*, *aventure* and *cas*. The Reeve, she claims, however, misunderstands the Miller's Tale, to see it as an attack upon himself. We may claim, however, that the Reeve offers us a glimpse of how men with insight may start to take control of their world, and should reflect after that on how we are subject to the influence of the writer as he scripts a role for the reader in the Miller's Prologue.

We ought, of course, to beware of imputing our own ideals of 'niceness' and liberalism to Chaucer: we should note, in this regard, the argument of Lee Patterson, who comes a long way towards recognizing the same thematization of social opposition in fragment I as is described here, but who suggests that Chaucer retreats from the dramatization of class antagonism in which he would have to take sides by using the Reeve as escape mechanism – a churl who produces division within his class, and who serves the seigneurial interest.[15] But this reading depends utterly on a reading of the Reeve's Tale "as the expression of an individual psyche" which is taken to be simply antagonistic to the Miller in the normal way.

15. Patterson L 1987 "No man his reson herde. . .", especially pp 466 and 481–2.

The Reeve and Miller, however, stand in a stable and balanced poise that is clearly definable, definable in particular by the contrasts between them as a pair and the target figures of their fabliaux that are supposed, antagonistically, to represent them. The narrator Miller and Carpenter/Reeve are intrinsically different from the carpenter and miller of their tales and stand figuratively at a point in between those characters – one of whom wishes to caricature himself as the faithful, content and unpretentious working man, the other who has his hopes of social climbing dashed with the 'disparaging' of his daughter. In our desire not to distort Chaucer into modern terms, we should not overlook the fact that he may have had a liberal mind comprehensible to modern inference and intuition.

THE COOK'S TALE

Fragment I of the Canterbury Tales ends in a rather confusing manner with the Cook's Prologue and fifty-eight lines of the Cook's Tale. There has been some discussion over whether this Cook's Tale is to be seen as a concluded piece of work or not and over whether it is the opening fragment of yet another fabliau or of some other form of tale. It has even recently been questioned whether Chaucer left it in this state or had in fact written more of it which has for some reason not survived.

Although a few manuscripts of the Canterbury Tales omit this prologue and tale altogether, we can at least be sure that it is in its right place in the Tales. The Cook's Prologue forms an unambiguous link with the Reeve's Tale, and a number of the sort of echoes and parallels that we have already noticed between the Knight's, Miller's and Reeve's Tales continue in the Cook's Prologue and Tale too. The theme of *pryvetee*, formerly "Goddes pryvetee" but now at the mundane level, emerges in the Prologue (4333–4, 4388). In the context of the Miller's and Reeve's Tales, too, the Cook's promise concerning his tale:

'I wol yow telle, as well as evere I kan,
A litel jape that fil in our citee.'

(4342–3)

with the "jape" and the urban context, necessarily raises expectations that a fabliau will follow. That the Cook has fabliaux to tell is indicated by his warning to the Host, named here for the first time, "Herry Bailly", that he can tell a tale "of an hostiler" by which "thou shalt be quit". But this, apparently, is a tale he will tell later on in the tale-telling game, not yet (4358–62).

In context, too, the Cook's Tale seems to start off as we might expect of a fabliau that follows the Miller's and Reeve's Tales. It opens with a description of the only major character in its short length, a fellow called Perkyn Revelour. The Reveler we can identify as a type that makes an occasional appearance amongst the French fabliaux, such as, for instance, in *Le Prestre et les deus ribaus*. Much of the initial portrayal of this character makes him appear colourful, vital and bright, with many echoes of the descriptions of Alison and Absolon in the Miller's Tale:

> Gaillard he was as goldfynch in the shawe,
> Broun as a berye, a propre short felawe,
> With lokkes blake, ykembd ful fetisly.
> Dauncen he koude so wel and jolily
> That he was cleped Perkyn Revelour.
> He was as ful of love and paramour
> As is the hyve ful of hony sweete. . .
>
> (4367–73)
>
> He loved bet the taverne than the shoppe. . .
>
> (4376)
>
> . . .in the toune nas ther no prentys
> That fairer koude caste a paire of dys
> Than Perkyn koude, and therto he was free
> Of his dispense, in place of pryvetee.
>
> (4385–8)

gaillard: jolly; shawe: forest; fetisly: neatly; cleped: called; dys: dice

The reference in the last line quoted here to a "place of pryvetee", however, momentarily introduces a serious shadow in the description, as the reader's mind turns back to the significant use of the term "pryvetee" in the Miller's Tale: not necessarily to discover some new perspective here on a theme developed earlier; it is sufficient just to check the flow of one's directed reading and wonder if any such productive connection can be made.

From the very next line of the Cook's Tale the tone definitely changes:

> That fond his maister wel in his chaffare
> For often tyme he foond his box ful bare. . .
>
> (4389–90)
>
> *chaffare*: business

A new perspective is introduced: that of the commercial interest of the master of this apprentice to the "craft of vitaillers". We are told then how the riotousness of an apprentice is at his master's expense, and how "revel and trouthe" are always at loggerheads. It is tempting, in context, to read the line that:

> thefte and riot, they been convertible
>
> (4395)

which simply states that theft and riot are so closely akin as to be interchangeable,[16] as implying also that theft and riot together are convertible into other terms, for instance into someone's (the master's) expense. Such a reading is possible, but it must be stressed that *convertible* does not develop its specifically economic sense until the late eighteenth century.

V. J. Scattergood has shown particularly well how the portrait of Perkyn Revelour can be likened to those of a particular type of "urban wastrel" which is familiar in satirical literature from the late fourteenth century through to the early sixteenth century. The closest parallel to Perkyn Revelour in Chaucer's writing is undoubtedly to be found in the three "riotoures" of the Pardoner's Tale, three drinking, whoring and gambling wastrels who find death, two murdering the third in order to deprive him of his share of a treasure of golden florins they have found before they die by his contrivance through drinking poisoned wine he has brought for them. The Pardoner's Tale is a dark, foreboding and tremendously powerful sermon, utterly different from the tone of the fabliaux with which the Cook's fragment on Perkyn Revelour is juxtaposed. Kolve's chapter on the Cook's Tale gives a useful survey of attempts by post-Chaucerian improvers or finishers of the Canterbury Tales to provide the Cook's Tale with a conclusion, showing how regularly they did so by providing the tale with an explicitly moral and homiletic ending. The tone of the tale becomes increasingly moralistic as it nears its abrupt end. The boy's wickedness is contrasted with his master's patience:

16. Cooper *The Canterbury Tales* p 120.

> This joly prentis with his maister bood,
> Til he wer ny out of his prentishood,
> Al were he snybbed bothe erly and late,
> And somtyme lad with revel to Newegate.

(4399–402)

> *bood*: remained; *ny*: nearly; *snybbed*: rebuked; *lad*: lead; *Newegate*: Newgate prison

Even his imprisonment is treated jocularly and with festivity. When his master finally has had enough of him, thinking on a proverb:

> 'Wel bet is roten appul out of hoord
> Than that it rotie al the remenaunt.'

(4406–7)

> *rotie*: should spread rot to

we see how far this character stands from the innocently amoral Alison of the Miller's Tale, whose:

> mouth was sweete as bragot or the meeth
> Or hoord of apples leyd in hey or heeth.

(3261–2)

and this is followed by a distinctly homiletic inference in the Cook's Tale:

> So fareth it by a riotous servaunt;
> It is ful lasse harm to let him pace,
> Than he shende al the servauntz in the place.

(4408–10)

> *shende*: corrupt

To corroborate our sense that the Cook's Tale has taken a distinctly moral turn in these lines we may remind ourselves that the Cook seems to have come on the Canterbury pilgrimage along with the five guildsmen (General Prologue: 361–81). His alliance with their interests, the prentice master's interests, is thus dramatically fitting.

There is little left of the tale after this – just nine lines after Perkyn leaves his master in which Perkyn moves home to dwell with:

> . . .a compeer of his owene sort,
> That lovede dys, and revel, and disport,
> And hadde a wyf that heeld for countenaunce,
> A shoppe, and swyved for hir sustenaunce.

(4419–22)

> *compeer* : friend; *for countenaunce*: for appearance's sake

Here ends the Cook's Tale, and the scribe of the Hengwrt manuscript of Chaucer seems to have concluded, after some doubt, "Of this Cokes tale maked Chaucer na moore". There have been attempts to explain the Cook's Tale as being in fact complete at this point. E. G. Stanley argued that the Cook narrow-sightedly perceives and adopts a theme of 'herbergage' from the preceding tales. In the incautious handling of herbergage John the carpenter and Symkyn the miller allow themselves to become the target figures of fabliau intrigue. The Cook by contrast produces a "recipe for carefree *herbergage*" after which "there is no more for him to say". Emily Jensen has suggested alternatively that the tales of fragment I show varying forms of male competition for a woman, a constant element in which is a "degenerative movement" from the Knight's Tale through the Miller's and Reeve's Tales to the Cook's, which concludes with the negation of male competition; a tale in which all cunning is excluded and male competition is reduced to a game of chance (dicing). Women are hired in a brothel, and the tale concludes where a woman has taken control of her own monetary and sexual affairs "and swyved for hir sustenaunce" – pretty much in the same way as the wife in the Shipman's Tale does.

While such interpretations may mean that no more is needed by the Cook's Tale as a thematic contribution to fragment I, they do not solve the problem that more is needed by the Cook's Tale as a narrative product: it conspicuously lacks the marked conclusion that all the preceding tales have had, either in a conclusion within the tale or in the form of an endlink. The only other tales of the Canterbury Tales that finish in this abrupt way are the interrupted tales: the Squire's Tale and 'Chaucer's' Tale of Sir Thopas. The Monk's Tale is also interrupted according to its endlink, which is also the Prologue to the Nun's Priest's Tale, although one would certainly not suppose the Monk's Tale to have been cut off from the internal evidence of the tale on its own. A simple solution to the curtailment of the Cook's Tale can be proposed, which draws on its associations with the fabliaux. In its final line we meet one of our marked fabliau terms, *swyved*, which has appeared in both the Miller's and the Reeve's Tales. If, as our analysis has suggested, the Cook's Tale makes an abrupt swing away from the fabliau in the direction of the moral tale after some twenty-four lines, then the word *swyved* is conspicuously out of place in its new generic context. The Cook has indecently broken the rules of literary decorum, and this provides a perfect excuse for an intervention to stop the tale-telling at precisely the point where it does stop. This is a breach of decorum quite different from that of the Miller's intervention at the end of the Knight's Tale; superficially the Miller, and the Reeve, confirm cultural norms by sounding like boorish churls.

Again we can find support for such an interpretation of the ending of the Cook's Tale by reference to the dramatic context, in particular to the characterization of the Cook. Despite Kolve's doubts about his presentation, he has an unwholesome physical and moral image in his General Prologue portrait, with his "mormal" on his shin – supposedly a sign of intemperancy and/or uncleanliness – and appears as a drunken slob in the Manciple's Prologue (IX: 1–92). The idea of scratching the Cook's back, introduced in his Prologue, is a particularly nasty one (4326). His feeling of such quasi-physical pleasure at the Reeve's Tale may also be read in terms of the extremity and confusion of feelings of pleasure that may come with drunkenness: he bursts out with wild thrill after the Reeve has finished to say that he too can tell a "litel jape", laughingly impervious to the Host's "ful sooth" on the Cook's flyblown and re-heated wares. In his comprehensive muddlement he has a lack of self-control and of self-knowledge that is wholly the opposite to that of the Reeve, his predecessor in the tale-telling game. He confuses the rules of the literary game, and this is why he is pulled up short.

The Summoner's and Merchant's Tales, and other adaptations of the fabliau by Chaucer

THE RELATIONSHIP OF THE SUMMONER'S AND MERCHANT'S TALES

Having studied, in the previous two chapters, three of Chaucer's Canterbury Tales which can be regarded as pure fabliau narratives irrespective of the complex uses to which Chaucer puts them, we come now to consider a number of cases of adaptation of the fabliau by Chaucer. There are two of the Canterbury Tales that contain a basic fabliau tale with something added on: a relatively simple example in the Summoner's Tale and a considerably more complicated one in the Merchant's Tale. There are also significant echoes of features of the fabliau dispersed within the remainder of Chaucer's writings, some of which are quite clear and sustained and of fundamental importance to a study of Chaucer's use of the genre in the Canterbury Tales.

The Summoner's and Merchant's Tales fall together here principally for reasons of orderliness and convenience, but having juxtaposed the two certain intriguing links between them become apparent. It is accepted that the two tales stand close together in the best order(s) of the Canterbury Tales, the Summoner's Tale at the end of fragment III (group D), following the contributions of the Wife of Bath and the Friar, separated from the Merchant's Tale at the end of fragment IV (group E) only by the Clerk's Tale. Both the Clerk's Tale – at least in its final version – and the Merchant's Tale contain explicit references to the Wife of Bath which make best sense if the Wife of Bath's Prologue and Tale have preceded them (IV: 1170ff, 1685–7). The classic 'marriage group' argument sees a sequence Wife of Bath–Clerk–Merchant as being 'interrupted' by the skirmish between the Friar and the Summoner.[1]

There are several clear echoes of each of these two tales in the other. The most important of these are anticipations in the friar's sermon on ire in the Summoner's Tale of images that are dispersed throughout the Merchant's Tale but which may be argued to lie close to the essence of the Merchant's Tale and its moral themes. Ire, for instance, sleeps in the bosom (III: 1993) and is like:

. . .the serpent that so slily crepeth
Under the gras and styngeth subtilly

(III: 1994–5)

while Damian, the "servant traytour" is:

Lyk to the naddre in bosom sly untrewe

(IV: 1786)

  naddre: adder, snake

Thomas is the name of the "goode man", apparently a well-off peasant, in the Summoner's Tale whom the friar bids emulate St Thomas the Apostle in church-building (III: 1974–80). The friar himself is not reluctant to liken himself to Christ and the Apostles. The Merchant swears by "Seint Thomas of Ynde" in his prologue (III: 1230), an oath which has been held to be of considerable significance in characterizing the Merchant-narrator and in the interpretation of his tale.[2] The compliant counsellor Placebo of the Merchant's Tale is anticipated by the friar's maxim:

Syngeth *Placebo* and 'I shal, if I kan',
But if it be unto a povre man

(III: 2075–6)

  placebo (Latin): I shall please; *povre*: poor

– and this moreover is in the context of an exemplary tale of a lord who is warned by one counsellor that his drinking is destroying his sight (cf. January's blindness) and other faculties. Soon after this comes another image that recurs in the Merchant's Tale:

---

1. Kittredge G L 1912 Chaucer's Discussion of Marriage, *MP* 9 (1911–12) pp 435–67.
2. Arrathoon 1986 pp 256–66, claims that the Merchant's swearing by Thomas of India, and his supposedly antimarital views, identify him as a (quasi-)Manichean heretic. But the Merchant immediately eschews the generalization of the antimarital maxim he has enunciated (III: 1228–32).

Hoold nat the develes knyf ay at thyn herte.

(III: 2090)

a warning which, like another important echo in the Parson's Tale (X: 859), underlines January's serious moral delusion:

A man may do no synne with his wyf,
Ne hurte hymselven with his owene knyf.

(IV: 1839–40)

The chronological and developmental relationship between the Summoner's Tale and the Merchant's Tale can only be a matter of speculation, though the prevailing opinion, for what it is worth, suggests they were written fairly close together, and put into their final form following the Wife of Bath's Prologue and Tale sometime around the mid-1390s. As we shall see, the Wife of Bath's Prologue also draws quite distinctly on fabliau material. It is tempting, in consequence, to imagine these tales as a product of a period of experimentation with fabliau: what has been called "Chaucer's greatest interest in his maturity".[3] It is not implausible that Chaucer came across themes and motifs in his composition of part of the Summoner's Tale which he was to exploit more profoundly in the Merchant's Tale.

THE SUMMONER'S TALE

Analogues and source

Contrary to a commonly repeated assertion, we can identify sufficient analogues to the Summoner's Tale, amongst the Old French fabliaux, to form a clear idea of an Old French source used – perhaps indirectly – by Chaucer for this tale. Jacques de Baisieux's early fourteenth-century *Dis de le Vescie a prestre*, 'Tale of a priest's bladder', is generally recognized to be similar. This is a tale comically asserted to be "un voir", 'a truth' not a fable, in which a dying priest is approached for a bequest by two begging Jacobin friars and decides in his anger at their shamelessness to bequeathe them his bladder. To shame them publicly he has them return to him, with their prior, and announces the bequest in front of the mayor and councillors of the town, creating the laughter of "tot

3. Brewer 'The Fabliaux' p 296.

chil ki la demorerent", 'all those who dwelt there'. Interestingly, the author's signature at the end of the *dis* includes the information that he has taken the tale from a Dutch source. A more distant analogue appears in *Les trois Meschines*, 'The three girls', where a face powder that three girls are to share is dispersed by a fart when one of them attempts to wet it with her urine.

Probably the most important analogue, however, is one that is strangely ignored or overlooked: a short fabliau by a French author of a generation or two before Jacques de Baisieux, Rutebeuf, the very title of which suggests a connection with the Summoner's Tale, *Le Pet au vilain*, 'The peasant's fart'. This anecdote explains how peasants' souls are barred from Hell – as well as from Heaven – after their death, because once a devil, sent to collect a dying peasant's soul, believing that the soul left the body "par le cul", 'through the arse', hung a leather sack on the peasant's backside into which the peasant farts, mightily. The devil carries this back to Hell, where he releases it to the offence of "chacun des maufiez", 'every single demon'. The devils then meet in "chapitre", 'chapter' – a term that is used of the conclave of a friary amongst other things (cf. the Summoner's Tale, line 1945) – and agree:

> Que jameis nuns arme n'aport
> qui de vilain sera issue:
> ne puet estre qu'ele ne pue.

> (That no one should ever fetch a soul
> that had come out of a peasant:
> it is impossible for it not to stink.)

The relevant details here are the deathbed 'gift' of a fart, and the fact that it is shared out in the devils' confraternity. A late fifteenth-century French play that is related to *Le Pet au vilain* is *La Farce du Munyer*, 'The farce of the miller'. This farce is discussed in more detail in the next chapter. It is pertinent to note here that like the Summoner's Tale it combines the so-called 'satiric legacy' of a scatological deathbed 'gift' with a scene of adulterous dalliance between the wife of the dying man and a cleric, in such a way as suggests that the combination was traditional rather than something re-invented for the play. It is significant, too, that Rutebeuf is particularly known as an antifraternal writer – a satirist or critic of the friars. In the Summoner's Tale, Chaucer builds his source(s) up into a powerful satirical assault upon the familiar type represented by its target figure, the greedy and luxurious friar John.

Antifraternal satire

The dramatic context in which this attack appears is that of a quarrel between the Friar and the Summoner – a context superficially similar to that of the Miller's and Reeve's Tales. The hostility between the Friar and the Summoner is one that is historically intrinsic to their two offices, rooted in the conflict between friars and secular clergy who both had the right to hear confession and to impose penance and restitution. Very early on in the Summoner's Tale we learn that the friar John urged the people in his sermons to give to the friars and explicitly not to "possessioners": to secular or monastic clergy living on endowments. Penance and restitution are prominent themes of the Summoner's Tale. In light of the clerkly character of the humour that we saw in the Miller's and Reeve's Tales, it is of interest to note that historical records reveal several summoners who were also designated *clericus*.[4] Although the portrait of Chaucer's Summoner has none of the wit and dexterity of the normal literary clerk of the fabliau, we may still suspect a touch of realism in the Summoner having recourse to this mode of attack on the Friar – just as it is appropriate for the Friar to assault the Summoner through a homily. The argument between the two characters surfaces at the end of the Wife of Bath's Prologue (III: 829–50), where an apparently innocent comment from the Friar provokes the Summoner to complain in general that:

A frere wol entremette hym everemo

(III: 834)

– which might be paraphrased as 'A friar must always shove his oar in'. This argument is then taken up again immediately after the end of the Wife of Bath's Tale, at the beginning of the Friar's Prologue.

The Friar's Tale that follows this is in fact a powerful sermon about a summoner who rides with a devil as his sworn brother bailiff, and who takes the summoner's soul to Hell after the summoner has sworn an oath "the foule feend me fecche" (1610)

4. Haselmayer 1937.

and been cursed by an old woman from whom he is trying to
extort money:

> 'Unto the devel blak and rough of hewe
> Yeve I thy body and my panne also!'

(1622–3)

Several critics have suggested that the Friar's Tale is itself a
fabliau,[5] but really neither it, nor the Pardoner's Tale to which it is
quite similar in certain respects, have much in common with the
fabliaux. There is deception in the Pardoner's Tale, as two of three
"riotoures" plot to murder their third companion to deprive him of
his share of a hoard of coins they have found, while he is away
fetching wine for them, which he poisons to kill them, but this
murderous conspiracy and device barely have the ingenuity in them
to merit calling a trick. The Pardoner's Prologue and Tale,
separately, and the Friar's Tale give haunting examples of the
beguiling nature of the confession of a threatening wickedness in
plain truth. The Pardoner declares his own corruptness; the old
man of the Pardoner's Tale points out for the "riotoures" the road
to death; the devil-yeoman of the Friar's Tale tells the summoner
the plain and shocking truth:

> 'Brother,' quod he, 'wiltow that I thee telle?
> I am a feend; my dwellyng is in helle. . .'

(1447–8)

This, as we shall see, especially in the context of German fabliau
tales, is paralleled in the medieval fabliau tradition. But here,
distinctly, the motif is used in an explicitly spiritual not a sexual
context, and consequently without any congruent fabliauesque
diction.

In the antifraternalism of the Summoner's Tale a great deal of
irony is deployed at the expense of the friar, but it is also ironic
that the moral criticism within the tale rebounds upon the
Summoner too. This happens much more clearly here than in the
supposedly parallel case of the Reeve. This ironic configuration

---

5. Dempster *Dramatic Irony* pp 42–5; Pearsall *The Canterbury Tales* pp 101 and 217–22.
   There is a medieval English reference to the story of the Friar's Tale, by one
   Robert Ripon of Durham, as "in parte iocosa", 'partly funny': quoted in
   Wenzel S 1979 The Joyous Art of Preaching; or, the Preacher and the Fabliau,
   Anglia 97 pp 304–25, on p 313.

appears in its simplest and most evident form in the theme of anger (Ire) and madness in the tale. The theme is clear in the opening lines of the Summoner's Prologue:

> This Somonour in hys styropes hye stood;
> Upon this Frere his herte was so wood
> That lyk an aspen leef he quook for ire.
>
> (1665–7)

and re-emerges within the Tale, firstly in the form of the anger of the "goode man", Thomas, from whom the friar is trying to wheedle more money. Thomas's wife effectively invites the friar to preach on ire by telling him that her husband "is as angry as a pissemyre [ant(!)]" (1825), an anger which, it is gradually revealed, can be attributed to a combination of Thomas's suffering in his illness, the death of a child, and the apparent ineffectiveness of all the gifts he has given the friars to alleviate any of this (1824–31, 1851–3, 1948–53). So the friar, after further admonitions to Thomas to give, particularly to himself (1954–80), preaches him a long sermon on the subject (1981–2093), ending with a direction to Thomas to confess to him. Anger and madness are linked again in a proverb of the friar's towards the end of his homily:

> 'Ne be no felawe to an irous man,
> Ne with no wood man walke by the weye,
> Lest thee repente.'
>
> (2086–8)

After hearing that Thomas has already confessed to his curate and done penance, the friar continues to beg gold – theatrically, on one knee – at which:

> This sike man wex wel ny wood for ire
>
> (2121)

and presents him with the gift of a mighty fart, for which the friar has had to grope beneath his buttocks. The friar's reaction continues the theme:

> The frere up stirte as dooth a wood leoun
>
> (2152)

> up stirte: started up

after which he goes off "with a full angry chere [countenance]", grinding his teeth with wrath (2158–61), and carrying his anger "in a rage" to the village manor house, to the lord of which he is also confessor (2162–9).

The friar's persistence and indulgence in a fault that he has just preached against is a simple instance of hypocrisy, and it is hypocrisy in general, rather than anger and ill-temper, that lies at the heart of this friar's faults. We have already seen an instance of it in the friar's *Placebo* maxim, telling poor men their vices, but flattering lords: a rule of thumb that does not save him from the ridicule of the lord's household at the end of the tale. The model friar was free of worldly possessions – hence the friars' dependence on begging – and such is the virtue this friar claims for himself and his brother friars:

'We lyve in poverte and in abstinence. . .'

(1873)

This friar, however, looks after his creature comforts well, driving the cat away from what is presumably the warm and comfy spot on the bench on which he wishes to sit while his companion and his "knave" go on into town to see to his lodgings (1770–80). The friar's shameless gluttony is amusingly revealed:

'Now, maister,' quod the wyf, 'er that I go,
What wol ye dyne? I wol go theraboute.'
'Now, dame,' quod he, 'now *je vous dy sanz doute*,
Have I nat of a capon but the lyvere,
And of youre softe breed nat but a shyvere,
And after that a roosted pigges heed –
But that I nolde no beest for me were deed –
Thanne hadde I with yow hoomly suffisaunce.
I am a man of litel sustenaunce;
My spirit hath his fostryng in the Bible. . .'

(1836–45)

je vous dy sanz doute: I tell you truthfully; *capon*: chicken; *shyvere*: thin slice;
hoomly suffisaunce: simple sufficiency; *sustenaunce*: consumption; *fostryng*: nour-
ishment

The poverty the friar claims contrasts grossly with his avarice for Thomas's money, an avarice that is neatly summed up by a telling rhyme:

'I walke and fisshe Cristen mennes soules
To yelden Jhesu Crist his propre *rente*;

To sprede his word is set al myn *entente*.'

(1820–2)

    yelden: yield, give

It seems that the friar adds lechery to his other indulgences, for there are abundant hints in the text that he enjoys a sexual relationship with Thomas's wife. He greets her intimately:

> The frere ariseth up ful curteisly,
> And hire embraceth in his armes narwe,
> And kiste hire sweete, and chirketh as a sparwe
> With his lyppes. . .

(1802–5)

    narwe: closely; *chirketh*: chirrups

– the sparrow's association with lechery is traditional, and is drawn on in the General Prologue portrait of the Summoner:

> As hoot he was and lecherous as a sparwe

(I: 626)

The subsequent conversation of the wife and the friar carries certain clear reminiscences of that between wife and monk in the Shipman's Tale; the wife offers intimate details of her failure to win "desport" of her husband in bed, despite offering him "al that he kan desire" (which sounds very much like the fabliau concept of "Goddes foyson" that we have seen in the Miller's Prologue (1826–31)), and the friar eventually responds in an appropriately conspiratorial way:

> 'I pray yow, dame, ye be nat anoyed,
> Though I so freendly yow my conseil shewe,
> By God! I wolde nat telle it but a fewe.'

(1848–50)

This, however, is enough to suggest the friar's sin in this regard, and the topic is not allowed to become a dominant one in the tale; the wife next deflects the direction of the conversation by revealing – in a remarkably unconcerned tone – the death of her child (1851–3).

    Hypocrisy is a form of lying, a theme that of itself is carefully identified and emphasized by a variety of comments on the use of 'text and gloss'. *Glosen*, 'to gloss', that is, initially meant to explain and comment upon some authoritative text, which was one of the most fundamental modes of medieval scholarship. By Chaucer's time it had taken on a clear alternative meaning of 'to lie', 'to deceive', no doubt through intermediary senses of 'to complicate', 'to mystify'. Again here we find ourselves faced with an aspect of medieval literary theory concerning *auctoritee*. The Summoner states his friar's dishonesty bluntly:

> He served hem with nyfles and with fables.
>
> (1760)

> *nyfles*: idle tales

which interestingly provokes the Friar into acknowledging his identification with the Summoner's target figure:

> 'Nay, ther thou lixt, thou Somonour!' quod the Frere.
>
> (1761)

> *thou lixt*: thou liest

The ambiguity of *glosen* makes the friar's general boast:

> 'Glosynge is a glorious thyng, certeyn. . .'
>
> (1793)

richly ironic, and we eventually come to see a specific example of a gloss/deceit by the friar in an exposition of one of the beatitudes of Matthew's gospel:

> 'But herkne now, Thomas, what I shal seyn.
> I ne have no text of it, as I suppose,
> But I shal fynde it in a maner glose,
> That specially oure sweete Lord Jhesus
> Spak this by freres, when he seyde thus:
> "Blessed be they that povere in spirit been".'
>
> (1918–23)

> *a maner*: a sort of

The key technique by means of which the friar's misrepresentation of sacred texts and images is exemplified in the Summoner's Tale is that of parody. The Summoner's friar is a thorough parody of the original Franciscan ideal and its New Testament apostolic prototypes. Before showing this in detail we might once again pause just to note that comparable parody may be used to reveal the misdeeds of the Summoner. P. A. Olson has pointed out that the linkage of the Summoner with the Pardoner (General Prologue: 623–714), with hints of homosexuality in their relationship, is reminiscent of the twin papal keys of punishment (the Summoner's field) and forgiveness/indulgence (the Pardoner's field). The pairing of these two corrupt ecclesiastics thus forms a grotesque parody of the Church.[6]

St Francis, who founded the fraternal movement, sought to model his brotherhood of friars on the apostolic model of the New Testament, particularly on Christ's directives given in Matthew 10 and Luke 9–10. The friar calls upon Thomas to emulate St. Thomas the Apostle (1974–80), and with a familiar pun on *sonne* (sun/Son) the friar does not scruple to claim likeness to Christ for himself and his brethren:

> 'For whoso wolde us fro this world bireve,
> So God me save, Thomas, by youre leve,
> He wolde bireve out of this world the sonne.'

(2111–13)

> *bireve*: remove

The Summoner's friar goes about "with scrip and tipped staf" (1737), the very opposite of the Biblical model:

> "Carry neither purse, nor scrip, nor shoes. . ."

(Luke 9:4)

> "Provide neither gold, nor silver, nor brass in your
> purses, nor scrip for your journey, neither two coats,
> neither shoes, nor yet staves. . ."

(Matthew 10:9–10)

The direction not to carry a purse is met by the friar being accompanied by a "sturdy harlot" carrying a sack (1754–5). John is preoccupied with extorting money from this sick man; Christ directed his disciples to "heal the sick" (Matthew 10:8; Mark 6:13; Luke 9:2). But the parody which is at the same time the most entertaining and the most shocking comes in the form of the gift of the fart to the friars, which in the Summoner's Tale is assimilated to the gift of the Holy Spirit to the apostles. The point is made in the coda to the tale, the scene in the manor house where the young squire presents a scheme for the sharing of the fart. Twelve other friars, like the twelve apostles, will sit round a wheel, to whom the fart will descend as the Holy Spirit descended. It has been noted that the apostles are often sitting in a circle in medieval depictions of Pentecost, and that a small number of representations of the

---

6. Olson *The Canterbury Tales and the Good Society* pp 183–213.

descent of the Holy Spirit show it coming down what look like the spokes of a wheel.[7]

The squire's stipulation that friar John should have the "firste fruyt" of the fart (2275–7) recalls the image of the "fruit of the [Holy] Spirit", used by St Paul (Galatians 5: 22–3). This fruit is "love, joy, peace, longsuffering, gentleness, goodness, faith, meekness, temperance" – all virtues which are markedly lacking in friar John. One of the most important gifts the Holy Spirit brings to the apostles at Pentecost is that of speaking in tongues: the ability to present and expound the gospel, to bring men to Christ and to prophesy, in all languages (Acts 2). This gift of "glosynge" is clearly abused by the friar, as in his showy habit of speaking in tongues, in Latin (1770, 1934, 2075, 2192) or French (1832, 1838). When the apostles first speak in tongues they are mocked: "These men are full of new wine" (Acts 2.13); it seems fitting, therefore, that the friar should use his Latin to represent an indulgent possessioner's burp:

'Lo, "buf!" they say, "*cor meum eructavit!*" '

(1934)

("*my heart has emitted!*")

and to produce what sounds like a drunken hiccup when he arrives at Thomas's house:

'*Deus hic!*' quod he. . . .

(1770)

('*God [be] here!*')

A study by John V. Fleming has also identified an iconographic reference of considerable thematic significance in the Summoner's Prologue, where a friar, taken to Hell in a vision, is shown the special nest of friars in that place, under Satan's tail, in his "ers", his 'arse'. This is a pastiche of depictions of *Mariae misericordia* (Mary's mercy) which show her sheltering and holding her loved ones under her cloak. *Misericordia*, it appears, is the antidote to the sin of Ire, and is in the gift of Mary; *misericordia*, further, is known as the first fruit of penance. The friar, in the Summoner's Tale, perverts the ritual of penance for worldly gain; it is heavily ironic, for

---

7. See Levitan 1971 and Cooper *The Canterbury Tales* p 177.

instance, that he should cite a maxim that concludes "*Lest* thee repente" (2086–8) immediately before directing Thomas to "lef thyn ire" and to:

> '. . . shewe to me al thy confessioun.'
>
> (2089–93)

Thematically linked to such depictions of the ideal and its inverse in the Summoner's Tale is a linguistic trait we have already met in Chaucer's fabliaux, most strikingly in the Shipman's Tale: the persistent reversion of certain terms to a basic carnal meaning as opposed to a more figurative and less crude sense. This of course is very much in line with the regular crudity and demystification of language and behaviour in the fabliau. Particularly striking examples include *grope*, used first by the friar as an elegant, figurative term for probing and examining a person's conscience in confession (1816–18) and later more crudely as the friar gropes around Thomas's anus for the promised gift (2147–9). Similarly, the friar claims to beg gold in order to complete a not yet "parfourned fundement", the unfinished foundations of his cloister, but *fundement* also has a scatological sense, 'excrement'. Even the "develes ers" of the Prologue is reduced by this scatological undercurrent from a nauseous, horrifying *image* of a place of torment to a more literal representation of the friars' world.

The organization of the antifraternal satire of the Summoner's Tale is, therefore, quite overt; what is very much harder to decide with confidence is how intense a condemnation this text presents. The Summoner's damnation of the friars is clear enough – he sends them into Satan's arse. But the Summoner's attitude is coloured by the same vice of anger as his tale reveals in his friar. We have seen the friar's appropriation of the role of Christ – the "sonne" – to himself and his brethren; are we to follow Alan Levitan in seeing the corrupt friar and his coven as Antichrist and his followers? Or are we rather to follow Helen Cooper in seeing here a less damning theme of the reduction of spiritual ideals to deformed earthly counterparts?[8] It is pertinent to note here that this problem is very similar to that faced in the Miller's Tale, with its extensive religious symbolism. In the case of the Miller's Tale it was argued that the religious dimension of the tale did assert the existence of a sure set

8. *Op. cit.* footnote 7.

of Christian values, but that the tale itself was still comic — a wry rather than a puritan view of human lowness, and a narrative exercise that may end in frank uninhibited laughter. The argument of consistency is a valid one in favour of taking the Summoner's Tale's portrayal of the friar in much the same terms. For Chaucer and his audience the character may be adequately punished, and chastened, by the laughter that falls upon him. Thoughts of the Devil are banished at the end: Thomas is not demon-possessed, but a man whose "heigh wit" has trumped the friar's truly "symple wit" (2290–2, 1789); and Jankyn the squire wins a new gown for genuinely 'amending' all of *this* jape.

It is worth noting briefly how Chaucer handles the denouement of the truly fabliau part of the Summoner's Tale technically, for we find much that is shared with the Miller's and Reeve's Tales. Between lines 2121 and 2161 we have a rapid dramatic denouement which nevertheless manages to bring to a climax many of the themes and motifs that have marked the Summoner's Prologue and Tale — and indeed the skirmish between the Friar and the Summoner at the end of the Wife of Bath's Prologue. Abundantly clear are the themes of anger and madness, found in Thomas at the start of this passage (2121) but transferred to the friar via the fart (2152–61). Equally clearly illustrated is the friar's avarice:

'A!,' thoghte the frere, 'that shal go with me!'
And doun his hand he launcheth to the clifte
In hope for to fynde ther a yifte. . .

(2144–6)

clifte: cleft, crack

The vulgar physicality of the fabliau world is clearly emphasized, particularly by repeated reference to the friar's hand, and by repetition of the word *grope*. This goes with characteristic fabliau language, either in the form of reference to the *clifte* and *tuwel* (anus) — or in the marked form, as in *fart*. The friar here is searching Thomas's backside for what he can find just as the friar of the Prologue asks a question the answer to which lies in Satan's arse. The friar's intimate intrusion under Thomas's bedclothes acts as a form of gloss on the Summoner's early outburst:

A frere wol entremette hym everemo

(III: 834)

and also echoes the suggestion of a sexual relationship with Thomas's wife; at the same time that echo is 'perverted' into a configuration with potential homosexual overtones – which in turn recalls the configuration of Summoner and Pardoner in the General Prologue. Adding cohesion to the denouement is an effective line of animal imagery: Thomas farting like a carthorse; the friar mad as a lion and foaming like a wild boar. And we should note too the comic speed and confusion with which the events of the denouement take place: the fart is let, "the frere up stirte", "his meynee (company) . . . cam lepying in", "and forth he gooth". Finally we can contrast the friar's wrathful departure from Thomas's house with Christ's instructions in the gospels to his apostles on leaving houses where they are not received: "but if [the house] be not worthy, let your peace return to you" (Matthew 10:13).

Thus Chaucer builds upon what he probably received as an antifraternal fabliau model to produce a complex and sophisticated antifraternal satire in the Summoner's Tale. Unlike his procedure with the Shipman's, Miller's or Reeve's Tales, however, Chaucer makes a substantial structural addition to the basic fabliau tale by the 133-line coda (2162–294). In a general way the contents of this reflect material in the French analogue, *Le dis de le Vescie a prestre*, in that the friar's disgrace becomes a matter of public mockery; much of the substance of the coda is provided by the pastiche of the descent of the Holy Spirit, however, and the motif of the witty squire's solution to a problem posed is perhaps more reminiscent of the resourceful youngest sons of folktale as of the wily characters (often women) of fabliau. The coda clearly repeats and deepens the fabliau joke: it begins with the lord seeking to 'amend' the friar's grief if he can (2175) but ends with the squire amending the jape in the way that Nicholas fails to do in the Miller's Tale. It keeps the redolence of the fabliau diction already noted, and plays with the word 'savour':

'Ye been the salt of the erthe and the savor'

(2196)

(this is the lord of the manor speaking of friars, again quoting from the Sermon on the Mount, immediately after the beatitudes: Matthew 5: 13), and:

. . .the soun or savour of a fart

(2226)

with an irreverent echo of the word 'Saviour' (Chaucer's *saveour*) present too.

In the light of our study of Chaucer's fabliaux up to this point, however, perhaps the most interesting and important aspect of the coda is the way in which it continues the unmasking of presumptions about the characters and capacities of men of different social ranks that was found to be such a major aspect of the Miller's and Reeve's Tales in fragment I of the Canterbury Tales. Thomas, who is initially introduced to us as a 'good man' (1768), is first called a "cherl" by the friar in his anger at the trick played on him (2153), and is then repeatedly and frequently given this designation throughout the coda. There he takes a place in a vignette with the lord of the manor and his lady and squire, bringing a broad social spectrum into view: the three estates of basic medieval sociology – clergy, knighthood and peasantry. In this vignette, the initial suppositions of the 'gentils' concerning the nature of the trick and its relationship to the trickster are perfectly clear:

'I seye a cherl hath done a cherles dede'

(2206)

says the lady of the house. This is followed by surprise that one from whom so little subtlety is to be expected could present the friar with the conundrum of how to share a fart out in equal portions:

'How hadde this cherl ymaginacioun
To shewe swich a probleme to the frere?'

(2218–9)

The Boethian concept of the place of 'imagination' in an intellectual hierarchy discussed in relation to the Nun's Priest's Tale (Chapter 3) is relevant here; it was a current supposition of some medieval socio-religious thought that churls were as brute beasts, possessed only of imagination rather than reason.[9] The general attitude seems to be that the churl has stumbled on this riposte to the friar blindly and sinfully: he is a "nyce [foolish, wanton], proude cherl" (2227, 2232) who is demon-possessed (2240); he can, in the end, be dismissed as of no consequence:

9. See Patterson "No man his reson herde. . ." pp 472–8.

'Now ete youre mete, and lat the cherl go pleye;
Lat hym go honge hymself a devel weye!'

(2241–2)

a devel weye: in the Devil's name

But the wit of the squire's solution to the apparently impossible challenge posed is not, as it could be, laid to the squire's credit alone:

The lord, the lady, and ech man, save the frere,
Seyde that Jankyn spak, in this manere,
As wel as Euclide /dide/ or Ptholomee.
Touchyng the cherl, they seyde, subtiltee
And heigh wit made hym speken as he spak;
He nys no fool, ne no demonyak.

(2287–92)

The tale ends with the recognition of the class-free human mental capacity of the 'churl', a wit that matches that of the squire, which indeed co-acts with the squire's glossing to produce the great amendment of the jape in the coda of the Summoner's Tale.

THE MERCHANT'S TALE

Although the critical literature on the Merchant's Tale is large, with the result that a relatively healthy range of dissent from the norm can be found, there still exists a clear, orthodox view of the Merchant and his tale which is very similar to that of the Reeve and his tale: that the Merchant, particularly as a result of the revelation of his character in his Prologue, is a bitter and twisted man, and that his tale follows suit, exposing the basest and most unpleasant aspects of humanity, not only in the characters and actions found within his tale but also in the Merchant's attitude towards them. As with the Reeve's Tale, it will be argued here that the Merchant's Prologue and Tale can be read differently. A case will be argued for the Merchant's Tale being essentially comic, and that far from Chaucer creating a distinctly bad pilgrim–narrator character in the Merchant in order to judge and condemn him, the greatly modulating narrative voice heard in the tale is a coherent, positive and Chaucerian whole like the narrative voice claimed for the Nun's Priest's Tale in Chapter 3. The tale is as complex in composition as the narrative voice. A major theme of the tale is that of sight and perception, a theme which reaches its climax at the very end of the tale. The greatest significance of this theme may lie less in the light in which it presents the one character, January, with his different forms of blindness, than in how it emphasizes the problem of interpretation; another ramification of the theme of textual *auctoritee*.

Literary parallels and their moral implications

The Merchant's Tale is rich in literary allusion and thus also in intertextual meaning. There is no mistaking the clear fabliau structure of the tale of the old man − becoming in the course of the tale a jealous old husband − who takes a young wife and is cuckolded, but who as a result of his wife's ingenuity is deceived into disbelieving the evidence of his own eyes and who ends the tale ridiculously happy in his delusion. Apt Old French parallels to cite are *Le Prestre qui abevete*, 'The priest who looked out for himself', in which a priest assures a peasant that when he has looked through a hole in the door at the peasant and his wife eating at the table they appeared to be fornicating, which lo and behold is just what the peasant sees too when he looks at the priest and his wife from the other side of the door, or *Le Chevalier qui fist sa dame confesse*, 'The knight who made his wife confess', in which a knight, disguised as a special confessor his wife asks for on her sickbed in order to test her apparent virtue, learns of her outrageous sexual misdeeds only then to be duped by the wife claiming to have seen through his disguise all along and to have hurt and punished him by a deliberate deception in this way. Several analogues are known to the actual device of the blind January's sudden discovery of his wife's adultery in the tree and his equally rapid delusion, none of them, however, amongst the French fabliaux. An early version appears in a twelfth-century Latin comedy, the *Comoedia Lydiae*, which was clearly the source for some later medieval vernacular versions, such as Day 9 tale 7 of Boccaccio's *Decameron*. Four versions are known from fifteenth-century Germany, in two of which it is God and St Peter who miraculously restore the blind cuckold's sight, a detail which is shared with a late thirteenth-century Italian novella that tells the tale. We should also note that a variant of this motif appears in the Anglo-Norman fabliau *La Gageure*, in which a lady to her horror discovers her maid fornicating beneath a pear tree.

One of the main planks in the argument for a severe moral censure of the actions of the Merchant's Tale is the variety of literary allusions to a world of fine spiritual and social ethics, a set of standards which the characters of the tale fall far short of. This is much the same as has been claimed for the Miller's Tale. Such aspects of the tale are supposed to reflect upon the Merchant as a bitterly cynical 'author' of the tale; having the sort of attitude that puts words from the Song of Solomon into January's mouth and then dismisses them as "olde lewed wordes" (2138–49). Although we may be aware of a potentially irreverent identification of the old man and his young wife in the Merchant's Tale, as in the Miller's Tale, with Joseph and Mary, there is a distinct leaning in the Biblical allusions of this tale towards the Old Testament, and one could argue that this blunts the edge of the Christian moral criticism that such echoes might otherwise invite. January's garden is a pastiche upon two Old Testament gardens, the garden of Eden, inhabited by the yet innocent Adam and Eve, in Paradise (Genesis 2–3) and the "garden inclosed" of the Song of Solomon (4: 12 and following). The latter is an image of the desirable female body that was allegorized by Christian exegetes as an image of the Virgin Mary, or of Ecclesia, the Church. It is an important point to appreciate that many motifs, actions, and even characters, are seen as projections of January's imagination. It is January who, like an eclectic artist, attempts to build a garden in which to enjoy "his paradys, his make", May (1822), and where he calls on his wife in the language of the Song of Solomon, "Rys up, my wyf, my love, my lady free!. . ."

The images of Old Testament theology could of course be given moral, typological and anagogical Christian meaning, and it is undeniable that as a realistic character January would be in serious spiritual error in making May his *summum bonum*, his highest good, his Paradise. At the intertextual level, one may also be acutely aware of the moral contrast between January's garden and the "jardin vray et delectable", the 'true and lovely garden' described by Repertoire de Science, 'the Body of Knowledge', in the source most extensively used by Chaucer for the Merchant's Tale, the *Miroir de Mariage* of his French contemporary, Eustache Deschamps. This is the garden to which Repertoire de Science urges another personified abstraction, Franc Vouloir, 'Noble Desire' or 'Free Will', to turn, away from women, who shortly before this in the poem are described as being as fragile as flowers. The spring in that garden, "la fontaine de conpunction", 'the fountain of contrition' (compare the "welle" in January's garden), pours out the Holy Spirit, nourishing the plants of virtue.[10]

Less distinctly a product of January's mind is the ironic citation of the Old Testament heroines Rebecca, Judith, Abigail and Esther as examples of the "good conseil" of women in the 'marriage encomium' in the early part of the Merchant's Tale (1360–74). January's young wife May is explicitly compared to these women during the marriage service when the priest bids her be like Sarah and Rebecca in wisdom and fidelity (1703–5). The irony here is simple. All of these women exercise deceit in some way – Rebecca, indeed, deceiving a short-sighted old husband – and they are cited shortly after the would-be husband has been assured that:

> He may nat been deceyved, as I gesse,
> So that he werke after his wyves reed.
>
> $(1356–7)$[11]

> *so that*: as long as; *reed*: counsel

The moral ambivalence that resides in the Old Testament examples and which allows them to be exploited to produce comic irony further diminishes the moral contrast between the events of the Merchant's Tale and the set of moral values that the Biblical references may recall. Not so amenable to this sort of witty reduction, however, is the contrast between May with her two 'lovers' in the garden and Susannah with two lecherous and dishonest judges in an orchard (Daniel 13). A distinct link between the two texts is formed by January and May's lovemaking alone in the garden "and no wight but they two", recalling what the two judges say to Susannah: "the gate is closed, and nobody sees us". The judges threaten Susannah that if she raises the alarm they will claim to have caught her there fornicating with a young man. Susannah preserves her honesty and is eventually vindicated by Daniel questioning the judges, separately, as to what sort of tree Susannah and the young man coupled under. May, conversely, escapes from one lecherous lover at the bottom of a tree to another

10. See *Miroir de Mariage* 5793–865, 6119–388 and 7205–15.
11. See especially Otten 1971, Brown (Jr) 1974 and Wentersdorf 1986 pp 37–9.

within it. It would go too far to suggest that this parallel *simply* brings a smile to the reading of the Old Testament by emphasizing the fabliau potential of the Biblical story.

For all the blatant error in his suppositions concerning the moral acceptability of his actions, January is presented as a thinking character who is acutely conscious of Christian moral doctrine and of the spiritual consequences of right and wrong behaviour in this life. His delusion is his confusion of these with sexual desire: a sort of confusion, indeed, of *lust* and *loore*. He seems honestly to believe that he is escaping lechery by pursuing it through marriage; he knows marriage is ordained for Man:

> . . .for they sholde leccherye eschue
>
> (1451)

– a line that is ironically echoed by repetition and rhyme as January laughably attempts to improve his performance of that sin:

> He drynketh ypocras, clarree, and vernage
> Of spices hoote t'encressen his corage;
> And many a letuarie hath he ful fyn,
> Swich as the cursed monk, daun Constantyn,
> Hath writen in his book *De Coitu*;
> To eten hem alle he was no thyng eschu.
>
> (1807–12)
>
> *ypocras, clarree, vernage*: types of wine; *corage*: spirit, vigour, determination;
> *letuarie*: drug; *fyn*: fine; *de coitu* (Latin): of sexual intercourse

This confusion runs throughout the speech in which January announces his intention to be wed (lines 1400–68), to end with a thumpingly ironic image:

> Though I be hoor, I fare as dooth a tree
> That blosmeth er that fruyt ywoxen be. . .
>
> (1461–2)
>
> *hoor*: hoary-headed; *ywoxen*: grown

January pursues both salvation and sexual gratification with a naive zeal. There is no explicit evidence that he *consciously* thinks he can simply outwit God.[12]

The confusion of the religious and the sexual in the garden created from January's imagination is found in another famous

---

12. Cf. Knapp *Chaucer and the Social Contest* pp 108–9.

garden of the literature of courteous romance. The garden in question is the garden of Deduit, 'Indulgence' (or "Myrthe" in what is thought to be Chaucer's translation of the text), in *The Romance of the Rose*. This is a dream poem in which the dreamer experiences love in the garden; and he suffers from his unsuccessful and unrequited love until, after 20 000 lines of verse by two authors, Guillaume de Lorris followed by Jean de Meun, the dreamer breaks into the rose garden and plucks the rose. January constructs a garden in which a less time-consuming version of this drama can be acted out. A concern with nobility and the introduction of the features of romance within the sexual relationship is fixedly a feature of January's imagination and no other character's. January and May are a knight and his lady, by social rank at least, and Damian a squire, and January is fully conscious of the social implications of his being able to get a legitimate heir for his "heritage" (1438–40). January portrays May in his thoughts in bed with the characteristic *effictio* and *notatio* (external and moral description) of a heroine of romance (1599–1604), and he sings May an aubade (a morning song) on the morning after their wedding night (1845).

January's confusion of the religious and the sexual is not just the depraved sickness of an individual mind; it is a dramatization of an ambiguity that resides in a deep-rooted medieval conception of love. January is typical of his age and of his culture in perceiving sexual love in religious terms. This may emerge in no more than the sacrilegious appropriation of the motifs of religion and of the respect and sense of duty due to Christianity in making a religion of the wholly mundane human desires and pleasures of sexual love. This is January's fault by a severe view of his personal behaviour. But at a more sophisticated, and orthodox and moral level, sexual love was conceived of and represented as an early step on a ladder of experience leading ultimately to the experience of divine love (*caritas*) and salvation.[13] January is hardly transfigured by the end of the Merchant's Tale. But he does achieve some moral progress through the tale, reflected particularly by the patience he eventually displays in his blindness:

13. The concept is thoroughly explored in Dronke P 1968 *Medieval Latin and the Rise of European Love Lyric* (Clarendon Press).

But atte laste, after a month or tweye,
His sorwe gan aswage, sooth to seye;
For when he wiste it may noon oother be,
He paciently took his adversitee. . .

(2081–4)

    sooth: truth

which balances structurally with the haste January shows to be married (1611–16, 1691–5, 1765–7 etc.). And January's continued blindness to his wife's misdeed at the end of the tale does not have to be seen solely in terms of his selfish stupidity; there is a touch of continued patience in this too; the sort of forbearance wrily recommended by the Miller (I: 3151–66) and perhaps enacted by the Shipman's merchant:

'. . .An housbonde shal nat been inquisityf
Of Goddes pryvetee, nor of his wyf.
So he may fynde Goddes foyson there,
Of the remenant needeth nat enquere.'

(I: 3163–6)

The Merchant as narrator

If we were to imagine the Merchant as the author of this tale, which is what we do if we judge him morally as a character on the basis of what the tale contains, it would be perverse to imagine him as a simpler character intellectually than the characters he has supposedly created, and as failing spiritually while at least one of them improves. There are echoes in the Merchant's Tale of the preceding tale in the Canterbury Tales, the Clerk's Tale, echoes which not only throw a critical light on to January's moral character, but which in realistic terms recall the dramatic context of the Merchant's Tale and thus re-emphasize the dramatic identity of the narrator as the Merchant. Walter, the husband of the Clerk's Tale who cruelly tests his wife Griselda, is "the gentilleste yborn of Lumbardye" (IV: 72) while January is also a knight of Pavia in Lombardy (1245–6). January copies Walter in choosing a wife of lowly origins:

Al were it so she were of smal degree;
Suffiseth hym hir yowthe and hir beautee.

(1625–6)

    smal degree: low social rank

There is a firm implication that January's impositions upon May are every bit as brutal as Walter's:

> How that he wroghte, I dar nat to yow telle,
> Or wheither hire thoughte it paradys or helle.
>
> (1963–4)

Beyond this adverse moral comparison of January, P. A. Olson views the Merchant as a character who sees only the literal tale of a patient wife in the Clerk's Tale and who thus fails to grasp the spiritual praise of the longsuffering of God's finest.

This reading is supported by an interpretation of the Merchant's explosive response to the comic imprecation upon the husband as a type at the end of the Clerk's Tale:

> '. . .And lat hym care, and wepe, and wrynge, and waille!'
>
> (1212)

with:

> 'Wepyng and waylyng, care and oother sorwe
> I knowe ynogh, on even and a-morwe. . .
>   . . .and so doon oother mo
> That wedden been. . .'
>
> (1213–16)[14]

as a pastiche of Boethius's opening lament in *de Consolatione Philosophiae*. The words, however, appear again, used of January, when he has been struck blind:

> He wepeth and he wayleth pitously
>
> (2072)

and they are not without pathos here. Most significantly, perhaps, we can spot another echo of the line in the description of Damian's woe in having fallen for May:

> But ther I let hym wepe ynogh and pleyne
>
> (1781)

This reflects ironically upon the Merchant's Prologue, for we now see weeping and wailing in both the husband and the bachelor. The relationship between the Merchant and the characters of this tale is not simply antagonistic. Despite all the rivalry and criticism at

14. *Op. cit.* footnote 6 pp 260–4.

the personal level, there is a seed of masculine solidarity growing here; all men are vulnerable to being "ravysshed", through their erotic imaginations, by the simple image of a beautiful girl like May (cf.1750 and 1774).

Having made his dramatic entrance at the end of the Clerk's Tale, the Merchant is further constructed in his prologue as he offers a portrait of himself in terms that are obviously related to the theme of marriage: a theme that runs at least from the Wife of Bath's Prologue at the start of fragment III to the Franklin's Tale at the end of fragment V. It is noticeable that the Merchant pretends at least to try to cut himself and his own self-reflection out at the end of his prologue:

> '. . .of myn owene soore,
> For soory herte, I telle may namoore.'

> (1243–4)

but we do not have here the equivalent of the disappearance of the Miller in the telling of his tale. It is easy to perceive the major male characters of the tale as projections of stages in the experience of a Merchant-narrator who is thus continuing to be characterized in the telling of his tale.

The three clearest and most distinct projections of the Merchant in the Merchant's Tale are January, Justinus and the narrator. The case for the reading of the Merchant's Tale as the bitter tale of a bitter character relies very much on the supposed antagonism between the last and the first of these, the narrator and January. The opening lines of the tale state the similarity between these two – a long-term bachelor decides to get married. The text then plunges into the long, well-known passage in praise of marriage, the 'encomium' (lines 1267–392), a passage which in fact problematizes the relationship between the narrator and January somewhat by creating a nice narratological complex: the narrator speaks, but the words sound like the character's. They express January's delusions about the blissful state of marriage, which by an act of interpretation we can take to generally resemble those of an earlier Merchant in his bachelor state; in realistic terms we might imagine the more experienced Merchant now rehearses them sarcastically, to reveal January's folly. So blatant is the sarcasm of this passage that when the narrator's voice converts from the mock encomium into plain antifeminism one can be excused for not

noticing any marked change of direction, particularly as the point is
approached in disguise, as it were, by way of a contrast between a
wife and the transient gifts of fickle Fortune:

> But drede nat, if pleynly speke I shal:
> A wyf wol laste, and in thyn hous endure,
> Wel lenger than thee list, paraventure.
>
> (1316–8)
>
> *thee list*: you wish

The sarcasm of the encomium is, however, moderated by the tale.
The encomium opens by comparing the sorrow and uncertainty of
bachelors with the supposed security of the married man (1273–85).
This ironically anticipates Damian's usurpation of January's
husbandly role, but the image painted of the bachelor here is
corroborated, not only in Damian's pain, but more covertly by the
desire of January, and the implied previous willingness of both the
Merchant and Justinus, to marry.

The more sophisticated narrative techniques displaying January's
error, such as this irony, tend to give way to plain description of
January's lust and ugliness around the point of his marriage with
May. His *effictio* of May already referred to (1600–4) is given a
disgusting, autoerotic turn by its context:

> And whan that he was in his bed ybroght,
> He purtreyed in his herte and in his thoght
> Hire fresshe beautee. . .
>
> (1599–601)

The similarity to Damian's taking to his bed (1779–82) is inescapable,
but the differences are significant: January is anticipating the
indulgence that will be his; Damian's action is his only available
substitute for – or way to – the desired union with May. No
commentary is needed with the ghastly picture of January singing
his aubade:

> The slakke skin aboute his nekke shaketh
> Whil that he sang, so chaunteth he and craketh
>
> (1849–50)

The modulating but insistent revelation of January's sordid obsession
can, however, inure the reader to this aspect of the character. It
certainly becomes something from which January can never be free.
Even when he performs a generous act that all must applaud:

And for that word hym blessed every man,
That of his bountee and his gentillesse
He wolde so conforten in siknesse
His squier, for it was a gentil dede.

(1916–19)

he spoils it; he sends May to Damian (ironically, for it brings
Damian and May together, just as his sympathy is, of course,
ironically misplaced) so that he can rest in order to be able to
indulge in more lovemaking afterwards (1920–66). Lechery in old age
is unlovely. We have already seen some consideration of this theme
in relation to the Reeve, and it was argued there that it was a topic
presented with more comic understanding than moral opprobrium.
Although the "olde lechour" – an intensification of the type-cast
senex amans, 'elderly lover' – is sufficiently familiar a figure for one
to see that January could be type-cast as a personification of a vice,
it is the case that the full direction of the three Chaucerian fabliaux
discussed so far is directly contrary to such type-casting. Just as
Chaucer distinguishes the individual from the social type, without
denying the 'reality' of the latter, so too he can distinguish the
individual from the moral type: January is more than just an "olde
lechour".

The older and wiser Merchant also makes a clear appearance in
Justinus, the wiser and more honest of January's counsellors. He has
much the same experience of marriage as the Merchant:

'For, God it woot, I have wept many a teere
Ful prively, syn I have had a wyf.'

(1544–5)

Justinus too has been condemned in recent studies, particularly for
his supposed obsession with marriage as a commercial transaction.[15]
This interpretation seems to overstress Justinus's opening words:

'. . .a man oghte hym right wel avyse
To whom he yeveth his land or his catel.'

(1524–5)

    catel: goods

as this argument is introduced as an element in a comparison
through which Justinus emphasizes what *is* more important:

15. See Aers *Chaucer, Langland and the Creative Imagination* p 152; Pearsall *op. cit.*
footnote 5 p 208.

And syn I oghte avyse me right wel
To whom I yeve my good awey fro me
Wel muchel moore I oghte avysed be
To whom I yeve my body for alwey.

(1526–9)

  good: property

Most of his subsequent counselling concerns the desirable *moral*
qualities in a wife, with occasional references to financial
considerations admittedly, but not as a major theme (i.e. 1535–6,
1547). Justinus is pragmatic and conservative; he knows the limits of
his ability to advise January (he does not clearly try to dissuade
him):

'Ye mowe, for me, right as yow liketh do.'

(1554)

and he, like January, is seen to be of his age, not better than it, as
he organizes the practical details of the marriage contract in a
contextually realistic way (1691–9). Crucially, whatever his rational
evaluation of January's plans:

Justinus, which that hated his folye. . .

(1655)

(actually a line with a telling ambiguity, for "his" could refer to
Justinus as well as to January), he ultimately has recourse to
comedy, answering "in his japerye" (1656), and reassuring January,
with his spiritual fears, with a nicely amusing image:

'She may be Goddes meene and Goddes whippe;
Than shal youre soule up to hevene skippe
Swifter than dooth an arwe out of a bowe.'

(1671–3)

  meene: intermediary

A narrative voice is insistently in evidence in the conspicuous
rhetorical flourishes within the Merchant's Tale. One of the
functions of rhetoric within the tale is (at least superficially) to
direct sympathy; in fact to share sympathy out, because the
direction of sympathy by this means is quite inconsistent. The voice
is consistent only in being sympathetic. One apostrophe warns
January of the "perilous fyr", the "famulier foo", and prays God to
reveal Damian's plot to him (1783–94); the next turns to "woful
Damyan" and prays "God be thyn helpe! I kan no bettre seye"

(1866–74). Several critics have commented on the staleness of Chaucer's oft-repeated line when applied to May:

> Lo, pitee renneth soone in gentil herte!
>
> (1986)[16]

but the narrator here does follow this up with an exposition of the feminine virtue of *pitee*, as idealized in the conventions of *fin amour*:

> Heere may ye se how excellent franchise
> In wommen is, whan they hem narwe avyse.
> Som tyrant is, as ther be many oon
> That hath an herte as hard as any stoon,
> Which wolde han let hym sterven in the place
> Wel rather than han graunted hym hire grace,
> And hem rejoysen in hire crueel pryde,
> And rekke nat to been an homycide.
>
> (1987–94)

franchise: generosity, nobility; *sterven*: die; *rekke*: care

A subtle embodiment of the masculine perspective of the narrator – and something that thus serves to associate him in general with the male part of his readership/audience – is the demarcation of May's difference, the woman being the one player in the eternal triangle who is not addressed directly. The narrator's next apostrophe is to a personified abstraction, Fortune:

> O sodeyn hap! O thou Fortune unstable!

which in a simple reading of rhetorical direction may be interpreted as directing blame away from the characters and somewhere into the vaguer nature of the cosmos (2057–68). The specific deed of Fortune in the tale is in fact to take January's eyesight, but the description of Fortune as a scorpion, with the sexual innuendos of its "head", "stynge", "tayl", "joye" and "sweete venim queynte", unmistakably paints a picture of a sexually charged hermaphroditic monster; an image of the force of intense, unbridled and *general* human sexuality.

16. Found also in the Knight's Tale (I: 1761), the Squire's Tale (V: 479), the *Legend of Good Women* (F: 503), and echoed in the Man of Law's Tale (II: 660).

Sexual difference

The Merchant's Tale is unusual amongst the Canterbury Tales in the number of its characters that seem to be personifications – January, May, Justinus and Placebo – and in the extent to which the tale might therefore seem to be allegorical. What is special about the Merchant's Tale – in comparison, for instance, to the Pardoner's Tale or *Melibee* – is the way in which it combines thematic generalization with a certain form of realism rather than with conventional idealism; in itself this combination may be claimed to be a peculiarly Chaucerian form of idealism.

January is associated by name and portrayal with age and decay, May, persistently, with spring and youth, freshness, fertility and growth; the latter in a real form, not a bowlderized one. Just as the May morning is the conventional setting for the experience of love in medieval literature – it is into such a morning that the dreamer 'awakens' in his dream in *The Romance of the Rose* – May, like Alison of the Miller's Tale, represents a certain conventional ideal of femininity. This is not the literary ideal of the courtly lady of romance – like White in *The Book of the Duchess* – but rather a model satisfying a recognizable masculine dream, an ideal that is expressed in the fabliau rather than the romance: a woman who is beautiful, irreticent in her sexuality, and therefore available to man. There is, for this view, one markedly problematic trait in the presentation of May, contrasted with Alison. May does not need to be introduced with the explosion of natural imagery that Alison does (Alison's name symbolizes nothing of itself), but May is characterized by the persistent repetition of the adjective *fresshe*, a practice that recalls the ambiguous *worthy* of the General Prologue and *hende* of Nicholas in the Miller's Tale. The drift of the usage of this term in the Merchant's Tale is at best towards irony, and at worst towards stale and sour sarcasm. Perhaps the best excuse we can make for May in this respect is to note that the term "fresshe" makes its first appearance as the first term of January's *effictio* – "hire fresshe beautee" (1601). The qualitative portrait we are given of May is consistently that of January's imagination. When May finally deceives January, she succeeds in doing so by encouraging him to return to his own self-deceit.

Alison represents the greatest imaginable sexual attraction for a man in a realistic contemporary urban setting. We soon see that

May is not the sexually alluring but frigidly *daungerous* lady of a romance but a wordly-wise girl who knows what to look for in and from a marriage. To put it crudely, as Jill Mann does, she has willingly married an old fool for his money. The indirect rhetorical question used to bring the reader to look through May's eyes at January as he sings his aubade after his wedding night:

> But God woot what that May thoughte in hir herte,
> Whan she hym saugh up sittynge in his sherte,
> In his nyght-cappe, and with his nekke lene
>
> (1851–3)

should not blind the reader to the declarative statement that answers the question in the next line:

> She preyseth nat his pleyynge worth a bene.
>
> (1854)

Given that "pleyynge" in this line can encompass all the sexual play of the wedding night, not just January's role-playing as the tuneful lover, we may find that May's reaction to January's whole performance as a lover is one of scorn or disappointment – she has some notion of what sort of playing would be worth something – but not of shock or disgust. When May falls, then, for and with Damian, plucking the fruit of the tree, her fall is no greater than Alison's.

The Merchant's Tale unfolds as a probing reflection upon the characteristics of man; it proves to be a thematic drama in which woman (represented by May) is a magnetic, influential but to a considerable extent psychologically unfathomable and certainly uncontrollable otherness that brings to a dramatic crisis one dominant characteristic of man: his sexuality – through which man habitually projects certain images and characters on to women.

All the male characters concerned with this tale converge into a single entity, man. The Merchant becomes projected as January, Justinus, and even Damian. When January purports to look around and outside of himself he looks only at a mirror of his own mind in preferring the counsel of Placebo (1478–518). This is also the way that he looks for a wife who best suits his fantasies (1577–616). Justinus, too, can be seen as the right side of January's mind, the side he wilfully rejects but which he might – like the Merchant – come to acknowledge. Even the Host joins in, in the Epilogue to the Merchant's Tale, generalizing primarily about woman's deceitfulness:

> 'Lo, whiche sleightes and subtilitees
> In wommen been! For ay as bisy as bees
> Been they, us sely men for to deceyve. . .'
>
> (2421–3)

sely: lucky, innocent, pitiable, foolish, feeble

but behind that expressing the same weaknesses in himself as are found in the Merchant, January, Justinus and, in due course, Damian: "I have a wyf. . .". David Aers has recognized this general thematic treatment of man in the Merchant's Tale, although his interests lie more in the nature of gender as a cultural construct and its social ramifications than in its psychological form.[17] He consequently interprets the fabliau-characteristic of the stripping of both religious and courtly motifs of their value-laden mystique as an embodiment "of the culture's disastrous fragmentation of love, sexuality and marriage" and emphasizes "the pervasive acceptance of capricious male power over women".

A crux in any consideration of the question of whether the two sexes are delineated as generalities and their relationship with one another explored in such a way as to reveal inequalities, injustice and the exploitation of woman by man, lies in the interpretation of the introduction of Pluto and Proserpina to January's garden: the *dei ex machina*, one of whom restores January's sight, the other of whom gives May her explanation. Their role in the tale undoubtedly extends beyond mere plot manipulation. They crystallize, in particular, a theme of "ravysshement" in the tale – a theme that we could call 'rape' in Modern English, although if we do so we must qualify the use of what is a highly charged term in our day by noting that the medieval English legal equivalent, *raptus*, covered both forced sexual intercourse and abduction. In May 1380, in fact, Chaucer was released from legal actions by one Cecelia Chaumpaigne *de raptu meo*, 'concerning my *raptus*'. We have already noted that both January and Damian are "ravysshed" by May (1750, 1774), and it is right there that January imagines himself as the peer of one of the epic amorous abductors of classical history, Paris (1752–4). The classical mythological tale of Pluto and Proserpina is

17. *Op. cit.* footnote 15 pp 151–60.

that Pluto abducted, "ravysshed" (2230), the young goddess Proserpina, daughter of Ceres the goddess of crops, and forced her into a marriage with him. The tale is told by Ovid (*Metamorphoses* 5,346–571; *Fasti* 4,417–620) and in a late classical poem referred to by Chaucer, *de Raptu Proserpinae* of Claudian (2232). Although *ravysshement* is first presented in the text as the effect of the female on the male, the dynamic force within this effect is the male erotic imagination, and the contrary direction is represented by the Paris/Helen and Pluto/Proserpina references.[18] Pluto's connection with January is expressed by his sympathy for the cuckold-to-be and his attempt to enlighten him; Proserpina's connection with May by her practical defence of the unfaithful wife. The image of January's marriage to May as a form of legalized *raptus* of the vulnerable sex by the powerful one readily forms itself.

It is justifiable, however, to stress the mythological implications of the motifs Pluto and Proserpina introduce above implications of male brutality and selfishness and female defencelessness. Significantly, the relationship between Pluto and Proserpina is ultimately one of accommodation, not one of continued strife. In Claudian, indeed, Proserpina's lamentations cause Pluto to experience feelings of sympathy and love rather than just desire (III: 273–306). The Pluto–Proserpina myth is an example – or an antitype – of a series of myths that are formed upon a *hieros gamos* model: the marriage of a male god, associated usually with the sky, with a female nymph, goddess or earth-mother figure; a recurrent myth that reflects the cycle of seasonal fertility and growth. Proserpina indeed is released by Pluto to her mother for the two seasons of growth – spring and summer – every year. The story remains the antitype of the essential, universal fertility myth, insofar as the marriage with Pluto remains a 'winter-prison'; it is away from Pluto that Proserpina takes on her association with growth. Part of the thematic relevance of this mythological reference lies in comically underlining the "unlikly elde", the 'ill-matched old-age', of January with his young wife and the improbability of his getting a child as he imagines he will, and in asserting the propriety, in the natural scheme, of May escaping to Damian, the virile young equivalent of the god of the new year. There is further comedy in the

---

18. Wentersdorf 1965 and 1986 notes also that the tale of Wade, mentioned by January (line 1423), is a tale of the abduction of a consenting maiden.

mythological allusions here too, however, as Damian, the lover hidden in the garden, merges with the phallic god Priapus, god of gardens (2035), another would-be divine ravisher but in this case a frustrated one, caught with his trousers down as it were.[19]

Medieval Christian moral exegesis of Ovid, such as the fourteenth-century French verse *Ovide Moralisé*, represents Pluto as the Devil and Proserpina as human nature "qui s'acoustume aus mortelz vices", 'which becomes habituated to mortal sins'.[20] We might, as a result, speculate upon the different exegetical ways one could interpret May's fellowship with the Merchant's wife:

> For thogh the feend to hire ycoupled were,
> She wolde hym overmacche, I dar wel swere.

> (1219–20)

> *hym overmacche*: be more than a match for him

But to follow this course of allegorical logic leads to unproductive confusion. Pluto and Proserpina replace God and St Peter as the *dei ex machina* of all the relevant analogues. The drama thus remains a comedy of the sublunary world; the pagan deities were the creation of Man seeking to comprehend the forces operative in his world.

The myth of the seasonal fertility ritual was also approached by Chaucer in the *Parlement of Foules*, in which all the birds have gathered in a garden distinctly similar to that of *The Romance of the Rose* for a parliament presided over by Nature, both goddess and "the vicaire of the almyghty Lord", in which each is to find its mate. The purpose of the parliament is first delayed by the contest between three noble eagles who all plead for the same female eagle, the 'formel', who sits on Nature's hand, and then frustrated when the formel is granted her own choice and chooses a year's respite before making a decision. Unlike this formel eagle, and the immature Proserpina, May follows a mating instinct and asserts her sexuality. She seems to accept January, although he is the reverse of ideal as a partner in sexual intercourse; she certainly accepts Damian more willingly. Ovid and Claudian's texts of the rape of Proserpina show full awareness of the importance of the maintenance of the seasonal relations of fructification. The taking of Proserpina by Pluto is plotted by Venus, with Jove in Claudian, tolerated by Jove

19. Compare Ovid *Fasti* I.391–440 and VI.319–48; Brown (Jr) 1970b.
20. *Ovide Moralisé* V: 2964–6; Dalbey 1974.

in Ovid, so that the rule of love, the proper pairing of male and female, should be furthered not resisted.

As far as fabliau is concerned, the mythic element in the composition of the Merchant's Tale turns the tale into what is practically a foundation myth for all fabliaux: Proserpina's gift is not to May alone,

> . . .I shal yeven hire suffisant answere,
> And alle wommen after, for hir sake,
> That, though they be in any gilt ytake,
> With face boold they shulle hem excuse,
> And bere hem doun that wolden hem accuse.

> (2266–70 et seq.)

It is thus a myth that explains certain dramatic and literary projections of the difference and the struggle (cf. May's "strugle", 2374–6!) between the sexes. The Merchant's Tale thus ends, teasingly, with two sweeping propositions about the nature of human affairs, one of which is intuitively recognizable as a fact, the other as an untruth. The former is a mature, wordly-wise recognition of the pervasiveness of human – not just male – silliness in matters of sexual instinct and attraction:

> For love is blynd alday, and may nat see.

> (1598)

The untruth is the wry rather than cynical proposition that a woman will always be able to talk her way out of a compromising situation.

Moral perspective in the Merchant's Tale

The merging of the Merchant with the other male characters is not a process that leads to the total disappearance of all realism and individuality in him as a character. But even on that premiss the notion of a bitter and misanthropic narrator can be rejected. The histrionic hyperbole of the Merchant's Prologue can rationally be read as a confident performance by an able raconteur; remember Dame Sirith and the Shipman's Tale as texts performed. With Laura Kendrick we can see the whole tale as an exercise by the Merchant in laughing at an image of himself, although there is no need to see this, with her, as a devious pretence that he (the Merchant) is somehow superior to January. A useful section of the text to consider in this respect is the fine, rhetorical description of the wedding feast (1709–41), with its epic similes, mythological machinery and hyperbolic apostrophe to the poet Martianus Capella, which climaxes with the wonderful duality of:

> When tendre youthe hath wedded stoupyng age,
> Ther is swich myrthe that it may nat be writen.
>
> (1738–9)

Reflection upon the construction and effect of this passage shows clearly that its humour does not lie in the details of the scene constructed but rather in their style of presentation – and thus in the tone, the attitude of the narrator/author to the fictional situation. The final point to be argued here is that the attitude and tone of the Merchant's Tale create and imply a narratorial character of authority and merit that is Chaucerian in a very real sense. As in the Nun's Priest's Tale, we have a profound adaptation of a familiar and simple literary genre presented deceptively as a casual composition, studded with extempore comments on events and situations.

The tale is brought to a comic end by artifice (the intervention of Proserpina) and in fiction (the untrue myth that that represents); a combination of artifice and fiction produced by a collaboration of the author with two mythical characters. Like Justinus, the author of the tale has seen the folly the tale encompasses and responds with japery. The narrator of the Merchant's Tale is a character who divides and contradicts himself; after his inconsistent rhetorical apostrophes that have been noted he finally denies himself as a rhetorician to produce the antirhetoric of a typical fabliau's linguistic climax:

> Ladyes, I prey yow that ye be nat wrooth;
> I kan nat glose, I am a rude man –
> And sodeynly anon this Damyan
> Gan pullen up the smok, and in he throng.
>
> (2350–3)

    throng: thrust

(This sort of language having been introduced, January picks it up in lines 2376–8.) The narrator divides into different voices just as the Merchant has divided into different characters (January, Justinus and Damian); as January divides (into Placebo and Justinus, and perhaps

into Damian too); and as Chaucer does, into Chaucer, 'Chaucer' –
and perhaps some of his narrator-pilgrims too. In the Merchant's
Tale, Justinus talks like 'Chaucer' (or Chaucer), with his "my wit is
thynne" (1682) and his reference to the Wife of Bath (1685–7). The
laughter of Justinus, the Merchant, Chaucer and the reader is a
healthy response to the absurd moral weaknesses of humanity that
are seen; this is the real antidote to the 'savage indignation' of the
disgusted satirist that some have claimed that Chaucer controls only
by placing it in the Merchant and dividing himself from his
creature.[21] Read thus, the Merchant's Tale expresses a view that is
tolerant, born out of sympathy, understanding *and* a firm
consciousness of personal responsibility and wrong; actually the
wrongs of the Merchant's Tale are more serious in their social and
biological aspects – broken faith, abuse of power, frustration of
nature – than in their spiritual ones. This Merchant's Tale offers
teaching, models of learning, and a 'snibbing' of wrongs that finds a
model in the Parson of the General Prologue (I: 477–528). It does
not damn the characters created for it. This is Chaucer's
unconventional idealism.

OTHER MANIFESTATIONS OF THE FABLIAU IN
CHAUCER'S WORK

It may appear something of an anticlimax to follow the conclusion
of a survey of all of Chaucer's works that can be called full-blown
fabliaux with some necessarily rather brief notices of the how,
where and why Chaucer draws upon characteristic features of the
fabliau in his other works. But this material is no miscellaneous
jumble, and is of great significance not only in making a general
assessment of Chaucer's perception and exploitation of this literary
genre but in determining the place of the fabliau in medieval
English literary history.

    There are two further places in the Canterbury Tales where we
suddenly find ourselves confronted by the sustained use of the
linguistic devices characteristic of the fabliau, and where we have to
consider whether these echoes of the genre imply any special tone.
The most extensive instance of this kind is found in the Wife of
Bath's Prologue. For the most part this takes the form of

21. See especially David *The Strumpet Muse* pp 170–81.

euphemistic sexual metaphors. The first instance comes in a set of six lines found only in a minority of manuscripts, but generally accepted as genuine (III: 44a–f), and is of considerable importance in corroborating the use of terms meaning 'purse' as sexual euphemisms by Chaucer:

> Of which [her five husbands] I have pyked out the beste,
> Bothe of here nether purs and of here cheste.
>
> (44a–b)
>
> *nether purs*: lower purse; *cheste*: [money]-chest

The Wife also uses "bacon" in a way that recalls the Old French fabliaux' use of the term (cf. Chapter 1):

> The bacon was nat fat for hem, I trowe. . .
>
> (217)

(cf. also line 418), and the image of grinding appears, recalling the Reeve's Tale and the French fabliau, *La Saineresse*:

> Whoso that first to mille comth, first grynt.
>
> (389)

More specifically Chaucerian is the use of "ese", implying sexual intercourse:

> What sholde I taken keep hem for to plese,
> But it were for my profit and myn ese?
>
> (213–4)

– a euphemism that is particularly characteristic of the Merchant's Tale in fact (IV: 1264, 1628, 1643). The most persistent and blatant fabliau term, however, is "queynte", a term that is in effect flaunted in the way that the Wife unhesitantly flaunts her own sexuality. Its first appearance comes in a passage which very clearly repeats – this time in the woman's voice – the Miller's argument about the undiminishing capacity of the female genitals to receive and provide sexual gratification, which he identifies, startlingly, as "Goddes foyson" (also anticipated or recalled in the Shipman's and Merchant's Tales, as noted above) (I: 3163–6):

> Have thou ynogh, what thar thou recche or care
> How myrily that othere folkes fare?

For certeyn, olde dotard, by youre leve,
Ye shul have queynte right ynogh at eve.

(329–32)

thar. need

The term and the argument is repeated in lines 443–4, and a pun on "queynte", 'strange, rare' appears in line 516. The wife introduces a new alliterating term for 'queynte' at line 608 with "*quoniam*", 'whatnot'. *Quoniam* is the Latin word for 'since', but is also a medieval and early Modern French slang term for *cunt*. There it looks like a comic, perhaps a deliberate, malapropism for the Latin pronoun *quidam*, 'a certain thing'. In the Wife of Bath's Prologue it allows the Wife of Bath to exploit the Latin of the clerk comically.

The Wife of Bath's Prologue also contains distinctive echoes of other fabliaux, particularly, and significantly, of the Merchant's Tale. An echo of a French fabliau, *Le Prestre crucifié*, 'The crucified priest' (in which a priest who is having an affair with the wife of a woodcarver tries to hide in the workshop as a crucifix figure when surprised by the husband, to be castrated when the husband notices an unseemly member he seems to have carved on one of his statues), in the claim by the Wife to have made "of . . . wode a croce" for her fourth husband may be coincidental, but the shared impiety and the fabliau potential of the Wife's story at this point are undeniable. The Wife claims that "Argus with his hundred yen" could never guard her adequately (357–61), a simile that is used too of the inability of January, blind or seeing, to inhibit May (IV: 2111–15). This simile is also of significance in the Merchant's Tale, as Argus was set by Juno, Jove's wife, as a watchman to watch over the heifer – formerly a nymph – Io, who had been raped by Jove. Not long after this the Wife clearly identifies herself as the sort of fabliau wife identified by the foundation myth of fabliaux in the Merchant's Tale:

They [her husbands] were ful glade to excuse hem blyve
Of thyng of which they nevere agilte hir lyve. . .
. . .For al swich wit is yeven us in oure byrthe.

(391–400)

blyve: directly, without disputing; *swich*: such

The order in which the Wife of Bath's Prologue and the Merchant's Tale were composed is indeterminable, but these echoes of the one in the other add very strongly to a sense of the coherency of fragments III and IV of the Canterbury Tales. That the Wife of Bath can present her own purported autobiography in fabliau terms shows also that Chaucer could and did conceive of the Wife as a teller of fabliau, supporting the theory that the Wife was the originally designated teller of what became the Shipman's Tale. An acknowledgement of the fabliau elements in the Wife of Bath's Prologue is, however, more important in the contribution it makes to the critical study of the Canterbury Tales as we have them rather than to speculation about the history of the composition of this work. Old French *fableors*, 'fabliau-tellers', and the perspective and narrators of the English fabliaux, are characteristically male. We see the Wife of Bath appropriating and employing various types of literature and discourse for her own ends. The Wife's use of familiar antifeminist material has been much discussed;[22] this is, however, one element in a comprehensive redeployment of literary models, including the fabliau, in her Prologue and the romance in her Tale. The appropriation of the fictional genre of the fabliau encourages one to emphasize the significance of her Prologue appearing dramatically as a fiction – the words she claims to use against her first three husbands, after all, come from her fifth husband's book – as well as being thematic in the terms of feminism and antifeminism, new and old.

The second place in the Canterbury Tales where the features of the fabliau are suddenly recalled to us is at the end of the Pardoner's Tale, where the Pardoner calls upon the pilgrims to purchase his pardon and kiss his relics, and asks the Host to begin (VI: 919–55, especially 941ff.). The Pardoner concludes his call quite literally, but with some familiar *double entendres*:

> 'Com forth, sire Hoost, and offre first anon,
> And thou shalt kisse the relikes everychon,
> Ye, for a grote! Unbokele anon thy purs.'

> (943–5)

Reliques is a familiar French substitute for *coilles*, 'balls', the uses of which are discussed at length, for instance, in a famous passage in Jean de Meun's continuation of *The Romance of the Rose* (6928–7180). The potentially bawdy double-meaning of the unbuckling of the

22. See, for instance, Mann *Geoffrey Chaucer* pp 48–51, 70–86 and 91–3, and cf. Delany S 1990 'Strategies of Silence in the Wife of Bath's recital' in *idem*, *Medieval Literary Politics. Shapes of ideology* (Manchester University Press) pp 112–29.

purse has been associated with the Host from as early as the Miller's
Prologue (I: 3114–15; cf. Chapter 4). The scurrilous metaphoric
implication of these lines is supported by the hints of the Pardoner's
homosexuality in the General Prologue. The Pardoner threatens to
disgrace the Host by embracing him in a form of sodomy. This
forms a transition between the cleanliness of the sermon text that
the Pardoner has recited and the literal crudeness of the Host's
explosive reply:

> 'Lat be,' quod he, 'it shal nat be, so theech!
> Thou woldest make me kisse thyn olde breech,
> And swere it were a relyk of a seint,
> Though it were with thy fundement depeint!
> But by the croys which that seint Eleyne fond,
> I wolde I hadde thy coillons in myn hond
> In stide of relikes or of seintuarie.
> Lat kutte hem of, I wol thee holpe hem carie;
> They shul be shryned in an hogges toord!'

(947–55)

> *so theech*: as I thrive (a common oath); *breech*: breeches; *fundement*: excrement;
> *depeint*: stained; *seintuarie*: a reliquary box; *lat kutte hem of*: have them cut off;
> *shryned*: enshrined

which maintains the focus on the anus and testicles, and which
verbally envelops the Pardoner, like Jouglet, in excreta. Castration
is a familiar punishment for the lecherous priest in the French
fabliau (cf. *Le Prestre crucifié*, above); the Pardoner is threatened with
a fabliau style of punishment matching both his ecclesiastical and his
homosexual promiscuity. The terms of the fabliau are appropriately
used by the Host for an anticlerical (counter-)attack.

The next nearest we come to the fabliau in the Canterbury Tales
is in lines 203–56 of the Manciple's Tale (fragment IX, group H).
These are the lines in which Phoebus Apollo's wife sends for and
receives her lover, and Phoebus's speaking crow witnesses their
lovemaking and tells his master what he has seen. More than half of
this passage is taken up with a discussion of the appropriate register
of terms to be used to describe the events: whether the wife's lover
should be accorded the title of 'lemman', and how a 'gentil'
woman may be called "his lady" in exactly the same situation in
which a poor woman would be called "his wenche or his
lemman". The variety of ways in which a characteristic fabliau
situation   may   be   viewed   are   not   dramatized   or   seriously

problematized here – they are plainly and explicitly stated. What is more, the moral seriousness of the situation of adulterous love is suggested by a simile linking it to inhuman destruction on an epic scale:

> . . .for the tirant is of gretter might
> By force of meynee for to sleen dounright,
> And brennen hous and hoom, and make al playn,
> Lo, therfore is he cleped a capitayn;
> And for the outlawe hath but smal meynee,
> And may nat doon so greet an harm as he,
> Ne brynge a contree to so greet mescheef,
> Men clepen hym an outlawe or a theef.

> (227–34)

meynee: strength; *sleen dounright*: slay outright; *brennen*: burn; *make al playn*: raze everything to the ground; *cleped*: called

The crow, subsequently, speaks like a *fableor* to Phoebus and does, in this way, "make al playn":

> '. . .on thy bed thy wyf I saugh hym swyve.'

> (256)

The response of Phoebus is to behave in the manner of the cuckold happy as long as he is ignorant, as predicted by the Miller's Prologue, the Merchant's Tale, and the Wife of Bath's Prologue: he kills his wife, and curses the crow, turning it black and taking away its "sweete noyse". The sweet illusion of the fabliau tale is broken here as Phoebus is disillusioned; the terms of the fabliau are used in the Manciple's Tale but the relationship of the tale with the genre is one of contrast. Significantly, Phoebus, the god of music and the guardian of the Muses, does not just destroy his wife:

> For sorwe . . . he brak his mynstralcye,
> Both harpe, and lute, and gyterne, and sautrie

> (267–8)

How different this is from the frank 'lustihede' of Nicholas's bedroom! The next move is symbolically anti-Cupidean:

> And eek he brak his arwes and his bowe

> (269)

eek: also

The Manciple's Tale is commonly held to be an early composition on the grounds of its supposed slightness of content and style. But it takes a deeply significant place in the final composition of the Canterbury Tales. It prepares us for the break from the sweet noise of poetry and the genres of poetic narrative to the solemn prose of the Parson and Chaucer's retraction "of the tales of Caunterbury, thilke that sownen into synne" (X: 1085).

There is, finally, one of Chaucer's minor and little studied works that contains distinct echoes of the fabliau: *The Complaint of Mars*. This tells a story, in both human and astronomical terms, of an adulterous liaison between Venus and Mars, with interesting emphasis, in this case, on their initial discovery by Phoebus (the sun) rather than their entrapment, *in flagrante*, by Vulcan, Venus's husband. A recognition of the fabliau potential of this tale, and of the motif of the cuckold happy as long as ignorant, is found in Jean de Meun's continuation of *The Romance of the Rose* (13823–74, 14161–86). *The Complaint of Mars* is tentatively dated on the grounds of the astronomical situation it surmises to *circa* 1385, which is close to the usual date ascribed to the Knight's Tale. We have in this poem a pair of rhetorical questions that are the equivalent, in structure, of questions in both the Knight's Tale and the Miller's Tale:

> Who regneth now in blysse but Venus,
> That hath thys worthy knyght in governaunce?
> Who syngeth now but Mars, that serveth thus
> The faire Venus, causer of plesaunce?
>
> (43–6)
>
> *regneth*: reigns

Cf. the Knight's Tale:

> Who looketh lightly now but Palamoun?
> Who spryngeth up for joye but Arcite?
>
> (I: 1870–1)

and 1454–6, 2652–3; and the Miller's Tale:

> Who rubbeth now, who froteth now his lippes
> With dust, with sand, with straw, with clooth, with chippes,
> But Absolon. . .?
>
> (I: 3747–9)

One cannot claim, for *The Complaint of Mars*, the same sort of significant contrastive echo as exists between the Knight's Tale and the Miller's Tale, but the connection allows one to suggest that it was indeed around the time of the composition of the Knight's Tale that Chaucer first began to develop the literary exploitation of the fabliau possibilities of romance — certainly he does so more in *The Complaint of Mars* than in *Troilus and Criseyde*, which was completed before 1388, perhaps by the spring of 1385. It is, admittedly, lightly done in just one pair of stanzas in *The Complaint of Mars*:

Up sterte Mars; hym liste not to slepe
When he his lady herde so compleyne,
But, for his nature was not for to wepe,
In stede of teres, from his eyen tweyne
The firi sparkes brosten out for peyne,
And hente his hauberk that ley hym besyde.
Fle wolde he not, ne myghte himselven hide.

He throweth on his helm of huge wyghte,
And girt him with his swerd, and in his hond
His myghty spere, as he was wont to fyghte,
He shaketh so that almost hit towond.
Ful hevy was he to walken over lond;
He may not holde with Venus companye
But bad her fleen lest Phebus her espye.

(92–105)

up sterte: up started; *brosten*: burst; *hente*: seized; *hauberk*: mailcoat; *fle, fleen*: flee; *wyghte*: weight; *girt*: girds; *towond*: shook to pieces

but these stanzas are sufficient to lend a comic colouring to the whole poem. Mars appears as a Priapic figure who "ne myghte himselven hide" and with "in his hond/His myghty spere" which "He shaketh so that almost hit towond" and "Ful hevy was he. . .". A phallic focus is well paralleled in the French fabliaux — cf. *Le Prestre crucifié, Le Pescheor de pont seur Saine* or *Le Fevre de Creil*, 'The blacksmith of Creil'. The complaint of Mars represents his frustration, and like Priapus and like Damian, this frustration makes him a comic figure.

These additional 'adaptations' of the stuff of fabliau by Chaucer are sufficient to impress upon us Chaucer's thorough awareness of the potential of fabliau in his later writing years; in fact in his most productive period from the mid-1380s to the end of his life.

Although a parallel between Pandarus in *Troilus and Criseyde* and the procurer/pimp of the *comoediae* and the fabliaux can be found, the characteristics of the fabliau genre are not exploited in that epic romance narrative poem, and this suggests that Chaucer *came to be* conscious of the use that could be made of the genre. The literary–historical circumstances in which this could come about will be considered in the following chapter. But Chaucer's exploitation of the fabliau seems always to be deliberate and significant; it has none of the appearance of a literary idiom into which Chaucer slips spontaneously and unconsciously.

Chapter 6

Fabliau: the history and spirit of a genre

As was promised at the end of the last chapter, an attempt will be made in this concluding chapter to set the appearance of fabliau as a genre in medieval England within a literary–historical context of broader geographical and chronological dimensions. A comparative study of transformations of the type between different literatures and through time may be hoped to sharpen our perception of the essential characteristics of fabliau. Eventually we must return to the problem noted at the start of the book: can we define 'fabliau'? A further question that can usefully be asked in addition is whether we can now identify something that Bédier called "l'esprit du genre": an essential *spirit* of fabliau that can be distinguished from the purely formal attributes of the genre. These perspectives, it is argued, strengthen the case for treating the English fabliau as a highly autonomous type.

OTHER EVIDENCE OF THE FABLIAU IN MIDDLE ENGLISH

Verse narrative

Up to this point, this study has been quite categorical in drawing a line around a small number of texts – *Dame Sirith*, and Chaucer's Shipman's, Miller's, Reeve's, Summoner's and Merchant's Tales – as being the only true representatives of the fabliau in Middle English. We do, however, have a number of narrative poems in English that are unquestionably identifiable with the genre, and which survive in versions of the late fifteenth and sixteenth centuries. One would hesitate to call these texts Middle English or medieval, although they may very well testify to the existence of more fabliaux within Middle English than the six texts we have studied in detail.

One of these poems is another version of the story found in Chaucer's Reeve's Tale. *A Mery Jest of the Mylner of Abyngton* was printed a number of times during the sixteenth century, first by Wynkyn de Worde, the successor to Caxton's press, in about 1522. It has been rather carelessly assumed and stated that the *Mery Jest* is simply a derivative of Chaucer's Reeve's Tale. There are, however, several substantial and significant differences between the two, and some points where the *Mery Jest* agrees with a French analogue against Chaucer's version. The two young men in the *Mery Jest* are identified as two sons of a poor widow, and their visit to the mill is an attempt to remedy their plight; this emphasis on poverty is matched in the French *Le Meunier et les deus clers*. The portrayal of the miller's daughter in the *Mery Jest* as fair and alluring agrees with the continental tradition against Chaucer, and there is a special scene where the one clerk talks his way into her bed which is similar, though in a rather general way, to what is found in *Le Meunier*. In the *Mery Jest* the clerk in this scene impersonates the daughter's real lover, Janekyn, the parish clerk. A gift is involved in the conquest of the girl too, although in the *Mery Jest* she actually ends up *giving* the clerk thirty shillings to make up the price of a gown she has demanded. Like *Le Meunier* and the Reeve's Tale, the cradle trick depends upon the wife getting up "water to make", although with *Le Meunier*, and against the Reeve's Tale, the wife in the *Mery Jest* rises *before* the second clerk moves the cradle. A significant parallel between the *Mery Jest* and the Reeve's Tale, however, is that when the first clerk and the miller are fighting in the dark, the wife is told by the second clerk to hit "him in the white": her husband has a white night-cap on. Some connection between the *Mery Jest* and the Reeve's Tale seems undeniable, but it is probable that the *Mery Jest* gives us a delayed glimpse of what a Middle English source for Chaucer's Reeve's Tale may have looked like. The location of the story, Abington, is, like Trumpington, near Cambridge. It is conceivable that Chaucer changed this name from his source to the similar Trumpington, a place whose relationship to the university town of Cambridge is much more like that of Oseney to Oxford and with a name that is not likely to be confused with the Abingdon near Oxford, thus strengthening the Oxford–Cambridge contrast between the Miller's and Reeve's Tales.

Two texts known in manuscript copies dating to the second half of the fifteenth century pose similar, and in one case quite teasing, problems of classification. Slightly the later of the two in its extant version is *The Lady Prioress*, a text preserved in a single copy, in British Library MS Harley 78, written in a hand dated to the last quarter of the fifteenth century. This contains a tale of which several continental versions are known, mostly of the sixteenth century, although many of those seem to derive from a fourteenth-century source: Day 9 tale 1 of Boccaccio's *Decameron*. *The Lady Prioress* is a more elaborate tale than Boccaccio's story of how a lady rids herself of the attentions of two suitors; and although there is some gaucheness in the composition of *The Lady Prioress* it is still quite successful as a comic poem. A beautiful prioress is persistently courted by a young knight, a parson and a merchant. The prioress's stratagem to rid herself of all three is to promise herself to each of them if they fulfil certain tasks: the knight is to lie for a night like a corpse in a secluded chapel; the priest is sent to perform his funeral and bury him; the merchant is sent to disrupt this service, on the pretext that the dead man owes the prioress money. The merchant is directed to do this by appearing at the church disguised as a devil, which produces a comic tumult of flight and misadventure as the priest, and then the knight, are terrified by the devil, while the merchant, and the priest, are terrified by seeing the 'corpse' rise. The characters' mishaps, it seems, just will not end: when, the following morning, the knight comes down from the treetop where he has taken refuge, he falls and injures himself. Thus all three men lose their bargain with the prioress; she maintains her chastity, and even succeeds in extorting money for her nunnery from the merchant in exchange for her silence.

Although it is most typical of fabliaux to be tales in which some misdeed is enacted by the lovers – or, in the case of several lecherous clerics, such a misdeed is painfully prevented or punished – there is a small subset of tales in which the essential trickery of the fabliau is deployed in order to preserve conventional womanly virtue and chastity: outstanding Old French examples are *Constant du Hamel* and, at least in part, *Le Segretain moine* (*NRCF: Le Sacristain*), 'The Sacristan'. In these, however, the punishment of the would-be lechers takes the form of extreme and shocking behaviour that represents the fabliau's characteristic treatment of the restraints of propriety. Constant du Hamel rapes the would-be lechers' wives in their husbands' presence; the lecherous sacristan is killed, and his body then follows the familiar course of the so-called 'circulating corpse', repeatedly hidden and rediscovered by new characters who believe that they are either responsible, or will be blamed, for the man's death. Boccaccio's tale has a real corpse, of a particularly loathsome and hideously deformed man, which the first lover is asked to displace and join in the tomb for one night. It is in the way in which *The Lady Prioress* so consistently and piously respects conventional standards of decency that it appears sufficiently untypical of the fabliau for one to hesitate over classifying it as such.

More similar to *Constant du Hamel* in its essential structure is a tale that is known in a copy dated to 1462, *The Wright's Chaste Wife*. This is the tale of a virtuous, lower-class woman wooed by three men of greater social status and power, a knight, a steward and a proctor. The woman accepts money from these three men for her favours, but sends them in turn into a room where they fall into a pit, and where they then have to work for the food and drink to keep them alive. When the men are to be released, the wright's wife sends for the knight's wife to witness her husband's shame. Added to this basic tale is the emblem of a garland of flowers belonging to the 'chaste wife' that will fade if ever the wife is untrue to her husband: this forms, in effect, a challenge to the three suitors; their efforts become a competition, as if to win a wager – a structural device we shall see more of shortly. Comparison between *The Wright's Chaste Wife* and *Constant du Hamel* shows clearly how all the fabliau features other than the deception that traps the would-be lechers are absent, leaving this English verse narrative as a clear and uncomplicated moral tale. In light of the particularly moral orientation of these two early post-medieval fabliau-like tales, we may also note how *The Mery Jest of the Mylner of Abyngton* ends with a lengthy coda detailing the grief of the miller's family at how they have been punished.

There are two further tales recorded in sixteenth-century copies that are worthy of attention. Both have clearly recognizable parallels amongst the Old French fabliaux. *Dane Hew, Munk of Leicestre* is known in a version printed sometime between 1560 and 1584. Its fabliau parallel is *Le Segretain moine* – a tale that in fact appears in four different fabliau versions in Old French as well as a fifteenth-century Italian version. A substantial difference between the French versions and *Dane Hew* is that much is made in the former of how the wife's tryst, for money, with the lecherous monk is the result of a serious and undeserved reversal of the husband and wife's fortunes, plunging them into poverty. That story is omitted from *Dane Hew*, but the wife still makes her arrangement with the monk in order to "get money". The omission of the preliminary story from *Dane Hew* therefore fails to shift the focus on to the punishment of the lecher from the self-centred motives of the husband and wife, if that is what it was intended to achieve.

The Friars of Berwick, which for some time was thought to have been written by the Scots poet William Dunbar (approx. 1456–1513), is found in two manuscript collections of the second half of the sixteenth century and in a printed version dated 1622. The poem is unquestionably a Scottish one, although there are a number of linguistic details that indicate that it was not written in the dialect that would be expected of south-eastern Scotland, the immediate vicinity of Berwick. The poem's most recent editor has argued that the praise of the town of Berwick and of its impregnability with which the poem opens means that the poem was probably written during the years 1461–82, when Berwick was part of the Scottish kingdom rather than the English.[1] But the poem is not political or nationalistic in any other way, and the praise of the town is a conventional rhetorical opening.

Its French fabliau parallel is *Le povre Clerc*, 'The poor clerk'. A poor travelling cleric – a *clerc* in the French story, one of a pair of friars in *The Friars of Berwick* – is refused hospitality at a house by a wife whose husband is away and who is expecting her own clerical lover. The husband returns inopportunely, and the poor clerk is able gradually to reveal firstly the presence of the food and drink the wife had prepared for her lover, and eventually of the now-hidden lover himself. In the French fabliau the information is revealed in plain terms and the husband punishes the priest-lover at the end; in *The Friars of Berwick* the young friar purports to conjure up the food and drink through a devilish servant he commands by means of necromancy. Eventually this servant is made to 'appear' in the form of a friar, and the husband is directed to thrash him as soon as he sees him. Thus the husband in the Scots poem never learns of his wife's infidelity. There are also significant parallels to the tale in German, dating from the first half of the thirteenth

1. Furrow *Ten Comic Poems* pp 321–5.

century to the mid-sixteenth century. In the pretended conjuring and the production of the hidden lover as a demonic spirit whom the husband should beat rather than as the wife's lover, *The Friars of Berwick* has a particularly close parallel in the fifteenth-century German *Van einem varndem Schüler*, 'Of a travelling student'.

Another poem, definitely one of Dunbar's, has been identified with a minor subtype found amongst the Old French and German fabliaux. This is *The Tretis of the Tua Mariit Wemen and the Wedo*, 'The Treatise of the Two Married Women and the Widow', which Roy J. Pearcy has compared positively with French fabliaux such as *Les trois Dames qui troverent un vit*, *Les trois Dames qui troverent l'anel*, *Le Jugement des cons*, 'The judgement of the cunts', *et al.*, as examples of tales in which three women compete in some way that requires a judgement to identify a winner. It is not, however, the presence of this structure that makes the French examples fabliaux. The three women who have found the ring compete in playing fabliau tricks on their husbands; in *Le Jugement des cons* the verbal and referential indecency of the text, and the violence of the rivalry between the three sisters, belongs to the fabliau world. Dunbar's poem presents the poet as narrator eavesdropping on a 'conversation' between two wives and a widow – all of them equally beautiful – each of whom presents a monologue of her experience in marriage. Where in *Le Jugement des cons* the male judge, the three sisters' uncle, is participating in a verbal form of pre-physical sexual initiation, virtually a form of sexual foreplay with the three girls in the test, there is a constant ironic emphasis in Dunbar's *Tretis* on the separation of the narrator from the ladies he is spying on. The narrator hides in a hawthorn hedge (ouch!) when he first hears the ladies. Their speeches are blunt and unadorned, as the first wife complains of her aged husband, the second of a husband who is worn out in his various amours, and the widow, who has twice been married, offers a self-dramatization that has all the assertiveness of Chaucer's Wife of Bath – which was presumably a model used by Dunbar, as January may have been for the portrait of the first husband. They can speak so openly for "ther is no spy nair [near]". Pearcy suggests an interpretation of this as more subtly ironic than a simple ignorance of the narrator's presence: we could imagine that the women were aware of the intruder thrusting himself hurriedly into the hawthorn hedge and are deliberately teasing and shocking him. All the time the narrator ironically attempts to maintain a simple, romantic and formulaic image of the women – calling them, for instance, "the semely", "the plesand", "this amyable" and "this eloquent wedow", despite what they say and how they say it. The idea of competition between the women is introduced only at the end, with the concluding question:

> Quhilk wald ȝe waill to ȝour wif gif ȝe suld wed one?

> (Which would you choose as your wife if you were to wed one?)

addressed solely to the readers. The conventional poetic forms of the debate and the comprehensive *demande d'amour* are common enough for Dunbar's *Tretis* to be a coincidental re-creation of a pattern found in French and German; and we are unquestionably a long way removed here from the material that is really typical of the fabliau.

In the drama

With one very unusual exception, there is no true sign in the surviving English drama of the fifteenth and earlier sixteenth centuries – primarily the great mystery cycles and the later interludes – of the fabliau's observable and inferrable association with dramatic performance in the late thirteenth and fourteenth centuries in England. Attention is paid in this present section only to the medieval mystery cycles of the fifteenth century; we shall come back to the Tudor interludes later in this chapter. There are two places in particular in the mystery cycle where fabliau influence is to be expected, in the parallel tales of a carpenter and his wife that provide the religious echoes in Chaucer's Miller's Tale: the stories of Noah and his shrewish wife, and of Joseph and Mary. The quarrelling of Noah and his wife during the building of the ark or when his wife refuses to enter the ark is a regular feature of this part of the mystery cycle, but their clashes are never presented in fabliau terms. More remarkably, the story of Joseph and Mary, with the old man coming to terms with the fact that his young wife is carrying a child that is not his, comes considerably closer to containing what we can recognize as the material of the fabliau. The degree to which this is so varies from cycle to cycle; echoes of the fabliau are strongest in the *Ludus Coventriae*, or 'N-town' cycle. In Play 12, *Joseph's Doubt*, Joseph laments at length that he will be scorned as an "olde cokwold" whose:

> . . .bowe is bent
> newly now aftyr the Frensche gyse
>
> (55–6)

and interprets the claims that the child is God's, and has been announced by an angel, as an absurd pretence:

> It was sum boy began þis game
>
> (75)

Soon after in the same cycle, in Play 14, *The Trial of Mary and Joseph*, Joseph is scorned in these terms, with explicit reference (lines 306–13) to the widely disseminated medieval *exemplum* of the Snow-child, in which a husband, absent from his wife for a long time, returns to find her with a child who cannot be his, which she claims was conceived by a snowflake landing in her mouth. This tale appears as a fabliau in Old French, in *L'Enfant qui fu remis au soleil*, 'The child who was given back to the sun'.

The exceptional play mentioned above is the famous Second Shepherds' Play (*Secunda Pastorum*) of the Towneley cycle, attributed to the 'Wakefield Master'. It is extraordinary that there should be two shepherds' plays in the one cycle, but the second play is not a superfluous indulgence in comedy; rather it is a skilful piece of art in which a fabliau-like tale is harnessed to the religious purpose of the mystery cycle, and in particular to the celebratory function of the Christmas-time plays. The central character in the fabliau-like episode is Mak, a sheep stealer who appears as a sort of spirit of disorder like Jouglet. Soon after Mak has joined the three shepherds in the play there is an echo of fabliau when he tells of his wife, who:

> Etys as fast as she can,
> And ilk yere that commys to men
> She bryngys furth a lakan –
> And, som yeres, two.
>
> (240–3)

> *etys*: eats; *ilk yere*: each year; *lakan*: baby

This echoes a widely repeated fabliau tale of a wife who gives birth very soon after her marriage – intervals of one day or three months are usual – after which her deluded husband decides to be more abstinent, sexually, as he cannot afford to have children so frequently. More significantly and substantially representative of fabliau, however, is the long episode (lines 269–637) in which Mak steals a sheep from the sleeping shepherds and takes it home to his wife, Gyll, who is to hide it in a cradle as her latest offspring. The shepherds, who come to search for their sheep, are initially deceived, but discover the trick when they return to give the child a gift and one stoops to kiss it:

> 3.pastor Gyf me lefe hym to kys, and lyft up the clowtt.
> What the dewill is this? He has a long snowte!
>
> (584–5)
>
> *clowtt*: cover

Mak and his wife still try to maintain the fiction, claiming the child has been elf-bewitched, but Mak is punished by a tossing in a blanket by the shepherds.

There is a clear parody here of the birth of Christ in the stable (with which the *Secunda Pastorum* play ends): the sheep baby contrasts with the heavenly babe who is the Lamb of God; Mak's stealing contrasts with God's gift; together these represent the disordered state of the world into which the Saviour is born. At the same time the play provides the audience with some lighthearted amusement appropriate to the joyous celebration of Christmas. The fabliau element resides in the thief's attempted deception, which in this case is unsuccessful. In an extremely general way fabliaux such as *Barat et Haimet* and *Le Bouchier d'Abeville* may be compared with the Towneley Second Shepherds' Play. The nearest medieval analogue of the Mak story that can be cited is an Italian novella published in 1483 in Sabadino de Arienti's collection *Le Porrettane*, in which the thieves are students and the stolen animal a pig, and the deception (the pig is passed off as a student sick with the plague) is successful. There are also much more recent ballad and folk-tale parallels.[2]

Exempla

We have already seen how closely fabliau tales and exemplary moral stories can be related, and it is important for us to remember that the basic tales that could be recomposed as fabliaux could circulate as *exempla*. There is no good reason for us to assume that if a fabliau tale is also found as an exemplum the latter is necessarily prior to the former, but empirically this seems quite often to be the

2. Cosbey R C 1945 The Mak Story and its Folklore Analogues, *Speculum* **XX**, pp 310–17.

case. In the case of *Dame Sirith*, for instance, the English version, rubricated as a "fablel", is the only deliberately comic and amoral fabliau rendition of this tale; all other known medieval versions are serious moral exempla.[3] An important, late-medieval English example of how such tales could circulate is provided by a large compilation of exempla translated into English from a Latin original, apparently of the early fourteenth century, called the *Alphabetum Narrationum* (English: *An Alphabet of Tales*) in the fifteenth century. This collection includes the 'weeping bitch' story of *Dame Sirith*, with Petrus Alphonsus explicitly cited as the source, as no.DXXXVII. As a matter of fact, the presentation of this story in English in the *Alphabet* lacks any clear moral interpretation except for the normal moral connotations of certain words used: in the end, we are told, the young man "had his luste & his desyre" and the old woman is called "þis false alde [old woman]". One moral interpretation, however, is made clear in the Latin rubric of the story: "Mulier mediatrix aliam ad peccatum inducit" – 'A lying woman leads another to sin'. The weeping bitch story makes its way into other collections of exempla found both in Latin and in various vernaculars: the *Gesta Romanorum*, 'The deeds of the Romans', and the *Historia Septem Sapientium*, 'The history of the seven sages'. There are Middle English versions of both of these collections, but in neither case is the weeping bitch story retold in English.

The Middle English versions of the *Seven Sages* do, however, include a version of a tale that appears in Western tradition first in the *Disciplina Clericalis*, and subsequently in Boccaccio's *Decameron*, as a fabliau tale.[4] It is the story of the Puteus, 'the well': the story of a cuckolded husband who locks his wife out of the house one evening as she returns from her lover. She drops a stone down the well, pretending she has thrown herself into it; he rushes out to the scene, for his wife to nip into the house and lock him out. She then publicly accuses him of having returned – late as usual – from drinking and whoring, to his shame and discomfiture. In the *Seven Sages*, this tale is told as an example of:

. . .hou ani wimmon
Miȝte bigile ani man. . .

(1391–2)

---

3. Tubach *Index Exemplorum* no. 661. See also Chapter 2, footnote 5.
4. Boccaccio, *Decameron* Day 7 tale 4.

and is used in its context as an example of how a man might be falsely accused and appear guilty. There is nothing comic in the *Seven Sages* version. Similarly the *Seven Sages* includes as *Vidua*, 'the widow' (2553–716), a version of the Matron of Ephesus story, which appears in the powerful French fabliau *De Cele qui se fist foutre sur la fosse de son mari*, in a thoroughly moralized version illustrating that a woman is not to be trusted. This was also collected amongst the *Exempla* of Jacques de Vitry.[5] In the moralized version, the widow's indifference to her husband's body, offering it to her lover to replace the lost body of a criminal he was meant to guard, leads to his rejecting her.

It is in the form of an exemplum that we get the nearest approach of Chaucer's distinguished contemporary English poet, John Gower, to the fabliau. *Confessio Amantis*, 'Lover's confession', is a large collection of tales presented as exempla through which a confessor, Genius, instructs and directs the lover, Amans. The one of these exempla that is truly fabliau-like appears early on in this work, in Book I, lines 761–1059: the story of Mundus and Paulina. This is a story whose source can be traced back to the ancient Latin historians, Josephus and Hegesippus. It tells of a lecherous duke who has his will of a beautiful, chaste, devout and gullible wife by impersonating the god Anubus. He braggingly reveals the deception to her; she cannot conceal her distress from her husband, who complains to the emperor. The result is that the priests who assisted the duke, Mundus, are put to death; the duke is given a lesser sentence of exile, as he was motivated by love. The tale is an exemplum against 'hypocrisy', or more specifically "deceipte" in love. It is not in any way presented as a comic story by Gower, but essentially the same story, with a lecherous friar impersonating a supposedly enamoured Angel Gabriel, is told comically by Boccaccio.[6] There again, however, the lecherous friar is exposed and punished.

One example of a fabliau-like exemplum used in a Middle English sermon has been reported by Siegfried Wenzel. A sermon ascribed to an earlier fourteenth-century English Dominican friar (the Dominicans were specifically a *preaching* order), Robert Holcot, includes a short anecdote:

5. Tubach *Index Exemplorum* nos. 5652–3.
6. Boccaccio, *Decameron* Day 4 tale 2.

Sed caveat laicus talis qui non videt nisi uno oculo quod non fiat de eo sicut de uno viro Oxonie qui habuit oculum tantum nequam. Cuius uxor dilexit unum cum duobus oculis, et existente illa cum amasio in camera, venit sponsus. Ipsa surgens imposuit viro suo quod potuit videre cum ceco oculo, et ipsa abscondit alium oculum, et interim amasius fugit. Hec mulier est mundus vel caro qui oculum dileccionis excecat.

(But let such a layman who sees with only one eye beware lest what happened to a one-eyed Oxford man should happen to him. This man's wife loved another man who had both his eyes, and while she was with him in the bedroom her husband arrived. She got up and persuaded her husband he could see with his blind eye; and while she covered the other eye her lover fled. This woman is the world or the flesh, that blinds the eye of love.)

(MS Peterhouse 210, fol.46v; ed. Wenzel 1979 p.318)

Note, with regard to Chaucer's Miller's and Reeve's Tales, and the *Mery Jest of the Mylner of Abyngton*, the clerkly, Oxford setting. The essence of this story is, again, found in Petrus Alphonsus, and is summarized in *An Alphabet of Tales* (no.DXXXV: "Mulier mala decipit virum suum" – 'A bad woman deceives her husband').[7] The most fabliauesque treatment of this story appears as nouvelle XVI of the mid-fifteenth-century French prose *Les cent nouvelles nouvelles*, 'The hundred new novellas', on which more below. We might, finally, note in this section the fabliau potential of *An Alphabet of Tales* no.XXXVI, "Adulterium punit deus in hac vita", 'God punishes adultery [or, possibly, the adulterer] in this life', a story of a man who impersonates his neighbour in order to lie with his wife after her husband has gone off to the fields.[8]

FABLIAU AND FABLIAU TALES IN OTHER EUROPEAN LITERATURE

Germany

Medieval German literature includes a substantial body of verse tales that unmistakably have characteristic features of fabliau. Some of these seem to differ from the Old French fabliaux only in being written in a different language. A good proportion of this collection

7. Tubach *Index Exemplorum* no. 1943.
8. Tubach *Index Exemplorum* no. 3455.

of German verse narratives is, however, rather different in nature from the French fabliaux in certain regular ways; other tales hover between these two categories. It is, as a result, quite impractical to attempt anything but the broadest numerical comparison of French fabliaux and their German counterparts; one can at least reasonably state that there is a similar number of Old French fabliaux and of medieval German tales that stand comparison with the French fabliaux by virtue of being relatively short verse narratives, usually of events including a deception and/or some misdeed, and quite often with clear analogues amongst the recognized French fabliaux. These German tales are sometimes referred to in scholarly literature as [Studenten]Abenteuer, '[students'] tales', or, rather more frequently and more appropriately, as Schwänke (singular Schwank), 'pranks' or 'tricks'. There is, however, a good deal of German Schwank literature that is quite dissimilar from fabliau. It seems significant that, in marked contrast to the situation in medieval French literature, there is no distinct medieval German concept of fabliau. The verse narratives in question usually refer to themselves as a maere (plural maeren, Modern German Mähre(n)): quite simply, as a 'tale'.

The birth of the German literary tradition of these fabliau equivalents is usually identified with an early to mid-thirteenth-century Franconian writer called der Stricker, a writer who practised his skills in many different genres and who is believed to have begun writing his Schwänke before 1240. Der Stricker arguably wrote no tales that would be identified as fabliaux by the terms that have been used in this book, but it is convenient to begin with der Stricker, especially to identify those characteristics of the German tradition that contrast most sharply with the nature of the French fabliau tradition while yet an undeniable analogousness between the stories remains.

Der Stricker belonged to the south of Germany; it appears that he spent some time at least in what is now Austria. His writings are in Middle High German, a literary language based in southern German dialects that is used for the great majority of medieval German Schwänke and fabliaux; very few examples survive written in the Low German that represents the vernacular of northern Germany. The most striking feature of der Stricker's individual Schwank pieces when set against the French fabliaux is their explicitly and seriously moral character. A clear example is his Drî wunsche, 'Three wishes', a version of the story told in the French

Les quatre Souhais Saint Martin. Der Stricker's tale is a clear moral example on the theme of foolishness: a peasant couple complain to each other of their state, and then to God:

> unz got ir tumpheit schande
> und in sînen engel sande

> (until God was offended by their foolishness
> and He sent them His angel)

and the wishes, which, as in *Les quatre Souhais*, cancel each other out, are granted to show them their foolishness. In a lengthy moral conclusion the couple are referred to simply as the *tôren*, the 'fools'. Indeed, the exposure and castigation of foolishness, and drunkenness, are very prominent characteristics of der Stricker's Schwänke, together with a reciprocal praise of *kündikeit*, 'astuteness'. *Der geafte pfaffe*, 'The priest tricked' (*alias Der kluge Knecht*, 'The clever lad'), an analogue to the Old French *Le povre Clerc*, thus concludes:

> Der vriuntlîche kündikeit
> mit rehter vuoge kan begân
> dern'hât dar an niht missetân.

> (Whoever is able to do a friendly deed
> astutely and with propriety
> does nothing wrong in that.)

Note here how the French fabliaux' supposed 'morality of efficacy' is qualified by additional criteria through the adverbs *vriuntlîche*, 'friendly', and *mit rehter vuoge*, 'with true decency'.

There are fabliau-like tricks in some of der Stricker's poems, such as *Man und wîp*, 'Man and wife' (*alias Ehe in Leben and Tode*, 'Marriage in life and death', or *Der erzwungene Gelübde*, 'The extorted vow') and *Der künig im bade*, 'The king in the bath'. In the former, a wife from whom the husband attempts to force a promise not to remain celibate after his death, astutely turns the tables by agreeing and suggesting they both enter the cloisters, and thus extorts a promise from him to allow her to have another man even while he lives before she will change her purpose. But having humbled her husband's pride and presumption, she resumes her life as a happy and faithful wife. The latter tale, too, has an extremely simple trick used to humble a proud king: an angel steals his clothes while he is in the bath, leaving him naked and an object of ridicule.

These tales come to a happy moral end. More haunting and ominous is *Daz heize îsen*, 'The hot iron'. This poem opens with a wife expressing her jealous fear that her handsome husband may be unfaithful, to be answered by a declaration of love and fidelity from her husband that is full of resonances of the courtly *Minnesang*, 'song of love'. The wife, however, makes the husband undergo the ordeal of holding heated iron to prove his fidelity; he cheats and passes the test. He then makes her take the test – and she fails. The poem ends with a speech from the husband "ûz grôzem zorne", 'in great anger', not with a moral. The implicit questions posed by the tale swamp any simplistic view of the poem as an example of hypocrisy exposed and punished. Are both husband and wife guilty? Or is the ordeal no test of virtue, and the wife simply foolish to have suggested it, perhaps trying to force her husband into subordinacy? A generation before der Stricker, Gottfried von Strassburg had produced an even more challenging moral study of the deceptive use of the hot iron ordeal as a test of marital fidelity, in his *Tristan*:

> dâ wart wol goffenbæret
> und al der werlt bewæret,
> das der vil tugenthafte Krist
> wintschaffen alse ein ermel ist

> (then it was clearly revealed
> and confirmed for all the world
> that the virtuous Christ
> bends with the wind like a sleeve)
>
> (Gottfried von Strassburg, *Tristan*. Ed. Marold K (1906)
> 3rd edn. 1969 (Walter de Gruyter: Berlin) 15737–40)

Of particular historical importance amongst der Stricker's innovations with the Schwank is a long narrative poem called *Der Pfaffe Âmis*, 'The parson Âmis'. Âmis is an English parson forced into exile who follows a career of adventures as a fraudster and trickster in a journey around the continent before finally returning to England and becoming an abbot. In a very general way Âmis's picaresque series of adventures can be seen as a pastiche or parody of the wanderings of a knight-errant of romance, but this is not especially thematized in the work. The prime focus of attention is, again, the human baseness and folly that Âmis exposes, with the added ingredient here of a comic toleration, or even covert praise, of the way he ingeniously profits from it. Rather than isolating individual target figures, Âmis tends to prey upon mankind *en masse* – taking a rich offering, for instance, by declaring he will receive nothing from wives who have been unfaithful to their husbands, or making the ailments of a host of sick people disappear by declaring he will kill the illest of them in order to make a medicinal powder to cure the rest (sections II and IV). The latter appears as no.CCLIV of Jacques de Vitry's *Exempla*. In an episode (section III) that is reminiscent of *Der künig im bade* he makes a fool of a king by offering him a miraculous painting that only the especially gifted can see: a variant of the well-known 'Emperor's clothes' story, told, for instance, by Hans Christian Andersen. Again, as in *Das heize îsen*, a more tantalizing and serious point is achieved in a parody of the gospel in an episode in which Âmis appears as a miracle worker, or when in the next episode he uses the appearance of true holiness to appear as something utterly strange in this world – and thus attracts more gifts (sections IX–X). It is at this point that we can be most sure that Âmis is not, simply, an alternative type of hero; he is a functional character showing the gullibility and debased nature of mankind, while at the same time, more poignantly, revealing mankind's residual yearning for the sort of holiness that he counterfeits.

A considerable number of medieval German fabliaux or fabliau-like tales are preserved for us in three great manuscript collections dating from the late fourteenth to the mid-fifteenth century. Some of these works are by known authors, but few of these stand out as writers in the way that der Stricker does. It is important to note that the composition, or re-composition, of fabliau tales in German continued in the second half of the fourteenth century at least down to the time of Chaucer's writing in England, while production of works of this genre in France seems to have ceased before 1350. At least two dozen of these German works have close parallels amongst the French fabliaux, and some of these, although having their own character as poetic narratives, can justifiably be called fabliaux. *Die hasen*, 'The hares', for instance, is a close parallel of the tale told in the French fabliau *Les perdris*, 'The partridges' (summarized in Chapter 1). It is instructive to compare the way in which the two versions deal with the motif of the husband's supposed threat to castrate the priest. In the French, the wife states the threat explicitly:

'. . .il vous voudra trenchier
Les coilles, s'il vous puet tenir.'

('. . . he will cut off
your balls, if he can catch you.')

In the German, it is more a matter of pleasingly comic innuendo:
the husband first pursues the parson shouting:

'Weiz got, ir lâzet sie bêde hie!'

('By God, you leave them both here!')

and then extracts a joke missed in the French:

'Eijâ, sô lâz mir doch den einen!'

('Alas, at least let me have the one!')

Of particular interest in the context of this book is *Irregang und
Girregar*, by one Rüdiger von Müner: a German version of the
story found in the Reeve's Tale and the *Mery Jest of the Mylner of
Abyngton*, in two versions amongst the Old French fabliaux, and in
Middle Dutch and Italian. This is the longest of the medieval
versions. As with the French *Gombert et les deus clers* and Boccaccio's
version in Italian, this is not set in a mill, and in agreement with
Boccaccio, the host's wife succeeds in persuading her husband that
the horrible truth he has inadvertently been told of his daughter's
company during the night was a deception – in this case
perpetrated by elves. With the concluding battle of most of the
analogues obviated in this way, the opportunity arises for more
deceptions; here one of the *knehte*, 'lads', enters the host's bed the
following night dressed as his wife, startling the host when he
gropes for his wife and finds a man – another elvish trick. The host,
"der wirt", who has started the tale characterized as "der alte", 'the
old man', is by the end characterized as "der tôre", 'the fool'.

This is not the only case where in certain respects we find closer
parallels between Italian and German 'fabliaux' than between either
of these and French examples: we may also note the tale of a naive
man who is persuaded he is pregnant, in the German *Der swanger
münch*, 'The pregnant monk', and Day 9 tale 3 of the *Decameron*.
But the German examples with close French parallels are more
numerous; there are also a number of these German tales that are
set in France, such as Ruprecht von Würzburg's *Von zwein*

koufmannen, 'Of two merchants', with characters with French names, partly set in Provins, or *Der schuolære ze Paris*, 'The student of Paris'.

There is a consistent, though not uniform, inclination in these German fabliau-like tales to move in a direction away from the anarchistic laughter that can often be found amongst the French fabliaux towards the greater moral, intellectual and emotional seriousness of the exemplum, and der Stricker. *Die drî münche von Kolmære*, 'The three monks of Kolmar', is a good example. It is a version of the returning corpse story found in French in *Estormi* and *Les trois Boçus*. Here the lecherous clerics who are punished with death meet the wife and make their advances when she is at confession, and a distinctly moralistic note is struck early on in an emphasis on her desire to confess fully: "als si solte", 'as she should'. When she is first seen acting deceptively – welcoming the first monk in to be relieved of the money he has offered her, and to meet his death trying to hide in a bath tub of boiling water – she is apologetically called "diu tungentbære", 'the virtuous woman'. "Ein varnder schuoler. . . der was trunken", 'a passing student who was drunk', is persuaded to dispose of the body, which he finds he has to do three times before meeting a fourth monk whom he takes to be the body returning yet again. Considerable emphasis is placed upon the innocence of this monk; he is on his way to matins, and, pathetically, is given speech and thought, telling the student:

> '. . .ich sage iu, ân allen spot,
> Ich wolt' dâ hin ze mattîn sîn,
> und gebuezet hân die sünde mîn.'

> ('. . .I tell you, honestly,
> I want to get on to matins,
> and to have done penance for my sins.')

and thinking:

> . . .'ach, lieber herre Got
> Waz wil der man an mir begân,
> dem ich kein leit hân getân?'

> (. . .'ach, dear Lord God,
> what does he intend to do with me,
> to whom I've given no offence?')

The poem is finally called a *bîspel*, an 'example', and the specific moral is drawn:

. . .der unschuldig' engelten
Muoz des schuldigen missetât.

(. . .the innocent has to pay
for the crime of the guilty.)

What more serious or fundamental Christian soteriological statement could be made?

This is not the place to expand upon this point in detail; one may, however, direct attention to examples such as the German *Daz heselîn*, 'The little hare', or *Der sperwære*, 'The sparrow-hawk', versions of the tale found in French as *Cele qui fu foutue et desfoutue, La Grue, Le Héron*, with pertinent moral endings, in one case with the deceived girl marrying her seducer, for "daz sîn sol, daz muoz gechehen", 'what should be must come about', in the other with a reflection that the old should understand the problems of the young; or to *Der Herrgottschnitzer*, 'The crucifix carver', like the French *Le Prestre teint*, a more moral version of *Le Prestre crucefié*, with a lecherous cleric manoeuvred into the trap by a faithful wife, and allowed (by the tale) to flee before castration. More intellectual is *Der borte*, 'The belt', by Dietrich von Glaz: here the beautiful wife of a knight is persuaded to commit adultery by another knight, who offers her a splendid jewelled belt. The husband learns of this and travels away; the wife then disguises herself as a knight, equipped with hunting dogs, hawks and other trappings of unparalleled quality, and in this disguise comes to her husband and brings him to covet her possessions: these she will give her husband if he will do anything for her – indeed to make love to her, for, as she truly says:

'. . .Ich minne gerne die man,
nic dehein wîp ich gewan. . .'

('. . . I love men;
I never had any woman.')

The knight, Konrad, agrees to this apparently homosexual act; the wife calls him a "kezzer", a 'heretic', for this, and identifies herself. The tale turns around the parallel and contrast between the wife's 'natural' heterosexual giving of herself for a gift and the husband's 'perverse' preparedness to give himself homosexually for equivalent gifts. It is this intellectual character that allows the tale to offer a practically unparalleled, tolerant contemplation of active homosexuality (one may compare, in French, the approaches to the subject in *Berengier au lonc cul*, or *Le sot Chevalier*, 'The sottish knight').

The initial misdeed of the wife in *Der borte* is also ameliorated by being wrapped in romantic, *minnelîch*, imagery and diction: she meets the knight with the belt in a garden, on a May afternoon; the knight 'burns' for her love, and is on the point of going demented or dying "von minne", 'of love'; the sexual act itself is elegantly and evasively covered by lines describing how the birds sang, the flowers laughed, and so on, for that time. This is representative of the recurrent and distinctive aristocratic orientation of the medieval German Schwänke. *Der ritter underm zuber*, 'The knight beneath the bath-tub', for instance, is a version of a simple tale told in the French fabliau *Le Cuvier*, where a wife hides her lover under a bath-tub and finds a device to allow him to escape her husband. In *Le Cuvier* the husband is a merchant, the lover is a "clers"; in *Der ritter underm zuber* the husband and wife are just a "wirt" and "wirtin", 'husband' and 'housewife', although the feigned journey of the latter – in order to catch his wife – may suggest a merchant, and the lover is a knight. There is a distinct echo of the *pastourelle*, a pastoral fantasy of knights dallying with beautiful shepherdesses, in this indulgence of a knight in amours with a beautiful woman of lower class; so too in, for instance, *Daz heselîn* or *Der sperwære*. In *Der ritter underm zuber* the husband, unlike his brothers, who inform on his wife, is emphatically not a jealous husband; he is, rather, foolish in his self-confidence:

> Der wirt sprach, 'dâ ist niht an,
> mîn wîp erminnet keinen man
> Anders, wærlîch, danne mich. . .'

> (The husband said, 'That is not so.
> Truly, my wife loves no man
> other than me. . .')

which is reinforced after his unsuccessful search for the lover. The wife then plays on the theme of befooling the husband by telling him her lover *is* under the bath-tub; he assumes she is teasing, and responds good humouredly: "'wiltu mich . . . machen zuo eime tôren?'", "do you want to make me a fool?" But the contrast between the husband

and the less pliant brothers stops the husband taking up the role of a real fabliau target figure; and this leaves instead room for the poem to function as a celebration of knightly pleasure.

Von zwein koufmannen, too, controls the impudence of fabliau by enveloping it in a framework that preserves the value of romantic *minne*, 'love'. The tale opens with 240 lines of the romantic tale of the betrothal and marriage of a young couple, Bertram and Irmengart, and then moves into a distinctly defined fabliau section that opens with the line:

Daz ich nû sage, daz ist wâr. . .

(What I shall say now is the truth. . .)

On a business trip to Provins, Bertram comes into a company of men who tell tales of the dreadful character of their wives. Bertram's romantic praise of Irmengart stands out in contrast. This leads the host to wager with Bertram that he can seduce Bertram's wife; she, in brief, escapes the otherwise irresistible pressure he puts her under − with her parents' connivance − by being replaced in bed by a prostitute. Startlingly, it is God who gives her this plan! Of course, the host's proof that he has slept with Irmengart − he cuts off a finger − proves false, and the tale ends with the prostitute, Amelîn, also becoming a 'proper wife' by being married to him. But romantic love can be tragic too, and this we see in *Der schuolære ze Paris*, where a fabliau device whereby a woman reveals her love to her chosen lover and sends him instructions on how to come to her by means of feigned rebuffals passed on by an innocent confessor is but one movement in a tragic tale wherein the young man's passion leads to his bleeding to death, with the girl, subsequently, dying of grief too.

The German Schwänke are characteristically milder than the French fabliaux, and the English, in their diction and their portrayal of sexual adventures, and in respect of the scatological. Marked language is very rare. The word *vut*, 'cunt', makes an appearance in *Der wîze rôsendorn*, 'The white rose-thorn': not itself a fabliau tale but one which with its anthropomorphized "vut" contains distinct echoes of *Le Chevalier qui fist parler les cons*. One may suspect, too, that the sexual connotations of the French *anel*, 'ring', and *corroie*, 'belt, money pouch' (cf. Chapter 1), may hover over the equivalent German terms too, as in *Der borte*, or in *Daz heselîn*, where the naive girl first offers the knight, amongst other things, a "vingerlîn", 'ring' and a "borte" that she keeps "in mîme schrîn", 'in my box'. The diction used to signify sexual intercourse is euphemistic, and remarkably modern-sounding: *ze samen slâfen*, 'to sleep together', or *gên ze bette*, 'to go to bed'; the act itself is often called the *bette spîl*, 'bed-play'. *Vrouwen list*, 'Woman's trickery', avoids describing the topic in a way that is exceptionally clear but essentially representative:

> In die kemenâten
> sie giengen: waz sie tâten
> Dar inne dô, dâ von wil ich
> niht vür baz sagen.
>
> (Into the bedroom
> they went; what they then did
> there, I think it better not to say.)

Castration is avoided as a topic, as we have seen, in *Der Herrgottschnitzer*, as too, except very allusively, in *Der vrouwen zuht*, 'The woman's disciplining', which corresponds to the French *La Dame escoillée*, except that here what is cut out of her (or is purportedly so) is not two testicles but two "brâten", two 'lumps of meat', that are her "übel", her 'evil'. The scatological is widely avoided too. An unusual exception is *Turandot*, a tale of massive defecation which is described with words like *schîzen*, 'to shit', and *ars*, 'arse'; there are also examples of the use of *netzen*, 'to piss', as in *Der blinde Hausfreund*, 'The blind familiar', where a lecher is punished when the husband rises to "netzen" on him.

The lines quoted above as marking the beginning of the fabliau section of *Von zwein koufmannen* are just one example in German of the assertion of the truth of the usually quite incredible tale that is being told that is very similar to what we find in Old French:

> Icil fableau ce est la voire
>
> (This fabliau is the truth)

A distinctive subset within the medieval German Schwänke that develops the theme of truth and falsehood is made up of tales in which the fabliau trick or device consists of telling the truth so honestly that it is simply not believed. This we have, for instance, in *Der ritter underm zuber*. Precisely the same device is used in a much simpler tale, *Der Liebhaber im Bade*, 'The lover in the bath', whose contents one can therefore virtually guess from the title alone. A somewhat different example appears in *Von dem ritter mit den nüzzen*, 'Of the knight with the nuts', which opens with the usual truth assertion:

> . . .merket ein bî spil,
> Wie ein ritter wart betrogen.
> Daz wil ich sagen unerlogen.
>
> (. . .attend to an example,
> of how a knight was deceived;
> I shall tell it truthfully.)

The tale is of how a wife shows her husband how she would really help a lover to escape from her unexpectedly returned husband, if, as she has 'pretended', she had one hiding in the bedroom, by covering her husband's eyes with her dress – symbolically blinding him with her sexuality, of course – which she does, and the lover escapes. We may note here the analogy with the anecdote used (*inter alia*) as an exemplum by the English Dominican Robert Holcot, quoted earlier in this chapter.

Unfortunately it appears difficult if not impossible to put close dates to many of the sort of German Schwänke we have been considering here, and thus to see how far these aspects of these tales represent phases of development. One known author, however, Heinrich Kaufringer, shows that in the second half of the fourteenth century at least there was some writing of German fabliaux that were generally less seriously inclined than most of the tales that have been referred to so far. The author is believed to be one of two Heinrich Kaufringers, a father and son, whose names appear as burgesses of Landsberg-am-Lech, near which is the small town of Kaufering, in Bayerisch-Schwaben, to the west of modern Bavaria, in records dated 1369 to 1404. Most of Kaufringer's Schwänke are simple, unoriginal and rather dull; in *Der Mönch als Liebesbote*, 'The monk as love-messenger', for example, he tells the tale embedded in *Der schuolœre ze Paris* of how a young lady communicates with her lover through an innocent confessor, and in *Der Schlafpelz*, 'The blanket', the story that has just been recounted of how a wife gives her lover an opportunity to escape by demonstrating how she would cover her husband's eyes. Significantly, however, Kaufringer omits the truth references, comments and imagery, etc., that so strongly create a more serious tone in the other medieval German Schwänke, and leaves the joke

– such as it is – to be 'enjoyed' on its own. He does, however, in *Chorherr und Schusterin*, 'The canon and the cobbler's wife', have the story of a wife, surprised by her husband's return while her lover is in the bath, telling him the truth which he does not believe.

Two of Kaufringer's Schwänke, however, stand quite apart in their complexity and quality. *Drei listige Frauen*, 'Three cunning wives', is a German example of the model Pearcy finds in Dunbar's *Tretis* and certain French fabliaux he calls *jugements* (above, this chapter). The tale is not original in that many of its parts can be closely paralleled elsewhere, but it is uniquely rich in Kaufringer's composition of these parts, and acutely effective in its exploitation of the outrageous excesses of fabliau behaviour. Three women compete in befooling their husbands. The first succeeds in drawing a healthy tooth from her husband's mouth, and then persuades him he is dead and has sexual intercourse with a "kneht", a 'lad', in front of him. This appears as a tale by itself in the twelfth-century Latin *Comoedia Lydiae*, whence it appears as tale 7 of Day 9 in the *Decameron*. The second wife tonsures her husband when he is drunk and persuades him he is a priest, who has to bury the 'dead' man (the first husband): compare *The Lady Prioress*, above, and Jacques de Vitry's *Exempla* no.CCXXXI. The third wife persuades her husband he is clothed when he is naked, and thus he goes to the funeral service in the church; he reaches to his scrotum/purse for his offering, but as he is too slow in producing anything his wife castrates him:

> sie schnaid im aus die hoden sein
>
> (she cut off his balls)

His scream brings the other husbands back to themselves – and everyone flees the apparently re-awoken dead, as, again, in *The Lady Prioress*. The insouciant moral has an acutely calm and simple inadequacy that contrasts painfully with the excesses of the tale:

> . . .sie alle ger trunken sind
> und mit sehenden augen plind.
>
> (. . .they are all dead drunk
> and blind with seeing eyes.)

Die Rache des Ehemanns, 'The husband's revenge', also starts with the unnecessary tooth-drawing motif, but the husband realizes the situation, and converts the Lydia story into a lecherous priest punished tale, feigning an absence and returning to castrate the priest and to tell him to bite off his wife's tongue.

Italy: novelle

In Italian literature the closest and truest analogues to the fabliaux of France, England and Germany appear in the form of short prose narratives of a type that is called the *novella* (plural *novelle*). It is generally agreed that the origins of this unusual form are to be found in medieval Latin prose exempla. A transitional stage between such Latin models and the vernacular novella would appear to be represented by the thirteenth-century Italian *Libro dei sette savi*, 'The Book of the Seven Sages', a translation of the *Historia Septem Sapientium*, whose occasional fabliau-like contents were discussed above with regard to the exemplum in England and the English *Seven Sages*. But ancestry alone is clearly insufficient to explain the quantity and range of fabliau tales that appear amongst the medieval Italian novellas. At the other end of the line of literary descent, the relationship of the medieval Italian novella to the novel in general has been, and continues to be, much debated. It is an issue we shall meet again in looking at post-medieval 'survivals' of the fabliau.

The Italian novella proper starts with a collection of short prose tales datable to the late thirteenth century and known as *Il Novellino*, literally 'the beginner'. Unfortunately our knowledge of the original form of this work is irretrievably obscured by a much confused chain of manuscript transmission behind the best copies that are now known to us. It is not clear whether it had a single author or not, and there is no reason to believe that the title by which it is known is original. Our primary sources for this collection differ in their contents; in fact some of the few fabliau-like tales that appear here occur only in one manuscript. There is, however, an authentic prologue to the collection which offers a valuable statement of its ostensible purpose: to offer for imitation "alquanti fiori", 'varied flowers', to make up a garden of fine words and deeds of courtesy, love *et al*. It is for the leisure and improvement of readers of noble hearts, to cheer them as well as to assist them. Here indeed is an equivalent of Chaucer's "tales of best sentence *and* moost solaas".

Amongst the fabliau-like tales found in just one early manuscript of *Il Novellino* is an analogue to the Merchant's Tale.[9] In itself this is a curiously mixed tale, certainly not readily recognizable as the equivalent of a fabliau. The husband to be cuckolded is quite briefly dealt with to begin with, and considerable emphasis is placed on the grace the lady shows to her 'dying' lover. But the device of a speaking tube, through which the lovers communicate, may seem simply grotesque, and when we come to the pear tree escapades the tone simply becomes crude: for instance the obvious sexual metaphor of the lady's "Io volea delle pere d'uno ramo. . .", 'I want some pears from one particular branch. . .'. The interference of God and St Peter does not, as in the Merchant's Tale, involve taking sides between husband and wife but functions rather to teach the point that the woman will always find an excuse, and the husband be taken in. Another fabliau analogue we might briefly note from *Il Novellino* is a short version of the tale found in French as *Le Chevalier qui fist sa dame confesse*.[10] Disappointingly – although perhaps significantly – censored even in the early manuscript is a story that looks to promise something far more fabliauesque concerning a "putta", a 'whore', and a man with a large member: but the story is never told.[11]

There is, then, very little in Italian literature up to the mid-fourteenth century to prepare us for the explosion of fabliau like tales that is to be found in Boccaccio's *Decameron*, written sometime after the year 1348 and, apparently, before Boccaccio's *Corbaccio*, 'The Raven', which is dated to 1354. There is also very little in Boccaccio's own earlier writings to prepare us for what appears in the *Decameron*. The *Decameron* is a collection of 100 tales, told by a "brigata", a 'party', of ten rich young townspeople, seven beautiful women and three men, who escape from Florence into the countryside during the plague of 1348 and who each tell one tale on each of ten days. Nearly one-third of the 100 tales of the *Decameron* could be counted as fabliau tales, and these are clearly grouped into clusters within the collection.[12] Several of these tales

9. MS Panciatichiano 32, no. XIX. Eds Bryant and Dempster *Sources and Analogues* pp 341–3.
10. Maghabechiano Strazzione II.III.343 no.V. Ed. Lo Nigro 1963.
11. MS Vaticano 3214 nos. XCVI and LXXXVI respectively. Ed. Lo Nigro 1963.
12. Most of the tales of Days 3, 7, 8 and 9 fall into this category. The only tale from another day that I would count here is Pampinea's tale of Friar Alberto, Day 4 tale 2, referred to above in connection with Gower's tale of Mundus and Paulina.

contain plots or motifs that we may be familiar with from other medieval literatures – indeed, the *Decameron* provides analogues to Chaucer's Shipman's, Miller's, Reeve's and Merchant's Tales. Although there is no conclusive evidence that Chaucer even knew of the *Decameron's* existence, so prominent a monument of fourteenth-century European literature is it that many cannot believe that Chaucer was not familiar with it, however little he may acknowledge it.

This is not the place to go into the sources and analogues of Boccaccio's fabliau tales in any detail; it is generally pertinent, however, to make a note of some salient examples of parallels to tales that are mentioned elsewhere in this book. Day 3 tale 3 is the familiar story of an innocent friar-confessor used by an amorous young woman to convey messages and guidance to her chosen young man; Day 3 tale 4, similar to part of the Miller's Tale, has a husband persuaded to gaze into the heavens while his wife commits adultery; Day 3 tale 8 has a husband persuaded he is dead by an adulterous wife and cleric; Day 7 tale 4 is the story of a wife deceiving her husband by dropping a stone down a well; Day 7 tale 5 has a husband disguised as a confessor to learn of his wife's adultery and eventually persuaded that this statement of the truth was a falsehood made only to tease him; Day 7 tale 7 contains the tale found in *La Bourgoise d'Orliens*, where an adulterous wife has her husband beaten, purportedly by her unwanted suitor, to make him a 'coccu battu et content'; Day 8 tale 4 has an ugly maidservant substituted for a beautiful young woman (a widow) in bed with a lecherous priest; Day 9 tale 1, as has been noted, has the basic tale found in the late fifteenth-century English *The Lady Prioress*. This is, of course, simply a selection.

The quantity of available literary analysis of Boccaccio's aims in composing the *Decameron* and the narrative prose style he develops there is immense, and it would be digressive to note more than the most basic points here. It is generally observed that the distinctive Boccaccian style includes an identifiable interest in the potential complexity of characterization within tales such as these. Hans-Jörg Neuschäfer, for instance, comparing Day 7 tale 7 with *La Bourgoise d'Orliens*, notes how the wife's foresight and control in Boccaccio's tale replace her astute but spontaneous response to crisis found in the French story; in the *Decameron*, the wife, Beatrice, calmly tells her husband of their servant's advances to her after the servant has entered their bedchamber and is cowering, terrified, in the dark beside her: thus she deliberately enjoys the heightened pleasure of daring, as she could easily have sent her husband out before the servant came to her, besides controlling a sequence of events in which she and her lover consummate their desires and her husband is reassured of the fidelity of both his wife and their servant. Beatrice acts out of sexual desire, but has her passion under control and can apply, and enjoy the exercise of, her intelligence all the time. In this, in Neuschäfer's terms, she represents a distinctly Boccaccian 'bipolarity' in character construction.

This tale can be taken as representative of what are broadly taken to be distinctive characteristics of Boccaccio's handling of these tales. Any move towards complex rather than monothetic character construction can be taken as a move towards realism, and Boccaccio's care in setting his tales in familiar and detailed contexts is generally recognized. Boccaccio tends to focus on the device or trick that is essential to the fabliau tale, and usually treats or portrays the sexual acts with which this device is involved with a refined sensuality rather than naked crudity. Thus the sexual climax of Day 7 tale 2, in which an adulterous wife has told her unexpectedly returned husband that her lover, hidden in a tub, has come to buy the tub, and has manoeuvred her husband into the tub, in place of the supposed customer, to clean it out, is brief but clear, with one of the more exotic positions for sexual intercourse denoted with a flourish through a fine classical simile, and with a deft parallelization of the scraping of the tub and the act of coitus:

> e a lei accostatosi, che tutta chiusa teneva la bocca del doglio, e in quella guisa che negli ampi campi gli sfrenati cavalli e d'amor caldi le cavalle di Partia assaliscono, a effetto recò il giovinil desiderio; il quale quasi in un medesimo punto ebbe perfezione a fu raso il doglio, e egli scostatosi e la Peronella tratto il capo del doglio. . .

> (. . .and he dressed her as she was keeping the whole mouth of the tub covered; and in the manner in which, in the wide open spaces, the unbridled stallions aflame with desire mount the Parthian mares, he brought his young man's desire up to its climax; which he had just completed when the tub was fully scraped out, and he slid back, and Peronella withdrew her head from the tub. . .)

Comparably, in Day 9 tale 10, a priest persuades a foolish peasant and his wife that he can magically turn the wife into a mare, gets her to adopt the appropriate posture, naked, and fondles her. In due course:

> risvegliandosi tale che non era chiamato e sù levandosi
>
> (someone awoke without being called and got up)

which, using another simile, is planted 'like a planting-stick in a furrow', to form the mare's tail. The peasant finally objects that he can do without the tail – but the 'essential juice with which all plants blossom had already come'. With rich ambiguity, the wife then upbraids her husband "di buona fé", literally 'in good faith' (meaning 'from her heart'? or 'in all simplicity'?):

> 'Bestia che tu se, perché hai tu guaste li tuoi fatti e'miei?'
>
> ('Animal that you are, why have you spoilt both your affairs and mine?')

It should be noted, briefly, that there is very little of the scatological in Boccaccio's fabliau tales: Day 8 tale 6 is about as much of an exception as we get, a tale in which a confection whose basic ingredient is a dog's turd is served up by a pair of jokers, Bruno and Buffalmacho, to their foolish workmate Calandrino, who is obliged to try to eat it.

Brevity and refinement in directions such as those noted here are the characteristics of Boccaccio's handling of the fabliau tale; expansive adaptation is very rare. An exceptional example of just that is Day 8 tale 7, an unusually long tale by the general standards of the *Decameron*, in which a scholar, who has wooed a vain and malicious widow without reward, to be befooled by her into spending a freezing night outside her house in the snow waiting for leave to come to her that never materializes, wreaks a carefully planned revenge on her, described in a tortuously drawn-out manner, by exposing her, naked, to the full heat of the summer sun for a whole day. Much space is given to the scholar's verbal admonishment of the widow as she begins to suffer, and although one can hear an echo of *Dame Sirith* in the tale's moral conclusion:

> E per ciò guardatevi, donne, dal beffare, e gli scolari spezialmente.
>
> (And so, ladies, I warn you against making fools of others, of scholars in particular.)

the emphasis in the tale lies on the horror of the scholar's revenge rather than its black comedy, and the tale functions principally as an urbane and humanistic exemplum.

Like Chaucer, Boccaccio was a highly talented interpreter and recaster of existing stories rather than a prolific originator of new stories. The abrupt appearance of such a fund of fabliau-like tales in the *Decameron*, together with the partly suppressed glimpses of similar material in the earlier *Il Novellino*, suggest that there was a store of such tales in Italy circulating and appreciated as fabliaux that was only occasionally finding expression in the forms of written literature that have survived for us in medieval Italian. It has been suggested that it is such tales that Boccaccio designates "favole" in his list of types of stories advertised in the *Proemio* to the *Decameron*. A firm example of material that Boccaccio has inherited from existing Italian tradition would seem to be provided by the set of 'Bruno and Buffalmacho' stories told on Days 8 and 9 of the *Decameron* (Day 8 tales 3, 6 and 9; Day 9 tales 3 and 5), most of which are distinctly fabliau-like. Bruno and Buffalmacho's role in the tales is that of a pair of tricksters, most of whose pranks are at the expense of one Calandrino; all three are described as painters (artists), and Bruno and Buffalmacho are identifiable with known painters of the earlier fourteenth century. It is not very plausible that Boccaccio himself selected these two deceased characters as the *dramatis personae* for a set of stories of this kind of his own. *Far Calandrino*, 'to paint Calandrino', becomes an idiom for 'to make a fool of somebody'.[13] And in the work which is thought to follow the *Decameron*, the *Corbaccio*, Boccaccio clearly invokes the notion of a great store of fabliau tales – certainly a greater store of corresponding tales than his *Decameron* alone contains:

> Quante già presummettero, e presummono tutto il giorno, or davanti agli occhi de' mariti, sotto le ceste o nelle arche gli amanti nascondere? Quante nel letto medesimo co' mariti farli tacitamente entrare? . . . E, che maggior vitupero è, veggenti i mariti, ne sono infinite che presummono fare i lor piaceri.

> (How many [women] have already dared, and dare day in day out, to hide their lovers from their husbands' eyes under baskets or in chests? How many have had them make their entrance silently, in the very same bed as their husbands lie in? . . . And, an even greater insult, there is an infinite number who dare to have their pleasure while their husbands are watching.)

13. See *Decameron*, ed. Branca 1976, notes, pp 1410–11.

Boccaccio has several distinguished successors as Italian *novellieri* in the later fourteenth, fifteenth and sixteenth centuries, but fabliau-like tales rarely appear more than sporadically in these authors' collections of novellas. From Franco Sacchetti (1335–1400), for instance, comes a now imperfect collection of 258 novellas known as the *Trecentonovelle*, 'The novellas of the 1300s', thought to date to *circa* 1376–97. The one truly interesting item amongst these in the context of the European fabliau is no.LXXXIV, a tale of adultery which moves in the direction of the French *Le Prestre crucefié* but which ends with the lover fleeing in panic in time to save his manhood, as in the German *Der Herrgottschnitzer* (above). Also of the later fourteenth century is Giovanni Fiorentino, who produced a collection of fifty novellas of which three appear to be derived from fabliau-like tales of the *Decameron*.[14] Giovanni Sercambi (1348–1424) produced a collection of 156 novellas organized according to an explicitly exemplary framework, but including a few more fabliau-like tales than the two writers just mentioned, among them an analogue (alongside *Decameron* Day 8 tales 1 and 2) to Chaucer's Shipman's Tale: a version that ends with a neat but teasingly ironic moral conclusion as Sofia, the wife, decides never to fall into the trap again, at least with someone who can outplay her in such a way.

One fifteenth-century Italian writer, however, who stands out in this respect is Masuccio Salernitano (1410–75), whose collection of fifty novellas, appropriately (again) entitled *Il Novellino*, was posthumously published in 1476. This collection includes one of the the analogues to Chaucer's Miller's Tale, at no.XXIX. The fifty novellas are divided into five groups of ten, the first supposedly illustrating the dark deeds of clerics (this includes a version of *Decameron* Day 4 tale 2 at no.II), the second how the jealous (in marriage) are made fools of, the third the faults of women; the fourth is presented as a mixture of tragic and comic tales, and the fifth as a collection of tales more elevated in tone and setting. Thus the collection starts firmly based in tales of love and sex with a set of themes that readily seem to have been suggested by a corpus of material that we can identify with the fabliau. Indeed, freeing ourselves from the stratification that the fivefold division tends to

14. Giovanni Fiorentino, *Novelle* nos.II. 2, III. 2 and V. 2; cf. *Decameron* Day 8 tale 7, Day 7 tale 7 and Day 9 tale 9 respectively.

impose on a view of Masuccio's *Il Novellino*, it may appear that Masuccio places the fabliau at one pole to be contrasted with the dignified and elevating tales that appear towards the end of the collection. The first three tales have strong fabliau links: the first is a version of the circulating corpse tale (cf. *Le Segretain moine, Dane Hew*, above); the second the tale that appears as Decameron Day 4 tale 2; the third is based on the situation where a lecherous friar leaves his trousers behind in a wife's bedroom: they are identified as a relic to befool the husband and carried to church in a solemn procession. This tale had been told in German by Kaufringer, as *Die zuruckgelassene Hose*, 'The trousers left behind'. But although tales which we can confidently treat as fabliau-like continue to appear in the collection (e.g. nos.IX, XII and XXIX), we subsequently find tales that are rather to be treated as examples or farces – tales of absurd misadventure in compromising situations rather than outrageously conceived and executed deceptions and misdeeds – than as fabliaux or their equivalents. Masuccio, though following very much in the master, Boccaccio's, footsteps, not least in dividing his collection into groups of ten, is rightly regarded as one of the most innovative of the early Italian *novellieri*, and comes closest to Boccaccio in his wide-ranging engagement with the greatly varying aspects of love as a literary theme. Hence the appropriateness of the title, *Il Novellino*, 'the beginner'.

In summary, an equivalent of the fabliau was a real enough presence in Italian literature from the late thirteenth to the late fifteenth century although – as, in very general terms, in England – its emergence in the collections of novellas, which was its only serious literary outlet,[15] was of a very sporadic nature. One can hardly fail to make a comparison between the supposed influence of Boccaccio's *Decameron* on Chaucer's fabliaux and the limited impact Boccaccio's innovations with fabliau-like tales had on Italian literature. It is, to recapitulate, only in the case of the Shipman's Tale that Italian literature offers the best and most appropriately dated analogues for there to be any question of their being a possible source; the pros and cons of this suggestion were considered in Chapter 3. The one place within Chaucer's fabliaux where we can be sure of derivation from Boccaccio comes in the

---

15. I discount here the comic literature of the *facetiae*, 'jokes', of, for example, Poggio.

Merchant's Tale, where the portrait of aged January seen through the eyes of the young wife is unquestionably drawn from Boccaccio's *Ameto* XXXII. In *Ameto* the young wife in May's situation is provided with a lover by Venus, to whom she prays, but the story is not developed as a fabliau: rather Ameto's response emphasizes the minor tragedy implicit in the tale, expressing his jealousy of both the husband and the lover, and noting how fate has hurt three people in this tale – the *vecchio*, 'old man', who has to repent, the girl, who is given, and himself (*ibid*. XXXIV). It is in fact in the *Corbaccio* again that we can find the germ of the development of the story as it appears in the Merchant's Tale; the mordant voice here records of women:

> Niuno vecchio bavoso, a cui colino gli occhi e triemino le mani e'l capo, sarà, cui elle per marito rifiutino, solamente che ricco il sentano, certissime infra poco tempo di rimanere vedove e che costui nel nido non dée lor soddisfare . . . al quale, se la già mancante natura concede figliuoli, sì n'ha; se non, può perciò morire sanza erede: altri vegnono, che fanno il ventre gonfiane. . .

> (There is no drooling old man whose eyes are runny and whose hands and head shake who they will refuse as a husband as long as they know he is rich, it being certain that they will be left as widows soon and that this man need not satisfy them in the nest . . . [and] if his now fading nature grants him sons, he gets them thus [sc. slobberingly]; if not, he cannot therefore die without heirs: others come who make the womb swell. . .)

Yet there remains one point of the deepest significance in Chaucer's handling of the fabliau for which a striking parallel is to be found in the *Decameron*. We have noted how Chaucer works with the motif of the contented cuckold, satisfied because he has as much sexual intercourse with his wife as he wants and as he can physically cope with; the woman, however, physically, has a greater capacity for sexual intercourse. Thus for the man:

> 'Of the remenant nedeth nat enquere'
>
> (I: 3166)
>
> ('There's no need to ask what is done with the rest')

We have found echoes of this theme, first stated in the Miller's Prologue (in the order of the Canterbury Tales), in the Shipman's and Merchant's Tales; a determined assertion of the argument is made by a female character in the Wife of Bath's Prologue (III:

323–36), and the inverse is stated in the Manciple's Tale. There is something comparable in Jean de Meun's continuation of *The Romance of the Rose* (7409–14), but undoubtedly the clearest parallel statement comes in Day 6 tale 7 of the *Decameron*, the tale of a wife taken in adultery and publicly charged in court with this as a crime, who defends herself with this question to the judge:

> '. . .domando io voi, messer podestà, se egli ha sempre di me preso quello che gli è bisognato e piaciuto, io che doveva fare o debbo di qual che gli avanza? debbolo io gittare a' cani? non è egli molto meglio servirne un gentile uomo che più che sé m'ama, che lasciarlo perdere o guastare?'

> ('. . .I ask you, sir, if he has always taken of me as much as he needs and is satisfied with, what am I to do with what is left over? Should I throw it to the dogs? Is it not much better for me to present it to a fine man who loves me more than he loves himself than to let it be lost or wasted?')

Chaucer did not need Boccaccio to provide him with fabliau models. But he may have found in the *Decameron* a theme that he was gradually to develop and examine from many sides in a serialized assessment of the moral worth of fabliau comedy as a literary type.

The Low Countries

There is a set of fabliaux written in Middle Dutch that survives amongst a group of tales that are collectively referred to as *boerden* (singular *boerde*). What was intended as a comprehensive collection of Middle Dutch boerden was edited and published by C. Kruyscamp in 1957; this collection contains nineteen boerden, of which a majority, some fifteen, can be identified as fabliaux. There may in fact be a few more fabliaux or fabliau tales in Middle Dutch, but as a group the boerden have been neglected, and texts are very inaccessible.[16] What is important here is that in Middle Dutch we have a literature in which fabliaux are definitely more numerous than in English, but markedly less so than the fabliaux or their near equivalents in French, German and Italian. The fabliau boerden published by Kruyscamp are found in four manuscripts.

---

16. See Dempster 1932; Hertog *Chaucer's Fabliaux as Analogues* p 107n.

The largest collection, eight fabliaux, comes from a famous and copious manuscript of *circa* 1400: the Hulthem manuscript now in the Royal Library of Brussels. Three more come from another manuscript in the same library, Brussels MS (K.B.) II,1171, and two each from two manuscripts in the Royal Library in The Hague. Several of these fabliaux have the word "boerde" in either their title or their rubric. The word is borrowed from Old French, *bourde*, which we might translate with English 'jest'.

Of the fabliaux or their equivalents in all other European literatures, it is the Middle Dutch boerden that show the closest relationship with the French fabliaux. Some of them are clearly derived from French originals. *Een bispel van .ij. clerken*, 'An exemplary tale of two clerks', subtitled "ene goede boerde", 'a good boerde', is a version of the early French *Gombert* by Jean Bodel, an analogue of the Reeve's Tale. In the Dutch version, accordingly, the two clerks come from Paris. It also preserves the name of the master of the house as "her Gobert". *Vanden vesscher van Parijs*, 'Of the fisherman of Paris', is likewise clearly derived from *Le Pescheor de Pont seur Saine*, 'The fisherman of Pont-sur-Seine'.

But there are French fabliaux dependent on Dutch sources too. It was noted, in connection with the Summoner's Tale, that Jacques de Baisieux states that his *Dis de la Vescie a prestre* is derived from the Dutch. The French *Barat et Haimet*, discussed in Chapter 1, again by Jean Bodel, has a close Dutch parallel in *Van .iij. ghesellen die den bake stalen*, 'Of three fellows who stole the bacon'. The relationship between these fabliaux was discussed by Jan de Vries in an old but still authoritative article, in which he showed the strength of various cases that can be made for this and other French fabliaux to be following Dutch sources. The major divergences between *Barat et Haimet* and *Van .iij. ghesellen* come at the beginning and the end, and they serve to give the Dutch version a much more coherent moral structure. The Dutch fabliau opens with one thief leaving his two companions because he wishes to earn an honest living, and not to end his life on the gallows. The to-ing and fro-ing of the stolen meat follows a very similar course in both versions until the final episodes, where in the Dutch the one man frightens the two thieves by sticking his naked "eers", 'arse', out of a window, which the thieves take to be the swollen face of the ghost of the dead mother of one of them, rather than impersonating their hanged father as in *Barat et Haimet*; when the thieves subsequently try to reach in and steal the meat back both lose an arm, cut off by the man inside the house. It is perfectly credible that this more predictably moral Dutch version stands closer to a common original for the two versions than does the relatively genial French fabliau.

Barat et Haimet, however, is one of the earliest datable French fabliaux; it was written by Jean Bodel and the most recently suggested date for its composition is 1190–94. What is known about Jean Bodel locates him for at least some time in Arras, in the Pas de Calais, in north-eastern France, not so very far from the Middle Dutch-speaking areas of Flanders (it is impracticable to attempt to separate Dutch and Flemish linguistically in the literature of this period). The historical implications of the possibility that Bodel may have used a Middle Dutch source for *Barat et Haimet* are substantial and radical indeed. Of course the Dutch version exists in a much later copy, and is rather unlikely to be a very close copy of any hypothetical twelfth-century source that Bodel may have drawn upon directly or indirectly.

This parallel, however, is not unique; another one of Bodel's fabliaux tentatively dated *circa* 1190–94, *Le Vilain de Bailleul*, 'The peasant of Bailleul', also has a close parallel in Middle Dutch, in *Van Lacarise den katijf die een ander sach bruden sijn wijf*, 'Of Lacarise the wimp, who saw another man take his wife'. This is the tale of a man who is persuaded by his wife that he is ill, and then by his wife and her lover, the priest, that he is dead, and thus lies still and closes his eyes as the priest and his wife fornicate in his presence. *Lacarise* is set in a place "op de Scelte", on the River Schelde in Flanders, now Belgium. It is uncertain in which Bailleul Jean Bodel set his fabliau: there are several in the north-eastern French regions along or near the border with the Dutch-speaking areas, although a Bailleul a few miles north-east of Arras seems the most probable candidate. Once again, *Lacarise* seems to have a more predictable or logical conclusion than Bodel's fabliau: it faces the question of what happens to Lacarise in the end, finally suggesting that he remained 'dead':

> Dits die vite van Lacarise;
> God bringhe ons ten eweghen paradise.

> (This is the life of Lacarise;
> God bring *us* to the eternal Paradise.)

while *Le Vilain de Bailleul* hits its comic climax with a wittily perceived paradox – the priest reassures the peasant that he must be dead, because the priest would obviously not screw his wife in front of his eyes if he were still alive; thus the fabliau ends. The burial of the husband alive is shockingly explicit in the next closest analogue to these tales: der Stricker's *Der begrabene Ehemann*, 'The buried husband'.

It is quite possible that, some time between the late twelfth and the late fourteenth centuries, copies of Bodel's fabliaux came to a Dutch versifier who reworked these two tales in Dutch; and even if both extant versions of the latter two fabliaux are derived from some earlier common ancestor, that ancestor could as well have been French as Dutch. At the very least, however, the connection between the Dutch versions and Bodel's versions of these two fabliaux must be close, for they are not fabliaux that are repeated and modified in a series of developed stories in French as are other fabliau tales.

A further outstanding French–Dutch fabliau parallel is that between *Le Foteor*, 'The fucker', and *Van den cnape van Dordrecht*, 'Of the lad from Dordrecht', subtitled "ene sotte boerde", 'a mad boerde'. Both of these fabliaux share the rare and striking motif of a professional male heterosexual prostitute, who declares himself shamelessly in either case when his identity or source of income is the subject of enquiry, explicitly in the French:

'Ge sui fouterres, bele suer!'

('I am a fucker, dear sister!')

euphemistically in the Dutch:

'Ic baenke om gelt der mannen wiven'

('I play games for the money of men's wives')

We might note in passing that this shameless lad from Dordrecht probably represents the closest parallel to Perkyn Revelour of Chaucer's Cook's Tale anywhere in European fabliau literature. The plot of how this youth comes to be in a particular man's house differs between the French and the Dutch fabliaux, but both tales end up with the same situation, as the husband has, to his shame, to pay off this stud-man who has come to service his wife. Thus the husband becomes a target figure, and since he has been present throughout the Dutch version – it is he, a "baeliu", 'bailly', who first enquires after the boy's means of support and who shows a prurient interest in his escapades before his wife becomes a customer – the Dutch appears as the more typical fabliau, and thus again probably closer to a model version, in this respect.

It is not our business here to evaluate such close relationships between French and Dutch fabliaux so as to try to reach a firm conclusion on the question of precedence and the direction of influence between the two, although it is a glaring omission in general studies of the French fabliau and its origins that these parallels are often never even mentioned. The important point for the present is that the French and Dutch fabliaux are in a general way as closely related to one another as their geographical provenance is contiguous. Six of the Dutch fabliaux are set in what is now Belgium; just two in Holland; and the two examples very clearly derived from French, *Een bispel van .ij. clerken* and *Vanden vesscher van Parijs* are located in or near Paris.

Other Middle Dutch fabliaux have more widespread analogues, and in some cases relationship with identifiable German and Italian literature is a real possibility. *Ic prijs een wijf*, 'I praise a wife', contains the familiar story that appears in the *Historia Septem Sapientium* and as the French fabliau *La Bourgoise d'Orliens*; in the German *Vrouwen stætikeit*, 'Wifely constancy', and *Der Herr mit dem vier Frauen*, 'The husband with four wives', as a serious moral exemplum; and in the *Decameron*, Day 7 tale 7. Unusually, the Dutch version is in stanzaic verse, and has the device that sends the cuckolded husband into the garden to be beaten originating with the young man, not the wife. *Wisen raet van vrouwen*, 'Wise counsel from women', has the story of a young woman complaining to an innocent confessor of the unwanted attentions a young man she desires is supposedly paying her; the confessor's subsequent warnings to the young man prove to be the means by which the lady can make her desires known to him, and to inform him how he can come to her. The tale appears in the German *Der schuolære ze Paris* and in the *Decameron*, Day 3 tale 3. Similarly, *Vander vrouwen die boven haren man minde*, 'Of the woman who had other lovers besides her husband', has a version of a widely told story in which a wife has a signalling system involving a piece of string tied to her foot running out of her bedroom window by which her lover can find out if it is safe to enter; one night the husband discovers the device, and traps the lover, or the wife – but a ruse is found by which they can escape punishment. The earliest fabliau version of this tale seems to be Herrand von Wildonie's *Der wirt*, 'The husband', a "maere" which he says was passed on to him by Ulrich von Liechtenstein (*circa* 1200–75), another famous Middle High German poet. *Der wirt* shares with *Vander vrouwen* the combination of the string trick and the substitution, in the dark, of an animal for the trapped lover. Herrand wrote another version of the tale in *Der Pfaffe mit der Schnur*, 'The priest with the string'. Both of Herrand's versions include the tale of the wife, after the lover's escape, getting another woman to take the physical punishment her husband then inflicts upon her – again in the dark – so that she, in the morning, can appear unharmed and innocent. The combination of this part of the story with the string trick appears in the *Decameron*, Day 7 tale 8; the substitution of an animal for a trapped lover, and the use of another woman to take the punishment of a guilty wife, but not the string trick, appear together in the French fabliau *Les Tresces*, 'The tresses'.

There is one instance of an exceptionally close parallel between a tale in the *Decameron* and a Dutch fabliau: between Day 8 tale 8 in the former and *Van enen man die lach gheborghen in ene scrine*, 'Of a man who lay hidden in a box'. These are the tale of a husband who surprises his adulterous wife with her lover, and knows that she has hidden the lover in a box in the bedroom; he forces his wife to bring the lover's wife there, whom he forcibly rapes on top of the box in which the lover is hidden. Remarkably, the final denouement in both cases is that this aggressive response is the basis for a reconciliation:

> Die goede knape van den huus
> Hi sprac: nu makens wi gene gerochte. . .
> Wi wisselden beide, dat mi dochte. . .
> Int spel van onser beider wiven.
> Gaet thuus te gader, leeft voert sochte
> Ende laet ons goede gevriende bliven.

> (The good man of the house
> said: 'now, let us not make a fuss. . .
> we've paid each other out, it seems to me. . .
> in screwing each other's wife.
> Go home together; get on with your lives in peace;
> and let us stay good friends.')

The French *Constant du Hamel* is analogous to this, but the case for this Dutch fabliau deriving from Boccaccio's novella is a persuasive one.

Although the number of fabliaux surviving in Middle Dutch is small, and although some of these are clearly adaptations of sources in another language, fabliau seems to have been a live and dynamic genre in medieval Dutch literature. As we have seen in other medieval European literatures that have been surveyed here, fabliaux or their equivalents follow some special course of development in each individual language. In Dutch this partly takes the form of producing, along with other erotic and scatological literature, the genre of the *boerde*. We might note as an example of the non-fabliau boerde *Dmeisken metten sconen vlechtken*, 'The maiden with the beautiful hair', a poem of six ten-line stanzas that apparently offers an *effictio* of a beautiful and courtly girl, but in reading which a reader steeped in fabliau can gradually become aware that the hair that the poet is obsessed with might be identified with the pubic hair. We also have in the Hulthem manuscript two in a series of 'sotternien', farce-like plays, in which we can recognize fabliau tales. *Lippijn* has a husband who has seen his wife with her lover persuaded that this is a product of "alfsgedrochte", an 'elvish illusion' – a device that is used in the German *Irregang und Girregar* (above) – and *Rubben* has a newly married wife giving birth after just three months of marriage, with the husband finally persuaded that these three months equal the nine months he expects a pregnancy to last. Here again we have a feature of medieval Dutch literature that anticipates the emergence of the dramatic farce in, most notably, French and German literature in the fifteenth and sixteenth centuries (see below).

The Middle Dutch fabliaux are also written with a vivacity, talent and variety that corresponds significantly with what is found in the French. They may contain a similar harsh undertone of black adult humour such as appears only rarely in medieval German or Italian. The image of the dead mother's ghost's face in *Van .iij. ghesellen*, or the notion that Lacarise may have been buried alive, are strong and disturbing motifs. In *Heile van Beersele*, the Miller's Tale's analogue, the 'misdirected kiss' is described with relish as the smith:

. . .custe spapen ers al dare
Met soe heten sinne,
Dat sine nese vloechder inne. . .

(. . .kissed the priest's arse right there
with such burning passion
That his nose shot right into it. . .)

In *Vander vrouwen die boven haren man minde*, after the over-eager
lover has unfortunately leapt between the husband's legs rather than
the wife's in the marital bed, the wife resourcefully:

. . .maecte hare orine
In tfier, soedat sijt wt brochte

(. . .passed her urine
on to the fire, so that she put it out)

to produce the necessary darkness. We also find a similar
exploitation of marked language to that of the French fabliaux; this
is particularly striking in *Vanden vesscher van Parijs*, where some
playing on the ways in which the penis can be represented
linguistically is found in the French original – the wife tries to refer
scornfully to:

'. . .vostre deable de pendeloche
qui entre les jambes vos loche. . .'

('. . .that devil of a tassel of yours
that swings between your legs. . .')

– seems to be picked up and developed in the Dutch. The husband
calls it:

. . .minen vrient
Die u dicke heeft gedient
Die tusschen mine bene staet

('. . .my friend
that has served you often,
which stands between my legs')

and part of the image is repeated when the fisherman takes the
penis from the corpse of a lecherous monk (it is a priest in the
French) whose adventures had led to his death:

Hi sneet den monec af dat let
Daer hi der vrouwen diende met
Dat men hiet sijn even oude. . .

(He cut off the monk's member
which he served the ladies with:
what men call their twin brother. . .)

When he throws the member at his wife's feet:

> Doe dochte der vrouwen geliken enen vede
> Bat dan enen andren lede

> (It clearly looked more like a prick to the woman
> than any other member)

But then she finds:

> J ding in sine broec raghen

> (A thing sticking out in his trousers)

a line that presents the wife's confusion better than the more explicit French:

> Puis sent le vit bochoier
> qu'entre les jambes li pantoise

> (Then she feels the prick swelling up
> which was knocking between his/her legs)

But the Dutch fabliau can also appear in less crude language without losing the insouciance of the genre. *Vanden monick*, 'Of the monk', and *Van de twee ridders*, 'Of the two knights', are examples of this: in the latter a poor but deserving knight succeeds in replacing a rich but "katijf", 'wretched', knight in a lady's bed when the latter has risen, not "te pissene", 'to piss', as Gobert does in *Een bispel van .ij. clerken*, but "sijn urine te maken", 'to pass her urine'.

The quality and the importance of the Middle Dutch fabliaux in medieval European literary history have been underestimated by Dutch and other European scholars alike. We should certainly not neglect the Middle Dutch tradition in looking for the historical context and even the sources for the English fabliau. The closest parallel to Chaucer's Miller's Tale, and its nearest analogue in date, is the Dutch *Heile van Beersele*. We also know that an analogue to the Summoner's Tale existed in Dutch. There are no specific details that could support any case that *Heile van Beersele* or the lost Dutch source of the *Dis de le Vescie a prestre* were direct sources of Chaucer's tales, although a somewhat tenuous connection has been drawn between the play, *Lippijn*, and the Merchant's Tale.[17] But

---

17. Beidler and Dekker 1989.

Middle English–Middle Dutch literary interaction is plausible in light of the economic connections between England and the Low Countries in the Middle Ages, and the existence of communities of "Flemminges" in medieval England. As was, coincidentally, noted in respect of *Dame Sirith*, there is considerable Middle Dutch lexical influence on the Middle English language. It is entirely possible that a literary tradition of the fabliau in England could have been strengthened, or even re-introduced, from the Low Countries via such connections. The Middle Dutch fabliaux are thus a significant and plausible rival to French and Anglo-Norman influence for identification as a source of the fabliau in English.

Wales

Although there is no identifiable influence one way or the other in respect of the fabliau in medieval English and Welsh, the geographical relationship of England and Wales justifies a quick look across the linguistic border in southern Britain to conclude this survey of the fabliau in other medieval European literatures. There appears to be just one true fabliau in medieval Welsh, *Y Dyn dan y Gerwyn*, 'The man under the tub': a tale readily recognizable as a version of the tale recorded in the Old French fabliau *Le Cuvier* and in German in *Der ritter underm zuber*. The Welsh version is short, just 42 lines long. A wife is surprised with her lover by the unexpected return of her husband, who works at farming: he seems to be identified as a ploughman. She hides the lover under a tub, and then lies on her bed and groans. In answer to the husband's tender enquiry after his "byd", his 'world', his 'precious darling', she directs him to tell a neighbouring woman she is suffering from the same "clwyf", 'wound, affliction', that she (the neighbour) suffered from a year before. In the French version the wife's refusal to return the bath-tub she has borrowed from her neighbour is sufficient for the neighbouring woman to perceive, intuitively, her predicament. So the neighbour lights a fire, in the corn-drying kiln in the Welsh, to create a diversion while the wife lifts the tub and the lover escapes. The conclusion of the Welsh poem focuses on the curtailment of the wife's misdeeds and the lover's lucky escape rather than celebrating the cunning that allows indulgence to flourish:

> colles y wraig ei llymaid,
> cafodd y dyn ei enaid

(the wife lost her titbit,
the man kept his life)

In the last line here, *enaid*, the object of the verb "cafodd", 'kept,
was allowed', can also carry the senses of 'soul' and 'beloved'. The
former has the more interesting connotations, as a reading of the
last line as 'the man got away with his soul' allows the word to
recall the Christian moral context within which all medieval
Western European literature belongs. This is not to suggest that the
poem has the simplistic moral happy ending 'sin was avoided';
rather that one may find here a wry reflection on the morally
flawed and vulnerable character of the sexually greedy *dyn*, 'man'.
In human terms, he's got away with his life, and soul – for now.
But there is no contrition or repentance for the sin committed, and
the ultimate judgement will not be evaded so impertinently.

It has also been claimed that the fabliau as a type is of
considerable influence in a number of works of Wales's foremost
lyric poet of the earlier and middle fourteenth century, Dafydd ap
Gwilym. The poems in question are collectively a set of
unsuccessful amorous adventures narrated in the first person; a good
example is *Trafferth mewn tafarn*, 'Trouble in a tavern', in which the
narrator tells us how he has made an arrangement in a tavern to
come to a beautiful girl's bed at night by whispering words of love
to her, but how he trips, falls and noisily knocks things over when
approaching her bed, after which he, now being hunted like a thief,
has to hide and slink back to his bed. Undoubtedly the erotic
theme, and the characters, of this and the similar adventures find
counterparts in the fabliau tradition, but the plots of these tales are
more appropriately associated with those that typify the farce: that
is, they represent a mishap or misadventure in connection with
illicit, usually amorous, exploits that is laughable; usually, in fact,
laughable primarily in sardonic terms. In comparison with the
fabliau, the discomfiture of the narrator-'hero' of these tales
produces a situation that is quite different from the victimization of
a target figure that is so characteristic of the fabliau, and the
deception and successful misdeed of fabliau is markedly lacking.

A more positive comparison of the range of medieval Welsh
erotic poetry noted here with continental literature can be achieved
by recognizing that as a whole it is a coherent and peculiarly Welsh
manifestation of a movement of literary exploration and licence that
elsewhere was contributing to the success of the fabliau and its

equivalents. Only in French do we begin to match the density of use of marked language that appears in certain medieval Welsh verses, and although the French fabliaux show some pleasure in exploring the linguistic range that can be brought to explicit sexual verse (cf. the discussion of *Le Pescheor du Pont seur Saine* and the Dutch *Vander vesscher van Parijs*, above), there is not the same intense interest purely in the art of generating a stream of images (actually a recognized technique of medieval Welsh verse called *dyfalu*) for, for instance, the male genitals, such as a medieval Welsh poet, perhaps Dafydd ap Gwilym again, produces in *Cywydd i Anfon y Gal a'r Ceillau'n Llatai*, 'A poem to send the prick and the balls as a love-messenger':

Cerdda, gal gron ddyfal ddu
â'm dwygaill yn ymdagu.
Rhydyn bin, rhed yn bennoeth
o flaen dau gabolfaen goeth
trwy dy gwcwll, trydwll tro,
syw faner, a saf yno.
Chwithau eich dwy, rwy reiol,
gwyliwch, anelwch yn ôl.
Mynnwch wledd i'ch arweddawdr,
meibion eillion llwydion llawdr.
Gwyllt bin ar fol dewingor,
gwst da, carn twca y tor,
distaw gal, dos di gulhoel
i mewn fel y clobren moel.

(Go, round black diligent prick
throttled by my two balls.
Rigid pin, run bare-headed
before two fine pumice-stones
through your hood, piercing deed,
splendid banner, and stand up there.
You two, regal leader,
watch out, bend backwards.
Demand a feast for your bearer,
pale bondmen of the trousers.
Wild pin on the belly of a wizard-dwarf,
good labour, belly's tuck-knife handle,
quiet prick, go you narrow nail
in like the bald nut-stick.)

(translation D. Johnston 1991)

It is difficult to resist comparison here with the development of erotic – and particularly erotic–comic – narrative and drama in Middle Dutch literature; in particular the narrative monologue as it appears in *Dmeisken metten sconen vlechtken* and other boerden.[18] The point of such comparison is not, let it be emphasized, to suggest any connection between the two groups of poems other than their essential similarity as the products of two relatively small but dynamic literary communities in which the impulses and licence noted just above were given rein to expand in rich and imaginative ways.

SURVIVALS: FROM THE FIFTEENTH TO THE EIGHTEENTH CENTURY

There is a continuity in the transmission of fabliau tales beyond the Middle Ages, into the fifteenth and sixteenth centuries and beyond, that is of great importance in identifying the boundaries and character of fabliau. A remarkably consistent pattern of transformation takes place across such literature in a range of different languages, leaving the fabliau tales fully recognizable in their newer forms, although rarely does it seem appropriate to separate them from other types of story in the same literary classes that these fabliau tales now occupy as the 'Renaissance-period fabliaux' of any language. The developments in French and German literature of the fifteenth and sixteenth centuries provide the best general guide to post-medieval developments against which the state of affairs in English literature can be assessed. Although not surveyed here, corresponding developments can also be traced in some measure in Italian, Dutch, Spanish and Scandinavian literature *et al.*

Germany: Schwänke

The medieval classification of German fabliaux and closely related tales within the category of *maeren*, and the later analytical inclusion of such tales within a larger corpus of *Schwänke*, appear to represent a historically real conception of a literary group of tales of misbehaviour and deception. The steady growth and reworking of

---

18. For example Kruyscamp 1957 nos. II, IV, XI and XVI; cf. also D Johnston's anthology *Canu Maswedd yr Oesoedd Canol/Medieval Welsh Erotic Poetry*.

the stock of Schwänke and Mähren from the thirteenth to the sixteenth century reflects the unique strength of continuity of fabliaux and related tales that there was in German literature. Tales that are truly fabliauesque, however, form very much a minority amongst the later Schwänke and Mähren. Besides examples in German, we should also remember the fabliau analogues written in Latin in Germany at this time, examples of which were cited in connection with the Merchant's Tale.

It is German literature that provides us with the only substantial case of continuity of these tales in verse form. Most prominent here are two picaresque 'cycles' of Schwank adventures, following the model of der Stricker's *Der Pfaffe Âmis: Neithart Fuchs* and the *Kahlenbergerbuch*. Closely related to these, although in prose and originating in Low rather than High German, is the book of *Dyl Ulenspiegel* (more commonly *Till Eulenspiegel*). The maintenance and reworking of such cycles of tales represents the strength of a striving for credibility that is so central in the German handling of the fabliau. Whole histories like this are more coherent and thus more realistic than isolated tales. The French fabliaux offer incredible tales in realistic settings; their German equivalents, in these cycles, attach themselves to historically real characters and represent themselves as true in a more persistent way. The historical basis for the legendary Neithart Fuchs is the early thirteenth-century poet Neidhart von Reuenthal, a poet whose lyrics are distinguished by his innovative though disdainful inclusion of scenes from country life and country folk. The *Kahlenbergerbuch* contains a set of stories that is believed to have clustered around the character of a parson Gundaker von Thernberg, parson of the parish of Kahlenberg, Austria in the earlier fourteenth century. A historical Tile Ulenspiegel of Brunswick died in 1350.

The *Kahlenbergerbuch*, a reworking of an earlier collection known as *Der Pfarrer vom Kahlenberg*, appeared in print around 1491. It shares with the typical fabliaux a few stories including sexual exploits – a bishop's, not the parson's – and violence and scatology. Possibly the most fabliauesque is the opening episode, in which the hero, still a student, brings a splendid fish as a gift to the prince. The doorman demands a share of whatever he gains from the prince in return for letting him in, so the student asks, in the first place, for a beating in payment: this is shared with the doorman. When the reason is revealed, he also asks for a parish, which he is given. Another tale tells how he intrudes on his bishop's lovemaking with his lady – 'blessing her chapel' – to obtain leave from the real versions of such services himself, so that he can spend more time with his own mistress. In a later tale, with echoes of *Jouglet*, he places filthy wine dregs in and around the backsides of some unwanted guests, leading them to accuse one another of shitting all over the place when they awake.

A now-lost Low German version of *Dyl Ulenspiegel* was apparently printed in 1478. A High German imprint from Strassburg of 1515 is now our primary German source. The stories of this collection are more persistently scatological. Time and time again one reads of how Ulenspiegel slights some other character by defecating in a 'suitable' place. Three anecdotes in this book are found earlier in *Der Pfaffe Âmis*: the healing of the sick, the miraculous painting for the king, and the acceptance of an offering only from faithful wives (Strassburg 1515 edition nos. XV, XXVII and XXVIII). Tale no. LXXI of the Strassburg edition is a version of the tale in the French fabliau *Les trois Aveugles de Compiegne* ('The three blind men from Compiegne'), and the cycle also includes an analogue of the Summoner's Tale: Strassburg edition no. XCII. Both the *Kahlenbergerbuch* and *Dyl Ulenspiegel* appeared in sixteenth-century English translations, the English *Howleglass* apparently being translated from the lost Low German version.

Neithart Fuchs, which also appeared in print in the late fifteenth century, is a more varied compilation of adventures and vignettes in which the Schwank is far from dominant and which are never truly of fabliau character. The closest we come to a fabliau is again in the opening episode, where the knight, Neithart, finds a violet which he wishes to preserve for a lady, and so he marks the spot and protects the flower by placing his cap over it. Certain "paurn", 'peasant men', who collectively are the fools of *Neithart Fuchs*, maliciously deposit a "*grossen merdum*", a 'large turd' (note the use of medieval Latin *merdus* for German *scheiss*), under the cap, to the knight's acute embarrassment when he reveals his present to the lady. This episode has a clear parallel in a medieval French verse "example" which is usually counted amongst the fabliaux, although it is not a representative case: *Les Chevaliers, les deus clers et les villains*, 'The knights, the two clerks and the peasants'. This is a brief tale in which two knights find a beautiful grove which they praise as a fine place for feasting; two clerks then praise it as a fine place in which to take one's pleasure of a lady; two peasants see it as a "biau lieu por chier", 'a beautiful place to shit'. And that is what they do. After a flimsy and lighthearted moral:

> . . .il n'est nus deduis entresait
> fors de chiier que vilains ait

> (. . .there's no pleasure at all
> that a peasant can have besides shitting)

a more substantial observation is made:

> nus n'est vilains se de cuer non:
> vilains est qui fet vilanie
> ja tant n'est de haute lignie

> (no one is a peasant if not by character:
> a peasant is one who does churls' acts,
> no matter how high his birth)

which in a reciprocal way matches the interpretation of Chaucer's presentation of the "cherles tales" of the Miller and the Reeve that has been offered in this study. A congruent perception is to be found in *Neithart Fuchs*. The absurd foolishness of the peasant men there is often represented by their participation in battles and their attempts to maintain an observance of honour – thus they parody chivalry, a set of conventions which are also cynically perceived and used as a mantle for his own less dignified desires and purposes by Neithart. In the vision of *Neithart Fuchs* life is thus is seen as subsisting in sets of conventions, from stereotyped stupidity of the peasant men to the 'nobler' stereotypes that they ape. Those for whom the chivalric culture is in this sense 'real', the aristocracy and the conservatives of a still highly aristocraticized society, are enabled and invited through the text to see that this culture is conventional: not natural; not even especially worthy.

One prolific author is a dominant figure in the history of the German Schwank in the sixteenth century: Hans Sachs (1494–1576), the *Meistersinger* (bard) of Nuremberg. Sachs produced a number of narrative poems that either offer a version of a fabliau, or clearly pick up fabliau themes. To the former category belongs *Die drei frauen mit dem borten*, 'The three ladies with the belt', which is a short version of Heinrich Kaufringer's *Drei listige Frauen*. Sachs presents the tale in a markedly more modest way than Kaufringer; where Kaufringer has one of the husbands castrated, Sachs has:

der Nacket auch gen Opfer ging,
doch ging es seines Beutels irr,
er sucht, griff ihm self um das Geschirr.

(the naked man also went up to the offering,
but he missed his pouch:
he groped, and laid hold of his equipment.)

Comic presentations of entry into heaven or escapes from hell that
have a basic connection with fabliaux such as *Le Vilain qui conquist
Paradis par plait, Le Pet au vilain* or *St Pierre et le jongleur* appear in
Sankt Peter mit den landsknecht im himmel, 'St Peter and the peasant
lad in heaven', and *Der teufel lässt kein landsknecht in die helle fahren*,
'The Devil lets no peasant lad come into Hell'.

But it is in Sachs's dramatic writing, in his *Fastnachtspiele*,
'Shrovetide plays', that we find the most extensive survivals of
fabliau models. A considerable number of his eighty or so surviving
Fastnachtspiele are Schwänke, and it is usually possible to identify
Sachs's sources for these. Boccaccio's *Decameron* seems to have been
a particularly productive source for him, underlying at least nine of
his Schwank plays: for instance the Bruno and Buffalmacho stories
of Day 8 tale 6 and Day 9 tale 3 produce *Der gstolen porchen*, 'The
stolen pig', and *Der schwanger Pauer*, 'The pregnant farmer'. Sachs
also uses der Stricker, *Neithart Fuchs* and *Till Eulenspiegel* as sources,
producing, for instance, a version of *Das heiss eisen*, 'The hot iron',
and *Der Neidhart mit dem feiel*, 'Neithart with the violet'. Scatology,
as in the latter play, and marked terms such as *ars* or *scheiss* are
occasionally used by Sachs, but generally he respects the bounds of
conventional propriety. Thus in *Der blind mesner*, 'The blind
sexton', a potential fabliau tale with many familiar echoes in which
a wife prays to a saint that her sexton husband could be made blind
in order to leave her free for her affair with the priest, the husband
impersonates the saint and tells his wife that she must give him food
and drink; he then feigns blindness, and in this state shoots the
lecherous priest. The fabliau plot emerges as a moralized farce.

France: the nouvelle and the farce

Something more than a century after the demise of the fabliau as a
medieval French poetic genre, a remarkable number of distinctly
fabliau-like tales occur in a collection of short prose narratives that
marks the birth of a new literary genre in French, the *nouvelle*. This

collection is *Les cent nouvelles nouvelles*, 'The one hundred new nouvelles', and its compilation is probably to be dated to the earlier 1460s. The collection is dedicated to the Duke of Bourgogne and Brabant – once more, in the north-east of France! – and a good proportion of the tales are set in his lands. Twelve of the hundred nouvelles would, if written in verse, pass any worthwhile test for identification as French fabliaux; eight are equivocal cases, and a further six have plots that have clear fabliau potential but do not develop as fabliaux.[19] Most of the latter diverge in the direction of clear and explicit moral seriousness (in their own cultural terms): nouvelle VIII, for instance, has the fabliau tale of *Cele qui fu foutue et desfoutue, La Grue* and *Le Héron*, but with the moralistic coda of the German *Daz heselîn*, with the seducer inviting the naive girl, whom he has made pregnant, to his subsequent wedding, and telling his betrothed the story as a comic tale, only for her to say she has done likewise many times; and so the greater justice is done: the man "s'en vint rendre a celle qu'il engrossa, et abandonna l'autre", 'he went to repay the girl he had made pregnant, and abandoned the other'.

Another interesting example is nouvelle LXXXVII, an analogue to the Merchant's Tale, and set in Holland(!). A young knight, with a beautiful chambermaid, whom he desires greatly, injures one eye. His surgeon considers it lost, but is assiduous in his visits as he too desires the maid; eventually he and the maid agree to blind the patient's other eye by covering it as a supposed cure, which they do, and take their pleasure passionately. This commotion is heard by the knight, who tears off the plaster, and asks:

> 'Et qu'est ce la . . . maister cyrurgien? . . . Doit estre mon œil gary par ce moien?'

> ('And what is this, mister surgeon? . . . Is my eye supposed to be healed by this means?')

In this version, no direct comic connection exists between the stolen sexual act and the wronged man's eventual recovery of the sight in his bad eye, but rather the two men – as two gentlemen – are able to laugh, make peace, and come to a suitable arrangement

---

19. The nouvelles I would put in these categories are 1: I, XVI, XXXIV, XXXVII, XXXVIII, XLIV, LVI, LXVI, LXXVIII, LXXXV, XCV; 2: III, IV, XIII, XX, XXXV, L, LXIV, LXXII; 3: VIII, IX, XXIX, LXV, LXXIII and LXXXVII.

to share the girl. In this case, a now distasteful piece of fraternal male arrogance represents a treatment of the misdeed as simply less serious, because inconsequential, in a way that contrasts with true fabliau. The strength of male fraternity in these nouvelles against class difference is strikingly shown in nouvelle III, in which a knight, who has repeatedly seduced a miller's wife, and the miller are reconciled after the miller succeeds in tricking the knight into allowing him to make a gross intrusion into the knight's wife's body.

The influence of the Italian novella, with its medieval origins, and of Boccaccio in particular, on the emergence of the French nouvelle has been much debated. The dedicatory preface to *Les cent nouvelles nouvelles* explicitly asserts such a derivation:

> . . .les cas descriptz et racomptez . . . de Cent Nouvelles avindrent la pluspart es marches et metes d'Ytaile . . . portant et retenant nom de Nouvelles
>
> (the adventures described and recounted as the *Cent Nouvelles* come mostly from within the bounds of Italy, carrying and retaining the name of novellas)

But this association with Italy could be a superficial one. Certainly it is a small minority of the French nouvelles of this and later collections that have any demonstrable dependence on known Italian sources, or are associable with Italy by containing tales located there. It is 1545 before the *Decameron* is translated into French. The French nouvelles do share features that have been identified as the special characteristics of the Boccaccian novella: most notably a concern for realism and proximity in the geographical and temporal location of the tales, and an interest in presenting characters with some psychological complexity. But these are hardly such arcane and extraordinary literary phenomena that they could not have been independently developed. They are, anyhow, the objects of artistic development in the transitional period between the Middle Ages and the Renaissance that appears in a much wider range than in literature alone.

Such features, therefore, do not define nor do they specially generate the nouvelle. More specific characteristic traits of the nouvelle are its presentation of a narrative with brevity, and, it seems, principally for the purposes of 'polite' entertainment, either comical or intellectual, with a *tour*, a pivotal trick or stroke, being an important narratological element. The same, or very similar features, are amongst the most typical traits of fabliau. A particularly clear and pertinent formulation of the relationship between fabliau and nouvelle in French literature is that put forward by Roger Dubuis in 1973. He sees the fabliau as an enabling genre for the emergence of the nouvelle: demonstrating, in the first place, that a tale can be both short and successfully entertaining, and secondarily providing a good stock of material that could be used in the nouvelles.

The second major new arrival in French literature of the second half of the fifteenth century is the dramatic farce: a short play, essentially, representing some ridiculous, often confrontational, mishap or misadventure. As a literary type, this differs most characteristically from fabliau in having less emphasis upon the trick, deception or ruse. It is also generally the case that the stories in farces are considerably tamer in sexual or scatological terms than the fabliaux. Perhaps this is an inevitable reflection of the different limits of propriety determining what could be represented in narrated literature and what could be imitated in theatrical performance. As we have noted, the dramatic farce had emerged in Dutch literature before the end of the fourteenth century, and it continued there through the fifteenth century into the sixteenth. By the sixteenth century it was flourishing in German literature too, most notably in Hans Sachs's plays. But the term *farce* itself derives from the label given to French plays of a type that flourished in the last decades of the fifteenth and the first half of the sixteenth centuries. Relatively few of these plays are definitely related to known fabliaux or contain familiar fabliau motifs. Amongst the more prominent or interesting examples in the present context we might note *De celuy qui se confesse a sa voisine*, 'Of the man who confessed to his neighbour', which has the motif of the disguised confessor learning of sexual misdeeds, or *Les trois amoureux de la croix*, 'The three lovers of the cross', a version of the tale found in English as *The Lady Prioress*.

The most important of the French farces in relation to the fabliau in English is *La Farce du Munyer*, 'The farce of the miller', recorded in a copy dated 1496, one of the neglected analogues to the Summoner's Tale. It is clearly closely related to Rutebeuf's *Le Pet au vilain*, telling (in part) the tale of a novice devil sent to fetch a dying miller's soul who supposes it will leave the body through the anus; rather than collecting a fart in this case he takes a turd back to Hell with him, leading to an interdict on bringing millers' souls to Hell. The most interesting feature of this farce in relation to Chaucer's fabliau is that the soul-collection scene is preceded by a scene between the miller lying dying in his bed, his unfaithful wife, and her lover, the *curé*, a scene which is initially scripted to exploit the comic irony of a situation in which the adulterous pair assume that the husband is dead before he actually is. When he interrupts their indiscreet behaviour, the wife tells her husband, with echoes of *Le Vilain de Bailleul*, "Paix, coquart'', 'Silence, fool'. Obviously, this is strikingly reminiscent of the connection of a love scene between the friar and the wife with the deathbed bequest scene in the Summoner's Tale. The preliminary scene is of course on a very familiar theme, and the version of it in the French farce has an early French (and Dutch!) analogue of which there is no trace in Chaucer's version. It is the case, however, that there is no thematic relationship between the two stories in *La Farce du Munyer* which could explain why they have been brought together in this farce; rather it appears likely that their association is inherited, with the sort of integration found in the Summoner's Tale having been effected at some stage in the transmission and subsequently having been quite lost, leaving only the juxtaposed scenes.

Perhaps the most individualistic aspect of the development of fabliau tales in the post-medieval French dramatic farce is the exploitation of comic irony as in *La Farce du Munyer*. In *La Farce de Resjouy d'Amours*, 'The farce of Joy-of-Love', we have a tale of a wife's secret lover, Resjouy, but the real comedy of the play comes in recurrent scenes in which this lover ironically shares the secret of his hidden love with a *confidant* – the lady's husband. In *La Farce de la Femme qui fut desrobée a son mari en sa hate et mise une pierre en son lieu*, 'The farce of the woman who was placed by her husband in his basket and who put a stone in her place', a simple labouring man places his wife in a pannier. A friar and a clerk succeed in substituting a stone for her there, and in persuading the simple husband that she has changed into it; as he prays for her return his prayers are answered by her climbing back into the basket. A similar device appears in a farce *Martin de Cambray*. But we also find, as in Hans Sachs's plays, a distinctly moral shift. A clear example comes with *De celuy qui se confesse a sa voisine*, where the disguised confessor is the mother of a girl who has been seduced by a neighbour; ironically, she hears his confession, and, morally, the farce ends with his being beaten.

England

A major factor governing the history of the transmission and dissemination of fabliau-like tales in England in the post-medieval period is the appearance of the printing press and the commercial enterprise of publishers. To a very considerable extent it is to relatively cheap chapbooks and broadsides, aimed, apparently, at as large a market as was practicable, that we must look to find such material. This material continues to be provided, along with many other forms of literature, as a form of popular entertainment. At the same time, we must remember that popular entertainment in narrative and song could exist and be transmitted independently of writing, in oral form; it is in the form of ballads, in particular, that a number of possible examples of this can be identified.

Prose: the jestbooks

English chapbooks containing prose narratives of a type that can at least be related to fabliau appear in the early sixteenth century. The earliest date that can be found for the appearance of most sixteenth- and seventeenth-century chapbooks is a record in the *Stationers' Register*, the records of the London Stationers' Guild, incorporated as the Stationers Company by Royal Charter in 1557. Later prints of the work, possibly under different titles and/or with modified contents, are often the only known versions. The earliest examples of chapbooks of interest to this study are translations into English from Low German of the adventures of Dyl Ulenspiegel, as *Howleglass* (*circa* 1516–20), and of *Der Pfarrer vom Kahlenberg* as *The Parson of Kalenborow* (*circa* 1520). The latter translation survives only in a single incomplete copy, but this fragment still provides examples of the tricks, and, importantly, of the scatology, that were noted above in the German original. *Howleglass* introduces into English a version of the tale that forms the French fabliau *Les trois Aveugles de Compiegne* (*Howleglass* no.34), and offers a retelling of the 'satiric legacy' story of the Summoner's Tale (no.45).

Overall, a survey of fabliau-like tales in this English prose literature reveals very little originality. The tales are almost uniformly familiar ones. It is not always possible to identify sources with absolute confidence as in the case of these translations; even where a particular source seems to be identifiable it is possible that the tales had passed through various translations and retellings, known and unknown, before the recension reproduced in the early printed English work. The general influence of Boccaccio's *Decameron* is abundantly evident notwithstanding. The earliest complete English translation of the *Decameron*, however, by an anonymous translator, did not appear until 1620.

In the early sixteenth century the book of 'jests', a type which can be referred to by the rather later term *jestbook*, appears as a type quite distinct from the translations such as *Howleglass* and *The Parson of Kalenborow*, although in due course this distinctiveness is eroded. The earliest of the English jestbooks is *A C. Mery Talys* of *circa* 1525, a collection of a hundred supposedly amusing anecdotes, ultimately drawn from widely differing sources. No.II, "Of the wyfe who lay with her prentys and caused him to beate her husbande disguised in her rayment", looks to be derived from *Decameron* Day 7 tale 7. No.LXXIV, "Of the husband that cryed ble under the bed", the tale in which a wife tells her husband of an importunate but unwanted lover, whereupon they make an appointment for the lover to come and be confronted by the husband, but when it comes to the point the husband is scared of a sword that the lover brings and so lies under the bed, like a sheep, while he is cuckolded. This had appeared in *Les cent nouvelles nouvelles* no.IV. A wider range of sources appears in a collection of *circa* 1535, *C. Tales and quicke answeres, very mery, and pleasante to rede*, republished in 1567 as *Mery Tales, Wittie Questions and Quicke Answeres, very pleasant to be Readde*, with, for instance, no.LI, "Of the inholders wyf and her ii lovers", a version of *Decameron* Day 7 tale 6; no.LXXIII, "Of the young man of Bruges and his spouse", a version of the tale found in the French fabliaux *Cele qui fu foutue et desfoutue*, etc., but in a form closest to the German *Daz heselîn* or *Les cent nouvelles nouvelles* no.VIII; or no.C, "Of a fryer that confessed the woman", a tale found in versions by Kaufringer, *Die zuruckgelassene Hose*, 'The trousers left behind', and, particularly, Masuccio, *Il Novellino*, no.III.

An important figure in the early history of English prose narrative is William Painter, whose *The Palace of Pleasure* published in 1566 and 1567, a collection of tales again drawn from diverse sources, was of much higher literary and moral pretensions than these jestbooks. Painter's tales include two derived from the *Decameron*: no.XXXVIII comes from *Decameron* Day 3 tale 9, and the tale can be summarized as in Boccaccio's rubric:

> Giletta of Narbonne cured the king of France of a fistula; she asks for Beltrano di Rossiglione as a husband, who, married against his will, goes off, resentfully, to Florence; there, he courts a young lady in whose place Giletta lies with him, and they have two sons; and so he, having come to love her, accepts her as his wife.

Although this is a tale of sexual deception, it is not presented as a fabliau tale by Boccaccio, nor by Painter, nor in Shakespeare's later version of it in *All's Well That Ends Well*. The other story is no.XCVII, a version of Day 8 tale 7, the story of the scholar's revenge (see above). A further tale with fabliau elements derived from Italian literature is Painter's no.XLIX, from his Italian contemporary Straparola, in which a would-be lover is put in his place by three faithful wives who repeatedly leave him naked and exposed somewhere; he then has his revenge by forcing the ladies to strip, and showing their bodies, but not their faces, to their husbands: they then have to lie to their husbands to claim that they were not the women whom they saw. This, at least, is comic, but nowhere does Painter show any sort of amused tolerance of marital infidelity as fabliaux so typically do.

Several new impulses come into this form of English writing in the decades around the turn of the sixteenth and seventeenth centuries, resulting in an especially productive phase which virtually sees the re-establishment of fabliau as a genre in English literature. The continuity of the more traditional form of jestbook is represented by the reprinting of a collection such as *Mery Tales of the Mad Men of Gotham* in 1613 and 1630, a collection which has a pale echo of the French *Les Tresces* and related medieval fabliaux at no.12: a husband seeks to cut off his wife's hair for no other reason that that "he did not love" her, but has her maid substituted on him in her place. *Scoggins Jests*, a revision of *The Geystes of Skoggan* of 1565–66, appeared in the same year. This collection is purportedly translated out of French and, like *Der Pfaffe Âmis*, follows the outrageous career of an English exile, reproducing material familiar from the *Decameron, Les cent nouvelles nouvelles, Till Eulenspiegel* and *Mery Tales, Wittie Questions and Quicke Answeres*. The creation of new, English characters such as Scoggin to fulfil the basic roles of adventurers such as Till Eulenspiegel or the Parson of Kalenborow is found as early as 1526 in *Twelve Merry Gestys of one called Edyth*, a collection which, however, contains no real fabliau tales.

One such character is Richard Tarlton, a sixteenth-century London wit and actor who died in 1588. *Tarltons Newes out of Purgatorie* was published in 1590. Tarlton appears in a dream to tell the stories of various characters he has met in Purgatory. This is an important example of the use of a frame narrative – the dream vision – as a context for the telling of a set of independent tales, rather than frame narrative and tale merging in a picaresque series of adventures as in *Scoggins Jests*. Three of the tales in this work could be described as fabliaux, and two of these are unmistakably derived from the *Decameron*: "The tale of Friar Onyon, why in purgatorie he was tormented with wasps" from Day 4 tale 2, and "Why the gentle woman of Lions sate with her haire clipt off in Purgatorie" from Day 7 tale 6. The third example is "The tale of two Lovers of Pisa, and why they were whipt in Purgatory with nettles", a tale which, despite its Italian setting here, also finds a parallel in the French *La Farce de Resjouy d'Amours*: the would-be adulterous lover continually, ironically, informs the husband of his plans, and is therefore repeatedly thwarted, although the husband is never able to confront the lover as the wife always finds a means for him to escape. The denouement of the tale, however, takes a motif from the husband-confessor stories: when a confrontation finally takes place, in public, the lover claims he knew the husband's identity all along and has pursued this charade to show him to be a "jealous foole". The husband soon dies of shame, and the lover can enjoy his lady.

Tarltons Newes out of Purgatorie precedes by a short time a series of especially interesting works which take up this frame-narrative model under the influence of a renewed interest in Chaucer. *The Cobler of Caunterburie* was also published in 1590, but it opens with references to *Tarltons Newes out of Purgatorie*, as well as to Chaucer and to Boccaccio's *Decameron*. It is a small scale imitation of the Canterbury Tales, representing a group's journey to Canterbury, the duration of which is to be whiled away by tale-telling. The great majority of these tales are distinctly fabliauesque. Three unmistakably borrow from the *Decameron*: the Gentlemans Tale, from Day 8 tale 7; the Old Wives Tale, from a blending of Day 7 tales 1 and 8; and the Somners Tale, from Day 3 tale 8. The Smiths Tale, however, contains a story that seems to make its earliest appearance in *Les cent nouvelles nouvelles*, as no.XXXVII, together with the feigned test motif of the *Decameron* Day 7 tale 7. There seem to be no immediate parallels to the first of the tales in this collection, the Coblers Tale. This is a fairly simple tale, in which a priest is able to pursue an adulterous relationship with a smith's wife by regularly bringing his laundry to her in disguise as a "scull", a servant lad; one day, however, the real scull has to go in his place, who also gratefully takes the opportunity to bed the wife. For this he is beaten; he then tells the tale to the smith, who beats the priest and the wife. Here, certainly, it is tempting to postulate a tale circulating in some form of English folk tradition as a source. It is worthy of note that the author of *The Cobler of Caunterburie* uses this tale first, and inserts it into a section where his Cobbler and his Smith use the fabliau with its target figure as weapons in a verbal battle, on the model of the skirmish between Chaucer's Miller and Reeve.

A response to *The Cobler of Caunterburie* was published by the prolific Elizabethan prosist Robert Greene in 1592. In *Greenes Vision* he notes that he has been "burdened with the penning of *Cobler of Canterbury*" and denies his authorship of the work. He then uses the dream-vision frame found in *Tarltons Newes out of Purgatorie*, portraying a dream in which he is visited by Chaucer and Gower together. In a description of *The Cobler of Caunterburie* he not only implies that he recognizes this work as representative of Chaucer's writing, but also offers an evaluation of such works that, somewhat covertly, offers less praise than blame:

> . . .a merrie werke, and made by some madde fellow, containing plesant tales, a little tainted with scurrilitie, such reverend *Chaucer* as your selfe set forth in your journey to *Canterbury*.

Chaucer's only immediate defence is that:

> 'Poets wits are free, and their words ought to be without checke. . .'

after which he and Gower are made to tell one tale each.

Chaucer's tale is *"Chaucer's tale of Jealosie"*. This is a carefully ambiguous narrative which might be either a fabliau or a fabliau-like exemplum. It tells of Tomkins, a wheelwright of Grantchester, near Cambridge. He begins as something of a gallant peacock, and succeeds in winning the hand of a milkmaid, Kate. After their marriage Kate continues to sell cream in Cambridge, and Tomkins grows so jealous of the "scholars" there "that he cut hir off from that vaine, and tyed hir to hir Distaffe, and caused hir to sit by him as hee wrought". His jealousy grows to madness; his wife grieves, but is patient, and "brookt his suspition, till she might with credit revenge". She then takes up in a sexually unspecified way with a scholar of Trinity, Cambridge, whom she asks to "devise some meane how he might rid her husband of his fonde suspition". This, of course, is ambiguous: is this to cure her husband of his ailment or to put him off the scent? In due course another student is put up to call Tomkins to his face "the moste famous Cuckould in all the countrey" and to appoint with him a time and occasion to see his wife's misbehaviour. Tomkins is brought to Cambridge where he is shown his wife sitting on her scholar's lap and eating cherries; he is then given a sleeping potion; Kate and the scholar "past away the time", somehow, and then take Tomkins home, after which Kate reveals the tale to her mother. She "laught, and said, the jealous fool was wel served". When Tomkins wakes up swearing in the presence of these two women they tell him he has been sick, and that "this disease is a mad bloud that lies in thy head, which is growne from jealousie". Tomkins asks for forgiveness, and vows never more to suspect Kate. "Thus was *Tomkins* brought from his suspition and his wife and hee reconciled". What we never know is whether or not Tomkins was truly cuckolded, and if the ending is a mutual reconciliation or leaves Tomkins as the happily deluded cuckold.

Greene's Chaucer then justifies this tale as "a good invective against jealousie": as an exemplum, in other words. Gower opposes him, not on the grounds of the ambiguity of the story, but because it is "too scurrilous . . . such fantasticall toyes be in the Cobler of Canterbury . . . Mens mindes are apt to follies . . . and such bookes are Spurres to pricke them forward in their wickednesse". Gower's tale that follows is his own "tale against Jelousie", a tale of a wife sorely tried by the mad jealousy of her husband, but who proves not just true but, in particular, patient. The debate is apparently concluded in "*The Authors answere to Gower and Chawcer*". Greene purports to reject Chaucer:

'. . .now I perceive Father Chawcer, that I followed too long in your pleasant vaine. . .'

and then another master, Solomon, appears, to tell him that
Wisdom is hard-won:

> 'Therefore be not wise in thine owne conceit . . . Devinitie . . . is
> true wisdom.'

This might seem to be the sage's perception that the superficial
scurrility of the Chaucerian fabliau covers writing of moral and
intellectual worth, but the structure of Chaucer and Gower's
commentary on the *"tale of Jealousie"* is that the moral is on the
surface and the scurrility is what is covert; a covertness that could
find its particular expression in the ambiguities noted. What Greene
calls to mind on awakening, "not onely the counsaille of *Gower*,
but the perswasions of *Salomon*", looks unambiguously
anti-Chaucerian, or at least anti-fabliau as Greene perceived the
fabliau. Interestingly, the wider context of this reflection by Greene
is that of a very Chaucerian late-life repentance and retraction of
the "foolishness" and "idle fancies" of his earlier life and works.
But the closest Greene had otherwise come to fabliau seems to be
in his tales of the fraudulence of his "cony-catchers".[20]

1603 saw the appearance of another quasi-Chaucerian collection
of tales, entitled *Westward for Smelts* by one "Kinde-Kit of
Kingstone". This is a small collection of tales purportedly told by a
group of fishwives, and again they are mostly fabliau-like, and quite
unoriginal although of varied origins. The Fishwife's Tale of
Brainford, for instance, is a long and very unfunny tale of marital
jealousy and cuckoldry, but it does include the device of a
substitute for a wife taking a punishment from the enraged husband
by having her nose cut: a feature of stories analogous to the French
fabliau *Les Tresces* or *Decameron* Day 7 tale 8, but specifically
reflecting the oriental tradition, such as the *Arabian Nights*, rather
than the Western European version. Other tales include the stone
in the well trick of *Puteus* in the *Seven Sages* (*et al.*, above), and the
castration of an adulterous friar.

First recorded as a publication in the Stationers' Register in
March 1597, but preserved in a reprint of 1626, is a work containing
a series of adventures composed by Thomas Deloney, *The pleasant*

---

20. See, for instance, the first tale in *The Thirde and Last Parte of Conny-Catching*,
    also dated 1592, in Grosart (ed.) *Complete Works*, vol.X, which initially uses the
    device of feigned blood-relationship found in the French fabliau *Boivin de
    Provins*.

Historie of John Winchcomb, In his younger yeares called Jack of Newbery, usually known by the latter name. Chapter VII of this book contains a fabliau tale, of an Italian merchant "Bennedicke", who falls for one of Jack of Newbury's "maidens" and who woos her in comic broken English. Disappointed of his desires, and seeking some poorly explained revenge, he seduces the wife of a weaver to whom the maid is related; this wife repents and tells her husband, and they have their revenge by bringing the merchant to bed with a drugged sow, who is supposed to be the desired maid, Jane. The range of literary echoes of this tale is fascinating: within the fabliau tradition the punishment of the lecher by such substition is found in *Le Prestre et Alison, Von zweim koufmannen* and *Decameron* Day 8 tale 4; the pig in the bed recalls Sabadino di Arienti's novella of 1483 — an analogue of the fabliau-like scene of the Towneley *Secunda Pastorum*; and the intertextual association of this lecherous Benedick with the confused young man of Shakespeare's *Much Ado about Nothing* is a suggestive one.

Comparable works of the earlier seventeenth century mostly continue to give familiar material set in familiar frameworks. Innovation is very sporadic. In *Tarltons Jests* (1600), for instance, we have one insouciant play with a marked word: in "How Tarlton answered a wanton gentlewoman", who threatens Tarlton with a "cuffe", he answers "spell my sorow backward then cuffe me and spare not". Again in "How a Maid drove Tarlton to a Non-plus" the simple indecency of a motif we have seen in the medieval fabliau is sufficient to justify extracting that motif and letting it stand alone, with the minimum of narrative context. The story reads:

> Tarlton meeting with a wily Country wench, who gave him quip for quip. Sweetheart (said he) would my flesh were in thine. So would I, Sir (saies shee) I would your nose were in my, I know where. Tarlton angred at this, said no more, but goes forward.

The Cobler of Caunterburie was republished in 1630 as *The Tincker of Turvey*, without the Old Wives Tale but with, in first place, a new Tinkers Tale, a prose version of a ballad of which a copy can be traced to 1616. This tells the tale of an old rich pedlar — the peasant seems no longer to be a social type characterized — who is gulled by three rogues of Gotham into giving away a stallion he has bought, and who has his revenge on the tricksters by enticing them to buy a supposedly trained goat of extraordinary talents from him. They lose the goat after their wives have bought meats in the market and put them on the goat, which they imagine will carry the goods home for them. The pedlar was originally persuaded to buy the horse by his "wench", Gillian, and although his revenge trick is not explicitly given him by her, the tale ends by extolling her female ingenuity is if it had been:

> The Pedlar at every Faire was commended, for overreaching them, that outstript him, and Gillians wit extoll'd beyond the wisedome of all the Wenches in Gotham.

The fate of the final target figures shows the power of judgement by ridicule; they:

> . . .saw how they were guld . . . one of their Wives laught, to see her Husband made such a Ninny . . . in a short time all the Towne was in a Hoobub. . .

– and they leave for London. But these fabliau features are joined in this tale with two elaborate frauds that owe much more to the recent Elizabethan tradition of 'coney-catching' satire; the three rogues are indeed called "Cunny-catchers", and Gillian tells the pedlar he has been "Cunny-catch'd".

Perhaps as puritanism grew to cultural ascendency in the first half of the seventeenth century even amongst those who consciously allied with the cavalier cause rather than the roundhead,[21] such writing failed to take deep root and to flourish in English literature. Symptomatic of the limp ending which this strand of writing came to in English literature is the brief prose synopsis, with some modification of detail and of characters' names, of Chaucer's Miller's Tale in Thomas Brewer's *The Merry Devill of Edmonton* of 1631, and the *Canterbury Tales* of "Chaucer Junior", known in a version dating from 1687, that contains cursory tellings of the Miller's and Merchant's Tales: the latter in fact with a degree of assimilation to Boccaccio's version of the cognate *Comoedia Lydia*. *The Sack-ful of News* (1673, though a jestbook of this title appeared over a century earlier) contains a simplified version of *Decameron*

---

21. See Thompson R 1979 *Unfit for Modest Ears. A Study of Pornographic, Obscene and Bawdy Works Written or Performed in England in the Second Half of the Seventeenth Century* (Macmillan) pp 8–17, and Thomas D 1969 *A Long Time Burning. The History of Literary Censorship in England* (Routledge & Kegan Paul) pp 8–33.

Day 7 tale 7 but with the sophisticated surprises of Boccaccio's version (see above) simply 'corrected' out. In the second half of the seventeenth century in France, fine prose and verse versions of such tales were still being produced by Saint-Évremond and La Fontaine, and Chaucer's fabliaux prove to be the most popular types subjected to eighteenth-century English "modernizations",[22] but it is the ballads that really carry the fabliau tradition on into the following centuries in England.

Drama

Compared with French and German literature of the fifteenth and sixteenth centuries, it is surprising how the farce fails to flourish in sixteenth-century English drama. Any connection between fabliau and dramatic performance that existed in medieval England would appear to have died out completely. There is only one Renaissance-period English play that has real claim to consideration in respect of the post-medieval survival of fabliau: a farce translated from French and attributed, a little uncertainly, to the dramatist John Heywood, preserved in printed versions dated 1533, *A mery play betwene Johan Johan, the Husbande, Tyb, his Wiffe, and Syr Johan, the Preest.*[23]

This is a play about a husband cuckolded by his wife and the priest. As a dramatic piece, however, the play concentrates on the comedy of the husband's anger and frustration at his wife's suspected adultery and further ways in which the wife and priest befool him. This anger is released in a scene of knockabout brawling at the end, with the characters finally removed from the stage by the wife and priest fleeing, pursued, after a short delay, by the husband. The husband is particularly vexed because he is a working man; he, unlike Syr Johan the priest, who has time for his liaison, has jobs to do. His wife explains her suspicious absence of which he complains at the beginning of the play by telling him that she has been with the priest and others making a pie; he is to set up the table and then go to invite the priest to eat it with them.

---

22. See Bornäs G 1972 Le Cocu battu et content. Étude sur un conte de La Fontaine, *SN* XLIV, 1 pp 37–61; Bowden B 1991 *Eighteenth-Century Modernizations from the Canterbury Tales* (Boydell & Brewer, Woodbridge).
23. Wilson F P 1969 *The English Drama 1485–1585* (Clarendon Press) pp 32–2.

Before he can go he is continually asked to do one more job after
another in a way that appears intended to tease and vex him – and
to show who is boss in the house. In the following scene, the priest
frustrates the husband by a leisurely spinning of yarns and a feigned
unwillingness to come; with a provocative double meaning he tells
Johan Johan of what he does with his wife:

> But I shall tell the what I have done, Johan,
> For that matter; she and I be somtyme aloft,
> And I do lye uppon her many a tyme and oft
> To prove her; yet could I never espye
> That ever any dyd worse with her than I.

(348–52)

But finally he comes.

Back at home, the husband is found more jobs to do. He is sent
out for water; he finds a hole in his bucket; and he sits down by
the fire to mend it while the wife and Syr Johan sit down to chat
and start eating. In due course the wife asks Syr Johan for a story,
and he tells a series of clearly fabliau-like anecdotes again hinting
impudently at his own escapades, for instance of a wife whose
husband is away for seven years and who returns to find her with
seven children:

> Yet had she not had so many by thre
> Yf she had not had the help of me

(547–8),

and of a child born to a wife five months after her wedding. Not
only does Johan Johan have to listen helplessly to these hints at his
own cuckolding, but while he works his dinner is eaten up. This is
the outrage that makes the worm turn; in anger he smashes the pail
he has mended and attacks the priest. Ironically, in the heat of this
moment, the priest forgets the veil of hints and allusions with
which he has been mocking the husband throughout the play and
calls him "horson kokold". When Johan Johan finally rushes off the
stage after his wife and the priest it is to continue battle; if we were
to see a general social satire to rest upon the fabliau tales in this
play, it would be in the representation of how the bodily
indulgence of the priest goes one step too far, beyond what can be
hidden by his cleverness, and how once his crime is revealed, the
hostility and vengeance of the exploited working man will always

remain. But the working man in this play is a passive fool, and is churlish in a way that Chaucer's "cherles", it is argued, are not. Thus his physical vengeance is the farcical limit of the response that he can make.

We should also note here a scene at the end of George Peele's play *Edward I* of 1593 that is readily recognizable as a descendant of a familiar medieval fabliau tale. This has a wife, Edward's Queen Eleanor, making a confession to her disguised husband of her infidelity to him. It is highly likely that Peele modelled this scene on a tale told in a ballad familiar in later copies as *Queen Eleanor's Confession* and noted in the following section, although the ballad tale is of Eleanor of Aquitaine, Queen of Henry II. Peele's presentation of the scene is utterly tragic, not comic.

Ballads

Ballads are verse narratives, generally intended to be sung, and the ballad is a constant and substantial feature of English popular literature at least from the sixteenth century to the nineteenth. Some of these popular ballads had earlier, medieval origins: considerable numbers of them contain tales, characters and motifs demonstrably handed down from the Middle Ages. It is, however, only with printing that these ballads come to be preserved in a durable form, particularly in the form of the broadside; a yet simpler and cheaper publication than the chapbook, and a form that seems to have enjoyed its greatest vogue in the later seventeenth and eighteenth centuries. In the ballads, then, we can be prepared to find material emerging into print from oral and folk-tale sources, besides material whose background is more literary.

In fact the ballads prove to be the most interesting and informative source we have on the tradition of fabliau tales in English literature from the Middle Ages down to the beginning of the industrial revolution and the Age of Romanticism. As we have noted to be the case with several other forms of 'survival' of the fabliau in the post-medieval centuries, there is a definite tendency to put fabliau-like tales of misbehaviour and deception to conventional moral use in the ballads. Examples of versions of tales that have been identified as possible Middle English fabliaux (though not in this study), that also emerge later in the ballad tradition, are *The Lancashire Cuckold*, in which an adulterous wife, her lover, and various other miscreants become stuck to an enchanted piss-pot, a tale related to the fifteenth-century *The Tale of the Basin*, and *A penny-worth of Wit*, related to a Middle English poem of the same title.[24]

The majority of cases of relationship between medieval fabliaux and later English ballads are identified by a perceptible similarity in the narrative plots. In the circumstances of preservation of these tales it is quite impossible in most cases to be sure of the course of transmisssion between the two. We might take, for instance, the ballad of *Queen Eleanor's Confession*, a particularly popular ballad to judge by the evidence of the number of broadside copies surviving from the late seventeenth and early eighteenth centuries.[25] This tale has the King and his Earl Martial disguised as friars to hear the deathbed confession of the Queen, Eleanor. King Henry learns that the Earl has cuckolded him, that one of her sons is the Earl's, and that she had poisoned the King's mistress, Rosamund. The King identifies himself in fury; the Queen shrieks in horror; but all characters have finally to face the shared knowledge of their misdeeds: the King in fact has sworn in advance not to hang the Earl. The disguised confessor has appeared in French fabliau, nouvelle and farce, and in the *Decameron*. As noted, this tale appears as the tragic finale of George Peele's play *Edward I* of 1593. It is also retold by La Fontaine amongst his verse *Contes et Nouvelles* of 1665. All of these could have contributed either materially or by way of suggestion to the re-emergence of the tale as a broadside ballad, but it is most likely that Peele's transference of the story to Edward's Queen Eleanor represents an adaptation of an extant ballad source.

A ballad of clearly literary and at least in part definitely English ancestry is *The Wanton Wife of Bath*.[26] This takes over Chaucer's character:

> In Bath a wanton wife did dwell
> As Chaucer he doth write

---

24. *The Lancashire Cuckold*: Ewing Collection 200; *The Tale of the Basin*: Furrow *Ten Comic Tales* pp 45–64; *A penny-worth of Wit, Collection* (1723) II, 37; the Middle English *A peniworþ of wit*, ed. Kölbing E 1884 in Kleine Publikationen aus der Auchinleck-HS, *Englische Studien* 7 pp 101–2. On the French analogue, '*La Bourse pleine de sens*' see especially Bloch *The Scandal of the Fabliaux* pp 72–3.
25. Childs *English and Scottish Popular Ballads* Book VII.
26. Childs *English and Scottish Popular Ballads* Book VIII.

and follows her soul up to Heaven after her death. There it enters into a tale of more distant literary ancestry, following the course of the peasant who won his way into Heaven by arguing in the French fabliau *Le Vilain qui conquist Paradis par plait*. The Wife of Bath points out the faults of a string of Biblical figures: Adam, Jacob, Lot, Judith, David, Solomon, Jonas, St Thomas, Mary Magdalen, St Paul and St Peter. The ballad ends, not with a comic view of the sinner's impudent justification by comparison with these, but rather with a pleasing change of tone to true reverence as she speaks to Christ Himself:

> 'My laws and my commandments,'
>   Saith Christ, 'were known to thee;
> But of the same, in any wise,
>   Not any word did ye.'
>
> 'I grant the same, O Lord,' quoth she;
>   'Most lewdly did I live;
> But yet the loving father did
>   His prodigal son forgive.'
>
> 'So I forgive thy soul,' he said,
>   'Through thy repenting cry;
> Come you therefore into my joy,
>   I will not thee deny.'

Other fabliau tales concerning the afterlife re-appear in ballad form too. The character rejected from Hell as being too intolerable even for Satan/Lucifer to live with is found in a Sussex ballad, *The Farmer's Old Wife* (a Scots parallel to which was recorded in 1892), in which the old woman assaults the imps or devils in Hell and is carried back to the world by Satan with the comment:

> 'I have been a tormentor the whole of my life,
> But I ne'er was tormented till I met with your wife.'[27]

A fainter Chaucerian echo can be found in *Room for a Jovial Tinker*, a probably seventeenth-century specimen in the Roxburghe ballad collection.[28] Here a travelling tinker works for a lady:

27. Childs *English and Scottish Popular Ballads* Book VIII; Sargent and Kittredge *English and Scottish Popular Ballads* no. 278.
28. Roxburghe Collection III, 20; Pinto and Rodway *The Common Muse* no. CXXXV.

> The lady lay down on the bed, so did the Tinker too:
> Although the Tinker knockt amain, the Lady was not offended,
> But before that she rose from the bed, her Coldron was well mended.

The lady has agreed to pay the tinker a mark for every time he "drives his nail"; she later tells the husband of the tinker:

> 'No fault at al this Tinker hath, but he takes dear for his work,
> That little time that he wrought here, it cost me twenty mark.'

The husband, not surprisingly, suggests she might be more prudent in the future, but he is satisfied by a response that recalls the final bedroom scene of the Shipman's Tale:

> 'Pray hold your peace, my lord,' quoth she, 'and think it not too dear.
> If you cou'd doo't so well 'twould save you forty pounds a year.'
> With that the lord most lovingly, to make all things amends,
> He kindly kist his lady gay, and so they both were friends.

One of the most frequent of the recognizable fabliau tales that turn up amongst the later English ballads is the tale familiar from French and German literature most aptly described by the title of one French fabliau version, *Cele qui fu foutue et desfoutue*, 'The girl who was fucked and unfucked'. Examples of related ballads are *The Fair Maid of the West* (*who sold her Maidenhead for a High-crown'd Hat*) and the *Leicester Chambermaid*.[29] While the former simply concentrates on the joke of the girl's naivety, the latter contains the moralizing coda to the tale that has been seen in the medieval German Schwank *Daz heselîn*, as the girl brings the young butcher who has fathered her child to justice, both in the civil court and in the form of public mockery:

> The company they laugh'd amain; the joke went freely round,
> And the tidings of the same was spread through Leicester town,
> The butcher was to a justice brought, who happened to live near,
> One hundred pounds he did lay down, before he could get clear.

We can also recognize an ancient fabliau motif in a probably eighteenth-century ballad, *The Merchant's Courtship to the Brazier's Daughter*, subtitled appropriately but probably on little authority "An old song".[30] The brazier's daughter accepts an arrangement proposed by her merchant lover:

---

29. Pinto and Rodway *The Common Muse* nos. cxc and cxcv; see also *The Astrologer*, in Holloway and Black *Later English Broadside Ballads* 2 no. 36.
30. Holloway and Black *Later English Broadside Ballads* 1 no. 77.

> You must tie a string unto your finger,
> And let the end hang out of the window,
> When I come and pull the string,
> You'll come down and let me in.

These arrangements are, however, overheard by Jack (a sailor?), who substitutes himself with his "cock'd pistol" for the merchant; indeed he seems to satisfy the brazier's daughter so well that they end up contentedly wed. The cunning substitution of one bedmate for another in the dark — as, for instance, with Symkyn's wife in the Reeve's Tale — is itself a recurring motif; further examples are *Glasgerian* and *Glenkindie* in F. J. Child's collection.[31] Examples of the wife substituting in the dark for a maid that her would-be adulterous husband is intending to bed appear in *The Frolicsome Farmer* and *The Unfortunate Miller*.[32]

Perhaps the most interesting of the later English ballads in relation to the medieval English fabliau is yet another tale that seems to belong to Summoner's Tale's family of analogues. A Restoration-period collection of songs and ballads entitled *Merry Drollery Compleat* includes a ballad called *The Gelding of the Divel*, a ballad also known in some broadside copies. A baker of Mansfield riding to market is asked by one of two devils why his horse is so swift; because it is gelded, is the answer. The foolish devil then asks the baker to geld him, but vows to geld the baker on their next meeting after experiencing the inevitable pain. The baker tells his wife of this threat; her "pretty trick" to prevent it is to go herself in her husband's place. When the devil prepares to geld her he sees her crotch and assumes she has already been gelded. He sympathetically observes that the wound ought to have been closed up; but while he goes for a salve, the other devil tries to knock a flea off her belly:

> And with that she let go a rowzing fart

so the devil dismisses her from him:

> Be gone, be gone, make no delay,
> For here thou shalt no longer stay.

It is the fart from which the devil recoils that relates this ballad

31. Childs *English and Scottish Popular Ballads* Book II no. 1a–b.
32. Pinto and Rodway *The Common Muse* nos. cx and clxxxiv.

to *Le Pet au vilain* and thus indirectly to the other analogues noted above. The nearest parallel of which I am aware to the woman's revealing her crotch to the devil in this challenging way comes in François Rabelais' mid-sixteenth-century *Quart Livre of Pantagruel*, chapters 45–7, where, on the island of Popefiggers (to *faire la figue* is to make an obscene gesture), a farmer is obliged to make a deal to share the profits from a field of his with the Devil, but twice outwits him to keep the whole real harvest for himself. The Devil then challenges the farmer to a 'scratching match', with the first to retire to forfeit his claim to the field. The farmer's wife comes up with the ruse of her intercepting the Devil, and showing the Devil the wound the farmer has supposedly made between her legs with one scratch of his little finger in practice. He has now, she tells the Devil, gone to the blacksmith to have his nails sharpened.

> Le Diable, voyant l'enorme solution de continuité en toutes dimensions, s'escria "Mahon, Demiourgon, Megare, Alecto, Persephone! il ne me tient pas! Je m'en voys bel erre. Cela! Je luy quitte le champ."

> (The Devil, seeing the enormous void, extending endlessly in all directions, cried out "Mahound, Demiurge, Megaera, Alecto, Persephone! He won't get me! I'm off, now! So! He can have the field.")

Even as an indirect source, however, this would not account for the concluding fart of the ballad, which were it not for the medieval analogues such as *Le Pet au vilain* might appear as a coarse invention by the English balladeer. Rabelais, however, was evidently familiar with the comic motif of the soul leaving the body through the anus. Immediately before the story from the island of Popefiggers he describes the island of Ruach, where the population "ne vivent que de vent", 'live on nothing but wind' (*Pantagruel* IV, chapters 43–4):

> Et meurent les hommes en pedent, les femmes en vesnent. Ainsi leur sort l'ame par le cul.

> (The men die with a loud fart, the women with a quiet one. Thus their soul leaves through the arse.)

Later, in Book V chapter 17 of *Pantagruel*, Rabelais tells of the death of a glutton who has burst to death with a report that is his "pet de la mort", his 'death fart'. The exact descent of *The Gelding of the*

Divel is of course unknown. But it does suggest yet again that the story of *Le Pet au vilain* was descending through the traditions of English narrative and literature. The tale in the ballad is of course very different, but the essential motif occurs too frequently for independent invention to be a convincing explanation.

THE FABLIAU IN ENGLISH AND ITS WORTH

Let us return to the question posed in the Preface to this study: what is a fabliau? With substantial reading, intuition becomes a reliable guide to what is more or less typical of fabliaux, but to be built on and communicated in any way, intuition has to be analysed methodically. Fabliaux have certain normal characteristics. Virtually universal in fabliau is a narrative that includes certain event types: a deception, and usually a misdeed. These event types usually occur in certain characteristic fields of human activity, most prominently the sexual and the scatological, and are often presented in a marked form of language created by certain words belonging to these semantic fields. While motivation of the action – desire, etc. – is of a familiar nature, the tricks and events tend to a preposterous excess. At virtually the same level of universality as these event types are certain character types: the duper/trickster – obviously implicit in the event-type *deception* – and the dupe, who significantly becomes a 'target figure'. In the realization of these event- and character types as particular dramatic events and characters we also find certain persistent and thus characteristic attitudes. Those which appear most significant in this study are a set of overlapping attitudes which can be labelled the *clerkly*, the *comic* (or, quite simply, a sense of humour), the *moral* and the *philosophical*.

An etymological sense of *defining* something is setting its limits. In practice, it has proved important to define the bounds of fabliau in respect of two adjacent genres: the exemplum and the farce. The fabliau is taken to differ from the exemplum in not being explicitly and directly morally correct according to the criteria of its date in both form and content, while the exemplum is. Historically, some fabliaux were adapted from exempla, and generally we find a tendency for fabliau to drift into exemplum across time, and perhaps space (e.g. from France into Germany). Amorality and immorality are not characteristics of fabliau, but what is characteristic is a level of toleration of immorality in conventional terms quite different from what is possible in exemplum. Farce of the kind considered in this book is historically younger than fabliau, and reflects, in general, a drift towards the moral tone of the exemplum. The definitive difference between farce and fabliau for our purposes, however, is a technical–narratological one: the opposition between the event types *deception* and *misadventure*. These contrastive definitions are simple and effective. The subtlest distinction that seems to need to be drawn is that between fabliau and the later French genre of nouvelle, some early examples of which, it was noted, are justifiably classified as fabliau. In general, one could suggest that there is an essential shift in attitude in the nouvelle, with the misdeed treated as less serious, and even less consequential; deliberate provocativeness gives way to polite, 'gentlemanly' delectation.

This brings us to something that could be called the 'spirit' of the genre: a set of attitudes that inheres within the formal characteristics of the genre in such a way that only subtle shifts in form – for instance the configurations of social types as the actants of the story – embody differences in attitude that *de facto* are associable with different genres. The contrast (such as it is) between fabliau and nouvelle may not simply be a feature of French literature; one could interpret the attitude towards the pedlar in the tinker of Turvey's tale, in the seventeenth-century English chapbook, as contrasting with the medieval fabliaux in the same way, noting at the same time that the treatment of the wheelwright, Tomkins, in the Elizabethan 'Chaucer's tale' of *Greenes Vision* maintains something more characteristic of fabliau in this respect.

As history stands, the spirit of the fabliau in English is primarily Chaucer's attitude as developed in and articulated through the fabliau. This is not something that can be summarized simply: it is, however, concurrently comic and reflexively critical of comedy. Contrasted with romance, fabliau offers an attractive comic myth in which the fulfilment of a simple desire, usually sexual pleasure, is relatively uninhibitedly sought by both sexes, and often easily achieved in circumstances that are both entertaining for the reader and reassuringly fairly harmless even for those who are 'injured' by the events: the target figures. This holds for *Dame Sirith* too. But the relatively untroubled target figure is gradually examined by Chaucer in the figure of the cuckold contented while ignorant, the man completely satisfied by having "queynte ynough", looking no further and thus being blinded by female sexuality. This strains the characteristic relations holding within fabliau, as the cuckold becomes potentially the supreme fabliau trickster in the Shipman's Tale, with a piece of indifference that is deliberately adopted by the Miller, the perceptive churl, in the words of his Prologue that are echoed by John the carpenter in his Tale. In the Merchant's Tale, sexually induced male (and female) foolishness is still comically viewed by the perceptive narrator there. But the course of time and the insistent pressure of the world break down this sophisticated, poised and contented attitude; this leads to a retraction in the penultimate tale of the Canterbury Tales, anticipating Chaucer's wider retraction at the very end of the book.

The history of the fabliau in English after Chaucer generally shows the pursuit of conventional, exemplary morality, or just the reduction of the complexity of the comedy of tales to the cursory 'merry jests' of the sixteenth century. *The Friars of Berwick* and *Dane Hew* preserve full fabliau tales paralleled in other literatures, and *The Friars of Berwick* does offer a laconic tone in presenting the story of human foolishness and malicious ingenuity that can have some of the moral effect suggested for the French *Les quatre Souhais Saint Martin*. *Dane Hew*, however, reads simply as a longer 'merry' anecdote. By the 1590s, Robert Greene seems to have seen a straightforward, exclusive polarity between morality and comedy in respect of fabliau-like tales, and the apparent revival of fabliau around this date did not succeed in re-establishing it in the range of 'high' English literature. A genuine tradition continued, however, in popular literature with the ballads. Here, however, besides some moralization, we generally find a tamer range of scenes and, in particular, language than in the medieval fabliaux. Probably a similar – if not the same – set of graded limits of tolerance respecting conventional decency of form as that noted for modern popular film and television comedy in Chapter 1 was a constraining force with this 'street literature'.

Several of the most characteristic features of fabliau as argued here have been detected in modern theatrical farce, albeit not in a very consistent way.[33] However, one outstanding example of a

33. See, for instance, Nelson T G A 1990 *Comedy. The Theory of Comedy in Literature, Drama and Cinema* (Oxford University Press) pp 25–7.

major writer in English, using and exploring the features of fabliau
like Chaucer, in 'high' literature of the twentieth century is to be
found in James Joyce's *Ulysses*. At first sight, to suggest any such
comparison between characteristically brief medieval verse tales and
a massive 'novel' of the earlier twentieth century which includes
within itself prose, poetry, drama and unclassifiable experimental
modes should seem incongruous to the point of absurdity. But
within the complex whole of *Ulysses*, as within the complex whole
of the Canterbury Tales, there are consistent moral ideas, and
consistent character types and situations that propound the
comparison. The overall narrative pattern of *Ulysses* is a
modification of that of the classical Greek heroic epic, Homer's
Odyssey. This retains the epic pretensions of the *Odyssey* to a
significant degree, provocatively relocating them in realistic urban
and domestic settings (like in the fabliaux) on a specified day in
Dublin, 16 June 1904. Realism is also expressed in *Ulysses* through
the mundanity of many of the events that are narrated and the
range of detail with which they are presented. Especially striking
because of conventions of decorum are events representing the
favourite topics of the fabliaux: sex and the scatological.

Most prominently of all, Joyce is one of the few writers of any
level of literature to present a version of the cuckold hero in
Leopold Bloom.[34] What *Ulysses* lacks in comparison with the
fabliaux is the trick or deception that foreshortens the narrative and
allows it to draw its force from one concentrated stroke; the
fulcrum of activity that turns dramatic crisis into dramatic
resolution. Leopold Bloom, too, is no concentrated, simplified
character. Through the events of the day, Bloom's mind is
presented in a huge and cumulative portrait as complex, and
internally contrastive. It is not, however, a place of conflict
between jarring contradictions. Overall, and most emphatically in
the end, after Bloom has achieved the satisfaction of finding a son
in Stephen Dedalus having lost his natural son, Rudy, as a baby ten
and a half years previously, Bloom's mind comes to "equanimity":
to a balanced state of contentment.

---

34. See Brown R 1985 *James Joyce and Sexuality* (Cambridge University Press) and
   Empson W 1982 'The Ultimate Novel' *London Review of Books* 4 nos. 15–16 (2
   parts), reprinted in *idem* 1984 *Using Biography* (Chatto & Windus) pp 217–59. See
   also Millington M I & Sinclair A S 1992 The Honourable Cuckold: Models of
   Masculine Defence *Comparative Literature Studies* 29(1) pp 1–19.

Bloom achieves equanimity in spite of the fact that he has been cuckolded (probably not for the first time) that same day by Blazes Boylan, whose imprint he can even still detect in his bed late at night (*Ulysses* 17: 2122–5).[35] In one view, his equanimity can be seen as being founded upon the moral weakness of the fabliau myth: that it is based upon a view of the world from which the worst things are excluded, leaving only a range of offences that can be trivialized, ridiculed or dismissed. The primary injury is the intangible loss of face of the target figure; loss of life and limb are momentarily painful incidents that befall those who deserve them, and the places of ultimate reward or punishment, Heaven or Hell, are simplistic and as absurd as Earth. One may note here the representation of Hades as the Municipal Graveyard (Ch.6) and the image of God in Heaven:

> He who Himself begot middler the Holy Ghost and Himself sent Himself, Agenbuyer, between Himself and others, Who, put upon by His fiends, stripped and whipped, was nailed like bat to barndoor, starved on crosstree, Who let Him bury, stood up, harrowed hell, fared into heaven and there these nineteen hundred years sitteth on the right hand of His Own Self but yet shall come in the latter day to doom the quick and dead when all the quick shall be dead already.
>
> (9: 493–9)

(The) reasons for Bloom's equanimity in face of his cuckolding are given:

> Equanimity?
> As as natural as any and every natural act of a nature expressed or understood executed in natured nature by natural creatures in accordance with his, her and their natured natures, of dissimilar similarity. As not so calamitous as a cataclysmic annihilation of the planet in consequence of a collision with a dark sun. As less reprehensible than theft, highway robbery, cruelty to children and animals, obtaining money under false pretences, forgery, embezzlement, misappropriation of public money, betrayal of public trust, malingering, mayhem, corruption of minors, criminal libel, blackmail, contempt of court, arson, treason, felony, mutiny on the high seas, trespass, burglary, jailbreaking, practice of unnatural vice, desertion from armed forces in the field, perjury, poaching, usury, intelligence with the king's enemies,

---

35. Line references and quotations are from *James Joyce, Ulysses. The Corrected Text*. Ed. Gabler H W 1986 (Penguin Books).

impersonation, criminal assault, manslaughter, wilful and premeditated murder. As not more abnormal than all other parallel processes of adaptation to altered conditions of existence, resulting in a reciprocal equilibrium between the bodily organism and its attendant circumstances, foods, beverages, acquired habits, indulged inclinations, significant disease. As more than inevitable, irreparable.

(17: 2177–94)

Note how the miscellaneous list of crimes that forms the centre of the answer is able to trivialize by taking the tone of a dry legal register, mixing contingent political pomposities – "misappropriation of public money"; "intelligence with the king's enemies" – with the humanly destructive – "wilful and premeditated murder" – and taking as one entry "cruelty to children and animals". With arguable or minor exceptions these 'crimes' are excluded from the events of *Ulysses*.

The great mass of human actions in *Ulysses* seems at worst to be sad, undignified, embarrassing or clumsy, not evil. Bloom is part Everyman, in part Noman (17: 2008). He is a literary character, crafted by Joyce out of the sources of literature and experience, presented as a 38-year-old Dublin man of Jewish ancestry shaped by a mass of determinative material and ideological factors. He is unusual enough to stand out and yet familiar enough in his actions, thoughts and fantasies to be quite mundane. If he does not personally encounter anything worse than his wife's infidelity, then he does in this way represent the limits of private injury and suffering of a majority in that time and place and many more times and places. This is the level at which life can be said to be like the fabliau world(s), and at which the Miller's and Reeve's Tales can be called 'realistic' in comparison with the Knight's Tale.

But greater human, intrasocial and interpersonal, evils are not excluded from *Ulysses*: they lurk as shadows in the background or the ambient of Bloom and Stephen's wanderings, physical and mental, through the day and the night. Joyce's signature to the work reflects his own wanderings:

Trieste–Zurich–Paris
1914–21

(18: 1610–11)

beginning in the year the First World War began, and partly

influenced by it.[36] The world of *Ulysses* could be regarded sentimentally as a world of relative innocence, before the Great War, and Dublin's Easter Rising of 1916 and its aftermath. But the material is there in *Ulysses* to see the book as a critique of such comic sentimentality rather than an expression of it. The Great War is symbolically evoked. In the surreal picture of the New Bloomusalem, Bloom mows down poppies (15: 1565–6). Above all, the number eleven, the cipher of the armistice at the eleventh hour of the eleventh day of the eleventh month of 1918, holds ominous overtones throughout the book. It is poignantly associated with Bloom's most painful and haunting loss, the death of his baby son Rudy, eleven days old, who would now have been in the eleventh year of his life. Bathetically, this loss is the immediate cause of Bloom's sexual problems (17: 2271–84). This concurrency of the immensely, immanently awful and the comically mundane is a version of the "ineluctable modality", the inescapable paradigmaticness, of human being: the alternation of "sad human ineffectiveness" with "vast inhuman cycles of activity" that Stephen Dedalus perceives in *A Portrait of the Artist as a Young Man*.

Essential to the moral style of *Ulysses* is a conception of life as an art form, and art as life: *artist* is a complete state of being. A true work of art in these terms could not be idealistic (like Bloom's dreams) and thus false to life. *Ulysses* represents a search for equanimity, an Arnoldian state of poise, and as a work it recognizes the compromises that have to be made in reaching that ideal. Compromise is a form of integration of opposites, and Bloom becomes an emblem of integration in his penultimate transformation, arguably his ultimate apotheosis, in the book:

> he said I was a flower of the mountain yes so we are flowers all a womans body yes that was one true thing he said in his life and the sun shines for you today yes that was why I liked him because I saw he understood or felt what a woman is
>
> (18: 1576–9)

In Molly Bloom's soliloquy, Bloom becomes a womanly man, and this leads to the final image of him as Molly re-creates him as the younger man (of 22, in fact, Stephen's age: twice eleven) she first

---

36. For a literary biography of Joyce see Ellmann R 1959 *James Joyce* (Oxford University Press).

gave herself to. Rather than the all-surpassing phallicism of the typical medieval fabliau heroes, including Chaucer's Shipman's merchant, this is how Bloom becomes the inverse of the fabliau hero, to 'triumph' in a remembered and re-enjoyed sexual conquest.

The history of the fabliau in English is a happy one in the sense that we do not see here a genre that suffers the tiresome reproduction of the elements of its stereotyped form to the extent that a mediocre mass surrounds and obscures examples of dynamic and creative exploration in the genre. Such dynamism and creativity thus in themselves become a normative feature of the fabliau in English. Between the late thirteenth and the late sixteenth centuries, from *Dame Sirith* to *Greenes Vision*, the fabliau in English does appear to follow the life cycle postulated by Russian Formalism: that genres that succeed in occupying a cultural high point gradually lose their effectiveness through mechanical reproduction, and are displaced by newer, rival genres, which often emerge from a lower, vulgar cultural level.[37] Thus the fabliau in English rises to challenge romance, and declines into exempla and merry jests, eventually to be subordinated to popular puritanism. But in alternative popular literature, in the ballads, the tales lived on. Despite his immense use of literary sources, however, Joyce did not detectably derive the similar features of his handling of the fabliau from this vulgar stratum; rather he re-invented them.

The importance of the fabliau in English, then, is reflected by the fact that as a literary mode, under that name or not, it has been seriously examined by two of the most pre-eminent writers in English literary history in their experimental investigations into the possibility of having concurrently comic, moral and realistic literature. Fabliau as produced and as presented by them in their supremely normative way is a form of comic myth that offers an ultimately unsustainable idealism. This is the limit of its worth. But it is able to bear the weight of an analysis and criticism of comedy itself, and this is its immense functional value.

37. Cf. Jauss, *op. cit.* Preface, footnote 1, pp 105–7.

Bibliography

The following abbreviations are used:

AM	*Annuale Mediaevale*
CR	*Chaucer Review*
EC	*Essays in Criticism*
ELH	*English Literary History*
ES	*English Studies*
JEGP	*Journal of English and Germanic Philology*
LSE	*Leeds Studies in English*
MÆ	*Medium Ævum*
MLN	*Modern Language Notes*
MLQ	*Modern Language Quarterly*
MLR	*Modern Language Review*
MP	*Modern Philology*
MR	*Marche romane*
MS	*Mediaeval Studies*
NM	*Neuphilologische Mitteilungen*
PMLA	*Publications of the Modern Languages Association of America*
PQ	*Philological Quarterly*
RES	*Review of English Studies*
SAC	*Studies in the Age of Chaucer*
SN	*Studia Neophilologica*
SP	*Studies in Philology*
TPS	*Transactions of the Philological Society*
UTQ	*University of Toronto Quarterly*

CHAPTER 1

The French fabliaux

Editions

Eichmann R and DuVal J ed. and trans. 1985 (2 vols) *The French Fabliau B.N. MS.* 837. Garland Publishing, New York (Garland Library of Medieval Literature).

Johnston R C and Owen D D R selected and ed. 1965 *Fabliaux*. Basil Blackwell (Blackwell's French Texts).

Levy B J ed. 1978 *Selected Fabliaux*. Department of French, University of Hull (Hull French Texts).

Ménard P ed. 1979 *Fabliaux français du Moyen Age*. Textes Littéraires Français, Geneva.

de Montaiglon A and Raynaud G 1872–90 *Recueil général et complet des fabliaux des XIIIe et XIVe siècles*. Paris.

Noomen W and van den Boogaard N 1982– *Nouveau Recueil Complet des Fabliaux*. van Gorcum, Assen/Maastricht.

Translations

Rouger G 1978 selected and trans. *Fabliaux*. Gallimard.

Scott N 1977 selected and trans. *Contes pour rire? Fabliaux des XIIIe et XIVe siècles*. Union Générale d'Editions, Paris.

Editions of individual French fabliaux cited in the book

EdV = Eichmann and DuVal; JO = Johnston and Owen; Mé = Ménard; MR = de Montaiglon and Raynaud; NRCF = Noomen and van den Boogaard. Where appropriate, a volume number is followed by the number of the poem in the collection.

Les deux Anglois et l'anel: MR II,46

Auburee: MR V,110; NRCF I,4; Levy 6

Les trois Aveugles de Compiegne: MR I,4; NRCF 2,9; Edv I,5

Barat et Haimet: MR IV,97; NRCF 2,6

Berengier au lonc cul: MR III,86 and IV,93; NRCF 4,34

Les trois Boçus: MR I,2; JO V; NRCF 5,47; EdV II,30

Boivin de Provins: MR V,116; NRCF 2,7; EdV I,4

Le Bouchier d'Abbeville: MR III,84; NRCF 3,18; EdV II,12

La Bourgoise d'Orliens: MR I,8; NRCF 3,19; JO VI; EdV II,13; Levy 5

La Bourse pleine de Sens: MR III,67; NRCF 2,8

Brunain: MR I,10; JO VIII; NRCF 5,40; EdV II,25

Cele qui se fist foutre sur la fosse de son mari: MR III,70; NRCF 3,20; Levy 8

Cele qui fu foutue et desfoutue: NRCF 4,30

Le Chevalier a la corbeille: MR II,47

Le Chevalier qui fist parler les cons: MR VI,147; NRCF 3,15

Le Chevalier qui fist sa dame confesse: MR I,16; NRCF 4,33; EdV II,22

Un Chevalier, sa dame et un clerc: MR II, 50

Le Chevalier, les deus clers, et les vilains: EdV II,33

Le povre Clerc: MR V,132

La Coille noire: MR VI,148; NRCF 5,46

Du Con qui fu fait a la besche: NRCF 4,22; EdV II,15
Connebert: MR V,138
Constant du Hamel: MR IV,106; NRCF 1,2
Le Cuvier: MR I,9; NRCF 5,44; EdV II,28
La Dame escoillee: MR VI,149
Les trois Dames qui troverent l'anel: MR I,5 and VI,138; MRCF 2,11; EdV I,8
Les trois Dames qui troverent un vit: MR V,112; Anglo-Norman version, MR
   IV, 51
La Damoiselle qui ne pooit oïr parler de foutre: MR III,65; NRCF 4,26
L'Enfant qu fu remis au soleil: MR I,14; NRCF 5,48; EdV II,31
L'Esquiriel: MR V,121
Estormi: MR I,19; NRCF 1,1; EdV I,1
Estula: MR IV,96; JO III; NRCF 4,38
Le Fevre de Creil: MR I,21; NRCF 5,42; EdV II,27
Le Foteor: MR I,28
La Gageure: MR II,48; NRCF 6,59
Gombert et les deus clers: MR I,22; NRCF 4,35
La Grue: see *Cele qui fu foutue et desfoutue*
Le Héron: see *Cele qui fu foutue et desfoutue*
La Housse partie: MR I,5; NRCF 3,16
Jouglet: MR IV,98; NRCF 2,10; EdV I,7
Le Jugement des cons: MR V,122; MRCF 4,23; EdV II,16
La Male Honte: MR IV,90; JO XII; NRCF 5,43
Les trois Meschines: MR III,64; NRCF 4,32; EdV II,21
Le Meunier et les deus clers: MR V,119; Mé VI
Les Perdriz: MR I,17; NRCF 4,21; EdV II,14; Levy 7
Le Pescheor de pont seur Saine: MR III,63; NRCF 4,28; EdV II,19
Le Pet au vilain: MR III,68; NRCF 5,55; EdV II,38
Le Prestre crucifié: MR I,18; NRCF 4,27; EdV II,18; Levy 9
Le Prestre et Alison: MR II,31; Mé V
Le Prestre et le leu: MR VI,145; Levy 10
Le Prestre et les deus ribaus: MR III,62; NRCF 5,45; EdV II,29
Le Prestre qui abevete: MR III,61
Le Prestre qui ot mere a force: MR V,125; NRCF 5,41; EdV II,26
Le Prestre teint: MR VI,132
La Saineresse: MR I,25; NRCF 4,36; EdV II,23
Saint Pierre et le jongleur: MR V,117; JO XIV; NRCF 1,3; EdV I,2
Le Segretain moine (Le Sacristain): MR V,123 and 136 and VI,150; Levy 12
Sire Hain et Dame Anieuse: MR I,6; NRCF 2,5; EdV I,3
Le sot Chevalier: MR I,20; NRCF 5,53; EdV II,36
Les quatre Souhais Saint Martin: MR V,133; NRCF 4,31; Levy 3
Les Tresces: MR IV,94; Mé VIII; NRCF 6,69
La vieille Truande: MR V,129; NRCF 4,37; EdV II,24
Le dis de le Vescie a prestre: MR III,59

Le Vilain asnier. MR V,114; JO II; Levy 1
Le Vilain de Bailleul: MR IV,104; NRCF 5,49
Le Vilain qui conquist Paradis par plait: MR III,81; NRCF 5,39; Levy 4

Critical studies

Bédier J 1895 *Les Fabliaux. Etudes de littérature populaire et d'histoire littéraire du moyen age* 2nd edn. Paris.

Benkov E J 1989 Language and Women: From Silence to Speech. In Wasserman and Roney L eds *Sign, Sentence, Discourse. Language in Medieval Thought and Literature.* Syracuse University Press, Syracuse pp 245–65.

Beyer J 1969 *Schwank und Moral. Untersuchungen zum altfranzösischen Fabliau und verwandten Formen.* Carl Winter, Heidelberg.

Bloch R Howard 1986 *The Scandal of the Fabliau.* University of Chicago Press.

Boutet D 1985 *Les Fabliaux.* Presses Universitaires de France (Études Littéraires).

Cooke T D and Honeycutt B L eds 1974 *The Humor of the Fabliaux. A collection of critical essays.* University of Missouri Press, Columbia.

Cooke T D 1978 *The Old French and Chaucerian Fabliaux. A Study of Their Comic Climax.* University of Missouri Press, Columbia.

Dronke P 1973 The Rise of the Medieval Fabliau: Latin and Vernacular Evidence. *Romanische Forschungen* 85 pp 275–97.

Eichmann R 1979 The Anti-Feminism of the Fabliaux. In *Authors and Philosophers.* University of South Carolina, Columbia (French Literature Series VI) pp 26–34.

Faral E 1924 Le Fabliau Latin au Moyen Age. *Romania* 50 pp 321–85.

Hart W M 1908 The Fabliau and Popular Literature. *PMLA* XXIII(3) pp 329–374

Jodogne O 1975 *Le Fabliau.* Brepols, Turnhout (Typologie des sources du moyen âge occidental, Fasc.13).

Johnson L 1983 Women on Top: Antifeminism in the Fabliaux? *MLR* 78 pp 298–307.

Kasprzyk K 1976 Pour la sociologie du fabliau: convention tactique et engagement. *Kwartalnik Neofilologiczny* XXIII(1–2) pp 153–61.

Lacy N J 1985 Fabliau Women. *Romance Notes* XXV(3) pp 318–27.

Lee C 1976 I Fabliaux e le Convenzioni della Parodia. In Lee C, Riccadonna A, Limentani A and Miotto A *A Prospettive sui Fabliaux. Contesto, Sistema, Reallizzazione.* Liviana, Padua pp 3–41.

Levy B J 1987 Black humour: the role of the devil in the fabliau. In Vitale-Brovarone and Mombello G (eds) *Atti del V Colloquio della International Beast Epic, Fable and Fabliau Society.* dell'Orso, Alessandria pp 129–46.

Lorcin M-T 1979 *Façons de sentir et de penser: les fabliaux français*. Honoré Champion (Essais sur le Moyen Age).

Ménard P 1983 *Les Fabliaux. Contes à rire du Moyen Age*. Presses Universitaires de France, Paris.

Muscatine C 1986 *The Old French Fabliaux*. Yale University Press, New York.

Noomen W 1978 Structures Narratives et Force Comique: Les Fabliaux. *Neophilologus* 62 pp 361–73.

Nykrog P 1957 *Les Fabliaux. Etude d'histoire littéraire et de stylistique médiévale*. Ejnar Munksgaard, Copenhagen.

Olson G 1974 The Medieval Theory of Literature for Refreshment and its Use in the Fabliau Tradition. *SP* LXXI pp 291–313.

Olson G 1982 *Literature as Recreation in the Later Middle Ages*. Cornell University Press, Ithaca.

Pearcy R J 1974 *Sentence and Solas* in the Old French Fabliaux. In Arrathoon L A ed. *The Craft of Fiction: Essays in Medieval Poetics*. Solaris Press, Rochester, Michigan pp 231–80.

Pearcy R J 1977 Investigations into the Principles of Fabliau Structure. In Ruggiers P G ed. *Versions of Medieval Comedy*. University of Oklahoma Press, Norman pp 67–100.

Pearcy R J 1990 *Connebert* and Branch I of *Le Roman de Renart*: the genesis of a fabliau. *MÆ* LIX(1) pp 73–90.

Rychner J 1960 *Contribution a l'Etude des Fabliaux. Variants, Remaniements, Dégradations* 2 vols. Université de Neuchatel, Geneva (Recueil de travaux publiés par la faculté des lettres).

Schenk M J S 1987 *The Fabliaux. Tales of Wit and Deception*. John Benjamins, Amsterdam/Philadelphia (Purdue University Monographs in Romance Languages).

Spencer R 1978 The treatment of women in the «Roman de la Rose», the «Fabliaux» and the «Quinze Joyes de Mariage». *MR* XXVIII pp 207–14.

van den Boogard N 1977 Le Nouveau Recueil Complet des Fabliaux (NRCF). *Neophilologus* 61 pp 333–46.

van den Boogard N 1978 Les Fabliaux: versions et variations. *MR* XXVIII pp 149–61.

White S M 1982 Sexual Language and Human Conflict in Old French Fabliaux. *Comparative Studies in Society and History* 24 pp 185–210.

The Anglo-Norman fabliau

Pearcy R J 1978 Chansons de Geste and Fabliaux. 'La Gageure' and 'Berenger au long cul'. *NM* LXXIX(1) pp 76–83.

van den Boogaard N 1981 Le Fabliau Anglo-Normand. In *Third International Beast Epic, Fable and Fabliau Colloquium, Münster* 1979. Cologne/Vienna pp 66–77.

Wailes S L 1972 The Unity of the Fabliau *Un Chevalier et sa dame et un clerk. Romance Notes* 14 pp 593–6.

CHAPTER 2

Dame Sirith, the Interludium de Clerico et Puella and the fabliau in English before Chaucer

Editions

Dame Sirith. Bennett J A W, Smithers G V and Davis N 1968 *Early Middle English Verse and Prose* 2nd edn. Oxford University Press pp 96–107 and 303–12.

Interludium de Clerico et Puella. Ibid. pp 196–200 and 370–3.

Analogues

Gesta Romanorum. Ed. Oesterley H 1872. Weidmannische Buchhandlung, Berlin.

Jacques de Vitry. *The Exempla, or Illustrative Stories from the Sermones Vulgares.* Ed. Crane T F 1890. David Nutt, London (Publications of the Folk-Lore Society XXVI).

Petronius *Satyricon.* Trans. Heseltine M 1913. William Heinemann. Loeb Classical Library.

Petrus Alphonsus *Disciplina Clericalis.* Eds Hilka A and Söderhjelm W 1911 *Die Disciplina Clericalis des Petrus Alfonsi.* Carl Winter, Heidelberg.

Studies

Axton R 1974 *European Drama of the Early Middle Ages.* Hutchinson & Co. (Hutchinson University Library) pp 17–24.

Bennett J A W and Gray D 1986 *Middle English Literature.* Clarendon Press (The Oxford History of English Literature) pp 17–22.

Bergner H 1972 Das Fabliau in der mittelenglischen Literatur. *Sprachkunst* 3 pp 298–312.

Boitani P 1982 *English Medieval Narrative in the Thirteenth and Fourteenth Centuries.* Cambridge University Press pp 28–35.

Busby K 1988 *Dame Sirith* and *De Clerico et Puella.* In Veldhoen N H G E and Aertsen H (eds) *Companion to Early Middle English Literature.* Free University Press, Amsterdam pp 69–81.

Canby H S 1906 The English Fabliau. *PMLA* XXI pp 200–14.

Furrow M 1989 Middle English Fabliaux and Modern Myth. *ELH* 56(1) pp 1–18.

Heuser W 1907 Das interludium de Clerico et Puella und das Fabliau von Dame Siriz. *Anglia* XXX pp 306–19.

Lewis R E 1982 The English Fabliau Tradition and Chaucer's "Miller's Tale". *MP* 79 pp 241–55.

Robbins R H 1970 The English Fabliau: Before and After Chaucer. *Moderna Språk* LXIV(3) pp 231–44.

Swanton M 1987 *English Literature before Chaucer*. Longman (Longman Literature in English) pp 226–32.

CHAPTERS 3–5

Chaucer

Editions

Benson L D *et al.* 1988 *The Riverside Chaucer*. Oxford University Press.

Robinson F N 1957 *The Works of Geoffrey Chaucer* 2nd edn. Oxford University Press.

The texts of the Canterbury Tales

Baker D C 1962 The Bradshaw Order of the *Canterbury Tales*. A Dissent. *NM* LXIII pp 245–61.

Benson L D 1981 The Order of *The Canterbury Tales*. *SAC* 3 pp 77–120

Blake N F 1985 *The Textual Tradition of the Canterbury Tales*. Edward Arnold.

Donaldson E T 1970 The Ordering of the Canterbury Tales. In Mandel J and Rosenberg B A (eds) *Medieval Literature and Folklore Studies. Essays in Honor of Francis Lee Utley*. Rutgers University Press, New Brunswick pp 193–204.

Keiser G R 1978 In Defense of the Bradshaw Shift. *CR* 12 pp 191–201.

Manly J M and Rickert E *et al.* 1940 *The Text of The Canterbury Tales*. 8 vols. The University of Chicago Press, Chicago.

Pratt R A 1951 The Order of the Canterbury Tales. *PMLA* LXVI pp 1141–67.

Sources and analogues: texts and criticism

Benson L D and Andersson T M 1971 *The Literary Context of Chaucer's Fabliaux. Texts and Translations*. The Bobbs-Merrill Company, Indianapolis and New York.

Bryan W F and Dempster G 1941 *Sources and Analogues of Chaucer's Canterbury Tales*. The University of Chicago Press, Chicago.

Boccaccio, Giovanni *Comedia delle Ninfe Fiorentine (Ameto)*. Ed. Quaglio A E 1964 *Tutte le opere di Giovanni Boccaccio*. Arnoldo Mondadori, Milan (I classici Mondadori). Vol.II pp 665–835.

Boccaccio, Giovanni *Decameron.* Ed. Branca V 1976 *Tutte le opere di Giovanni Boccaccio.* Arnoldo Mondadori, Milan (I classici Mondadori). Vol. IV.

Boccaccio *The Decameron.* Trans. McWilliam G H 1972. Penguin Classics.

Claudian *De Raptu Proserpinae.* Ed. Hall J B 1969. Cambridge University Press (Cambridge Classical Texts and Commentaries).

Claudian *De Raptu Proserpinae.* Trans. Platnauer M 1922. Heinemann. (Loeb Classical Library). *Claudian* vol.II pp 292–377.

Deschamps, Eustache *Le Miroir de Mariage.* Ed. Raynaud G 1894 *Oeuvres Complètes de Eustache Deschamps.* Société des Anciens Textes Français, Paris. Vol.IX.

Limentani A 1976 I *Fabliaux* di Rutebeuf. In Lee C, Riccadonna A, Limentani A and Miolto A *Prospettive sui Fabliaux. Contesto, Sistema, Reallizzazione.* Liviana, Padua pp 83–98.

de Lorris, Guillaume and de Meun, Jean *Le Roman de la Rose.* Ed. Langlois E 1914–1924. Paris. 5 vols.

de Lorris, Guillaume and de Meun, Jean *The Romance of the Rose.* Trans. Dahlberg C 1971. Princeton University Press, Princeton.

McGrady D 1977 Chaucer and the *Decameron* Reconsidered. *CR* 12(1) pp 1–26.

Ovid *Fasti.* Trans. Frazer J G 1967. Heinemann (Loeb Classical Library).

Ovid *Metamorphoses.* Trans Miller F J 1928–29. Heinemann (Loeb Classical Library). 2 vols.

Ovide Moralisé. Ed. de Boer C 1915–1938. Verhandelingen der Koninklijke Akademie van Wetenshapen te Amsterdam, Amsterdam. 5 vols.

Regalado N F 1970 *Poetic Patterns in Rutebeuf: A study in noncourtly poetic modes of the thirteenth century.* Yale University Press, New Haven.

Serpes A 1969 *Rutebeuf. Poète satirique.* Klincksieck, Paris (Bibliothèque française et romane. Centre de Philologie romane de la Faculté des Lettres de Strasbourg. Serie C: Etudes Littéraires).

Chaucer's fabliaux and their context: general works

Aers D 1980 *Chaucer, Langland and the Creative Imagination.* Routledge & Kegan Paul.

Aers D 1986 *Chaucer.* Harvester Press (New Readings).

Benson C D 1986 *Chaucer's Drama of Style. Poetic variety and contrast in the Canterbury Tales.* The University of North Carolina Press, Chapel Hill.

Benson L D 1984 The "Queynte" Punnings of Chaucer's Critics. In Strohm P and Heffernan T J eds *Reconstructing Chaucer.* The New Chaucer Society, the University of Tennessee (Studies in the Age of Chaucer, Proceedings No.1) pp 23–47.

Brewer D S 1968 Class Distinction in Chaucer. *Speculum* XLIII pp 290–305.

Brewer D S 1979 The Fabliaux. In Rowland B ed. *Companion to Chaucer Studies* revised edition. Oxford University Press pp 296–325.

Burlin R P 1977 *Chaucerian Fiction*. Princeton University Press, Princeton.

Cooper H 1983 *The Structure of the Canterbury Tales*. Duckworth.

Cooper H 1989 *The Canterbury Tales*. Clarendon Press (Oxford Guides to Chaucer).

Craik T W 1964 *The Comic Tales of Chaucer*. Methuen & Co.

David A 1976 *The Strumpet Muse. Art and Morals in Chaucer's Poetry*. Indiana University Press, Bloomington.

Dempster G 1932 *Dramatic Irony in Chaucer*. Reprinted 1959. The Humanities Press, New York.

Hansen E T 1992 *Chaucer and the Fictions of Gender*. University of California Press, Berkeley.

Hertog E 1991 *Chaucer's Fabliaux as Analogues*. Leuven University Press, Leuven (Mediaevalia Lovaniensa Series I/Studia XIX).

Howard D R 1976 *The Idea of the Canterbury Tales*. University of California Press, Berkeley.

Huppé B F 1967 *A Reading of the Canterbury Tales* revised edition. State University of New York.

Joseph G 1970 Chaucerian "Game" – "Earnest" and the "Argument of Herbergage" in *The Canterbury Tales*. *CR* 5(2) pp 83–96.

Kean P M 1972 *Chaucer and the Making of English Poetry*. Routledge & Kegan Paul. 2 vols.

Kendrick L 1988 *Chaucerian Play. Comedy and Control in the Canterbury Tales*. University of California Press, Berkeley.

Kittredge G L 1912 Chaucer's Discussion of Marriage. *MP* 9 pp 435–67.

Knapp P 1990 *Chaucer and the Social Contest*. Routledge.

Lawler T 1980 *The One and the Many in the Canterbury Tales*. Archon Books.

Lindahl C 1987 *Earnest Games. Folkloric Patterns in the Canterbury Tales*. Indiana University Press, Bloomington and Indianapolis.

Mann J 1973 *Chaucer and Medieval Estates Satire. The Literature of Social Classes and the General Prologue to the Canterbury Tales*. Cambridge University Press.

Mann J 1991 *Geoffrey Chaucer*. Harvester Wheatsheaf (Feminist Readings).

Martin P 1990 *Chaucer's Women. Nuns, Wives and Amazons*. Macmillan.

Mehl D 1986 *Geoffrey Chaucer. An Introduction to his Narrative Poetry*. Cambridge University Press.

Muscatine C 1957 *Chaucer and the French Tradition. A study in style and meaning*. University of California Press, Berkeley.

Olson P A 1986 *The Canterbury Tales and the Good Society*. Princeton University Press, Princeton.

Patterson L 1987 "No man his reson herde": Peasant Consciousness, Chaucer's Miller and the Structure of the *Canterbury Tales*. *South Atlantic Quarterly* 86 pp 457–95.

Pearcy R J 1986 The Genre of Chaucer's Fabliau-Tales. In Arrathoon L A ed. *Chaucer and the Craft of Fiction*. Solaris Press, Rochester (Michigan) pp 329–84.

Pearsall D 1985 *The Canterbury Tales*. George Allen & Unwin (Unwin Critical Library).

Pearsall D 1987 Versions of Comedy in Chaucer's *Canterbury Tales*. In Fichte J O ed. *Chaucer's Frame Tales: The Physical and the Metaphysical*. D.S.Brewer pp 35–49.

Richardson J 1970 *Blameth Nat Me. A Study of Imagery in Chaucer's Fabliaux*. Mouton, The Hague (Studies in English Literature).

Robertson D W (Jr) 1963 *A Preface to Chaucer. Studies in Medieval Perspectives*. Princeton University Press, Princeton.

Rogers W E 1986 *Upon The Ways: The Structure of The Canterbury Tales*. University of Victoria, Canada (ELS Monograph Series).

Rowland B 1978 Distance and authentication in Chaucer's comic tales. *MR* XXVIII pp 199–206.

Rowland B 1979 What Chaucer Did to the Fabliau. *SN* LI(2) pp 205–13.

Ruggiers P G 1967 *The Art of the Canterbury Tales*. University of Wisconsin Press, Madison.

Stilwell G 1955 The Language of Love in Chaucer's Miller's and Reeve's Tales and in the Old French Fabliaux. *JEGP* LIV pp 693–9.

Strohm P 1989 *Social Chaucer*. Harvard University Press, Cambridge (Massachusetts).

Thro A B 1970 Chaucer's Creative Comedy: A Study of the *Miller's Tale* and the *Shipman's Tale*. *CR* 5(2) pp 97–111.

Traversi D 1983 *The Canterbury Tales. A Reading*. The Bodley Head.

Whittock T 1968 *A Reading of the Canterbury Tales*. Cambridge University Press.

The Shipman's Tale

Abraham D H 1977 *Cosyn* and *Cosynage*: Pun and Structure in the *Shipman's Tale*. *CR* 11(4) pp 319–26.

Adams R 1984 The Concept of Debt in *The Shipman's Tale*. *SAC* 6 pp 85–102.

Braswell M F 1988 Chaucer's "Queinte Termes of love": A Legal View of the *Shipman's Tale*. *CR* 22 pp 295–304.

Copland M 1966 *The Shipman's Tale*: Chaucer and Boccaccio. *MÆ* XXXV pp 11–28.

Fichte J O 1987 Chaucer's *Shipman's Tale* Within the Context of the French Fabliaux [*sic*] Tradition. In Fichte J O ed. *Chaucer's Frame Tales: The Physical and the Metaphysical*. D.S. Brewer pp 51–66.

Guerin R 1971 *The Shipman's Tale*: The Italian Analogues. *ES* LII pp 412–19.

Hahn T 1986 Money, Sexuality, Wordplay and Context in the *Shipman's*

Tale. In Wasserman J N and Blanch R J eds. *Chaucer in the Eighties*. Syracuse University Press, Syracuse. pp 235–49.

Joseph G 1983 Chaucer's Coinage: Foreign Exchange and the Puns of the *Shipman's Tale*. *CR* 17 pp 341–57.

Keiser G R 1978 Language and Meaning in Chaucer's *Shipman's Tale*. *CR* 12(3) pp 147–61.

Lawrence W W 1958 Chaucer's *Shipman's Tale*. *Speculum* 33 pp 56–68.

McClintock M W 1970 Games and the Players of Games: Old French Fabliaux and the *Shipman's Tale*. *CR* 5(2) pp 112–36.

Nicholson P 1978 The "Shipman's Tale" and the Fabliaux. *ELH* 45 pp 583–96.

Scattergood V J 1976–77 The Originality of the *Shipman's Tale*. *CR* 11 pp 210–31.

Silverman A H 1953 Sex and Money in Chaucer's *Shipman's Tale*. *PQ* XXXII(III) pp 329–36.

Stilwell G 1944 Chaucer's 'Sad' Merchant. *RES* XX pp 1–18.

Fragment VII of the Canterbury Tales

Astell A W 1992 Chaucer's "Literature Group" and the Medieval Causes of Books. *ELH* 59(2) pp 269–87.

Baum P F 1958 *Chaucer: A Critical Appreciation*. Duke University Press, Durham, N.C. pp 74–84.

Gaylord A T 1967 *Sentence* and *solaas* in fragment VII of the *Canterbury Tales*: Harry Bailly as horseback editor. *PMLA* 82 pp 226–35.

CHAPTER 4

The Miller's Tale

Beichner P E 1950 Absolon's Hair. *MS* XII pp 222–33.

Bloomfield M W 1970 The Miller's Tale – An UnBoethian Interpretation. In Mandel J and Rosenberg B A eds. *Medieval Literature and Folklore Studies. Essays in Honor of Francis Lee Utley*. Rutgers University Press, New Brunswick pp 205–11.

Bolton W F 1962 The "Miller's Tale": An Interpretation. *MS* XXIV pp 83–94.

Donaldson E T 1951 Idiom of Popular Poetry in the Miller's Tale. Reprinted in Donaldson E T 1970 *Speaking of Chaucer*. The Athlone Press, University of London pp 12–29.

Farrell T J 1989 Privacy and the Boundaries of Fabliau in the *Miller's Tale*. *ELH* 56 pp 773–95.

Fletcher A J 1992 The faith of a simple man: Carpenter John's Creed in the Miller's Tale. *MÆ* LXI(1) pp 96–105.

Gallacher P J 1983 Perception and Reality in the *Miller's Tale*. *CR* 18 pp 38–48.

Harder K B 1956 Chaucer's Use of the Mystery Plays in the *Miller's Tale*. *MLQ* XVII(3) pp 193–8.

Kaske R E 1962 The *Canticum Canticorum* in the *Miller's Tale*. *SP* LIX(3) pp 479–500.

Kiernan K S 1975 The Art of the Descending Catalogue, and a Fresh Look at Alisoun. *CR* 10(1) pp 1–16.

Miller R P 1970 *The Miller's Tale* as Complaint. *CR* 5(2) pp 147–60.

O'Connor J J 1956 The Astrological Background of the *Miller's Tale*. *Speculum* XXXI pp 120–5.

Olson P A 1963 Poetic Justice in the *Miller's Tale*. *MLQ* XXIV pp 227–36.

Rowland B B 1970 The Play of the *Miller's Tale*: A Game within a Game. *CR* 5(2) pp 140–6.

Rowland B B 1974 Chaucer's Blasphemous Churl: A new interpretation of the *Miller's Tale*. In Rowland B B ed. *Chaucer and Middle English Studies in Honour of Russell Hope Robbins*. George Allen & Unwin pp 43–55.

Siegel P N 1960 Comic Irony in *The Miller's Tale*. *Boston University Studies in English* IV pp 114–20.

The Reeve's Tale

Baird J L 1969 Law and the *Reeve's Tale*. *NM* LXX pp 679–83.

Beidler P G 1992 *The Reeve's Tale* and its Flemish Analogue. *CR* 26(3) pp 283–92.

Brewer D 1987 The Reeve's Tale. In Fichte J O ed. *Chaucer's Frame Tales: The Physical and the Metaphysical* D.S. Brewer pp 67–81.

Burridge R T 1972 Chaucer's *Reeve's Tale* and the fabliau "Le Meunier et les .ii. clers". *AM* 12 pp 30–6.

Copland M 1962 *The Reeve's Tale*: Harlotrie or Sermonyng? *MÆ* XXXI pp 14–32.

Delany S 1967 Clerks and Quiting in *The Reeve's Tale*. Reprinted in Delany S 1990 *Medieval Literary Politics. Shapes of Ideology*. Manchester University Press pp 104–11.

Friedman J B 1967 A Reading of Chaucer's *Reeve's Tale*. *CR* 2 pp 8–19.

Garbáty T J 1973 Satire and Regionalism: The Reeve and his Tale. *CR* 8(1) pp 1–8.

Goodall P 1980 The *Reeve's Tale*, *Le Meunier et les ii Clers* and the *Miller's Tale*. *Parergon* 27 pp 13–16.

Hart W M 1908 The Reeve's Tale. A Comparative Study of Chaucer's Narrative Art. *PMLA* XXIII(1) pp 1–44.

Kaske R E 1959 An Aube in the *Reeve's Tale*. *ELH* 26(3) pp 295–310.

Lancashire I 1972 Sexual Innuendo in the *Reeve's Tale*. *CR* 6 pp 157–70.

Olson G 1969 "The Reeve's Tale" and "Gombert". *MLR* 64(4) pp 721–5.

Olson G 1974 The *Reeve's Tale* as a Fabliau. *MLQ* XXXV pp 219–30.

Olson P A 1962 *The Reeve's Tale*: Chaucer's *Measure for Measure*. *SP* LIX(1) pp 1–17.

Plummer J F 1983 Hooly Chirches Blood: Simony and Patrimony in Chaucer's *Reeve's Tale*. *CR* 18 pp 49–60.

Tolkien J R R 1934 Chaucer as a Philologist: *The Reeve's Tale*. *TPS* 1934 pp 1–70.

Fragment I of the Canterbury Tales

Curry W C 1920 Chaucer's Reeve and Miller. *PMLA* XXXV(2) pp 189–209.

Hill B 1973 Chaucer: *The Miller's* and *Reeve's Tales*. *NM* LXXIV pp 665–75.

Jensen E 1990 Male Competition as a Unifying Motif in Fragment A of the *Canterbury Tales*. *CR* 24(4) pp 320–8.

Jones T 1980 *Chaucer's Knight. The portrait of a medieval mercenary*. Weidenfeld and Nicolson.

Knight S 1980 Chaucer and the Sociology of Literature. *SAC* 2 pp 15–51.

Kolve V A 1984 *Chaucer and the Imagery of Narrative. The First Five Canterbury Tales*. Edward Arnold.

Owen C A (Jr) 1954 Chaucer's *Canterbury Tales*: Aesthetic Design in Stories of the First Day. *ES* XXXV pp 49–56.

Parr J 1954 Chaucer's *cherles rebellyng*. *MLN* LXIX pp 393–4.

Scheps W 1977 Chaucer's Theseus and the *Knight's Tale*. *LSE* NS9 pp 19–34.

Schweitzer E C 1986 The Misdirected Kiss and the Lover's Malady in Chaucer's *Miller's Tale*. In Wasserman J N and Robert J B eds. *Chaucer in the Eighties*. Syracuse University Press, Syracuse pp 223–33.

Siegel M 1985 What the Debate is and Why it Founders in Fragment A of *The Canterbury Tales*. *SP* LXXXII(1) pp 1–24.

Wordsworth J 1958 A link between the Knight's Tale and the Miller's. *MÆ* XXVII p 21.

The Cook's Tale

Scattergood V J 1984 Perkyn Revelour and the *Cook's Tale*. *CR* 19(1) pp 14–23.

Seymour M C 1990 Of this Cokes Tale *CR* 24(3) pp 259–62.

Stanley E G 1976 'Of This Cokes Tale Maked Chaucer Na Moore'. *Poetica* 5 pp 36–59.

CHAPTER 5

The Summoner's Tale

Adams J F 1962 The Structure of Irony in *The Summoner's Tale*. *EC* XII(ii) pp 126–32.

Andreas J 1990 "Newe Science" from "Olde Bokes": A Bakhtinian Approach to the *Summoner's Tale*. *CR* 25(2) pp 138–51.

Birney E 1960 Structural Irony within the *Summoner's Tale*. *Anglia* 78 pp 204–18.

Clark R P 1976 Wit and Witsunday in Chaucer's *Summoner's Tale*. *AM* XVII pp 48–57.

Fleming J V 1966 The Antifraternalism of the *Summoner's Tale*. *JEGP* LXV pp 688–700.

Fleming J V 1967–68 The Summoner's Prologue: an Iconographic Adjustment. *CR* 2 pp 95–107

Hanning R W 1985 Roasting a Friar, Mis-taking a Wife, and Other Acts of Textual Harassment in Chaucer's *Canterbury Tales*. *SAC* 7 pp 3–21.

Haselmayer L A 1937 The Apparitor and Chaucer's Summoner. *Speculum* XII pp 43–57.

Levitan A 1971 The Parody of Pentecost in Chaucer's *Summoner's Tale*. *UTQ* XL(3) pp 236–46.

Szittya P R 1974 The Friar as False Apostle: Antifraternal Exegesis and the *Summoner's Tale*. *SP* LXXI(1) pp 19–46.

Williams A 1953 Chaucer and the Friars. *Speculum* XXVIII pp 499–513.

Zietlow P N 1966 In Defense of the Summoner. *CR* 2(1) pp 4–19.

The Merchant's Tale

Arrathoon L A 1984 Antinomic Cluster Analysis and the Boethian Verbal Structure of Chaucer's *Merchant's Tale*. *Language and Style* 17(1) pp 92–120.

Arrathoon L A 1986 "For craft is al, whoso that do it kan": The Genre of *The Merchant's Tale*. In Arrathoon L A ed. *Chaucer and the Craft of Fiction*. Solaris Press, Rochester (Michigan) pp 241–328.

Baugh A C 1937 The Original Teller of the Merchant's Tale. *MP* XXXV pp 15–26.

Beidler P G 1971 January, Knight of Lombardy. *NM* LXXII pp 735–8.

Bleeth K A 1974 The Image of Paradise in the *Merchant's Tale*. In Benson L D ed. *The Learned and the Lewed. Studies in Chaucer and Medieval Literature*. Harvard University Press, Cambridge, Massachusetts (Harvard English Studies) pp 45–60.

Bleeth K A 1986 Joseph's Doubting of Mary and the Conclusion of the *Merchant's Tale*. *CR* 21(1) pp 58–66.

Bronson B H 1961 Afterthoughts on the Merchant's Tale. *SP* LVIII(3) pp 583–96.

Brown E (Jr) 1970(a) Why Was Januarie Born "Of Pavye"? *NM* LXXI pp 654–8.

Brown E (Jr) 1970(b) *Hortus Inconclusus*: The Significance of Priapus and Pyramis and Thisbe in the *Merchant's Tale*. *CR* 4(1) pp 31–40.

Brown E (Jr) 1974 Biblical Women in the Merchant's Tale: Feminism, Antifeminism, and Beyond. *Viator* 5 pp 387–412.

Brown E (Jr) 1978/79 Chaucer, the Merchant, and their Tale: Getting Beyond Old Controversies (2 parts) *CR* 13 pp 141–56 and 247–62.

Brown P 1984 An Optical Theme in *The Merchant's Tale*. In Strohm P and Heffernan T J eds. *Reconstructing Chaucer*. The New Chaucer Society, The University of Tennessee, Knoxville (Studies in the Age of Chaucer, Proceedings, No.1) pp 231–43.

Brown P and Butcher A 1991 *The Age of Saturn. Literature and History in the Canterbury Tales*. Basil Blackwell, especially pp 157–204.

Burnley J D 1976 The Morality of *The Merchant's Tale*. *The Yearbook of English Studies* 6 pp 16–25.

Burrow J A 1957 Irony in the Merchant's Tale. *Anglia* 75 pp 199–208.

Dalbey M A 1974 The Devil in the Garden: Pluto and Proserpina in Chaucer's 'Merchant's Tale'. *NM* LXXV pp 408–15.

Donaldson E T 1970 The Effect of the Merchant's Tale. In Donaldson E T *Speaking of Chaucer*. University of London, Athlone Press pp 30–45.

Donovan M J 1957 The Image of Pluto and Proserpina in the Merchant's Tale. *PQ* XXXVI(1) pp 49–60.

Edwards R R 1991 Narration and Doctrine in the Merchant's Tale. *Speculum* 66(2) pp 342–67.

Harrington N T 1971 Chaucer's Merchant's Tale: Another Swing of the Pendulum. *PMLA* 86 pp 26–31.

Hartung A E 1967 The Non-Comic *Merchant's Tale*, Maximianus and the Sources. *MS* XXIX pp 1–25.

Jordan R M 1963 The Non-Dramatic Disunity of the *Merchant's Tale*. *PMLA* LXXVIII(4) pp 293–9.

Kellogg A L 1960 Susannah and the *Merchant's Tale*. *Speculum* XXXV pp 275–9.

Lowes J L 1910 Chaucer and the *Miroir de Mariage*. *MP* VIII pp 165–86.

McGaillard J C 1946 Chaucer's *Merchant's Tale* and Deschamps' *Miroir de Mariage*. *PQ* XXV(3) pp 193–220.

McGaillard J C 1946 Chaucerian Comedy: The *Merchant's Tale*, Jonson, and Molière. *PQ* XXV(4) pp 343–70.

Neuse R 1989 Marriage and the Question of Allegory in the *Merchant's Tale*. *CR* 24(2) pp 115–31.

Olson P A 1961 Chaucer's Merchant and January's "Hevene in Erthe Heere". *ELH* 28(3) pp 203–14.

Otten C F 1971 Proserpina: *liberatrix suae gentis*. *CR* 5(4) pp 277–87.

Pace G B 1965 The Scorpion of Chaucer's *Merchant's Tale*. *MLQ* XXVI pp 369–74.

Pittock M 1967 The Merchant's Tale. *EC* XVII(1) pp 26–40.

Richmond V B 1979 Pacience in adversitee: Chaucer's Presentation of Marriage. *Viator* 10 pp 323–54.

Rosenberg B A 1971 The "Cherry-Tree Carol" and the *Merchant's Tale*. *CR* 5(4) pp 264–76.

Schleusner J 1980 The Conduct of the *Merchant's Tale*. *CR* 14(3) pp 237–50.

Schroeder M C 1970 Fantasy in the "Merchant's Tale". *Criticism* XII(3) pp 167–79.

Sedgewick G C 1948 The Structure of *The Merchant's Tale*. *UTQ* 17 pp 337–45.

Stevens M 1972 "And Venus laugheth": An Interpretation of the *Merchant's Tale*. *CR* 7(2) pp 118–31.

Tatlock J S P 1936 Chaucer's *Merchant's Tale*. *MP* XXXIII(4) pp 367–81.

Wentersdorf K P 1965 Theme and Structure in The Merchant's Tale: The Function of the Pluto Episode. *PMLA* LXXX(5) pp 522–7.

Wentersdorf K P 1986 Imagery, Structure, and Theme in Chaucer's *Merchant's Tale*. In Arrathoon L A ed. *Chaucer and the Craft of Fiction*. Solaris Press, Rochester, Michigan pp 35–62.

White G M 1965 "Hoolynesse or Dotage": The Merchant's January. *PQ* XLIV(iii) pp 397–404.

Wurtele D 1978/79 Ironical Resonances in the *Merchant's Tale*. *CR* 13 pp 66–79.

The Pardoner's Tale

Owen N H 1967 The Pardoner's Introduction, Prologue and Tale: Sermon and *Fabliau*. *JEGP* LXVI pp 541–9.

The Complaint of Mars

Clemen W 1963 *Chaucer's Early Poetry*. Methuen pp 188–97.

CHAPTER 6

Other evidence of the fabliau in Middle English

Verse narrative: texts and studies

Dunbar, William *The Tretis of the Tua Mariit Wemen and the Wedo*. In Kinsley J ed. 1979 *The Poems of William Dunbar*. Clarendon Press No.14.

Furrow M M ed. 1985 *Ten Fifteenth-Century Comic Poems*. Garland Publishing, New York (Garland Medieval Texts).

Dane Hew, Munk of Leicestre. Ed. Furrow *Ten Fifteenth-Century Comic Poems* pp 155–74.

The Friars of Berwick. Ed. Furrow *Ten Fifteenth-Century Comic Poems* pp 313–62.

The Lady Prioress. Ed. Furrow *Ten Fifteenth-Century Comic Poems* pp 1–43.

A Mery Jest of the Mylner of Abyngton. Ed. Hazlitt W C 1866 *Remains of Early Popular Poetry of England*. John Russell Smith, London (Library of Old Authors). Vol.3 pp 98–118.

Pearcy R J 1980 The Genre of William Dunbar's *Tretis of the Tua Mariit Wemen and the Wedo*. *Speculum* 55(1) pp 58–74.

The Wright's Chaste Wife. Ed. Furnivall F J (1865) *The Wright's Chaste Wife*. Early English Text Society (OS12).

Plays: texts and studies

Baird J L and Baird L Y 1973 Fabliau Form and the Hegge *Joseph's Return*. *CR* 8(2) pp 159–69.

Cosbey R C 1945 The Mak Story and its Folklore Analogues. *Speculum* XX pp 310–7.

Spector S ed. 1991 *The N-Town Play. Cotton MS Vespasian D*.8. Early English Text Society (SS11-12). 2 vols.

Richardson C and Johnston J 1991 *Medieval Drama*. Macmillan (English Dramatists).

England G and Pollard A W eds. 1897 *The Towneley Plays*. Early English Text Society (ESLXXI).

Cawley A C 1958 *The Wakefield Pageants in the Towneley Cycle*. Manchester University Press (Old and Middle English Texts).

Exempla

An Alphabet of Tales. Ed. Banks M M 1904–5. Early English Text Society (OS126-7). 2 vols.

Gesta Romanorum. Ed. Herrtage S J H 1879 *The Early English Versions of the Gesta Romanorum*. Early English Text Society (ESXXXIII).

Gower, John. *Confessio Amantis*. Ed. Macaulay G C 1900 *The English Works of John Gower*. Early English Text Society (ES81). 2 vols.

The Seven Sages. Ed. Brunner K 1933 *The Seven Sages of Rome (Southern Version)*. Early English Text Society (OS191).

Tubach F C 1969 *Index Exemplorum. A Handbook of Medieval Religious Tales*. Suomalainen Tiedeakatemia, Helsinki (FF Communications Vol.LXXXVI No.204).

Wenzel S 1979 The Joyous Art of Preaching; or, the Preacher and the Fabliau. *Anglia* 97 pp 304–25.

Medieval German Schwänke

Texts

von der Hagen F H 1850 *Gesammtabenteuer. Hundert altdeutsche Erzählungen.* J G Cotta, Stuttgart and Tübingen. Reprinted 1961 as *Gesamtabenteuer.* Wissenschaftliche Buchgesellschaft, Darmstadt. 3 vols.

Niewöhner H 1937 *Neues Gesamtabenteuer* 2nd edn. 1967. Weidmann, Dublin and Zürich.

der Stricker. Fischer H ed. 1960 *Der Stricker: Fünfzehn kleine Verserzählungen.* Max Niemeyer, Tübingen (Altdeutsche Textbibliothek).

Kaufringer, Heinrich. Sappler P ed. 1972 *Heinrich Kaufringer: Werke.* Max Niemeyer, Tübingen.

Editions of individual texts cited in this book

F: der Stricker, ed. Fischer; GA: von der Hagen, *Gesammtabenteuer,* NGA: Niewöhner, *Neues Gesamtabenteuer,* S: Kaufringer, ed. Sappler.

Daz heselîn: GA XXI

Der blinde Hausfreund: NGA 32

Der Herr mit dem Vier Frauen: NGA 29

Der Herrgottschnitzer: NGA 33

Der Liebhaber im Bade: NGA 25

Der schoulære ze Paris: GA XIV

Der sperwære: GA XXII

Der swanger münch: GA XXIV

der Stricker, *Daz heize îsen*: GA XLVI, F V

der Stricker, *Der begrabene Ehemann*: F IV

der Stricker, *Der geafte pfaffe*: GA LXI, F VIII

der Stricker, *Der künig im bade*: GA LXXI

der Stricker, *Der Pfaffe Âmis*: In Lambel H ed. 1883 *Erzählungen und Schwänke.* F.A.Brockhaus, Leipzig (Deutsche Classiker des Mittelalters 12) pp 22–102.

der Stricker, *Drî wunsche*: F I

der Stricker, *Man und wîp*: GA XXXIII, F II

Der vrouwen zuht: GA III

Der wîze rôsendorn: GA LIII

Die drî münche von Kolmære: GA LXII

Die hasen: GA XXX

Dietrich von Glaz, *Der borte*: GA XX

Heinrich Kaufringer, *Chorherr und Schusterin*: S 9

Heinrich Kaufringer, *Der Mönch als Liebesbote*: S 7

Heinrich Kaufringer, *Der Schlafpelz*: S 15

Heinrich Kaufringer, *Die Rache des Ehemanns*: S 13

Heinrich Kaufringer, *Drei listige Frauen*: S 11

Herrand von Wildonie, *Der Pfaffe mit der Schnur.* NGA 22
Herrand von Wildonie, *Der verkêrte wirt:* GA XLIII
Jakob Appet, *Der ritter underm zuber.* GA XLI
Rüdiger von Müner, *Irregang und Girregar.* GA LV
Ruprecht von Würzburg, *Von zwein koufmannen:* GA LXVIII
Turandot: GA LXIII
Von dem ritter mit den nüzzen: GA XXXIX
Vrouwen list: GA XXVI
Vrouwen stætikeit: GA XXVII

Studies

de Boor H 1962 *Die Deutsche Literatur im Späten Mittelalter. Zerfall und Neubeginn. Erster Teil* 1250–1350. C.H.Beck, Munich (Geschichte der Deutschen Literatur von der Anfängen bis zur Gegenwart 3/1).

de Boor H 1966 *Die Höfische Literatur. Vorbereitung, Blüte, Ausklang* 1170–1250. C.H.Beck, Munich (*ibid.*).

Fischer H 1957/58 Zur Gattungsform des 'Pfaffen Amis'. *Zeitschrift für deutsches Altertum* 88 pp 291–9.

Glier I 1986 *Die Deutsche Literatur im Späten Mittelalter 1250–1370. Zweiter Teil: Reimpaargedichte, Drama, Prosa.* C.H.Beck, Munich (Geschichte der Deutschen Literatur von der Anfängen bis zur Gegenwart III/2).

Stehmann, W 1909 *Die mittelhochdeutsche Novelle vom Studentenabenteuer.* Mayer & Müller, Berlin (Palaestra LXVII).

Medieval Italian novelle *and related texts*

Texts and translations

(See also Bibliography, Chapters 3–5, Chaucer, Sources and Analogues, for editions and translations of Boccaccio.)

Boccaccio, Giovanni *Corbaccio.* Ed. Marti M 1972 *Giovanni Boccacio, Opere Minori in Volgare.* Rizzoli, Milan (I Classici Rizzoli). Vol.IV pp 199–308.

Boccaccio, Giovanni *Corbaccio.* The *Corbaccio* trans. and ed. Cassell A K 1975. University of Illinois Press, Urbana.

Boccaccio, Giovanni *Decameron.* Ed. Branca V *Tutte le opere di Giovanni Boccaccio.* Arnoldo Mondadori, Milan (I classici Mondadori). Vol. IV.

Ser Giovanni Fiorentino *Il Pecorone.* Ed. Esposito E 1974. Longo, Ravenna (Classici Italiani Minori).

Masuccio Salernitano *Il Novellino.* Ed. Mauro A 1940, reprint ed. Nigro S S 1975. Laterza & Figli, Bari (Scrittori d'Italia Reprint 3).

Il Novellino. Ed. Lo Nigro S 1963 *Novellino e Conti del Duecento.* Unione Tipografico-Editrice Torinese, Turin (Classici Italiani).

Sacchetti, Franco. *Opere* ed. Borlenghi A 1957. Rizzoli, Milan (I Classici Rizzoli).

Sercambi, Giovanni. *Novelle* ed. Sinicropi G 1972. Laterza & Figli, Bari (Scrittori d'Italia). 2 vols.

Studies

Branca V 1976 *Boccaccio. The Man and His Works.* The Harvester Press, New York.

Caporello-Szykman C 1990 *The Boccaccian Novella. Creation and Waning of a Genre.* Peter Lang, New York (Studies in Italian Culture).

Neuschäfer H-J 1969 *Boccaccio und der Beginn der Novelle. Strukturen der Kurzerzählung auf der Schwelle zwischen Mittelalter und Neuzeit.* Wilhelm Fink, Munich (Theorie und Geschichte der Literatur und der Schönen Kunst).

Quaglio A E 1970 Retorica, Prosa e Narrative del Duecento. In Mineo N, Pasquini E and Quaglio A E *Il Duecento. Dalle origini a Dante.* Laterza & Figli, Bari (La Letteratura Italiano Storia e Testi). Vol.I(2) pp 255–428.

Tateo F 1972 La Litteratura in Volgare da Masuccio Salernitano al Chariteo. In Nigro S S, Tateo F and Benvenuti A T *Il Quattrocento. L'età dell'Umanismo.* Laterza & Figli, Bari (La Letteratura Italiano Storia e Testi). Vol.III(2) pp 543–608.

Middle Dutch boerden and related texts

Texts

Kruyscamp C (ed.) 1957 *De Middelnederlandse Boerden.* Martinus Nijhoff, The Hague.

Moltzer H E 1875 *De Middelnederlandse Dramatische Poezie.* J.B.Wolters, Groningen.

Verwijs E 1860 *Dit sijn X goede Boerden.* Martinus Nijhoff, The Hague.

Verwijs E 1871 *Van Vrouwen ende van Minne. Middelnederlandse Gedichten uit de XIVde en XVde Eeuw.* J.B.Wolters, Groningen.

Studies

Beidler P G and Decker T 1989 *Lippijn*: A Middle Dutch Source for the *Merchant's Tale? CR* 23(3) pp 236–50.

Dempster G 1932 Some Old Dutch and Flemish Narratives and their Relation to Analogues in the Decameron. *PMLA* XLVII pp 923–48.

Lodder F J 1982 De moraal van de boerden. *De nieuwe taalgids* 75(1) pp 39–49.

de Vries J 1926 De Boerde van .III. Ghesellen, die den Bake Stalen. *Tijdschrift voor Nederlandsche Taal- en Letterkunde* XLV pp 212–62.

Welsh fabliaux and related texts

Texts and translations

Dafydd ap Gwilym. Parry T ed. 1952 *Gwaith Dafydd ap Gwilym.* University of Wales Press.

Dafydd ap Gwilym. Loomis R M 1982 *Dafydd ap Gwilym. The Poems. Translation and commentary.* Center for Medieval and Early Renaissance Studies, Binghampton, NY (Medieval and Renaissance Texts and Studies).

Y Dyn dan y Gerwyn. Ed. and trans. Johnston D 1991 *Canu Maswedd yr Oesoedd Canol/Medieval Welsh Erotic Poetry.* Tafol. No.19.

Studies

Bromwich R 1986 Aspects of the poetry of Dafydd ap Gwilym. Garland, New York.

Dronke P 1975 Serch *fabliau* a serch cwrtais. In Rowlands J ed. *Dafydd ap Gwilym a Chanu Serch yr Oesoedd Canol.* University of Wales Press pp 1–17.

Fulton H 1989 *Dafydd ap Gwilym and the European Context.* University of Wales Press.

Later German Schwänke

Texts

Kahlenbergerbuch. Ed. Bobertas F 1884. In *Narrenbuch.* W. Spermann, Berlin and Stuttgart (Deutsche National-Literatur vol.11) pp 1–86.

Neithart Fuchs. Ed. Bobertas F 1884. *Ibid.* pp 141–292.

Sachs, Hans. *Fastnachtspiele.* Ed. (and modernized) Schiller K M. Philipp Reclam Jun., Leipzig.

Sachs, Hans. *Werke in zwei Bänden.* Aufbau, Berlin and Weimer.

Sachs, Hans. *Zeitgedichte und Schwänke.* Ed. (and modernized) Schiller K M. Philipp Reclam Jun., Leipzig.

Till Eulenspiegel. (Low German) *Ulenspiegel* ed. Kromann W 1952. Karl Wachholtz, Neumünster (Drucke des Vereins für niederdeutsche Sprachforschung).

Till Eulenspiegel. (High German) *Dyl Vlenspiegel. In Abbildung des Drucks von 1515.* Alfred Kümmark, Göppingen (Litterae Göppinger Beiträge zur Textgeschichte).

Studies

Jöst E 1976 *Bauernfiendlichkeit. Die Historien des Ritters Neithart Fuchs.* Alfred Kümmark, Göppingen (Göppinger Arbeiten zur Germanistik).

MacMehan A 1889 *The Relation of Hans Sachs to the Decameron, as shown in thirteen shrovetide plays drawn from that source.* Nova Scotia Printing Company, Halifax, Nova Scotia.

Rupprich H 1970 *Die Deutsche Literatur vom Später Mittelalter bis zum Barock. Part 1: Das ausgehende Mittelalter, Humanismus und Renaissance 1370–1520.* C.H.Beck, Munich (Geschichte der Deutschen Literatur von der Anfängen bis zur Gegenwart 4/1).

Rupprich H 1973 *Die Deutsche Literatur vom Später Mittelalter bis zum Barock. Part 2: Das Zeitalter der Reformation.* C.H.Beck, Munich (Geschichte der Deutschen Literatur von der Anfängen bis zur Gegenwart 4/2).

The French nouvelle

Editions

Les Cent Nouvelles Nouvelles. Ed. Sweetser F P 1966. Libraire Droz, Geneva (Textes Littéraires Français).
Saint-Évremond. Ternois R ed. 1962–69 *Œuvres en prose de Saint-Évremond.* Marcel Didier, Paris. 4 vols.

Studies

Dubuis R 1966 La Genèse de la Nouvelle en France au Moyen Age. *Cahiers de l'Association des Etudes Françaises* 18 pp 9–19.

Dubuis R 1973 *Les Cent Nouvelles Nouvelles et la Tradition de la Nouvelle en France au Moyen Age.* Presses Universitaires de Grenoble, Grenoble (Collection Theta).

French farces

Editions

Cohen G 1949 ed. *Recueil de Farces Françaises inédites du XVe Siècle.* The Medieval Academy of America, Cambridge, Mass.

Fournier E 1872 ed. *Le Théâtre Français avant La Renaissance. Mystères, Moralités et Farces.* Reprinted Burt Franklin, New York (Research and Source Works Series).

Jacob P L 1859 ed. *Recueil de Farces Soties et Moralités du Quinzième Siècle.* Alphonse Delahays, Paris.

Picot É 1902–12 ed. *Recueil Général des Sotties* 3 vols. Société des Anciens Textes Français, Paris.

Editions of individual plays cited in this book

C: Cohen; F: Fournier; J: Jacob; P: Picot.
De celuy qui se confesse a sa voisine: C II
La Farce de la Femme qui fut desrobée a son mari en sa hote et mise une pierre en son lieu: C XXIII
La Farce du Munyer: J pp 233–65; F pp 162–71
La Farce de Resjouy d'Amours: C XVIII
Les trois amoureux de la croix: C VIII
Martin de Cambray: C XLI

English jestbooks and related prose

Texts

Brewer, Thomas 1631 *The Life and Death of the Merry Devill of Edmonton. With the pleasant prancks of Snug the Smith, Sir John, and mine Host of the George, about the stealing of Venison.* Ed. Proescholdt L 1884 Eine prosäische Nachbildung der 'Erzählung des Müllers' aus Chaucer's Canterbury Tales. Anglia VII pp 116–19.

A C. *Mery Talys* Ed. Hazlitt W C 1864 *Shakespeare Jest-Books.* Willis & Southeran, London. Vol.I., and Zall P M ed. 1963 *A Hundred Mery Tales and Other English Jestbooks of the Fifteenth and Sixteenth Centuries.* University of Nebraska Press, Lincoln pp 57–150.

C. *Tales and quicke answeres, very mery, and pleasant to rede. circa* 1535. In Zall P M ed. 1963 *A Hundred Mery Tales and Other English Jestbooks of the Fifteenth and Sixteenth Centuries.* University of Nebraska Press, Lincoln pp 239–322.

Chaucer Junior *Canterbury Tales.* Imprint of 1687 edn. In Thompson R 1976 *Samuel Pepys' Penny Merriments.* Constable & Co. pp 156–61.

The Cobler of Caunterburie. Ed. Creigh G and Belfield J 1987 *The Cobler of Caunterburie and Tarltons Newes out of Purgatorie.* E.J.Brill, Leiden (Medieval and Renaissance Texts).

Deloney, Thomas 1597 *The pleasant Historie of John Winchcomb, In his yonger yeares called Jack of Newbery.* Imprint of 1626 edn. In Mann F O 1912 *The Works of Thomas Deloney.* Clarendon Press pp 1–68.

Fenton, Geoffrey 1567 *Certain Tragical Discourses of Bandello.* D.Nutt, London, 1898 (The Tudor Translations). 2 vols.

The Gestes of Skoggan 1565–66. Ed. Hazlitt W C 1864 *Shakespeare Jest-Books.* Willis & Southeran, London. Vol.II.

Greene, Robert. Grosart A B ed. 1881–86 *The Life and Complete Works in Prose and Verse of Robert Greene, M.A.* Cambridge and Oxford. 15 vols. The Huth Library. Reprinted 1964 Russell & Russell, New York.

Greene, Robert 1592 *Greenes Vision.* Ed. Grosart A B (*ibid.*) vol.XII pp 189–281.

Howleglass, circa 1516–20. In Zall P M ed. 1963 *A Hundred Mery Tales and Other English Jestbooks of the Fifteenth and Sixteenth Centuries.* University of Nebraska Press, Lincoln pp 151–237.

Kinde-Kit of Kingstone 1603 *Westward for Smelts.* Imprint of 1620 edn. Halliwell J O 1848. Percy Society vol.XXII.

Mery Tales of the Mad Men of Gotham. Imprint of 1630 edn. Hazlitt W C 1864 *Shakespeare Jest-Books.* Willis & Southeran, London. Vol.III.

Mery Tales, Wittie Questions and Quicke Answeres, very pleasant to be Readde 1567. Ed. Hazlitt W C 1864 *Shakespeare Jest-Books.* Willis & Southeran, London. Vol.II.

Painter, William 1566–67, revised and enlarged 1575 *The Palace of Pleasure.* Ed. Miles H 1929. The Cresset Press, London.

The Parson of Kalenborow circa 1520. Ed. Schröder E 1888 'Der Parson of Kalenborow und seine niederdeutsche Quelle' *Jahrbuch des Vereins für niederdeutsche Sprachforschung* XIII pp 129–52.

The Sack-ful of Newes 1673. Imprint of 1685 edn. In Thompson R 1976 *Samuel Pepys' Penny Merriments.* Constable & Co. pp 162–4.

Scoggins Jestes. Printed by Raph Blower, London, 1613.

Tarltons Jests 1600. Printed by Andrew Cook, London, 1628.

Tarltons Newes out of Purgatorie. Eds. Creigh G and Belfield J 1987 *The Cobler of Caunterburie and Tarltons Newes out of Purgatorie.* E.J.Brill, Leiden (Medieval and Renaissance Texts).

The Tincker of Turvey, in his merry Pastime in his passing from Billingsgate to Graves-End. Printed by Nath. Bultler, London, 1630.

Twelve Merry Gestys of one called Edith 1526. Ed. Hazlitt W C 1864 *Shakespeare Jest-Books.* Willis & Southeran, London. Vol.III.

Studies

Farnham W 1926 *The Merchant's Tale* in Chaucer Junior. *MLN* XLI(6) pp 392–6.

Kahrl S J 1966 The Medieval Origins of the Sixteenth-Century English Jest-books. *Studies in the Renaissance* XIII pp 166–83.

Wilson F P The English Jest-books of the sixteenth and early seventeenth centuries. In Wilson F P (ed. Helen Gardner 1969) *Shakesperian and Other Studies.* Clarendon Press pp 285–324.

Drama

Heywood, John (attributed) *A mery play betwene Johan Johan, the Husbande, Tyb, his Wyfe, and Syr Johan, the Preest.* Imprint of 1533 edn. In Adams J Q 1924 *Chief Pre-Shakespearean Dramas.* The Riverside Press, Cambridge, Massachusetts pp 385–96.

Peele, *George Edward I.* Ed. Hook F S 1961. In Pronty C T (general editor)

The Life and Works of George Peele. Yale University Press, New York. Vol.2 pp 1–212.

Ballads

The Bagford Ballads ed. Ebsworth J W 1876–78. The Ballad Society, London. 2 divisions.

Childs F J 1861 *English and Scottish Ballads.* Sampson Low, Son, & Co., London. 8 vols.

A Collection of Old Ballads, Corrected from the best and most Ancient Copies Extant 1723. J. Roberts & D. Leach, London. 3 vols.

The Euing Collection of English Broadside Ballads. 1971, University of Glasgow Publications.

Holloway J and Black H eds. 1975–79 *Later English Broadside Ballads.* Routledge & Kegan Paul. 2 vols, Vol.1 not numbered.

Merry Drollery Compleat, being Jovial Poems, Merry Songs, &c. Final (3rd) edn. 1691. Ed. Ebsworth J W 1875. Robert Roberts, Boston, Lincs.

Pinto V de Sol and Rodway A E 1957 *The Common Muse: an anthology of popular British ballad poetry.* Chatto & Windus.

The Roxburghe Ballads. Ed. Chappell W 1871–99. The Ballad Society, London. 9 vols.

Sargent H C and Kittredge G L 1904 *English and Scottish Popular Ballads edited from the collection of Francis James Childs.* Houghton, Mifflin & Co., Boston and New York.

Index